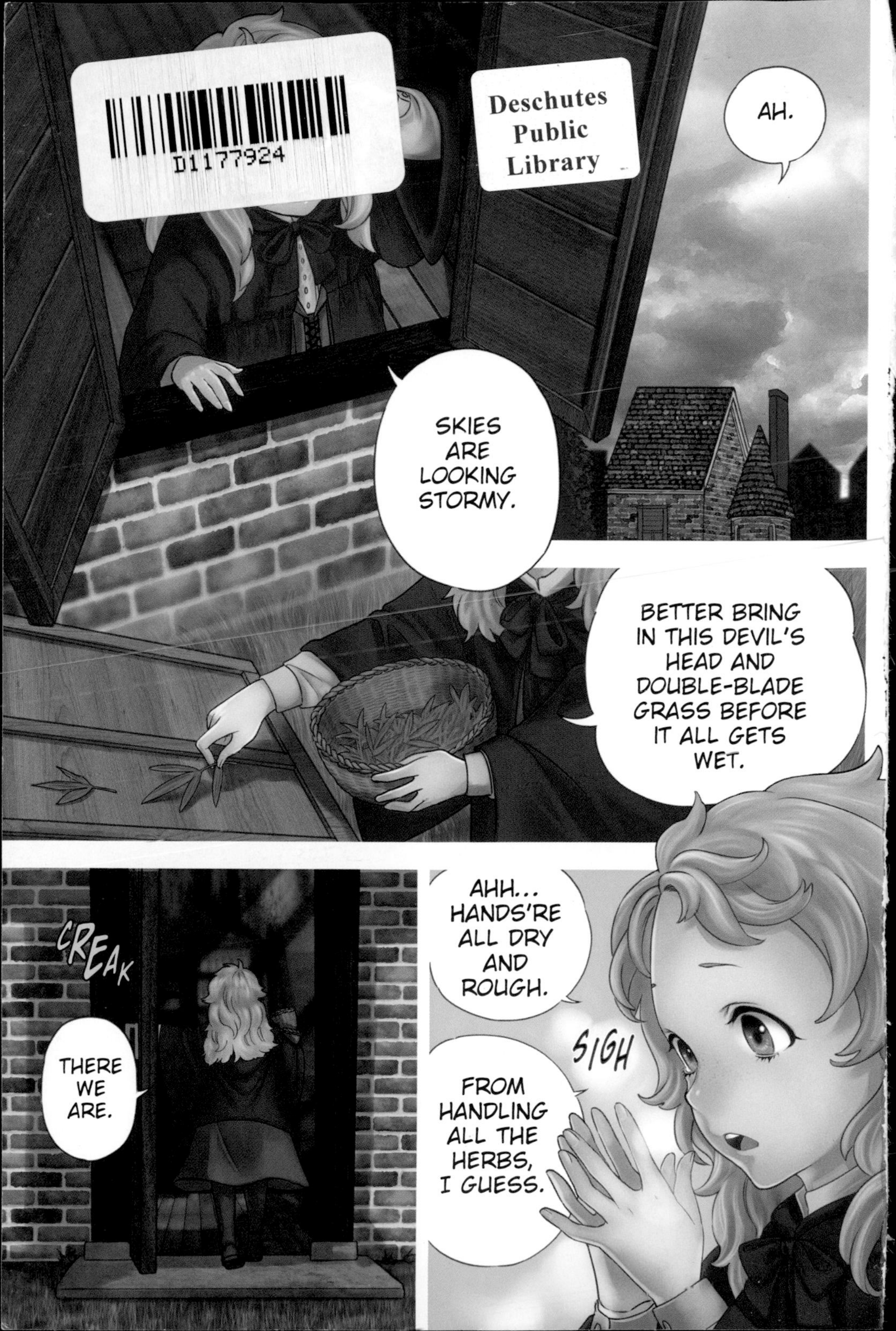
AH.
SKIES ARE LOOKING STORMY.
BETTER BRING IN THIS DEVIL'S HEAD AND DOUBLE-BLADE GRASS BEFORE IT ALL GETS WET.
AHH... HANDS'RE ALL DRY AND ROUGH.
SIGH
FROM HANDLING ALL THE HERBS, I GUESS.
CREAK
THERE WE ARE.

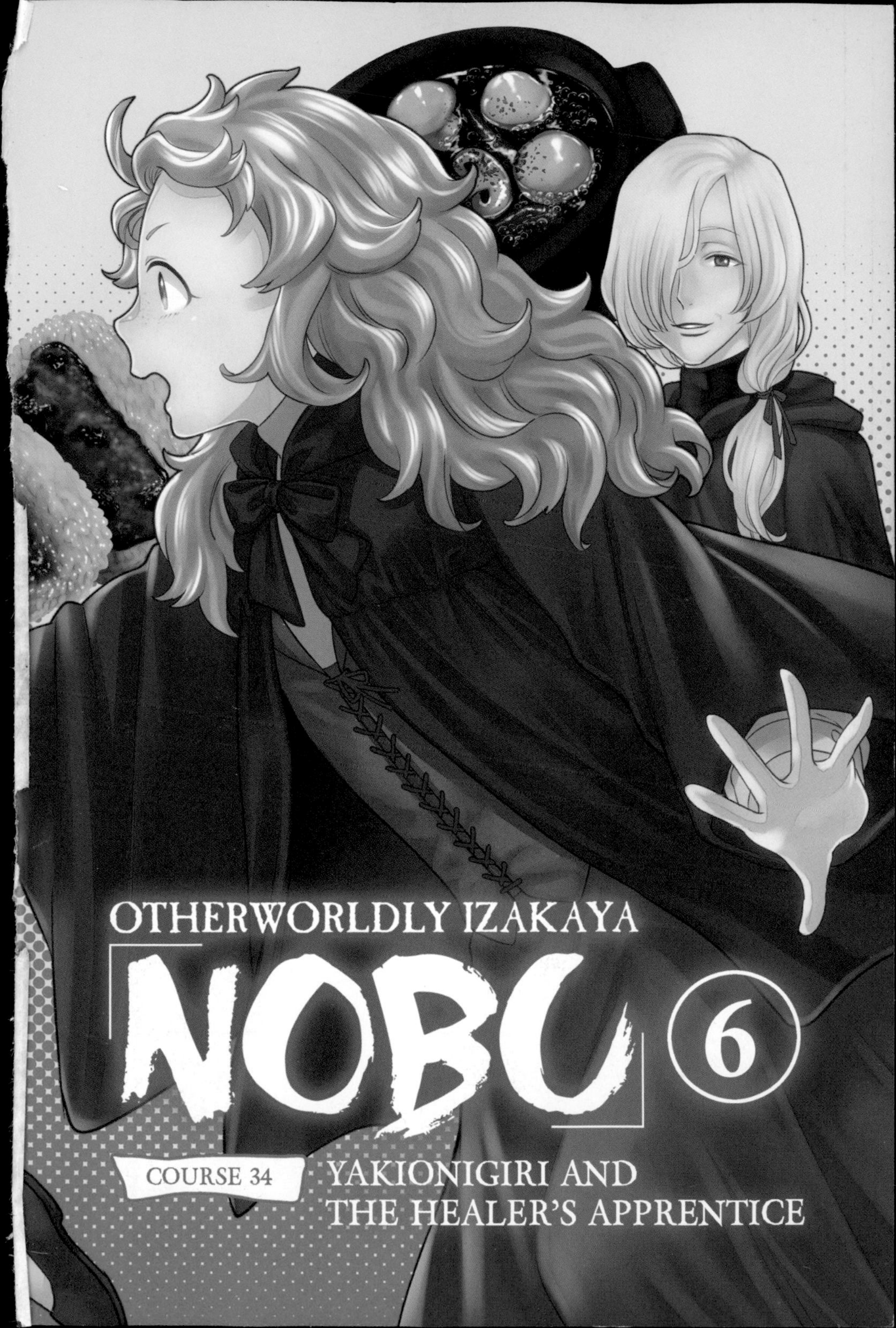
OTHERWORLDLY IZAKAYA
NOBU 6
COURSE 34
YAKIONIGIRI AND
THE HEALER'S APPRENTICE

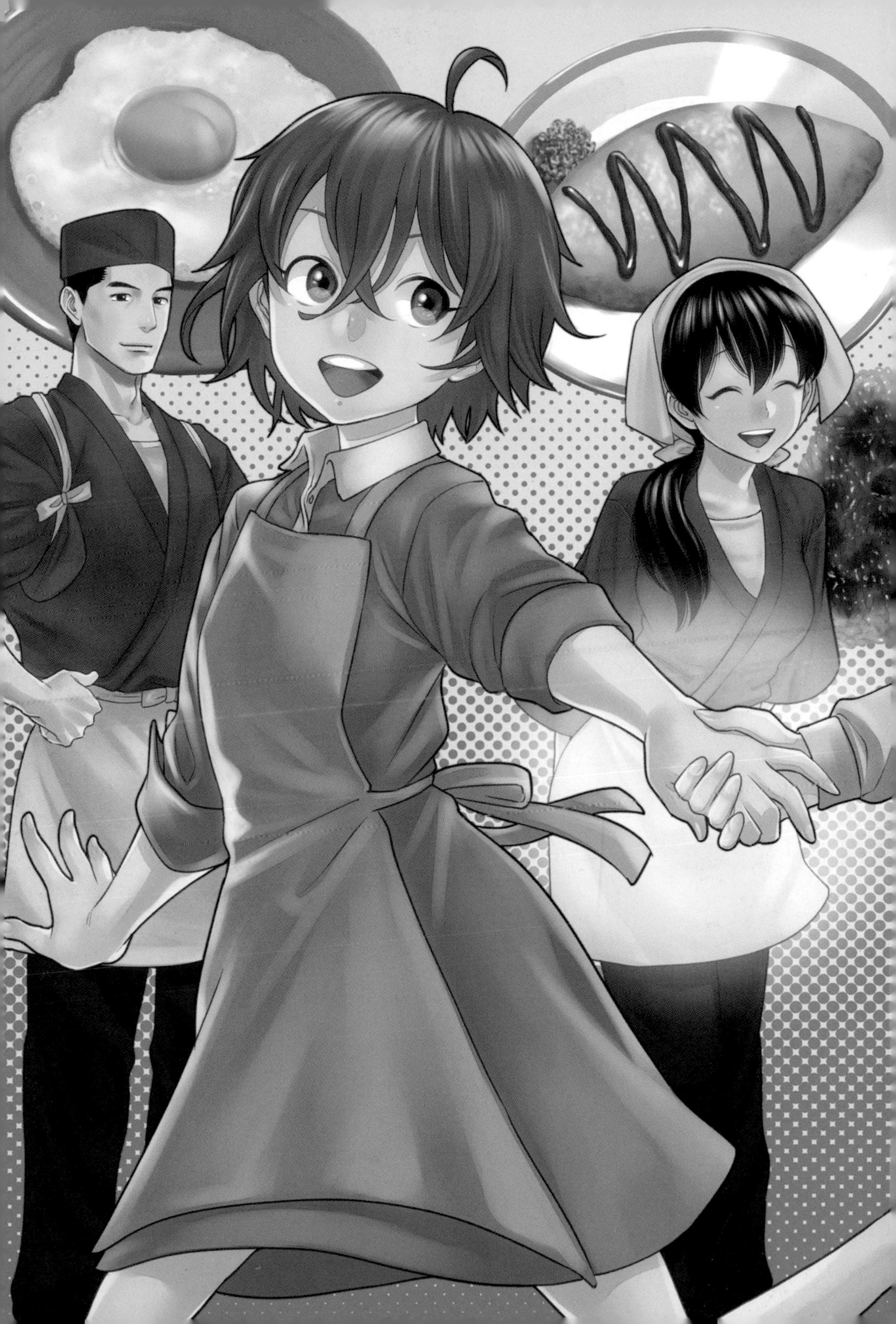

MENU

OTHERWORLDLY IZAKAYA

NOBU ⑥

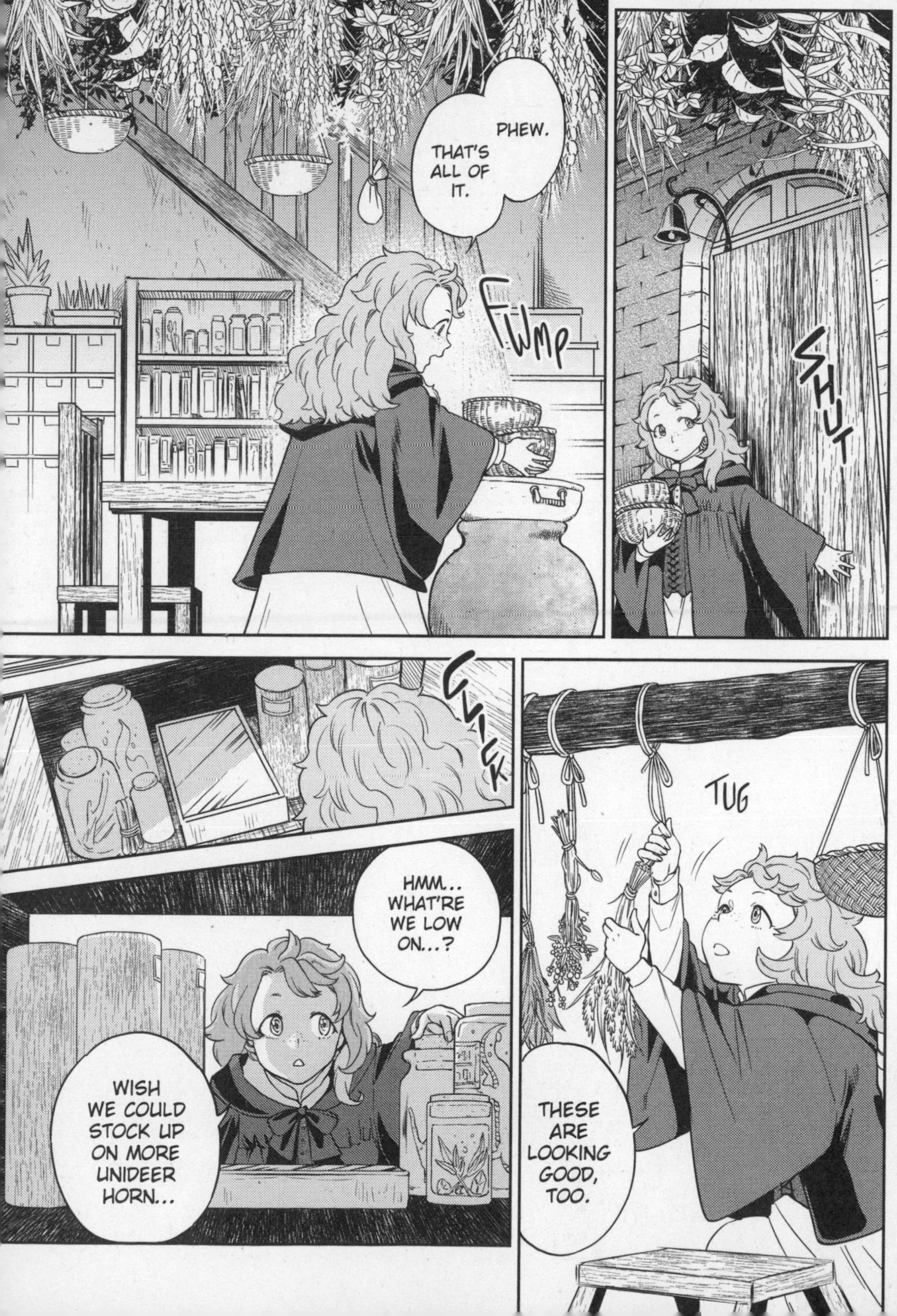
SHUT
PHEW. THAT'S ALL OF IT.
FWMP
TUG
THESE ARE LOOKING GOOD, TOO.
CLICK
HMM... WHAT'RE WE LOW ON...?
WISH WE COULD STOCK UP ON MORE UNIDEER HORN...

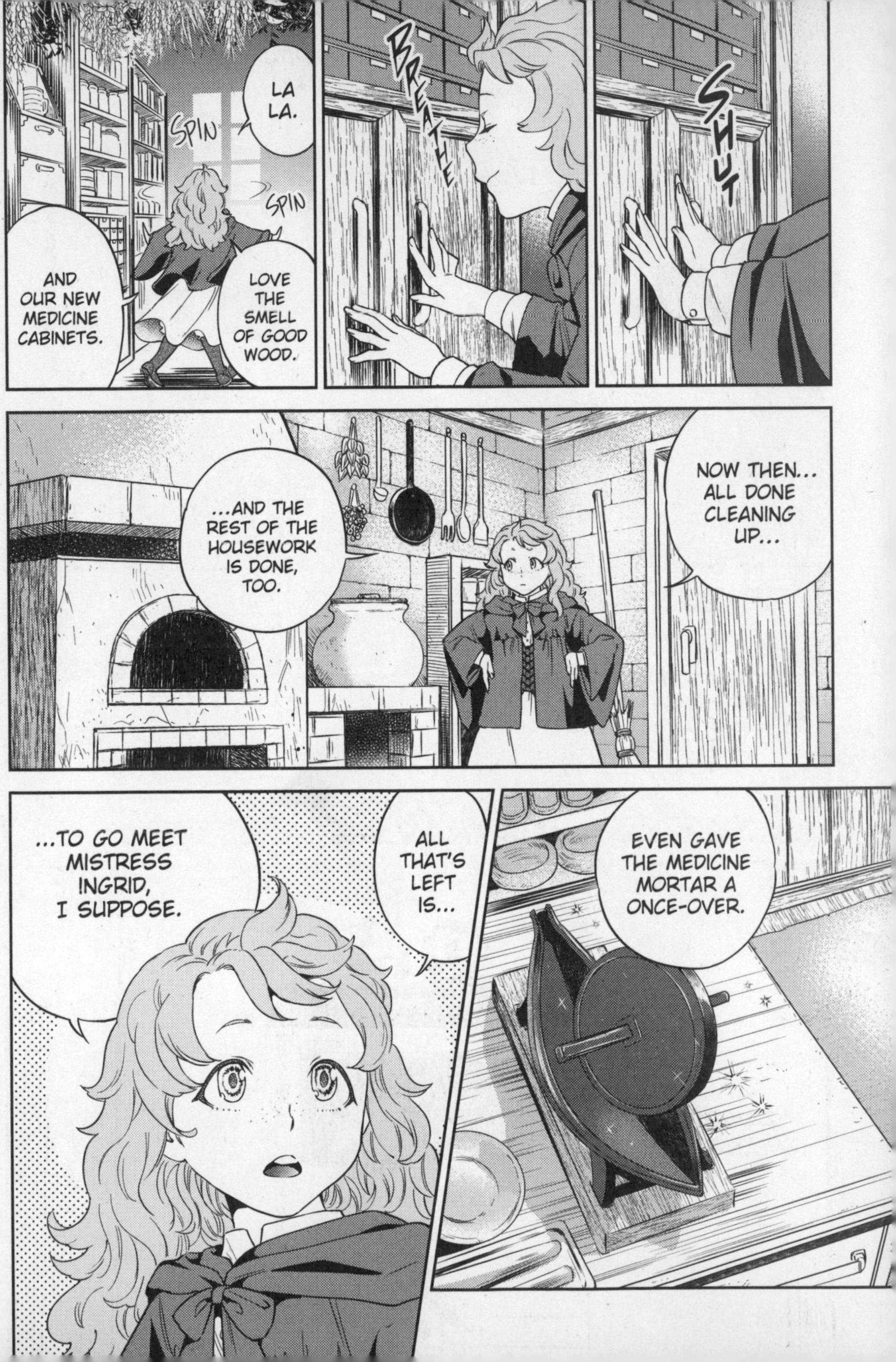
SHUT
BREATHE
LA LA.
SPIN
SPIN
LOVE THE SMELL OF GOOD WOOD.
AND OUR NEW MEDICINE CABINETS.
NOW THEN... ALL DONE CLEANING UP...
...AND THE REST OF THE HOUSEWORK IS DONE, TOO.
EVEN GAVE THE MEDICINE MORTAR A ONCE-OVER.
ALL THAT'S LEFT IS...
...TO GO MEET MISTRESS INGRID, I SUPPOSE.

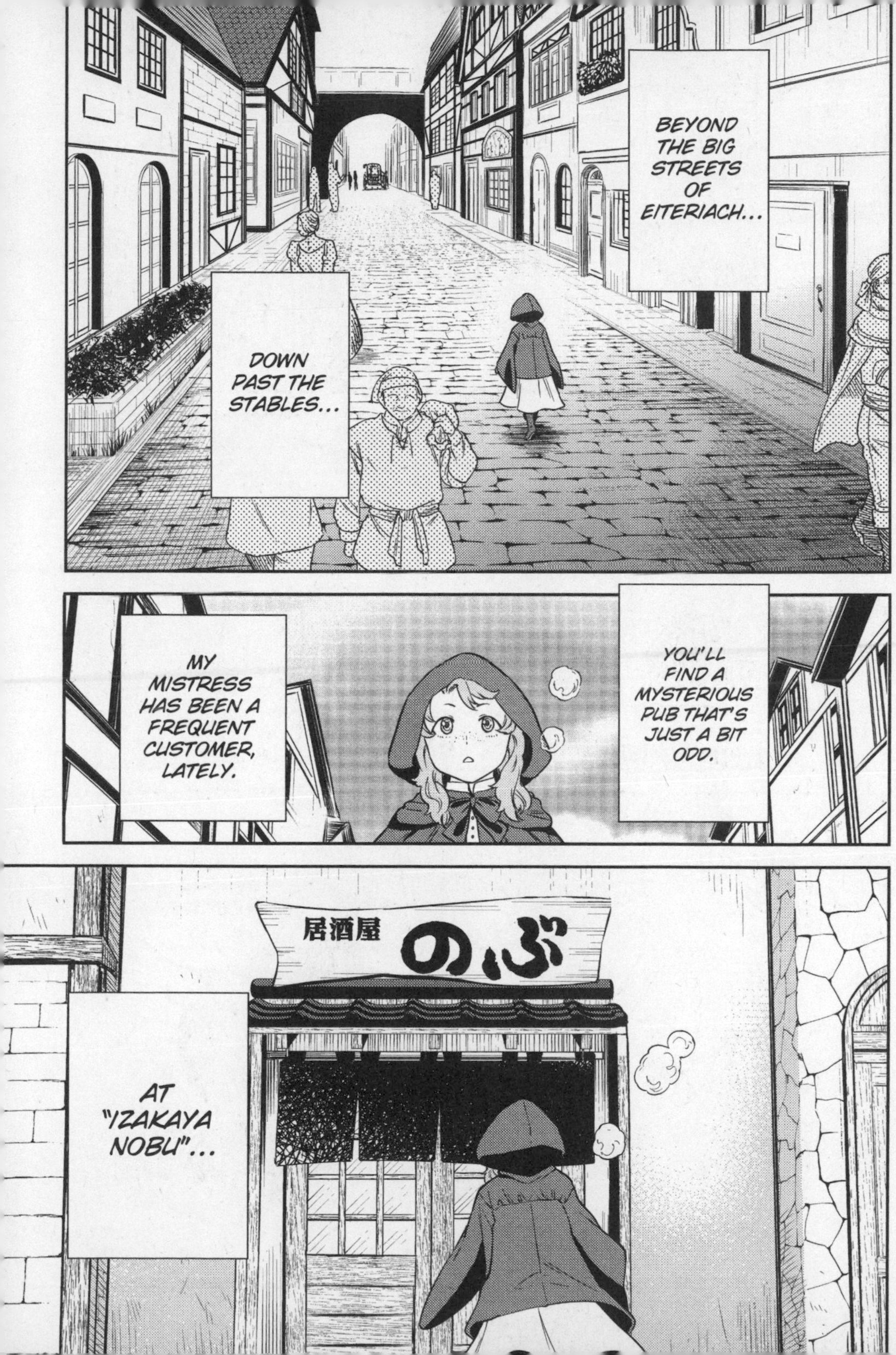
BEYOND THE BIG STREETS OF EITERIACH...
DOWN PAST THE STABLES...
YOU'LL FIND A MYSTERIOUS PUB THAT'S JUST A BIT ODD.
MY MISTRESS HAS BEEN A FREQUENT CUSTOMER, LATELY.
居酒屋 のぶ
AT "IZAKAYA NOBU"...

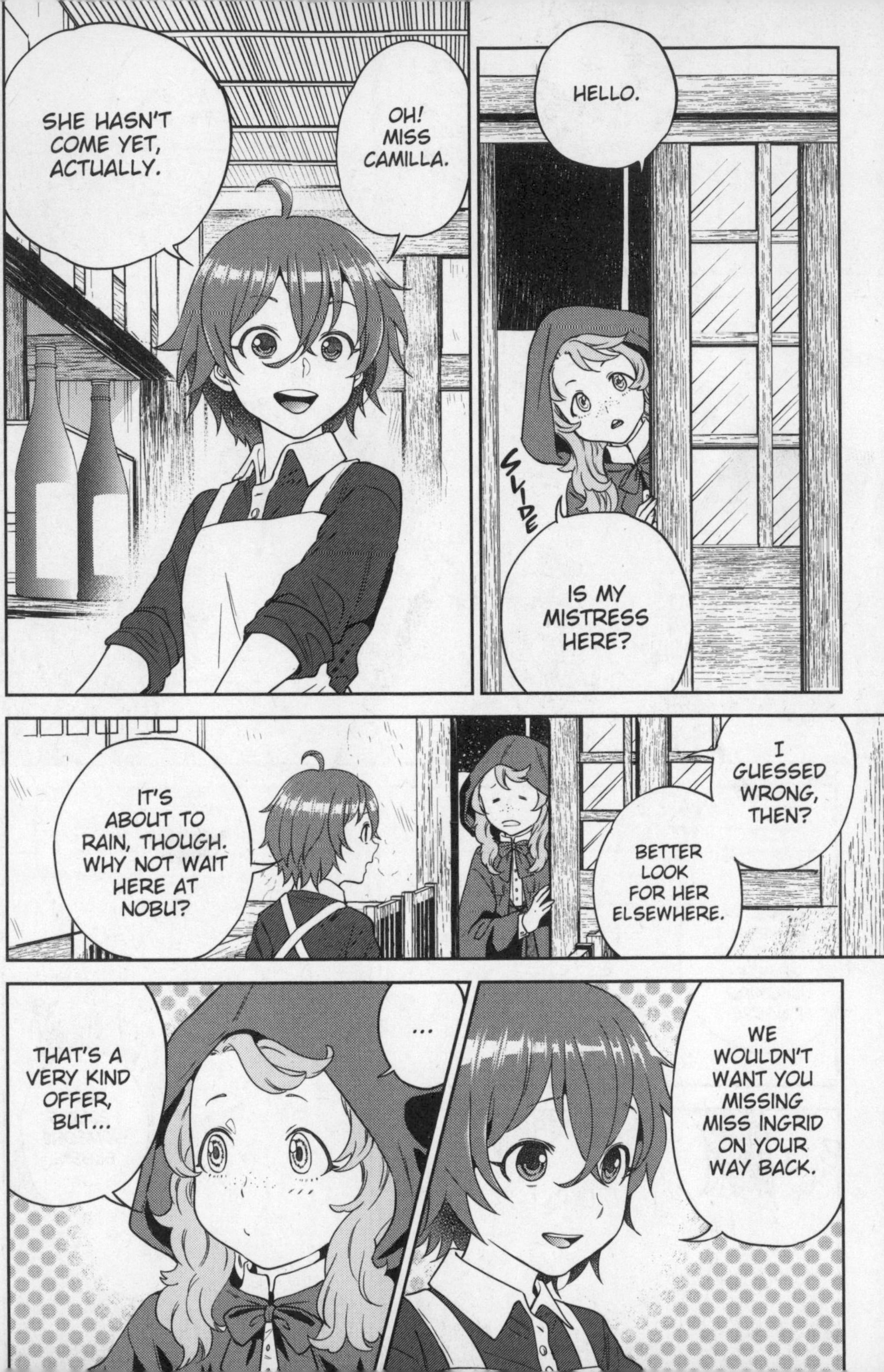
HELLO.
SLIDE
IS MY MISTRESS HERE?
OH! MISS CAMILLA.
SHE HASN'T COME YET, ACTUALLY.
I GUESSED WRONG, THEN?
BETTER LOOK FOR HER ELSEWHERE.
IT'S ABOUT TO RAIN, THOUGH. WHY NOT WAIT HERE AT NOBU?
WE WOULDN'T WANT YOU MISSING MISS INGRID ON YOUR WAY BACK.
...
THAT'S A VERY KIND OFFER, BUT...

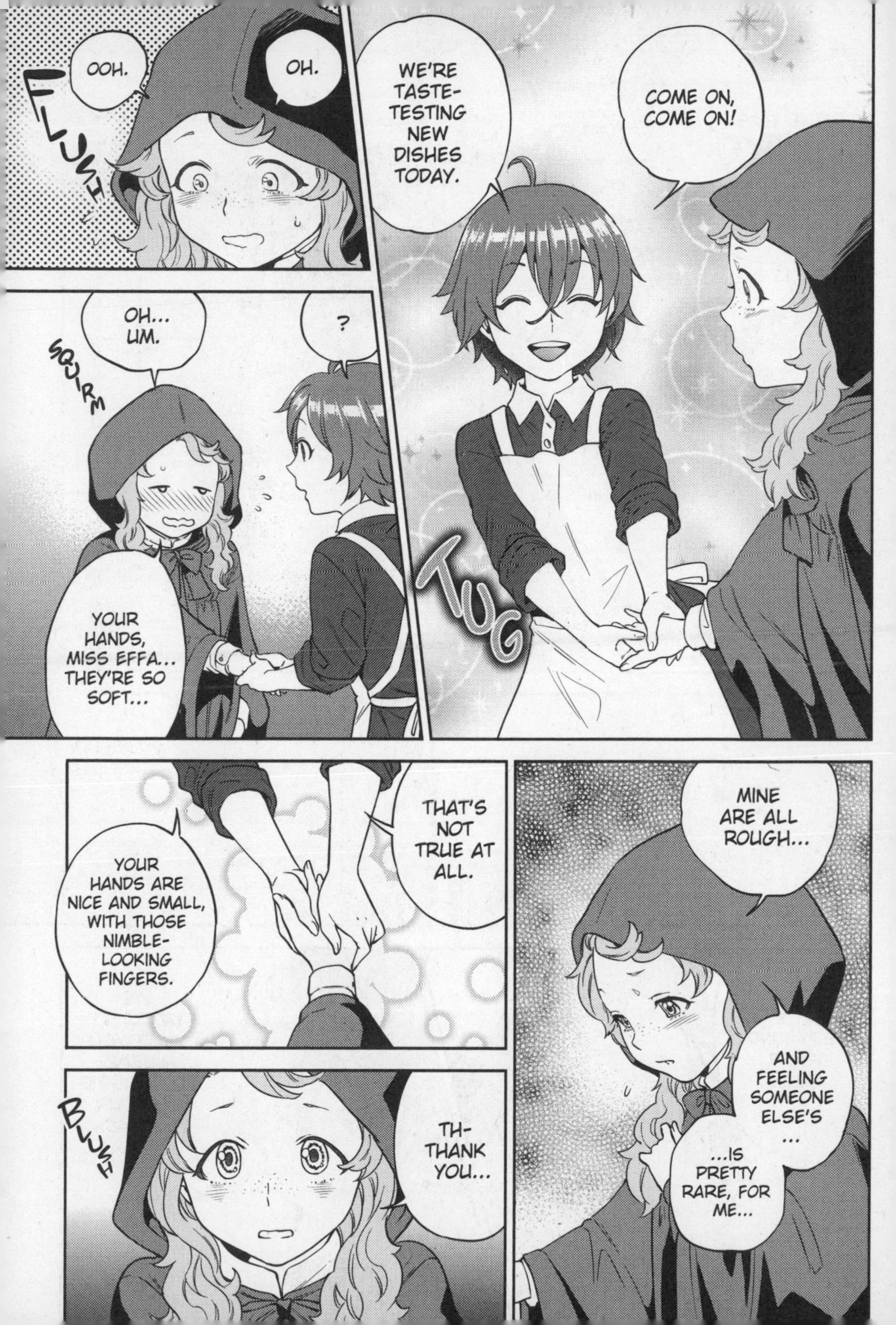
COME ON, COME ON!
WE'RE TASTE-TESTING NEW DISHES TODAY.
TUG
OH.
OOH.
FLUSH
?
OH... UM.
SQUIRM
YOUR HANDS, MISS EFFA... THEY'RE SO SOFT...
MINE ARE ALL ROUGH...
AND FEELING SOMEONE ELSE'S ...
...IS PRETTY RARE, FOR ME...
THAT'S NOT TRUE AT ALL.
YOUR HANDS ARE NICE AND SMALL, WITH THOSE NIMBLE-LOOKING FINGERS.
TH-THANK YOU...
BLUSH

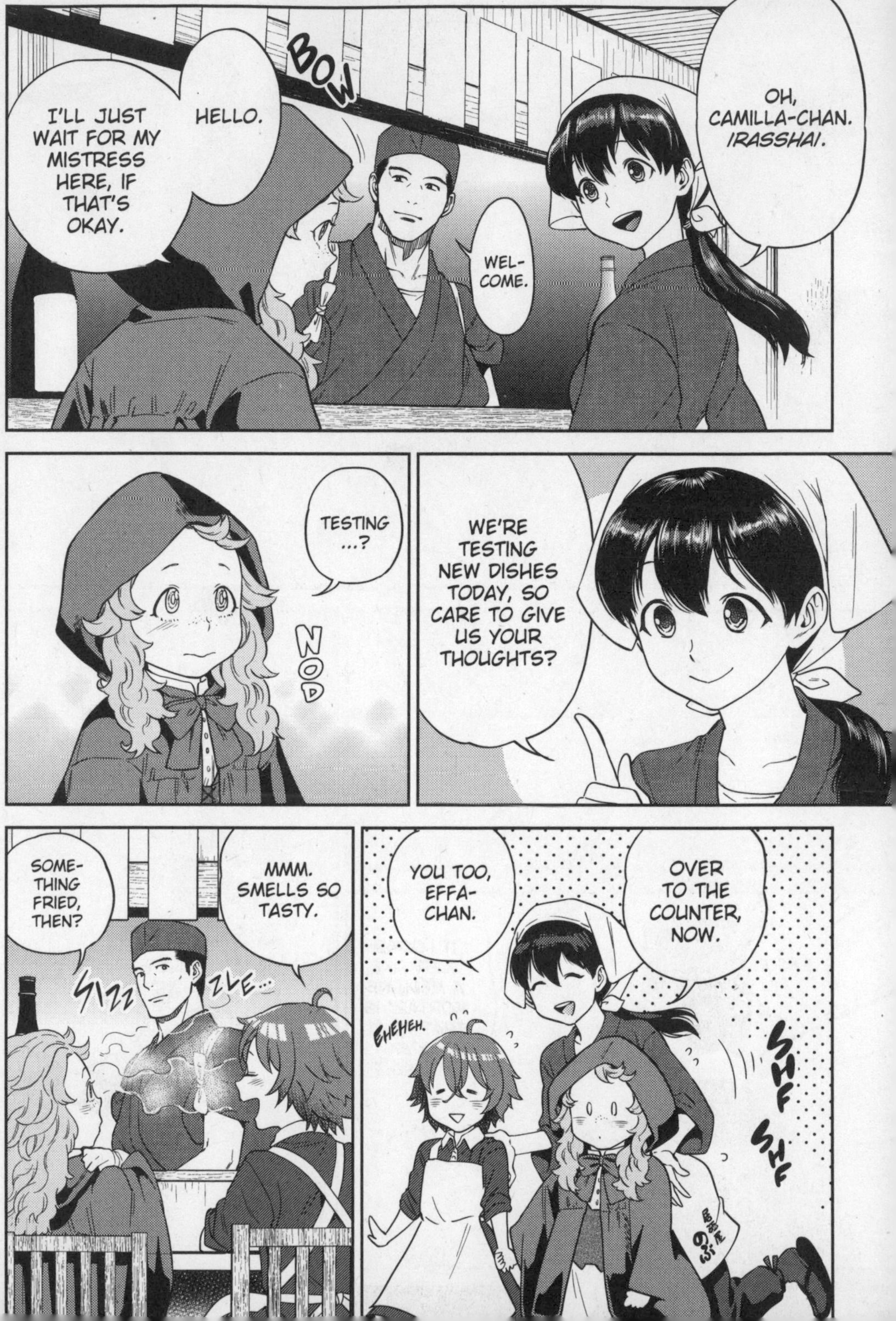
OH, CAMILLA-CHAN. IRASSHAI.
BOW
WEL-COME.
HELLO.
I'LL JUST WAIT FOR MY MISTRESS HERE, IF THAT'S OKAY.
WE'RE TESTING NEW DISHES TODAY, SO CARE TO GIVE US YOUR THOUGHTS?
TESTING ...?
NOD
OVER TO THE COUNTER, NOW.
SHF SHF
YOU TOO, EFFA-CHAN.
EHEHEH.
居酒屋のぶ
MMM. SMELLS SO TASTY.
SOME-THING FRIED, THEN?
SIZZLE...

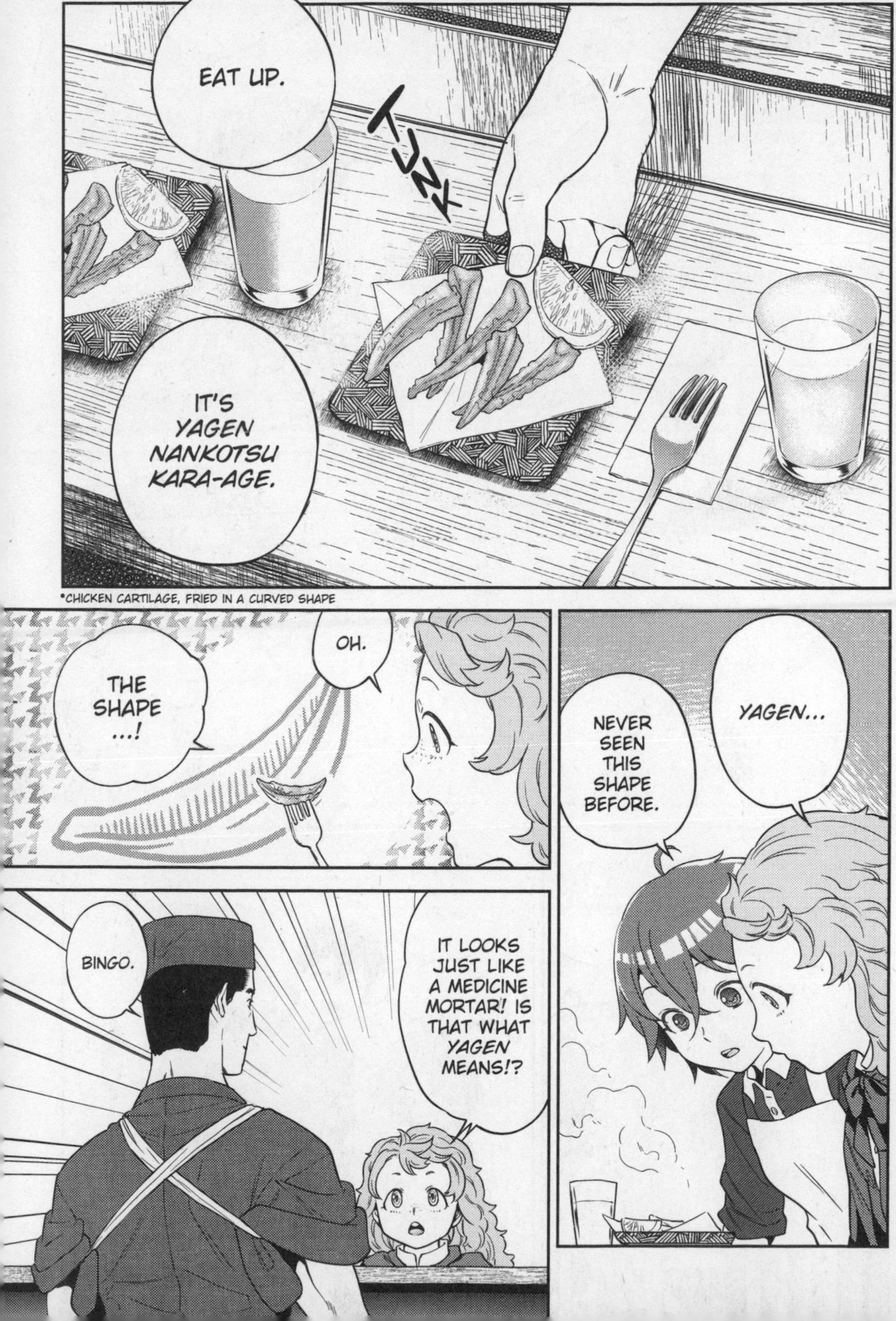
EAT UP.
TUNK
IT'S YAGEN NANKOTSU KARA-AGE.
*CHICKEN CARTILAGE, FRIED IN A CURVED SHAPE
YAGEN...
NEVER SEEN THIS SHAPE BEFORE.
OH.
THE SHAPE ...!
IT LOOKS JUST LIKE A MEDICINE MORTAR! IS THAT WHAT YAGEN MEANS!?
BINGO.

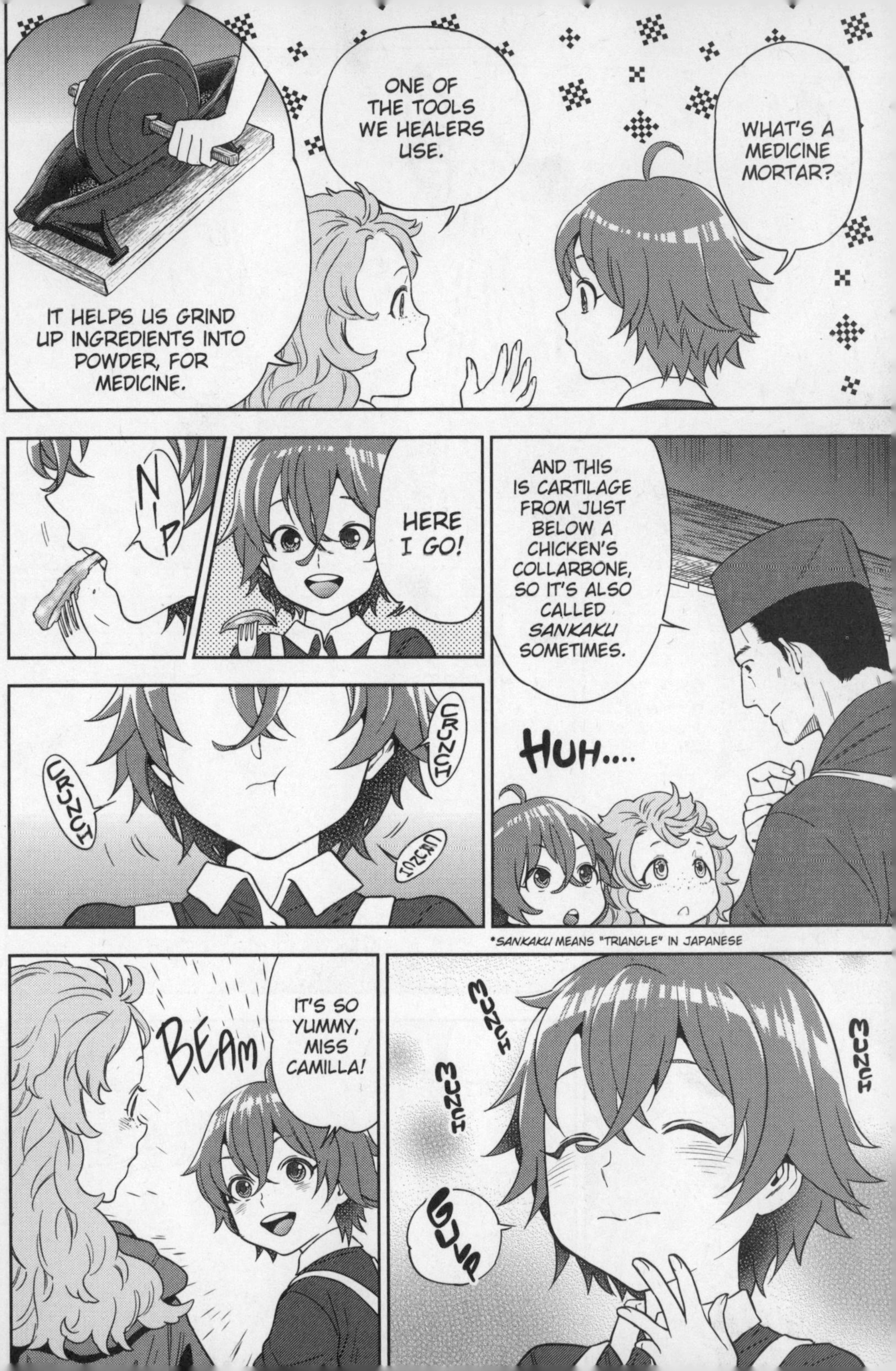
WHAT'S A MEDICINE MORTAR?
ONE OF THE TOOLS WE HEALERS USE.
IT HELPS US GRIND UP INGREDIENTS INTO POWDER, FOR MEDICINE.
AND THIS IS CARTILAGE FROM JUST BELOW A CHICKEN'S COLLARBONE, SO IT'S ALSO CALLED *SANKAKU* SOMETIMES.
HUH....
HERE I GO!
NIP
CRUNCH
CRUNCH
CRUNCH
MUNCH
MUNCH
MUNCH
GULP
BEAM
IT'S SO YUMMY, MISS CAMILLA!

**SANKAKU* MEANS "TRIANGLE" IN JAPANESE

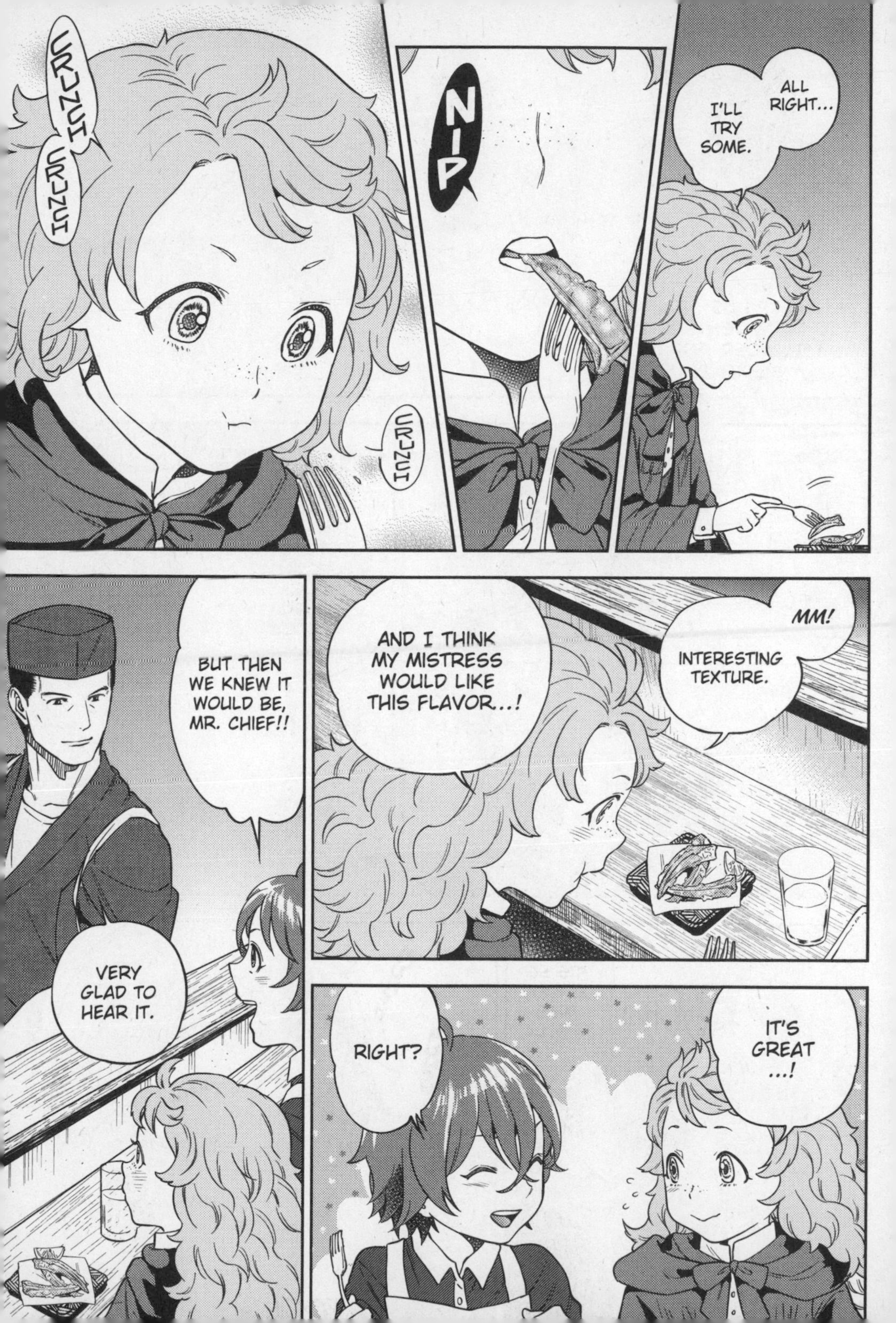
ALL RIGHT... I'LL TRY SOME.
NIP
CRUNCH
CRUNCH CRUNCH
MM! INTERESTING TEXTURE.
AND I THINK MY MISTRESS WOULD LIKE THIS FLAVOR...!
IT'S GREAT ...!
RIGHT?
BUT THEN WE KNEW IT WOULD BE, MR. CHIEF!!
VERY GLAD TO HEAR IT.

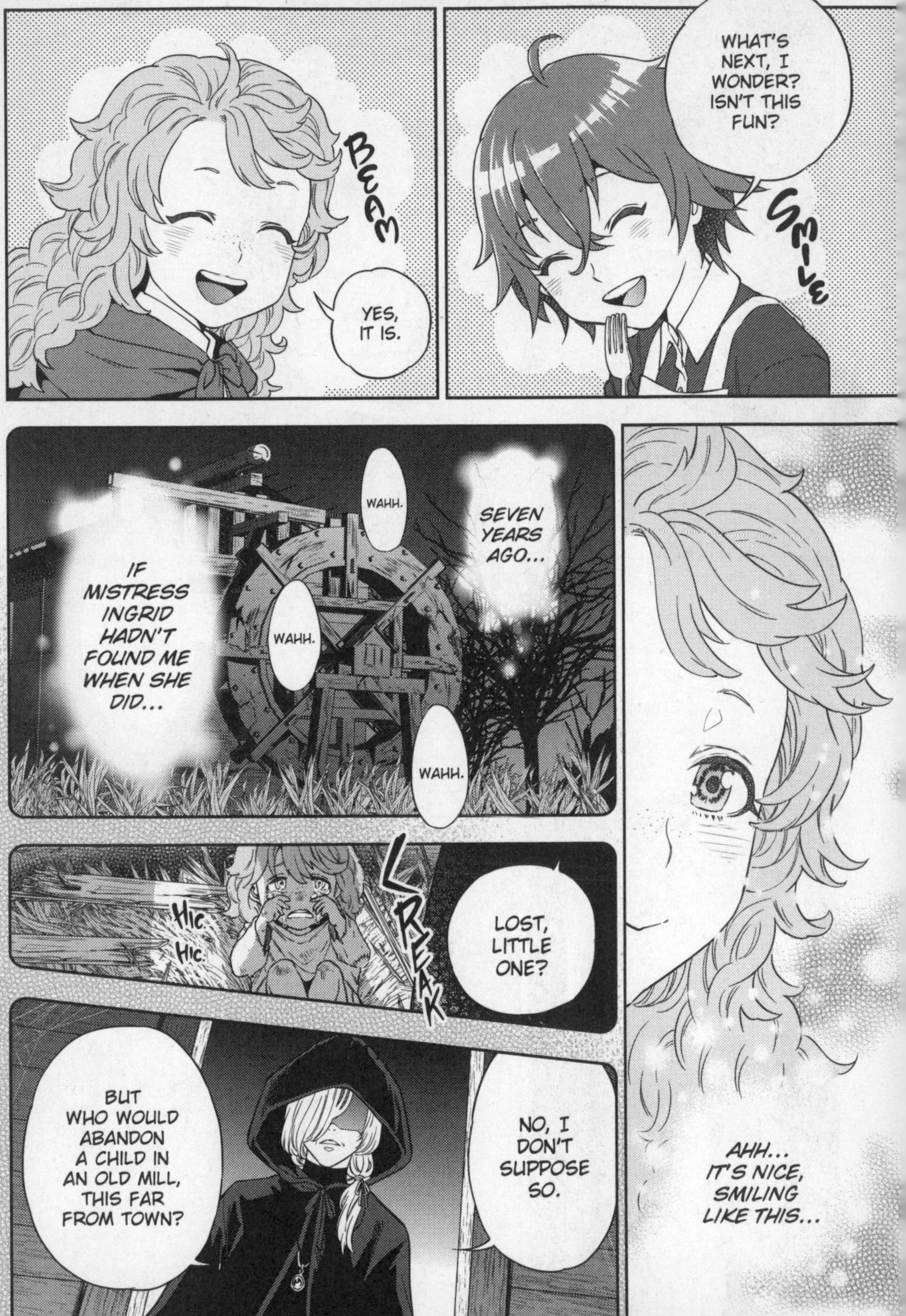
WHAT'S NEXT, I WONDER? ISN'T THIS FUN?
SMILE
BEAM
YES, IT IS.
AHH... IT'S NICE, SMILING LIKE THIS...
SEVEN YEARS AGO...
WAHH.
WAHH.
WAHH.
IF MISTRESS INGRID HADN'T FOUND ME WHEN SHE DID...
LOST, LITTLE ONE?
CREAK
HIC HIC.
NO, I DON'T SUPPOSE SO.
BUT WHO WOULD ABANDON A CHILD IN AN OLD MILL, THIS FAR FROM TOWN?

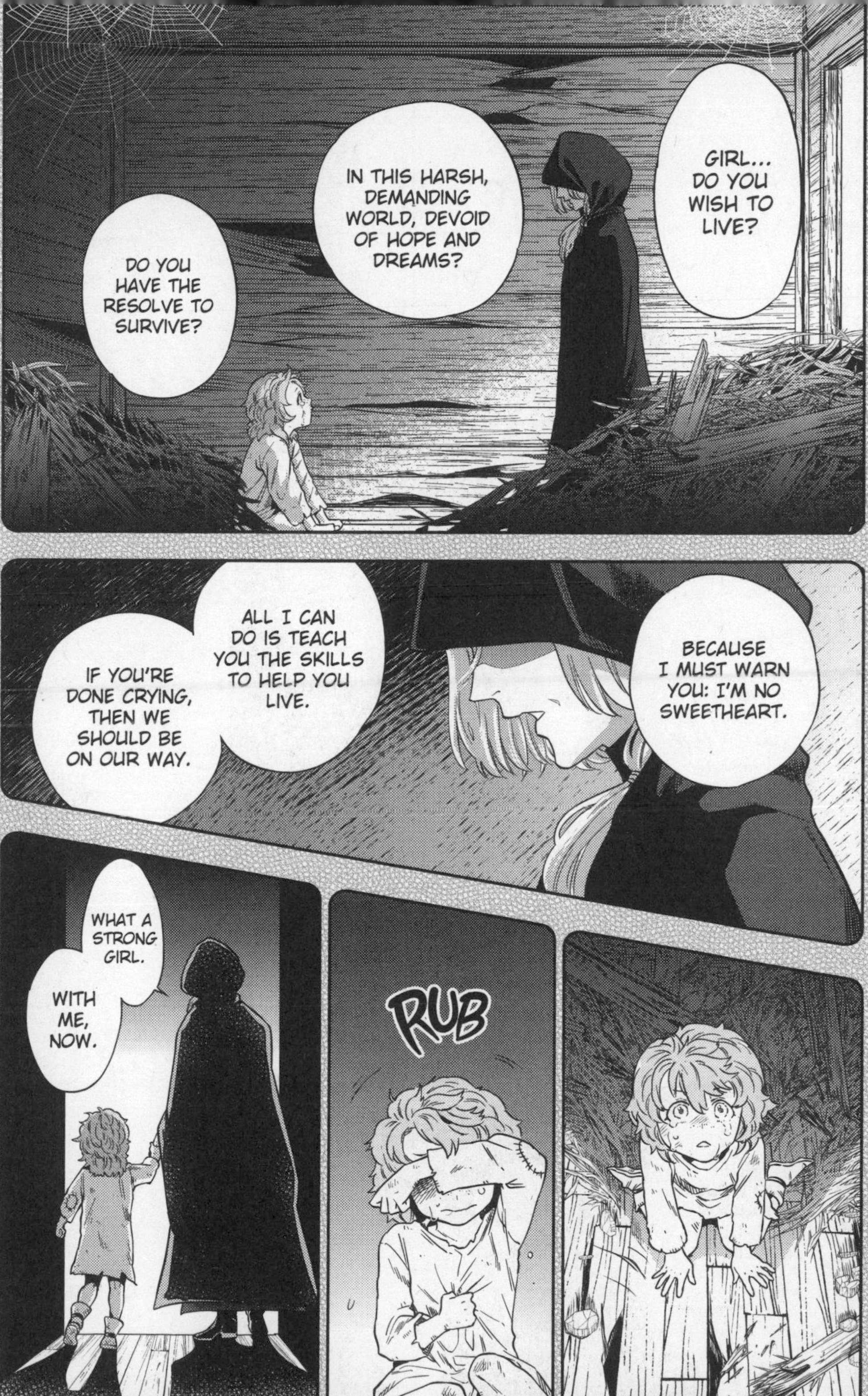
GIRL... DO YOU WISH TO LIVE?
IN THIS HARSH, DEMANDING WORLD, DEVOID OF HOPE AND DREAMS?
DO YOU HAVE THE RESOLVE TO SURVIVE?
BECAUSE I MUST WARN YOU: I'M NO SWEETHEART.
ALL I CAN DO IS TEACH YOU THE SKILLS TO HELP YOU LIVE.
IF YOU'RE DONE CRYING, THEN WE SHOULD BE ON OUR WAY.
RUB
WHAT A STRONG GIRL.
WITH ME, NOW.

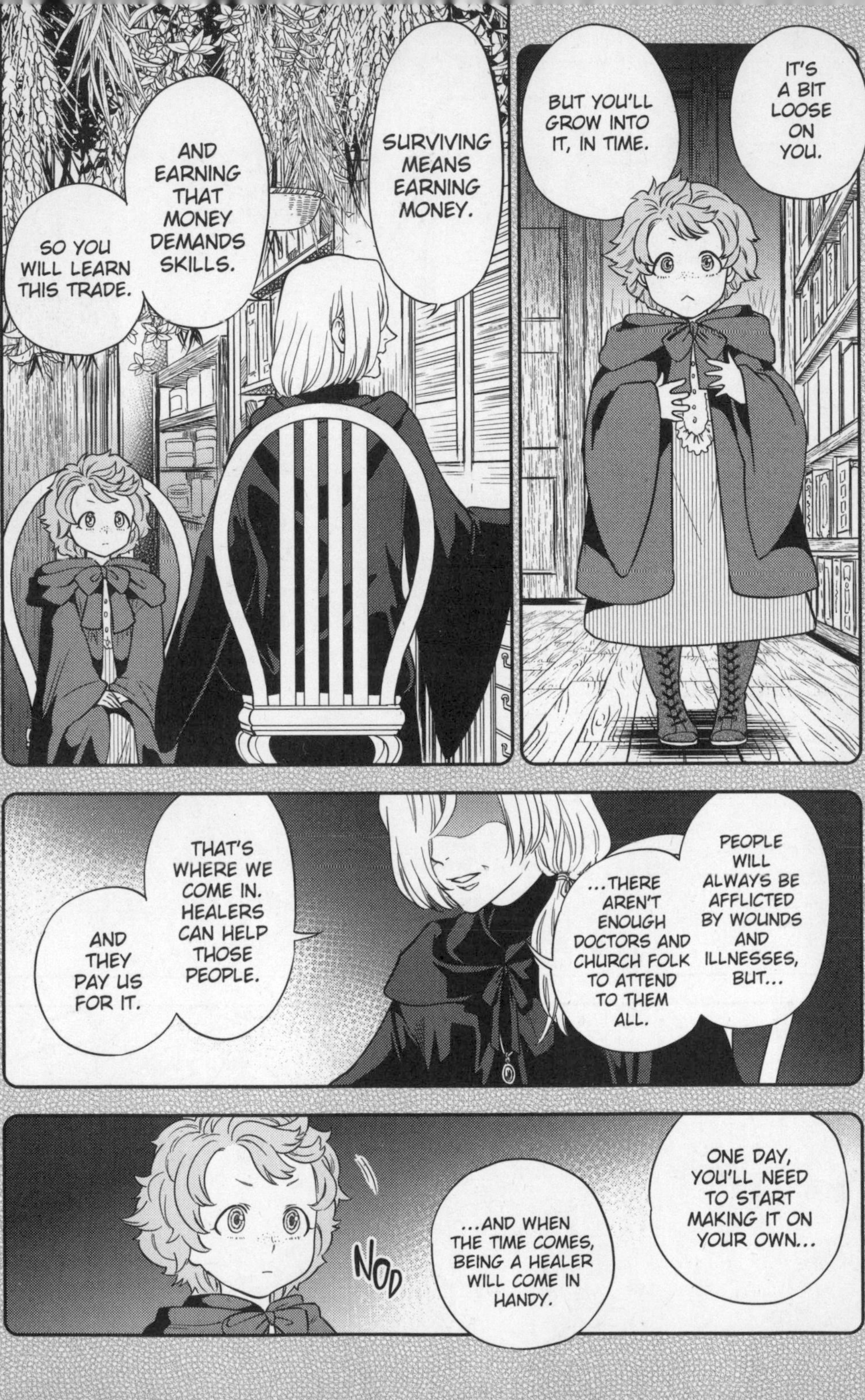
IT'S A BIT LOOSE ON YOU.
BUT YOU'LL GROW INTO IT, IN TIME.
SURVIVING MEANS EARNING MONEY.
AND EARNING THAT MONEY DEMANDS SKILLS.
SO YOU WILL LEARN THIS TRADE.
PEOPLE WILL ALWAYS BE AFFLICTED BY WOUNDS AND ILLNESSES, BUT...
...THERE AREN'T ENOUGH DOCTORS AND CHURCH FOLK TO ATTEND TO THEM ALL.
THAT'S WHERE WE COME IN. HEALERS CAN HELP THOSE PEOPLE.
AND THEY PAY US FOR IT.
ONE DAY, YOU'LL NEED TO START MAKING IT ON YOUR OWN...
...AND WHEN THE TIME COMES, BEING A HEALER WILL COME IN HANDY.
NOD

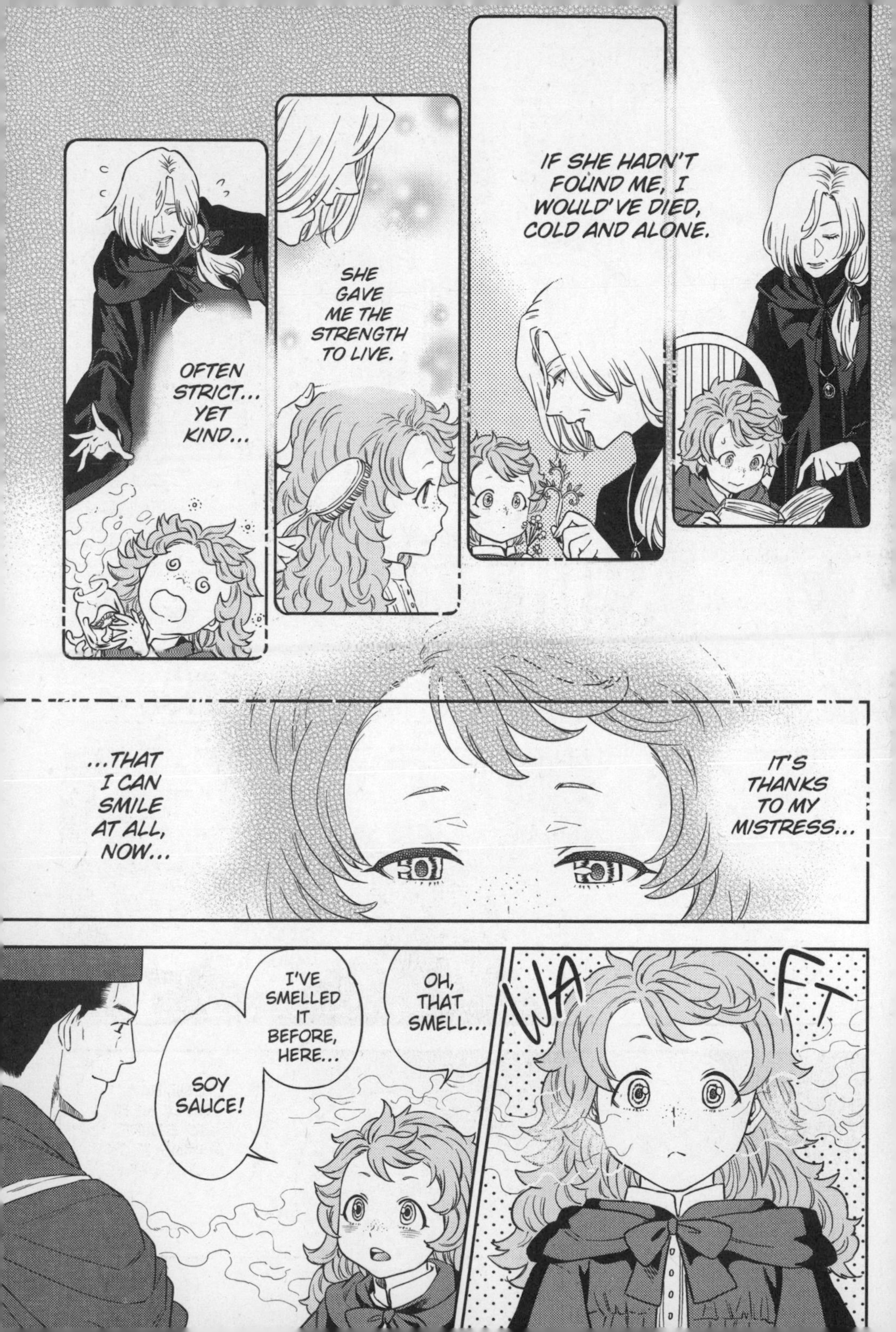
IF SHE HADN'T FOUND ME, I WOULD'VE DIED, COLD AND ALONE.
SHE GAVE ME THE STRENGTH TO LIVE.
OFTEN STRICT... YET KIND...
IT'S THANKS TO MY MISTRESS...
...THAT I CAN SMILE AT ALL, NOW...
WAFT
OH, THAT SMELL...
I'VE SMELLED IT BEFORE, HERE...
SOY SAUCE!

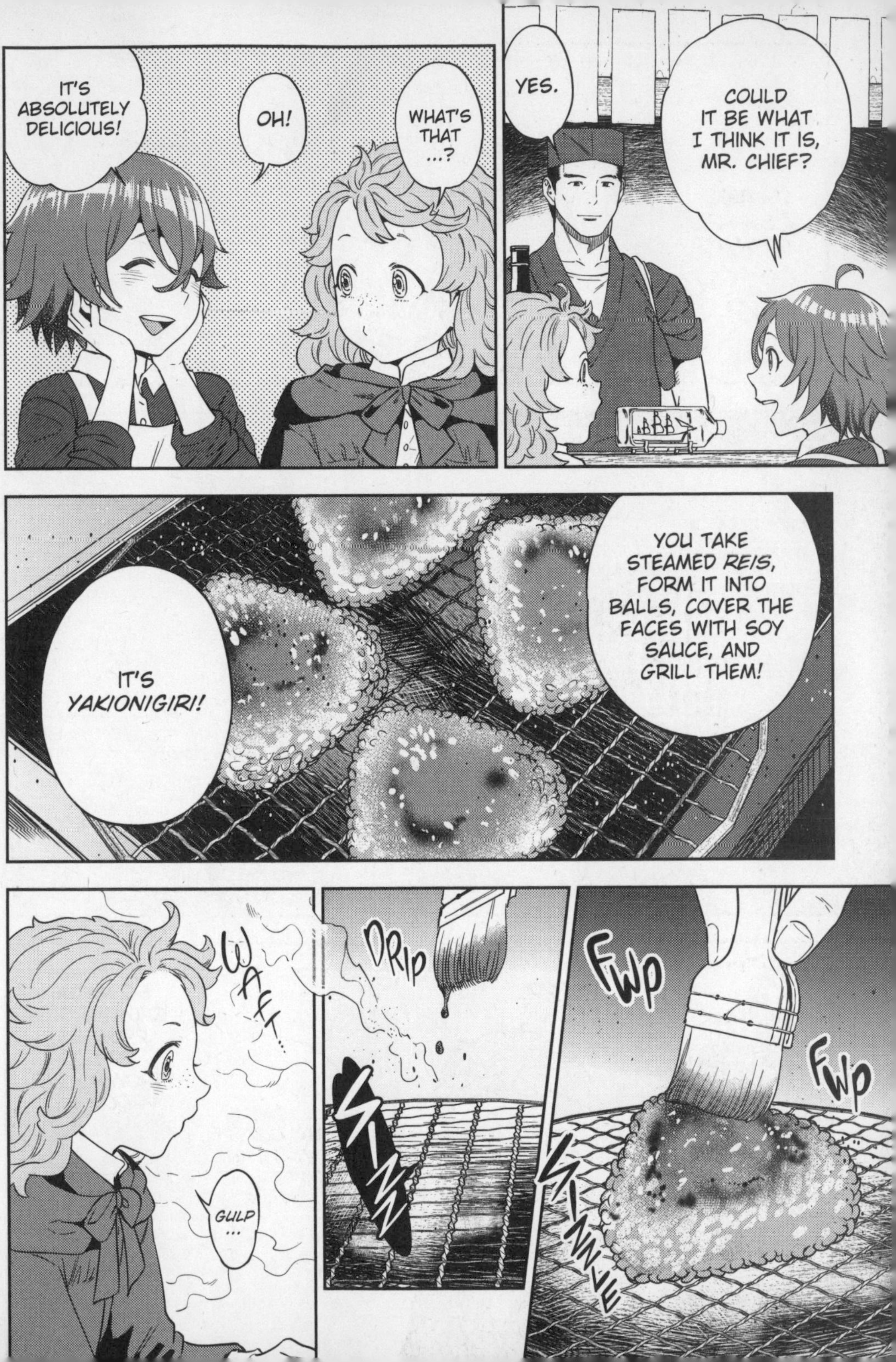
COULD IT BE WHAT I THINK IT IS, MR. CHIEF?
YES.
WHAT'S THAT ...?
OH!
IT'S ABSOLUTELY DELICIOUS!
YOU TAKE STEAMED *REIS*, FORM IT INTO BALLS, COVER THE FACES WITH SOY SAUCE, AND GRILL THEM!
IT'S *YAKIONIGIRI*!
FWP
FWP
DRIP
WAFT...
GULP ...

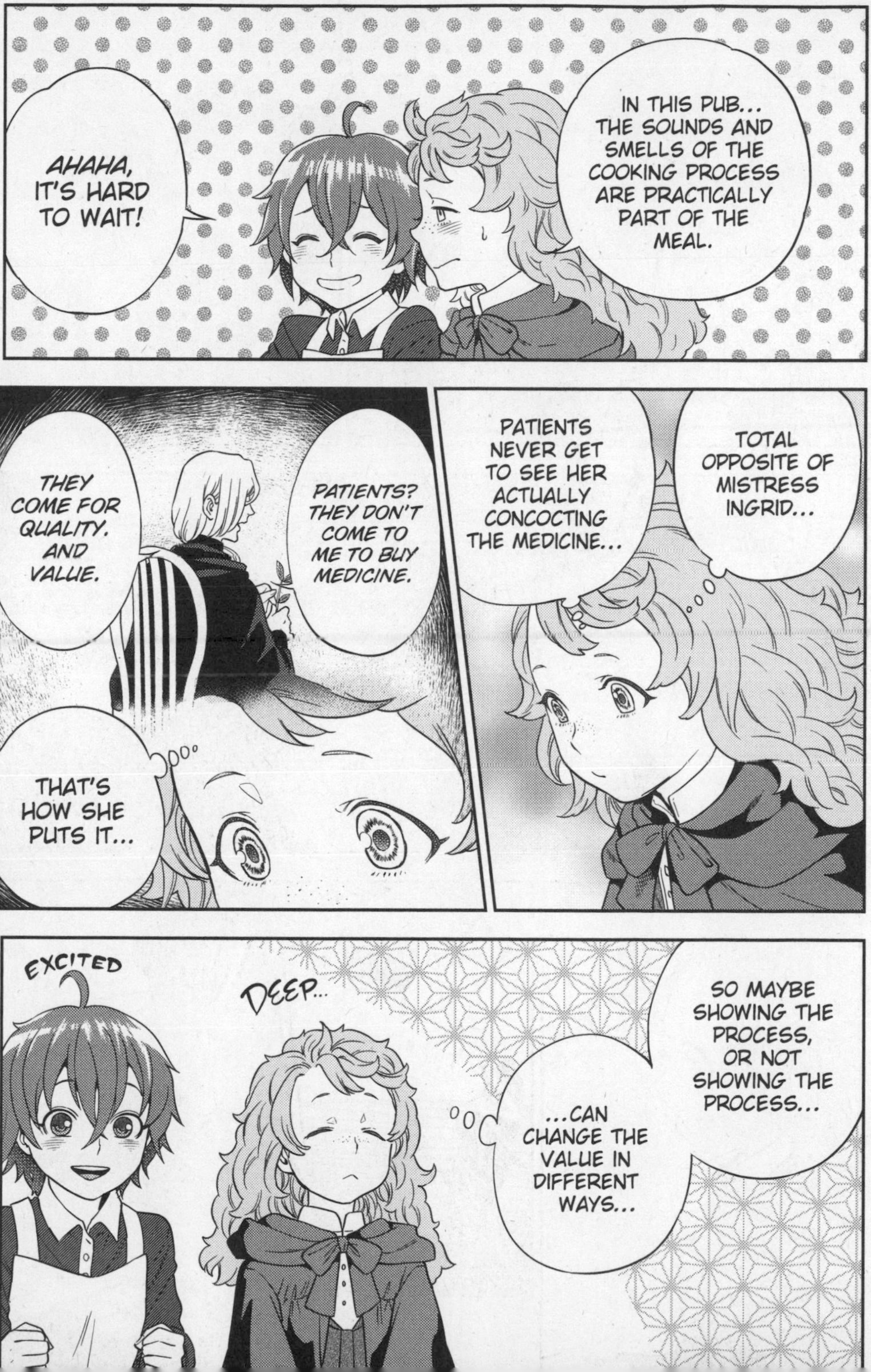
IN THIS PUB... THE SOUNDS AND SMELLS OF THE COOKING PROCESS ARE PRACTICALLY PART OF THE MEAL.
AHAHA, IT'S HARD TO WAIT!
TOTAL OPPOSITE OF MISTRESS INGRID...
PATIENTS NEVER GET TO SEE HER ACTUALLY CONCOCTING THE MEDICINE...
PATIENTS? THEY DON'T COME TO ME TO BUY MEDICINE.
THEY COME FOR QUALITY. AND VALUE.
THAT'S HOW SHE PUTS IT...
SO MAYBE SHOWING THE PROCESS, OR NOT SHOWING THE PROCESS...
...CAN CHANGE THE VALUE IN DIFFERENT WAYS...
DEEP...
EXCITED

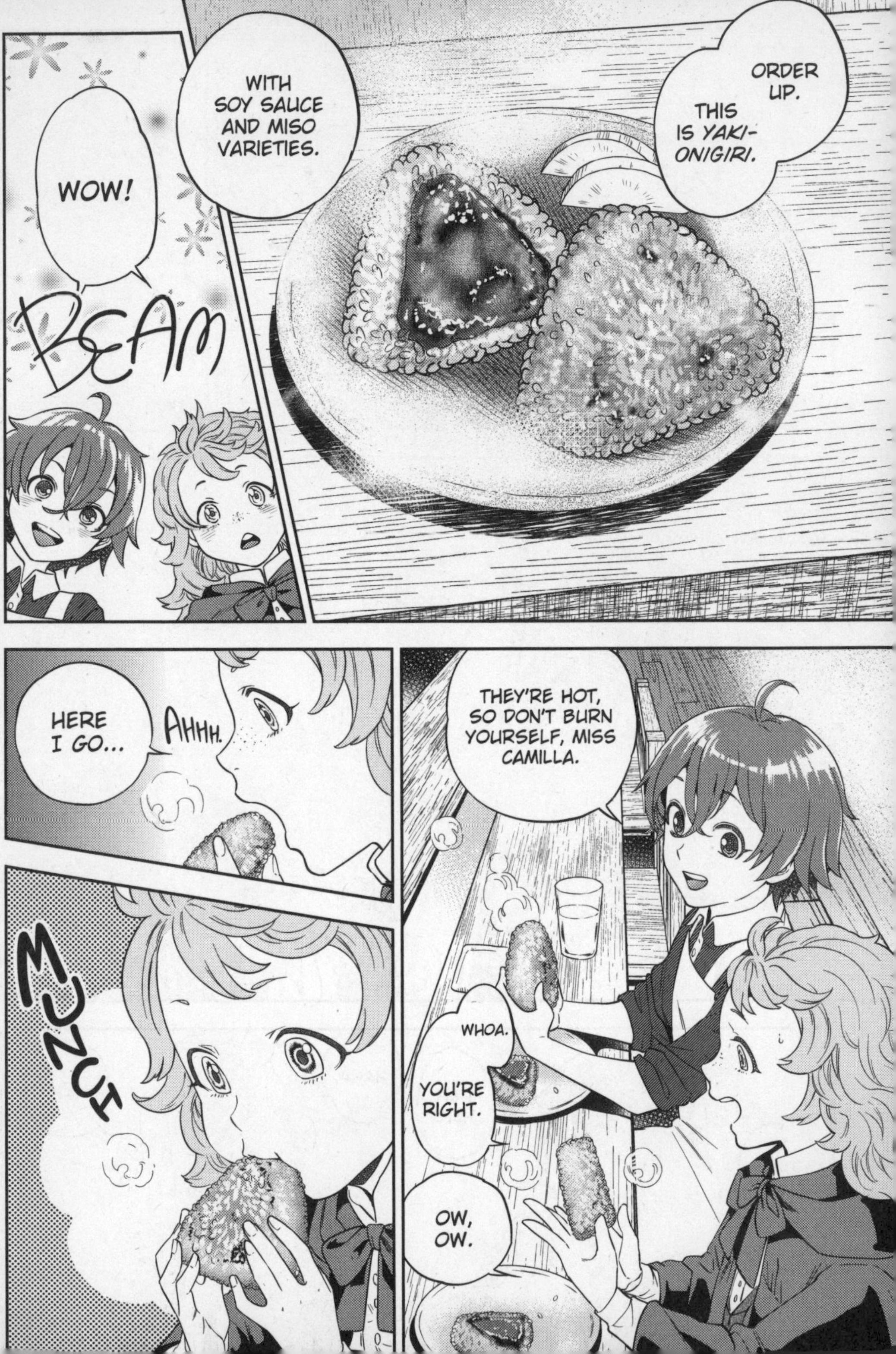
ORDER UP.
THIS IS YAKI-ONIGIRI.
WITH SOY SAUCE AND MISO VARIETIES.
WOW!
BEAM
THEY'RE HOT, SO DON'T BURN YOURSELF, MISS CAMILLA.
WHOA.
YOU'RE RIGHT.
OW, OW.
HERE I GO...
AHHH.
MUNCH

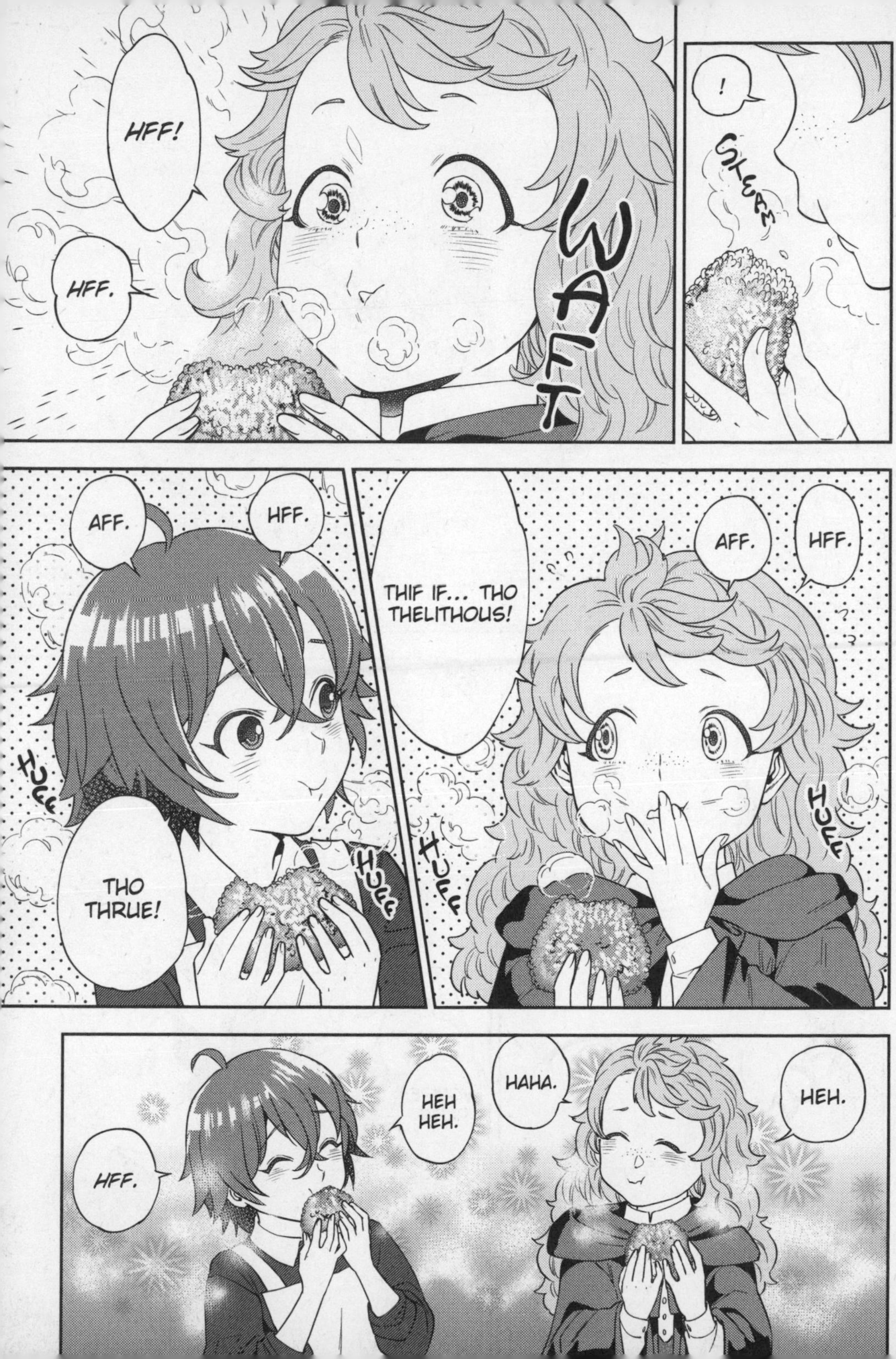
!
STEAM
HFF!
HFF.
WAFT
HFF.
AFF.
THIF IF... THO THELITHOUS!
HUFF
HUFF
HFF.
AFF.
HUFF
HUFF
THO THRUE!
HEH.
HAHA.
HEH HEH.
HFF.

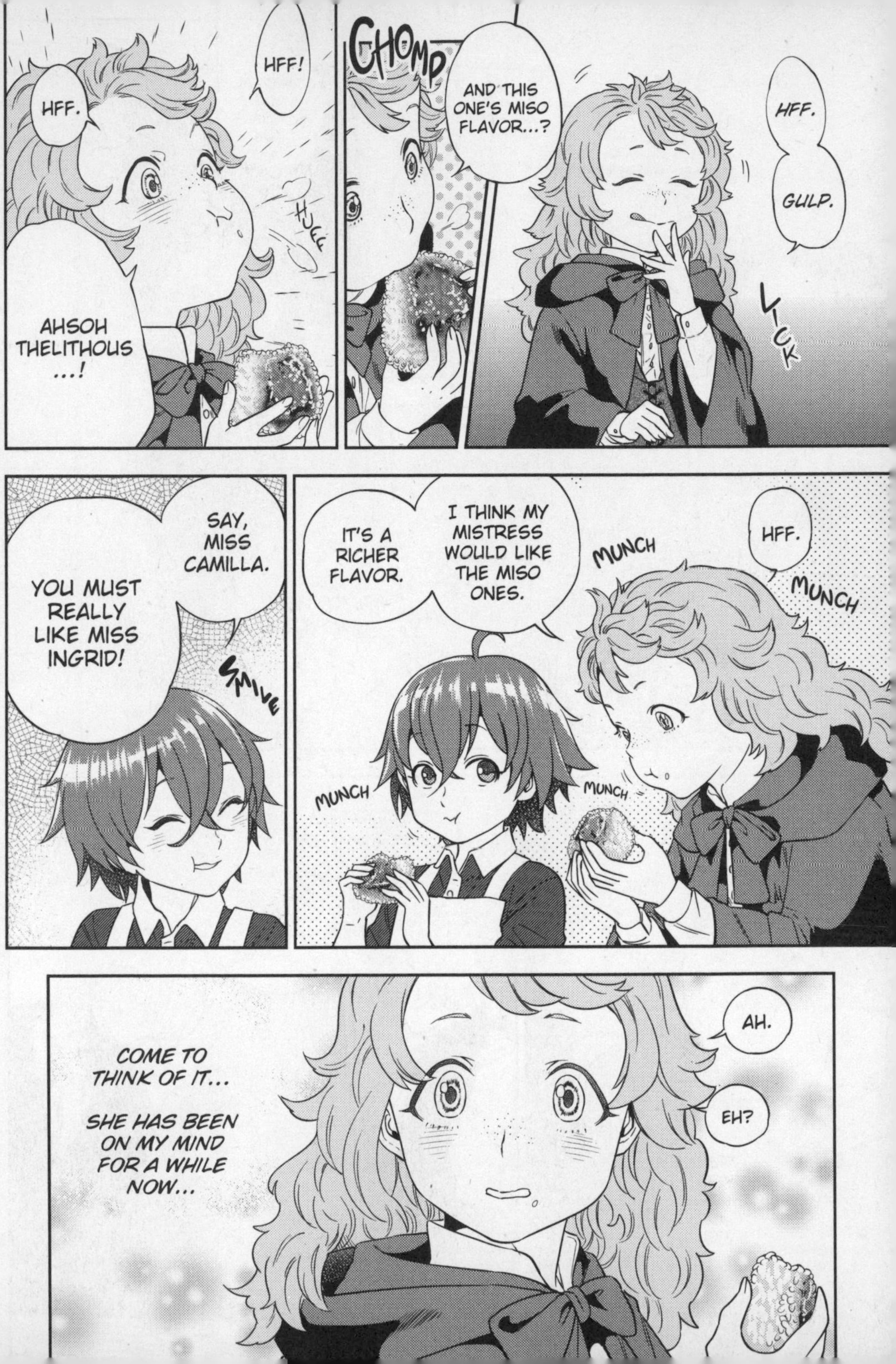
HFF.
GULP.
LICK
CHOMP
AND THIS ONE'S MISO FLAVOR...?
HFF!
HFF.
HUFF
AHSOH THELITHOUS ...!
HFF.
MUNCH
MUNCH
I THINK MY MISTRESS WOULD LIKE THE MISO ONES.
IT'S A RICHER FLAVOR.
MUNCH
MUNCH
SAY, MISS CAMILLA.
YOU MUST REALLY LIKE MISS INGRID!
SMILE
AH.
EH?
COME TO THINK OF IT...
SHE HAS BEEN ON MY MIND FOR A WHILE NOW...

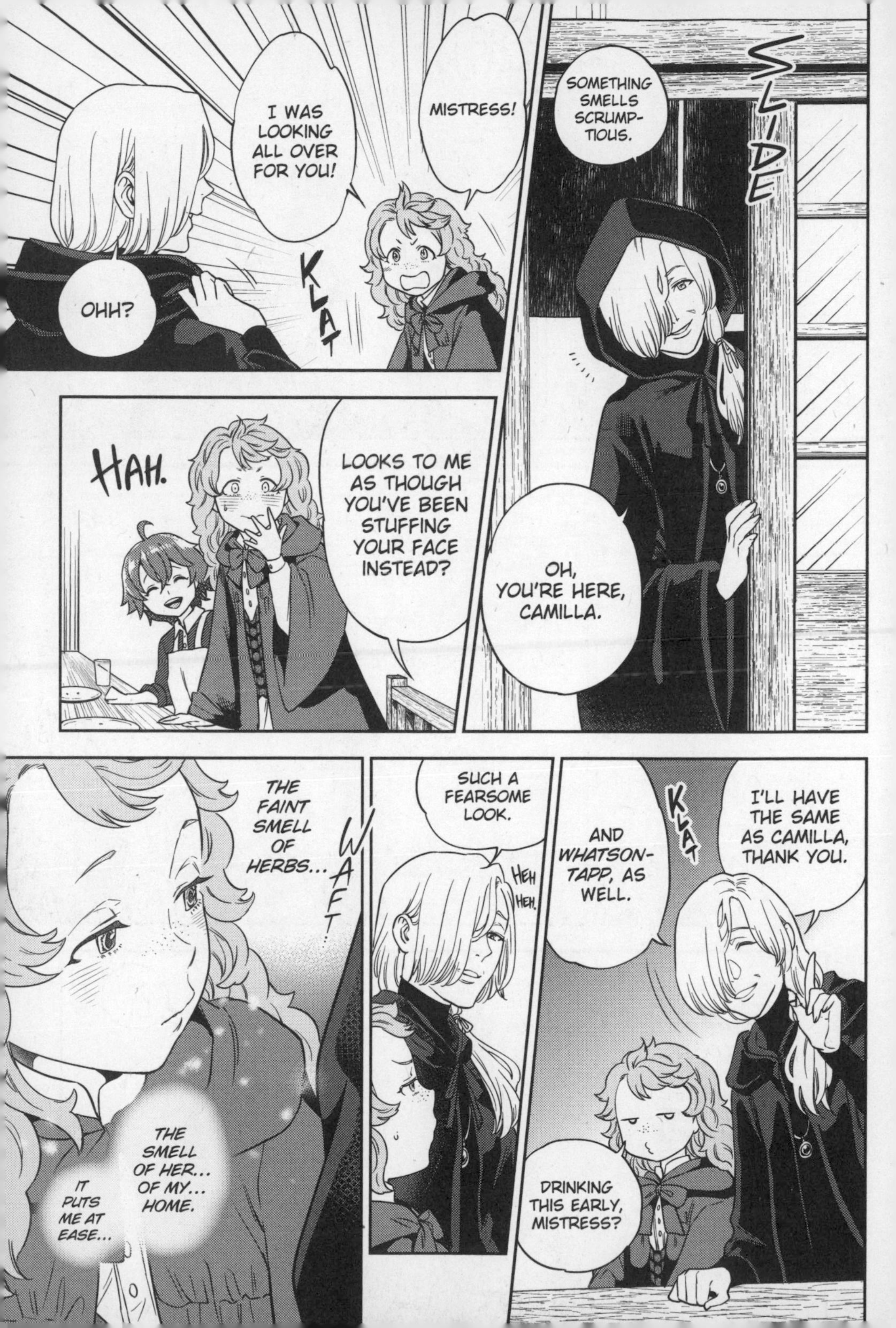
SLIDE
SOMETHING SMELLS SCRUMPTIOUS.
OH, YOU'RE HERE, CAMILLA.
MISTRESS!
I WAS LOOKING ALL OVER FOR YOU!
KLAT
OHH?
LOOKS TO ME AS THOUGH YOU'VE BEEN STUFFING YOUR FACE INSTEAD?
HAH.
I'LL HAVE THE SAME AS CAMILLA, THANK YOU.
KLAT
AND WHATSON-TAPP, AS WELL.
DRINKING THIS EARLY, MISTRESS?
SUCH A FEARSOME LOOK.
HEH HEH.
THE FAINT SMELL OF HERBS...
WAFT
THE SMELL OF HER... OF MY... HOME.
IT PUTS ME AT EASE...

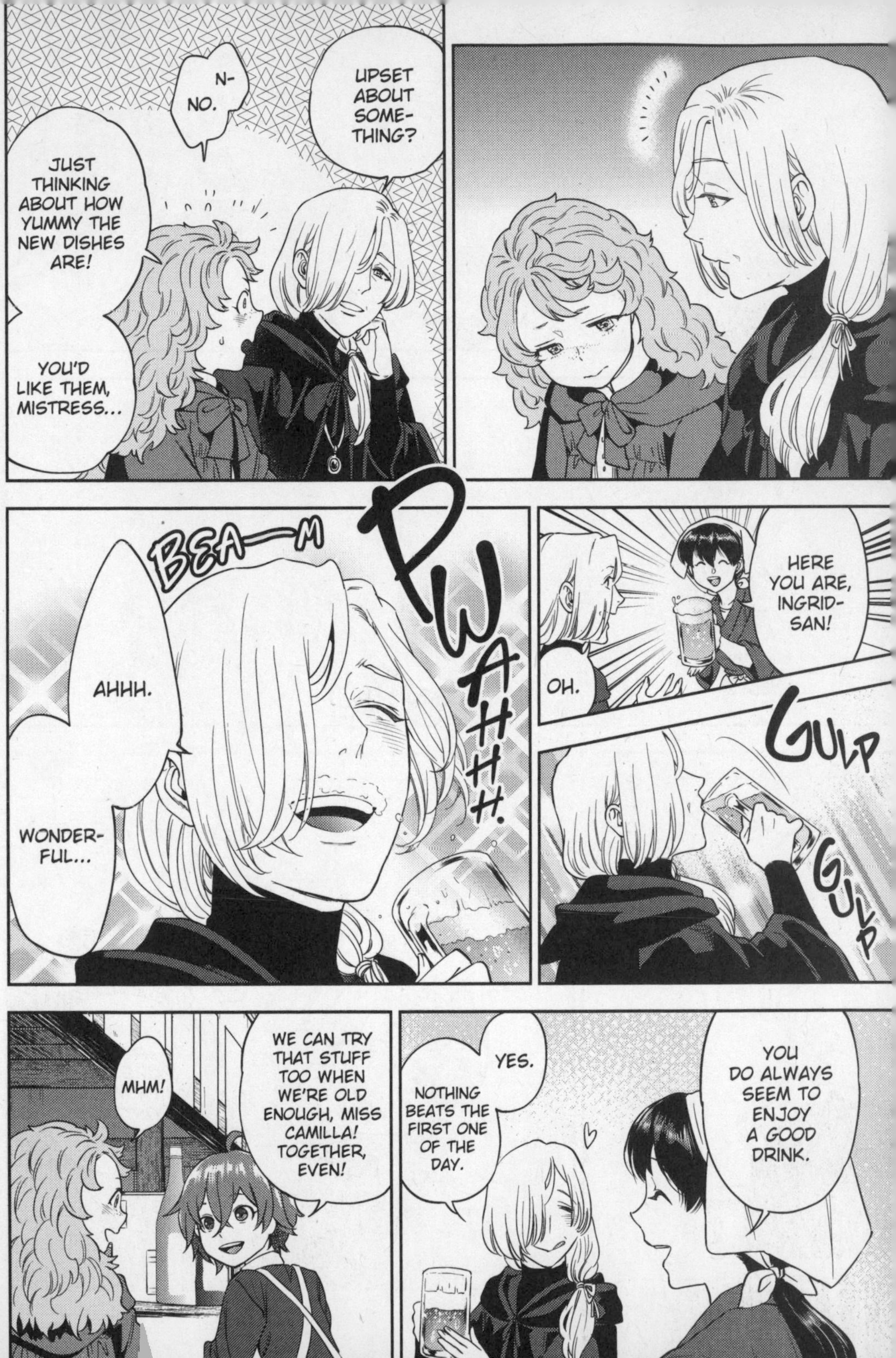
UPSET ABOUT SOMETHING?
N- NO.
JUST THINKING ABOUT HOW YUMMY THE NEW DISHES ARE!
YOU'D LIKE THEM, MISTRESS...
HERE YOU ARE, INGRID-SAN!
OH.
GULP
GULP
PWAHHH!
BEA—M
AHHH.
WONDERFUL...
YOU DO ALWAYS SEEM TO ENJOY A GOOD DRINK.
YES.
NOTHING BEATS THE FIRST ONE OF THE DAY.
WE CAN TRY THAT STUFF TOO WHEN WE'RE OLD ENOUGH, MISS CAMILLA! TOGETHER, EVEN!
MHM!

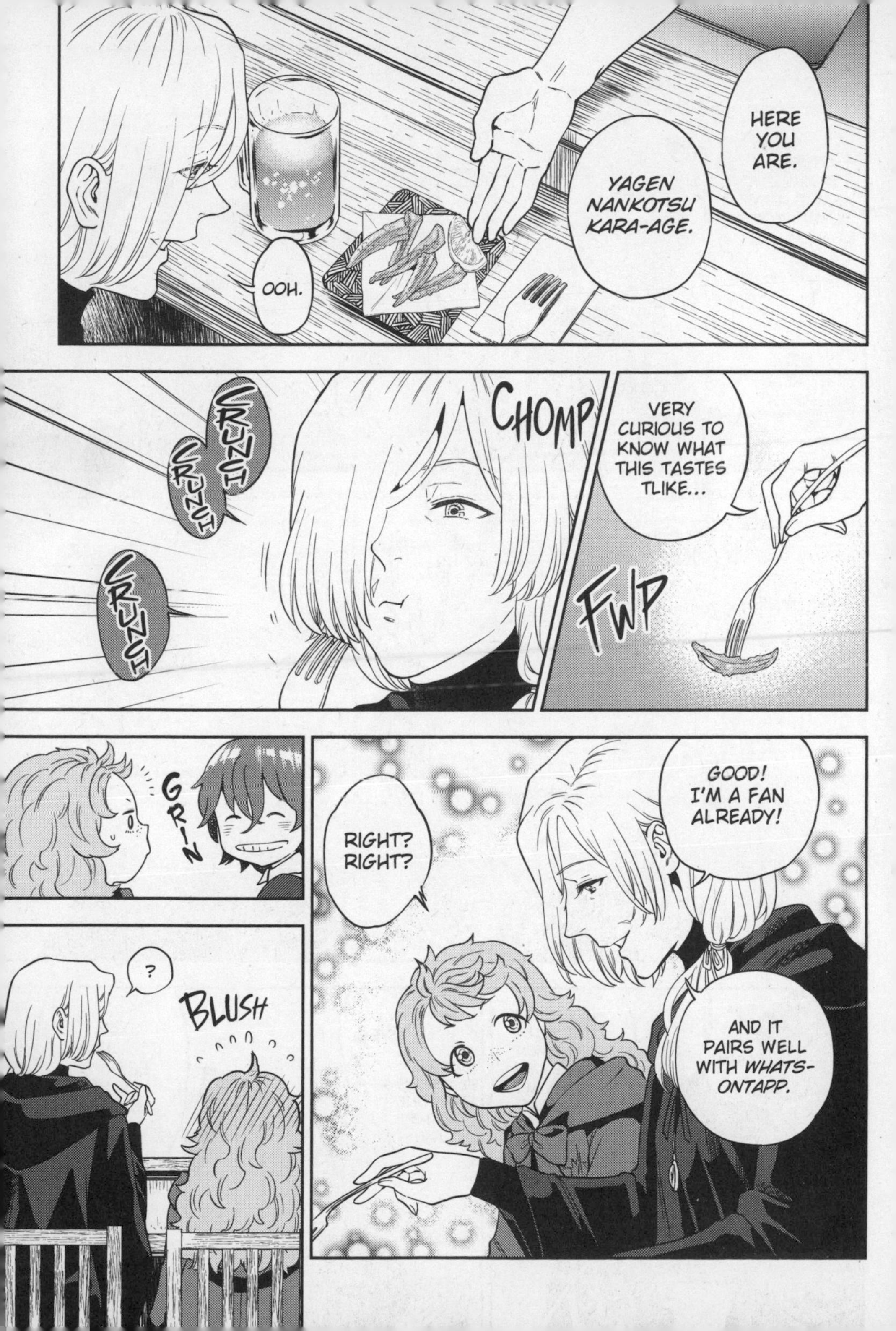
HERE YOU ARE.
YAGEN NANKOTSU KARA-AGE.
OOH.
VERY CURIOUS TO KNOW WHAT THIS TASTES TLIKE...
FWP
CHOMP
CRUNCH
CRUNCH
CRUNCH
GOOD! I'M A FAN ALREADY!
RIGHT? RIGHT?
AND IT PAIRS WELL WITH WHATS-ONTAPP.
GRIN
?
BLUSH

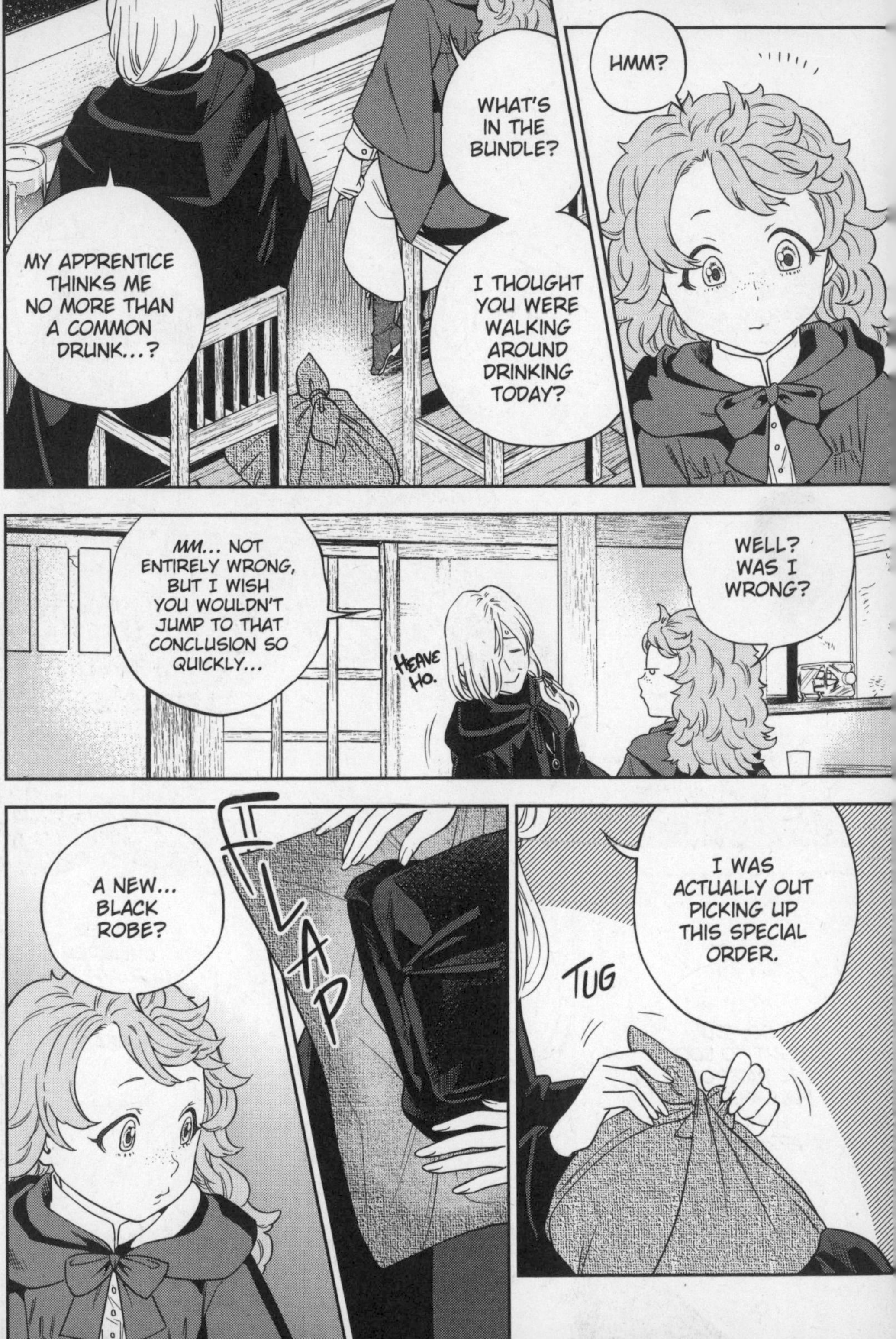
HMM?
WHAT'S IN THE BUNDLE?
I THOUGHT YOU WERE WALKING AROUND DRINKING TODAY?
MY APPRENTICE THINKS ME NO MORE THAN A COMMON DRUNK...?
WELL? WAS I WRONG?
MM... NOT ENTIRELY WRONG, BUT I WISH YOU WOULDN'T JUMP TO THAT CONCLUSION SO QUICKLY...
HEAVE HO.
I WAS ACTUALLY OUT PICKING UP THIS SPECIAL ORDER.
TUG
FLAP
A NEW... BLACK ROBE?

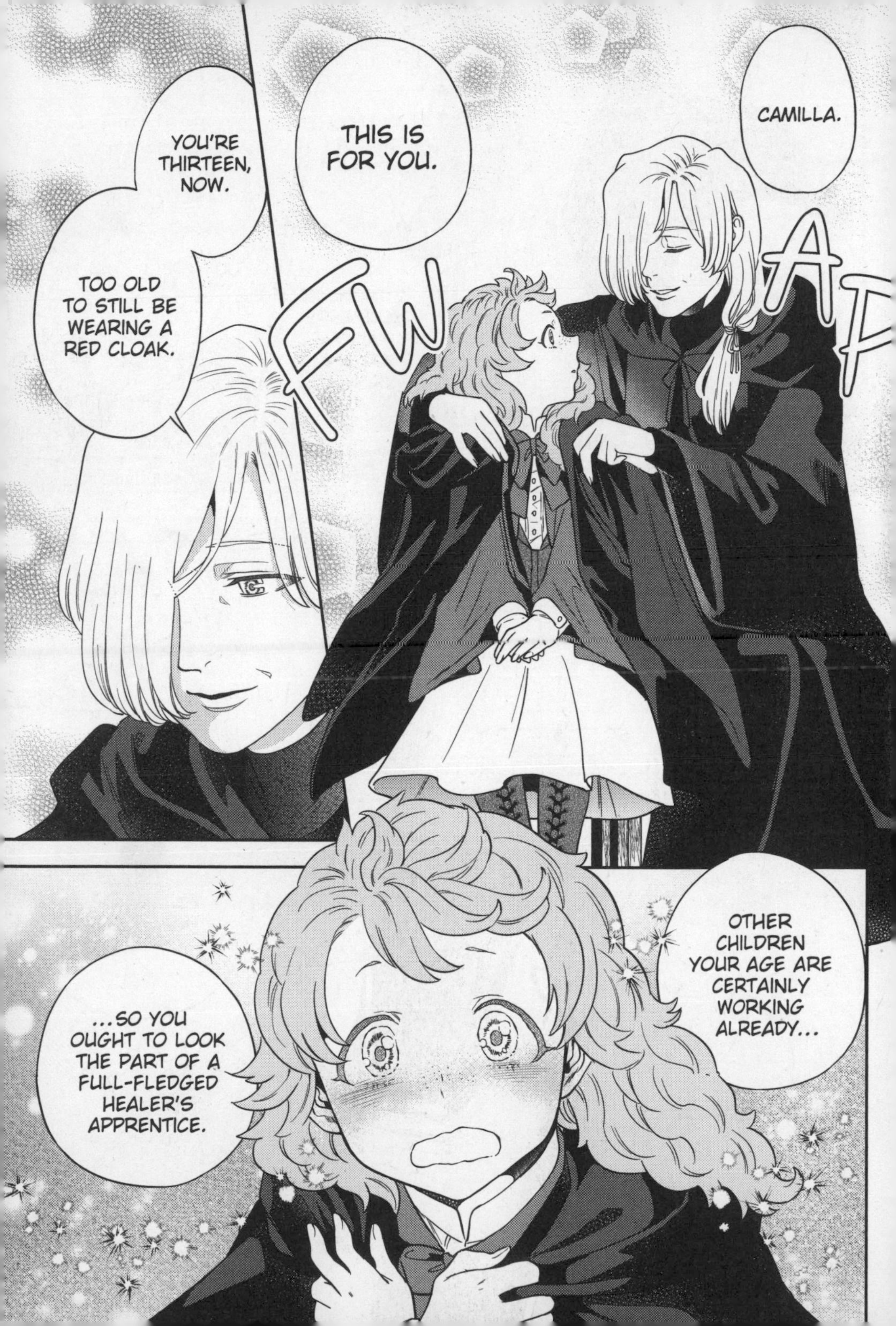
CAMILLA.
THIS IS FOR YOU.
FWAP
YOU'RE THIRTEEN, NOW.
TOO OLD TO STILL BE WEARING A RED CLOAK.
OTHER CHILDREN YOUR AGE ARE CERTAINLY WORKING ALREADY...
...SO YOU OUGHT TO LOOK THE PART OF A FULL-FLEDGED HEALER'S APPRENTICE.

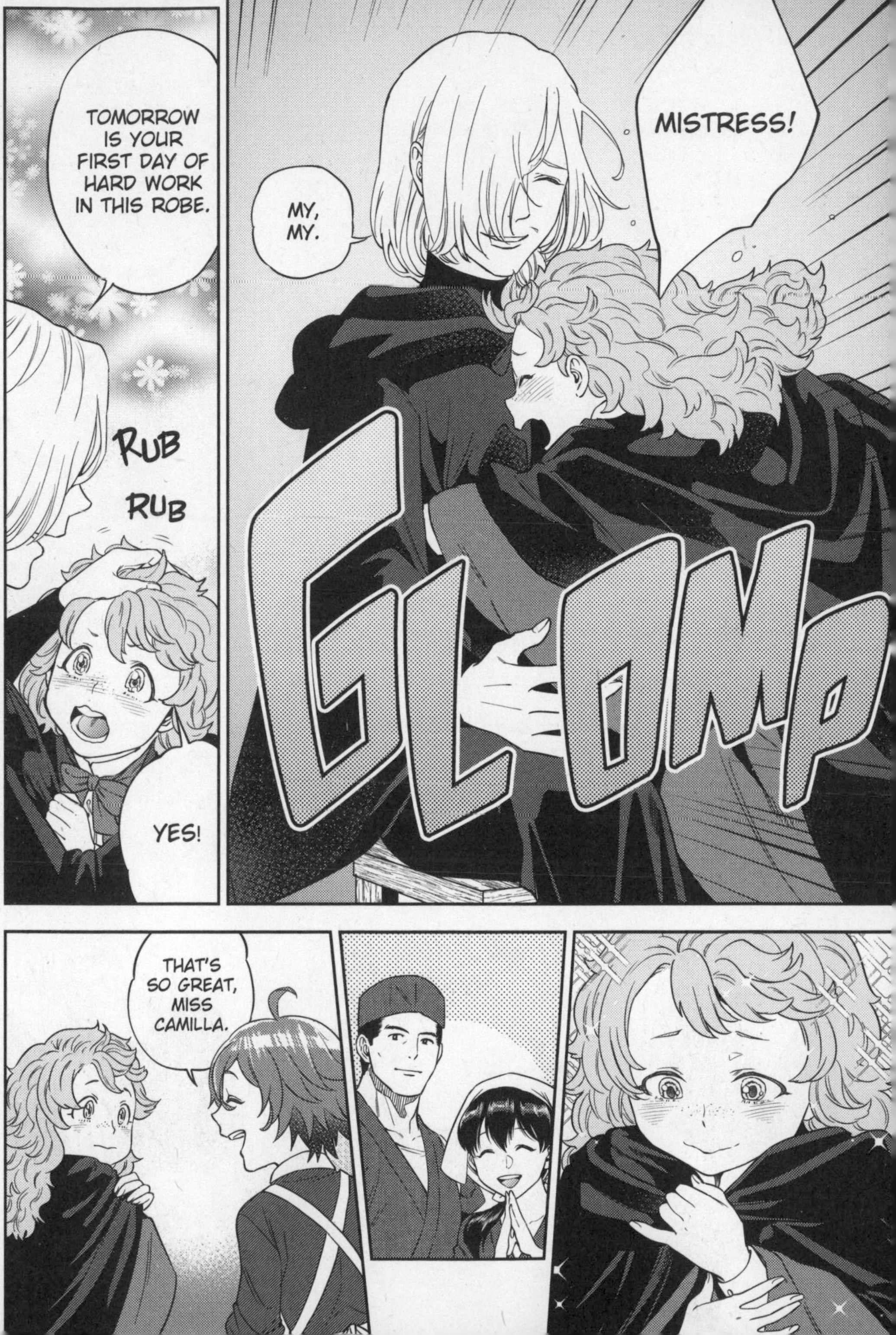
MISTRESS!
MY, MY.
GLOMP
TOMORROW IS YOUR FIRST DAY OF HARD WORK IN THIS ROBE.
RUB
RUB
YES!
THAT'S SO GREAT, MISS CAMILLA.

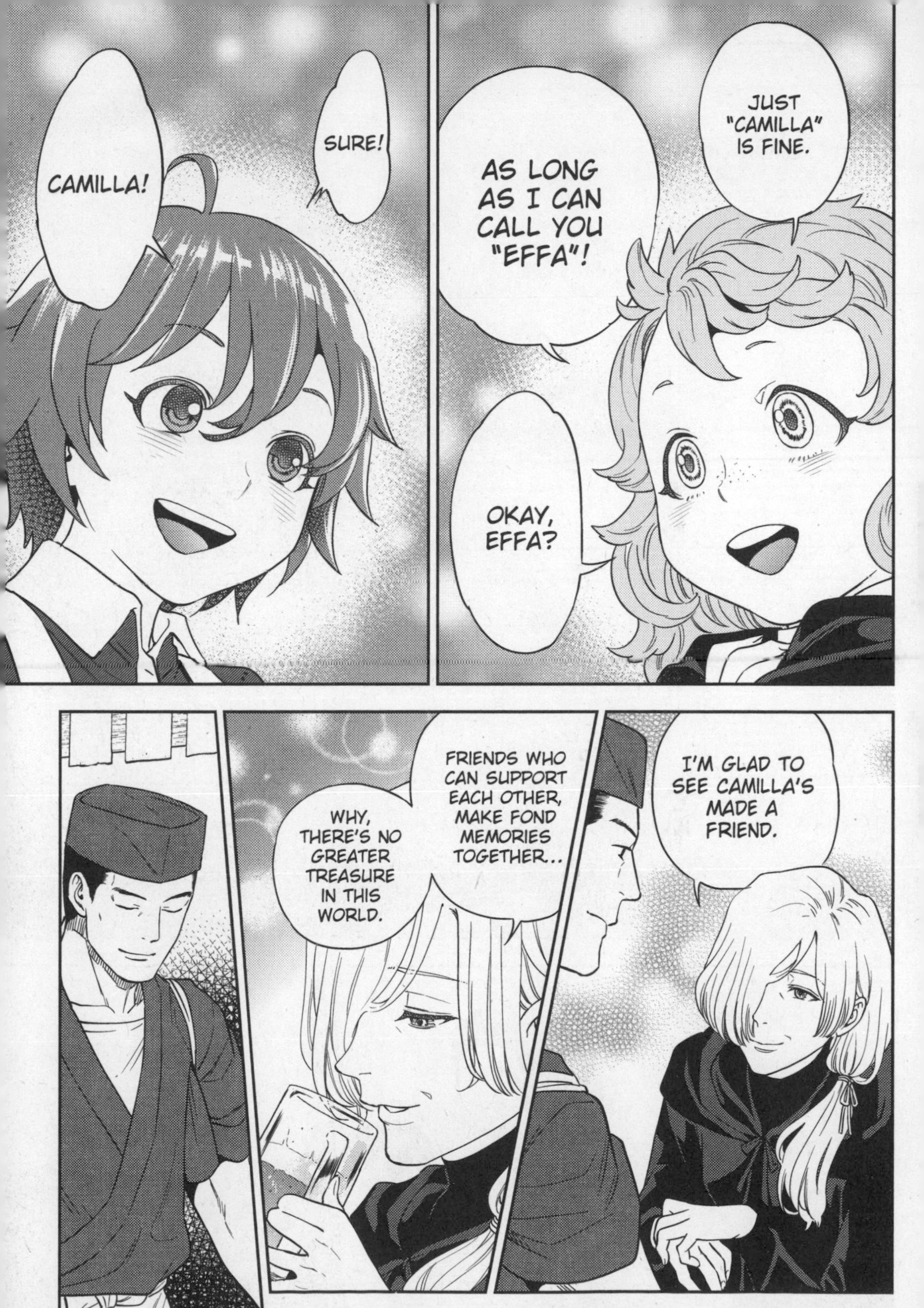
JUST "CAMILLA" IS FINE.
AS LONG AS I CAN CALL YOU "EFFA"!
OKAY, EFFA?
SURE!
CAMILLA!
I'M GLAD TO SEE CAMILLA'S MADE A FRIEND.
FRIENDS WHO CAN SUPPORT EACH OTHER, MAKE FOND MEMORIES TOGETHER...
WHY, THERE'S NO GREATER TREASURE IN THIS WORLD.

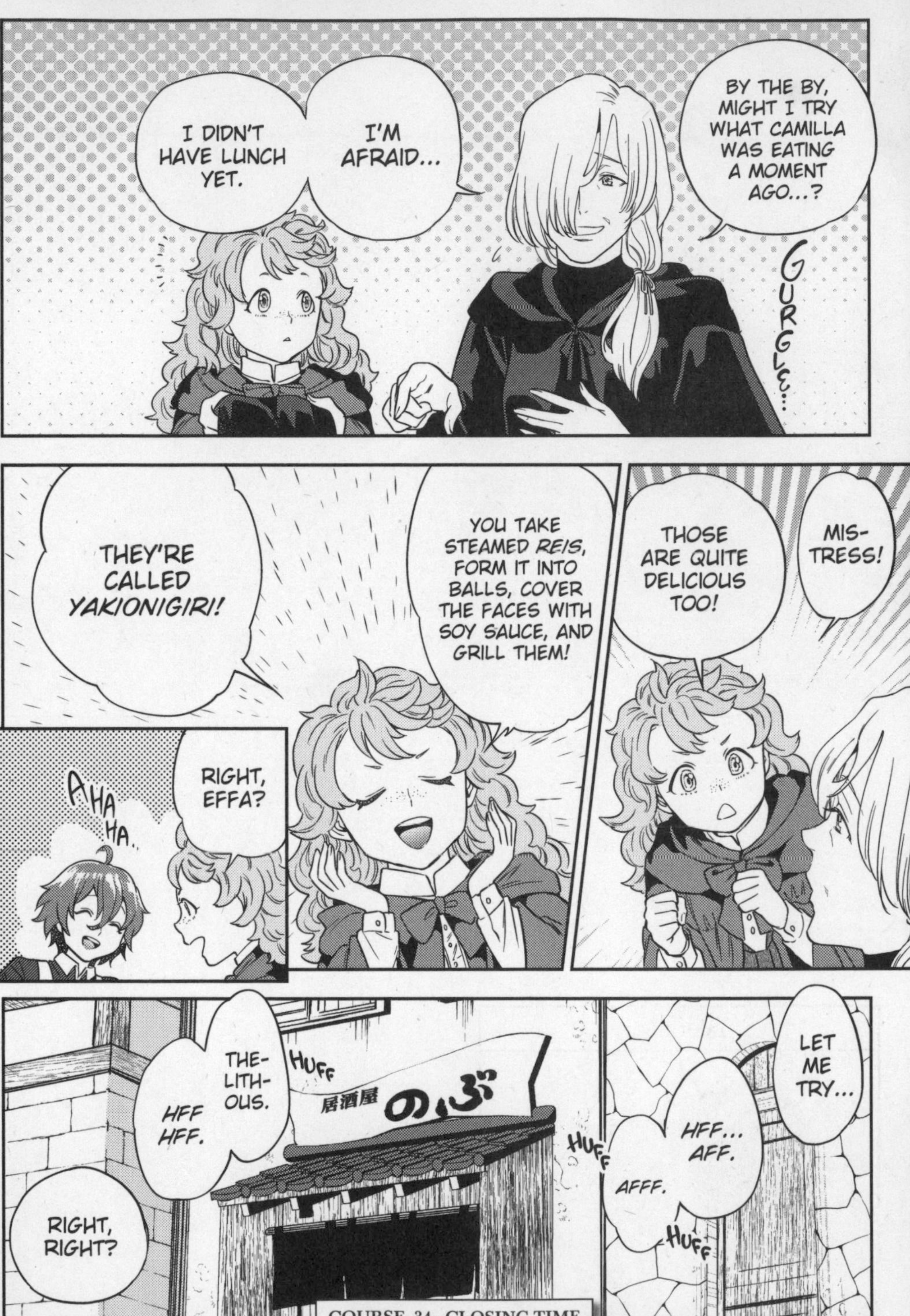
BY THE BY, MIGHT I TRY WHAT CAMILLA WAS EATING A MOMENT AGO...?
GURGLE...
I'M AFRAID...
I DIDN'T HAVE LUNCH YET.
MIS-TRESS!
THOSE ARE QUITE DELICIOUS TOO!
YOU TAKE STEAMED *REIS*, FORM IT INTO BALLS, COVER THE FACES WITH SOY SAUCE, AND GRILL THEM!
THEY'RE CALLED *YAKIONIGIRI*!
RIGHT, EFFA?
AHAHA..
LET ME TRY...
HFF... AFF.
HUFF
AFFF.
HUFF
THE-LITH-OUS.
HUFF
HFF HFF.
居酒屋 のぶ
RIGHT, RIGHT?

COURSE 34 - CLOSING TIME

Yakionigiri

OTHERWORLDLY IZAKAYA

NOBU

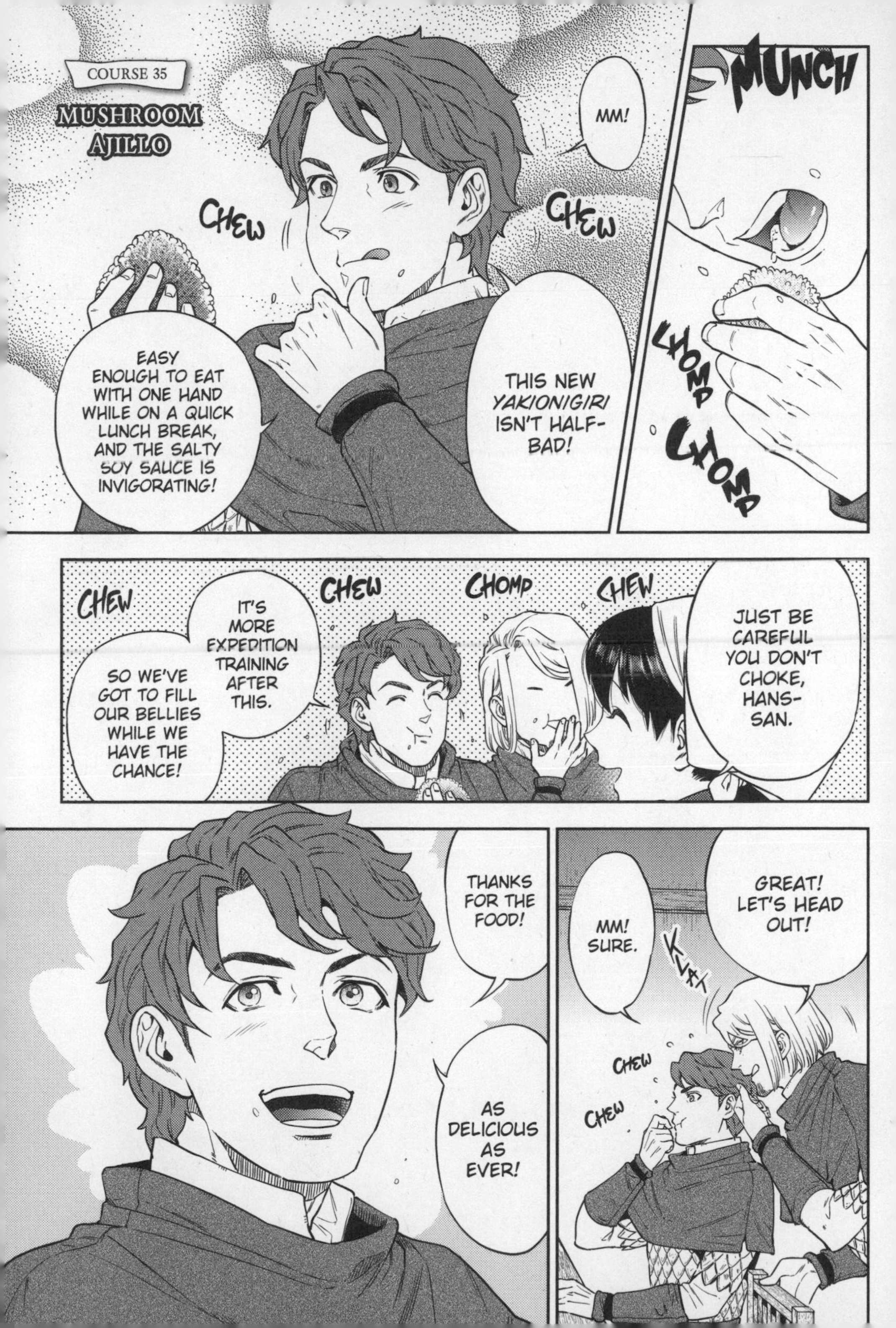
MUNCH
CHOMP
CHOMP
COURSE 35
MUSHROOM AJILLO
MM!
CHEW
CHEW
THIS NEW *YAKIONIGIRI* ISN'T HALF-BAD!
EASY ENOUGH TO EAT WITH ONE HAND WHILE ON A QUICK LUNCH BREAK, AND THE SALTY SOY SAUCE IS INVIGORATING!
JUST BE CAREFUL YOU DON'T CHOKE, HANS-SAN.
CHEW
CHOMP
CHEW
IT'S MORE EXPEDITION TRAINING AFTER THIS.
SO WE'VE GOT TO FILL OUR BELLIES WHILE WE HAVE THE CHANCE!
CHEW
GREAT! LET'S HEAD OUT!
MM! SURE.
CHEW
CHEW
THANKS FOR THE FOOD!
AS DELICIOUS AS EVER!

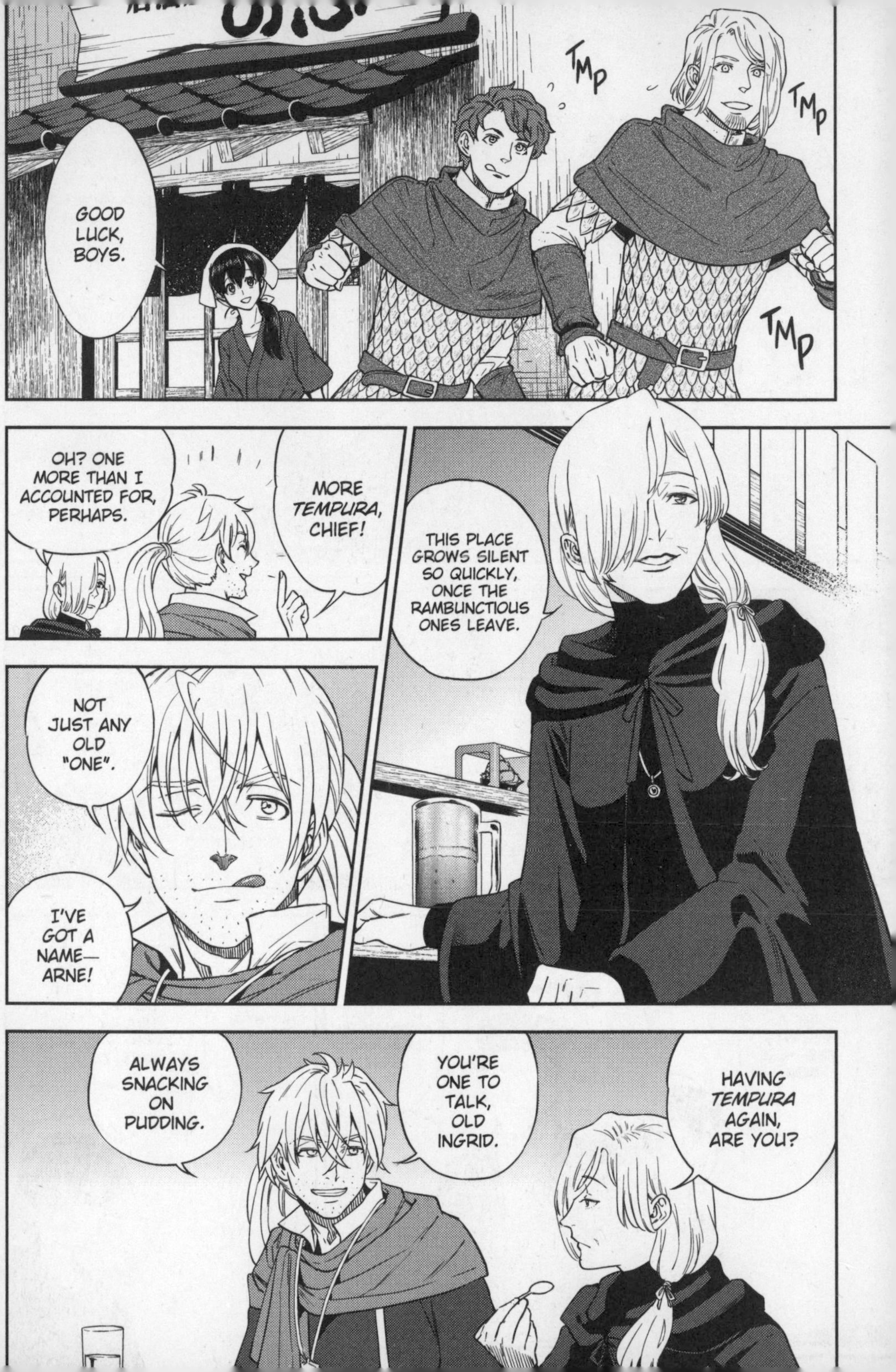
TMP
TMP
GOOD LUCK, BOYS.
TMP
THIS PLACE GROWS SILENT SO QUICKLY, ONCE THE RAMBUNCTIOUS ONES LEAVE.
MORE *TEMPURA*, CHIEF!
OH? ONE MORE THAN I ACCOUNTED FOR, PERHAPS.
NOT JUST ANY OLD "ONE".
I'VE GOT A NAME—ARNE!
HAVING *TEMPURA* AGAIN, ARE YOU?
YOU'RE ONE TO TALK, OLD INGRID.
ALWAYS SNACKING ON PUDDING.

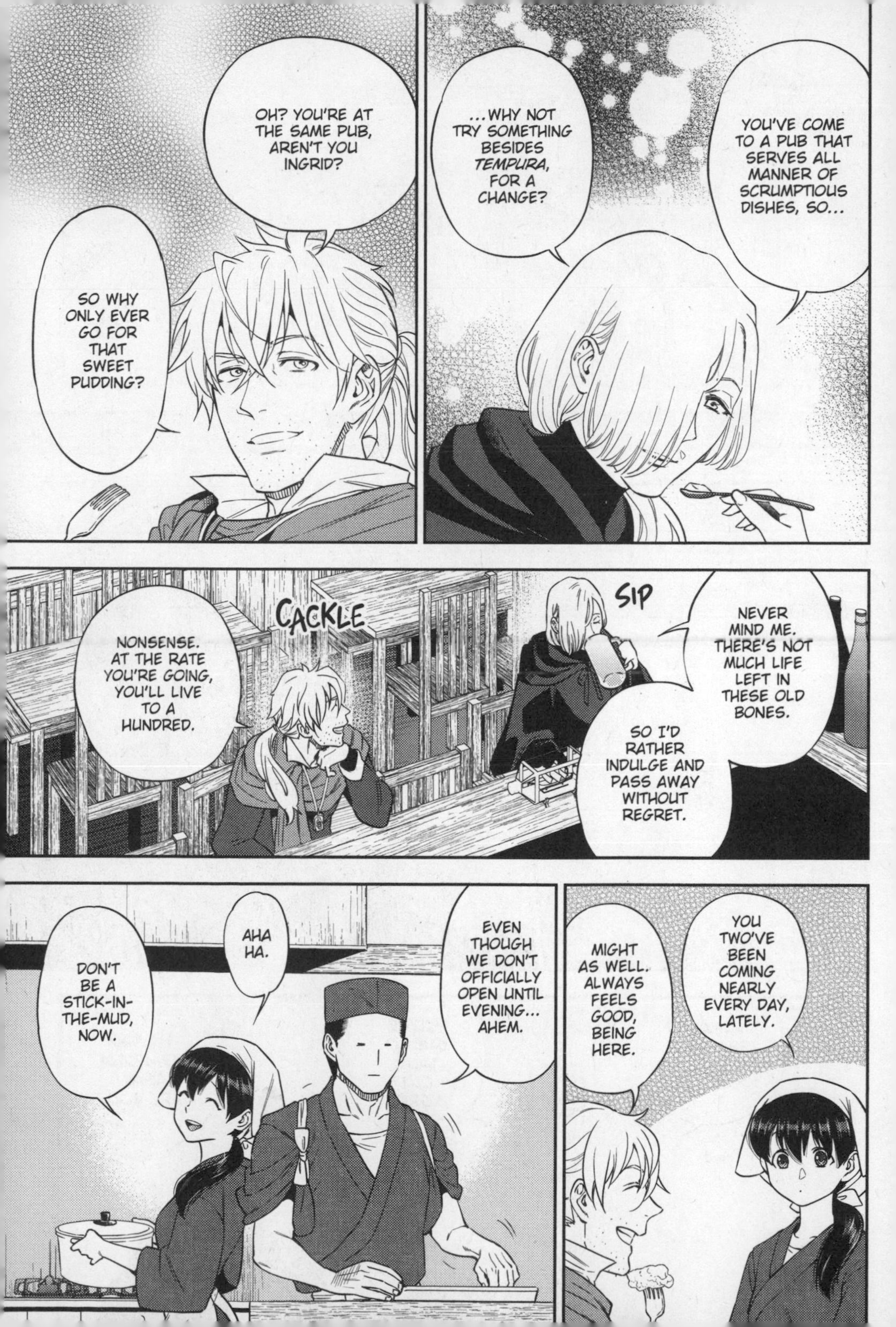
YOU'VE COME TO A PUB THAT SERVES ALL MANNER OF SCRUMPTIOUS DISHES, SO...
...WHY NOT TRY SOMETHING BESIDES *TEMPURA*, FOR A CHANGE?
OH? YOU'RE AT THE SAME PUB, AREN'T YOU INGRID?
SO WHY ONLY EVER GO FOR THAT SWEET PUDDING?
SIP
NEVER MIND ME. THERE'S NOT MUCH LIFE LEFT IN THESE OLD BONES.
SO I'D RATHER INDULGE AND PASS AWAY WITHOUT REGRET.
CACKLE
NONSENSE. AT THE RATE YOU'RE GOING, YOU'LL LIVE TO A HUNDRED.
YOU TWO'VE BEEN COMING NEARLY EVERY DAY, LATELY.
MIGHT AS WELL. ALWAYS FEELS GOOD, BEING HERE.
EVEN THOUGH WE DON'T OFFICIALLY OPEN UNTIL EVENING... AHEM.
AHA HA.
DON'T BE A STICK-IN-THE-MUD, NOW.

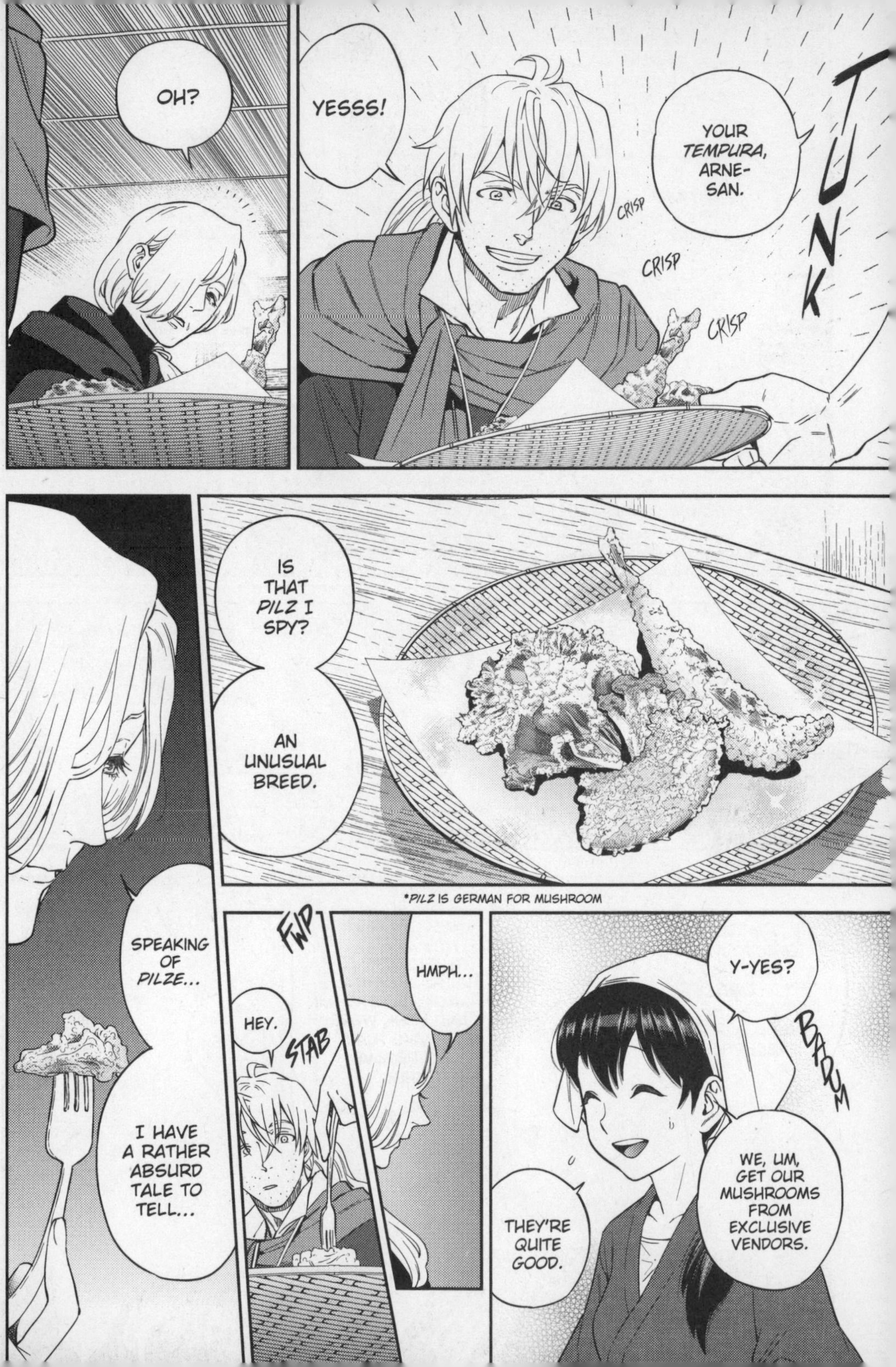
JUNK
YOUR TEMPURA, ARNE-SAN.
CRISP
CRISP
CRISP
YESSS!
OH?
IS THAT PILZ I SPY?
AN UNUSUAL BREED.
Y-YES?
BADUM
WE, UM, GET OUR MUSHROOMS FROM EXCLUSIVE VENDORS.
THEY'RE QUITE GOOD.
HMPH...
FWP
HEY.
STAB
SPEAKING OF PILZE...
I HAVE A RATHER ABSURD TALE TO TELL...

*PILZ IS GERMAN FOR MUSHROOM

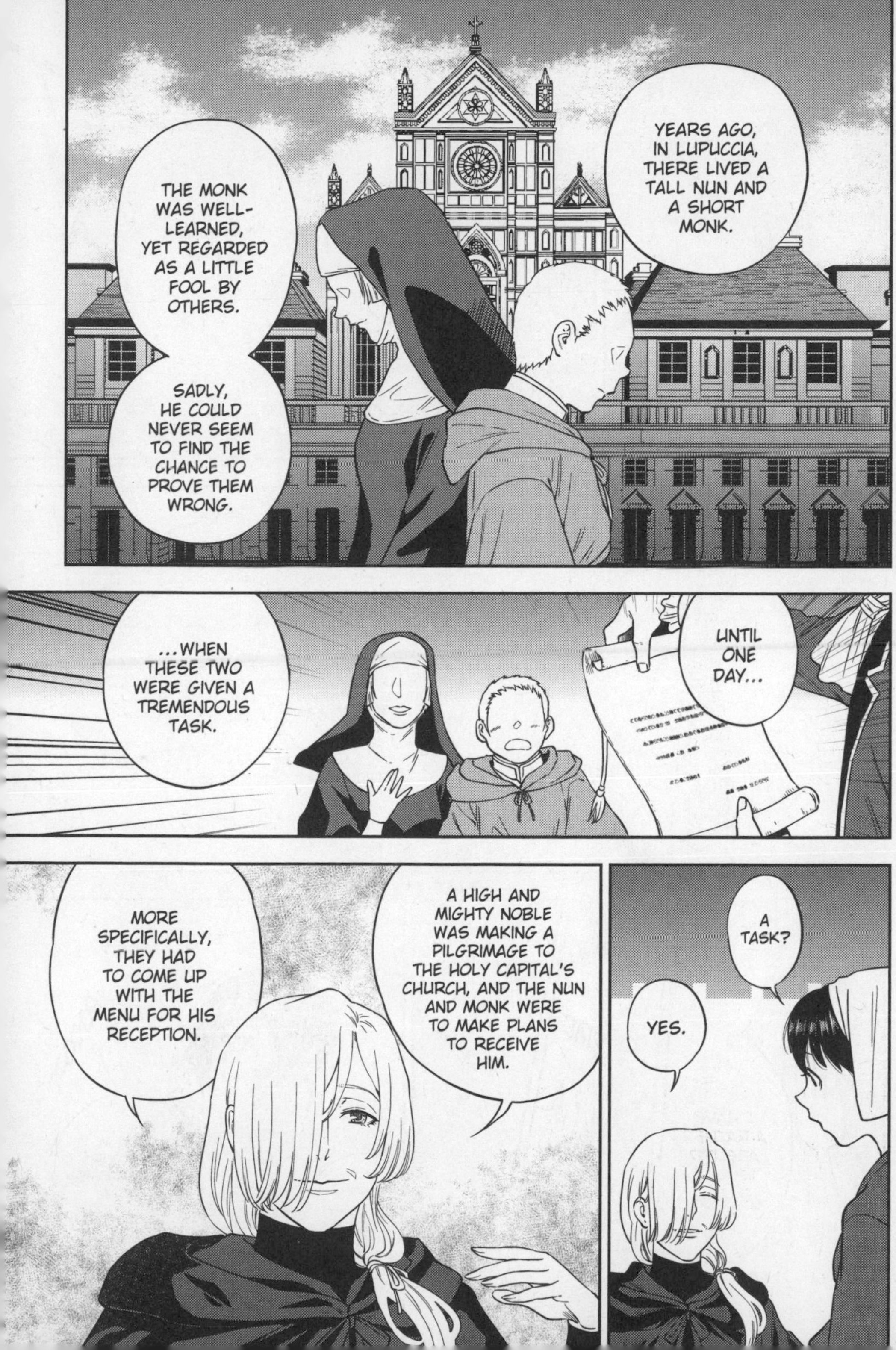
YEARS AGO, IN LUPUCCIA, THERE LIVED A TALL NUN AND A SHORT MONK.
THE MONK WAS WELL-LEARNED, YET REGARDED AS A LITTLE FOOL BY OTHERS.
SADLY, HE COULD NEVER SEEM TO FIND THE CHANCE TO PROVE THEM WRONG.
UNTIL ONE DAY...
...WHEN THESE TWO WERE GIVEN A TREMENDOUS TASK.
A TASK?
YES.
A HIGH AND MIGHTY NOBLE WAS MAKING A PILGRIMAGE TO THE HOLY CAPITAL'S CHURCH, AND THE NUN AND MONK WERE TO MAKE PLANS TO RECEIVE HIM.
MORE SPECIFICALLY, THEY HAD TO COME UP WITH THE MENU FOR HIS RECEPTION.

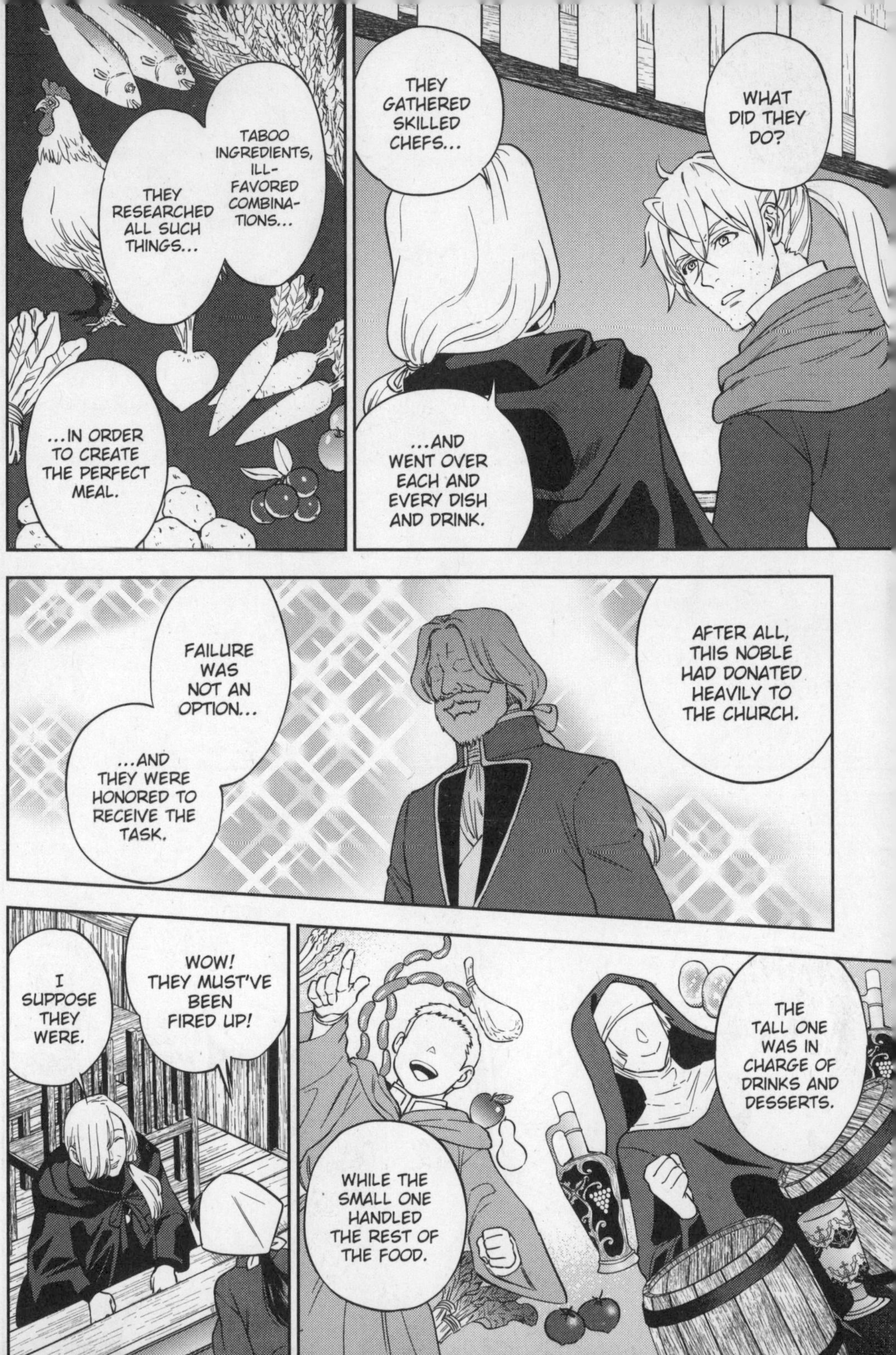
WHAT DID THEY DO?
THEY GATHERED SKILLED CHEFS...
...AND WENT OVER EACH AND EVERY DISH AND DRINK.
TABOO INGREDIENTS, ILL-FAVORED COMBINATIONS...
THEY RESEARCHED ALL SUCH THINGS...
...IN ORDER TO CREATE THE PERFECT MEAL.
AFTER ALL, THIS NOBLE HAD DONATED HEAVILY TO THE CHURCH.
FAILURE WAS NOT AN OPTION...
...AND THEY WERE HONORED TO RECEIVE THE TASK.
THE TALL ONE WAS IN CHARGE OF DRINKS AND DESSERTS.
WHILE THE SMALL ONE HANDLED THE REST OF THE FOOD.
WOW! THEY MUST'VE BEEN FIRED UP!
I SUPPOSE THEY WERE.

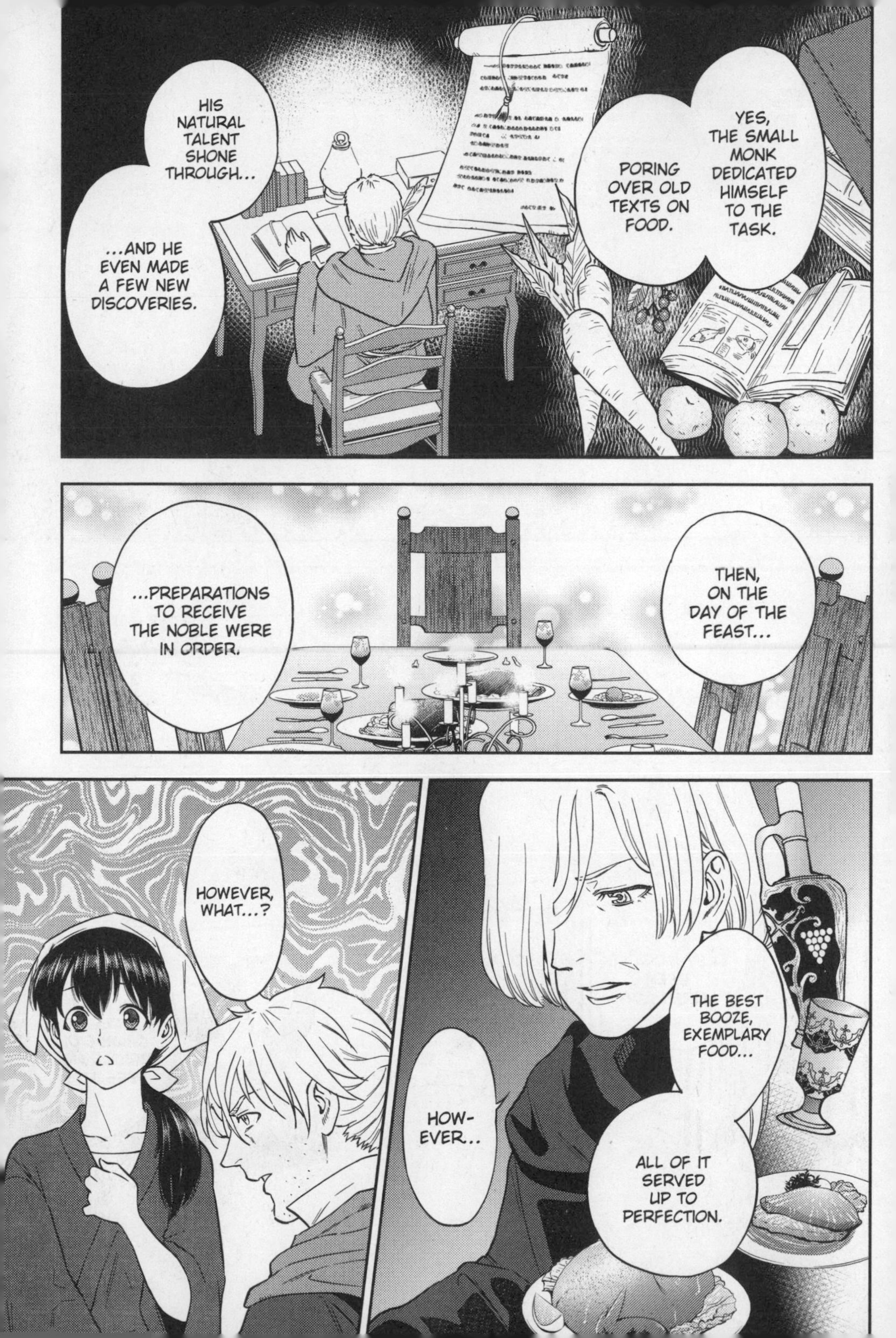
YES, THE SMALL MONK DEDICATED HIMSELF TO THE TASK.
PORING OVER OLD TEXTS ON FOOD.
HIS NATURAL TALENT SHONE THROUGH...
...AND HE EVEN MADE A FEW NEW DISCOVERIES.
THEN, ON THE DAY OF THE FEAST...
...PREPARATIONS TO RECEIVE THE NOBLE WERE IN ORDER.
THE BEST BOOZE, EXEMPLARY FOOD...
ALL OF IT SERVED UP TO PERFECTION.
HOW-EVER...
HOWEVER, WHAT...?

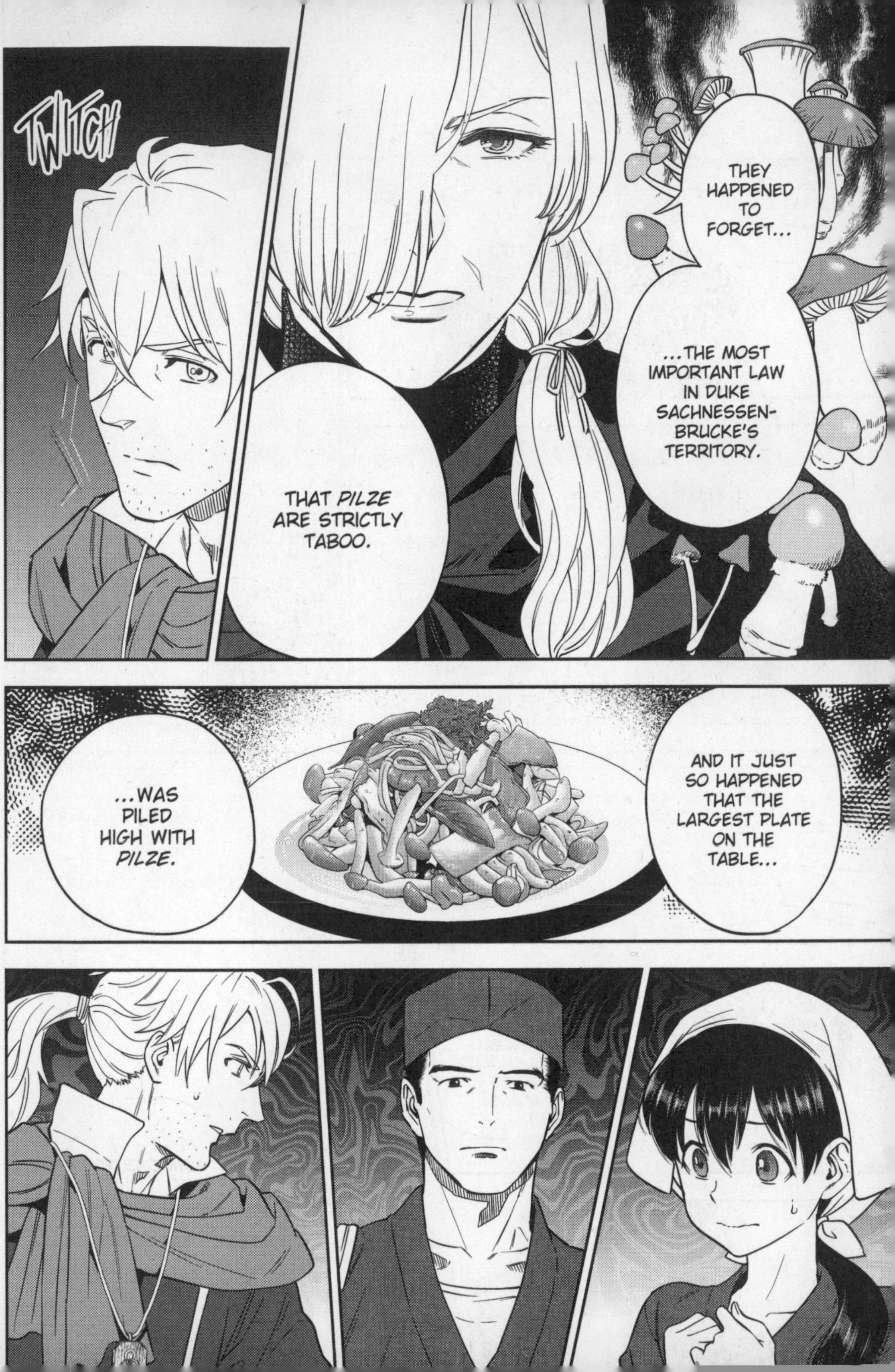
THEY HAPPENED TO FORGET...
...THE MOST IMPORTANT LAW IN DUKE SACHNESSEN-BRUCKE'S TERRITORY.
THAT *PILZE* ARE STRICTLY TABOO.
TWITCH
AND IT JUST SO HAPPENED THAT THE LARGEST PLATE ON THE TABLE...
...WAS PILED HIGH WITH *PILZE*.

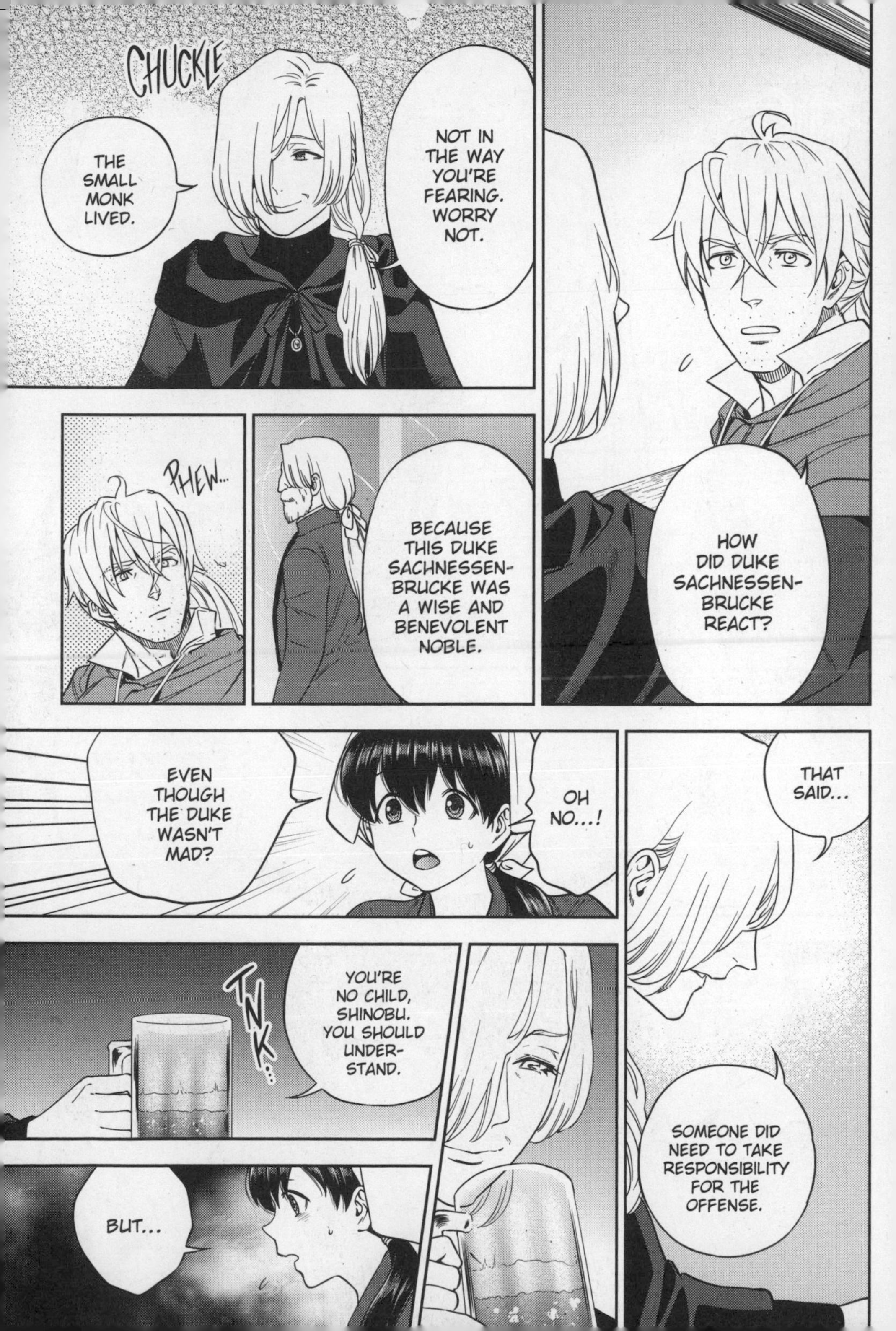
HOW DID DUKE SACHNESSEN-BRUCKE REACT?
CHUCKLE
NOT IN THE WAY YOU'RE FEARING. WORRY NOT.
THE SMALL MONK LIVED.
BECAUSE THIS DUKE SACHNESSEN-BRUCKE WAS A WISE AND BENEVOLENT NOBLE.
PHEW...
THAT SAID...
SOMEONE DID NEED TO TAKE RESPONSIBILITY FOR THE OFFENSE.
OH NO...!
EVEN THOUGH THE DUKE WASN'T MAD?
YOU'RE NO CHILD, SHINOBU. YOU SHOULD UNDER-STAND.
TNK...
BUT...

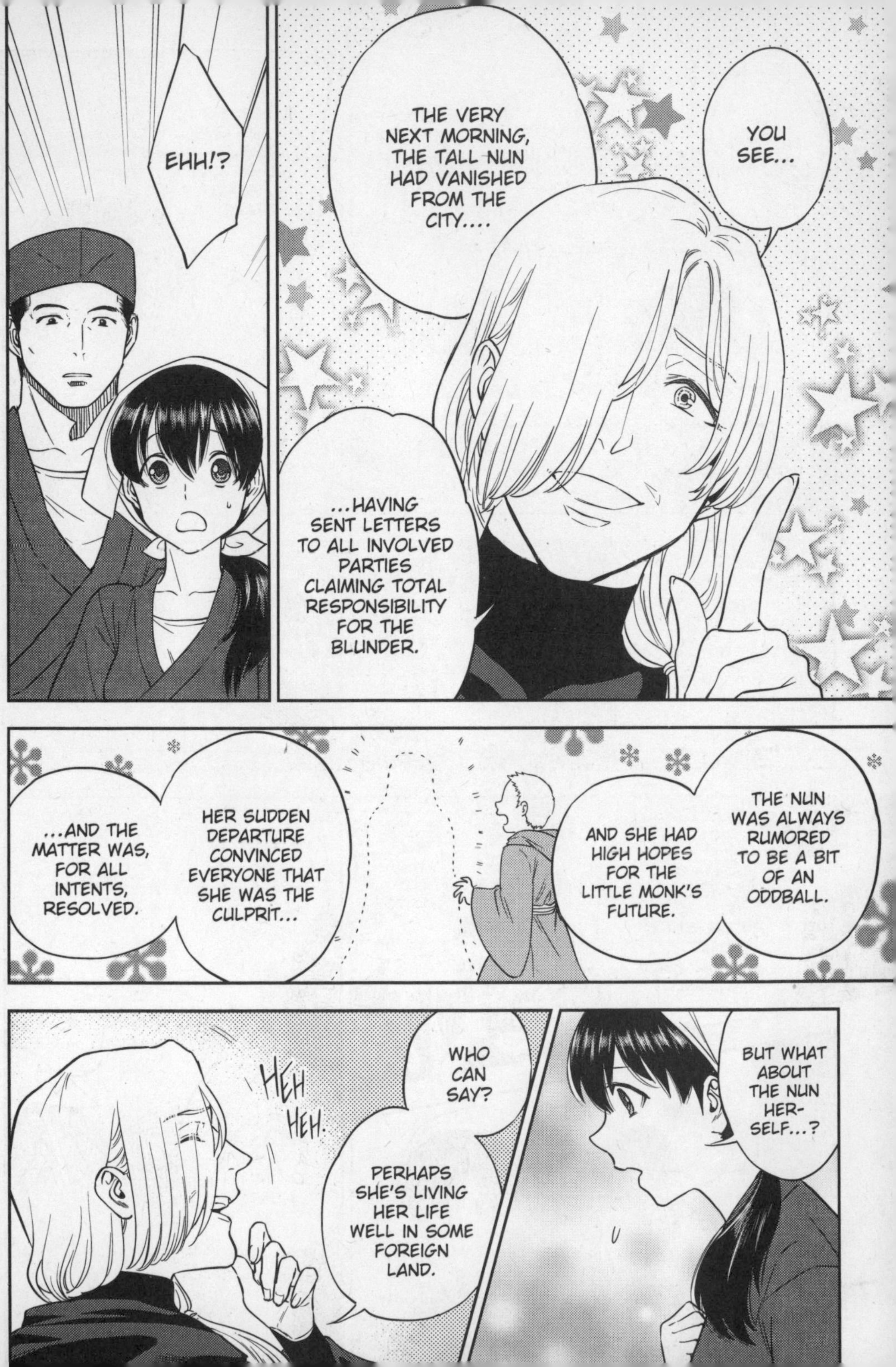
YOU SEE...
THE VERY NEXT MORNING, THE TALL NUN HAD VANISHED FROM THE CITY....
...HAVING SENT LETTERS TO ALL INVOLVED PARTIES CLAIMING TOTAL RESPONSIBILITY FOR THE BLUNDER.
EHH!?
THE NUN WAS ALWAYS RUMORED TO BE A BIT OF AN ODDBALL.
AND SHE HAD HIGH HOPES FOR THE LITTLE MONK'S FUTURE.
HER SUDDEN DEPARTURE CONVINCED EVERYONE THAT SHE WAS THE CULPRIT...
...AND THE MATTER WAS, FOR ALL INTENTS, RESOLVED.
BUT WHAT ABOUT THE NUN HER-SELF...?
WHO CAN SAY?
HEH HEH.
PERHAPS SHE'S LIVING HER LIFE WELL IN SOME FOREIGN LAND.

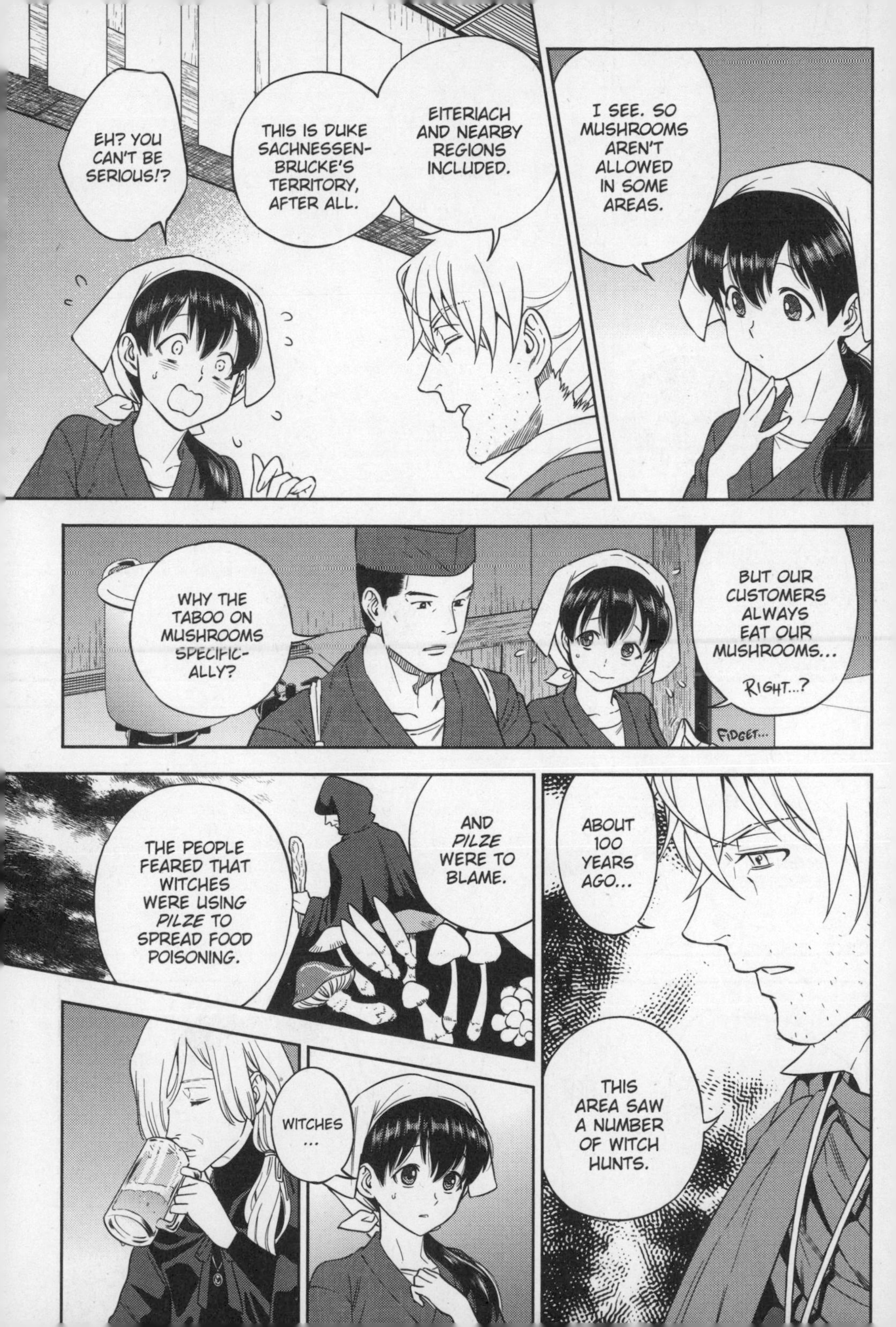
I SEE. SO MUSHROOMS AREN'T ALLOWED IN SOME AREAS.
THIS IS DUKE SACHNESSEN-BRUCKE'S TERRITORY, AFTER ALL.
EITERIACH AND NEARBY REGIONS INCLUDED.
EH? YOU CAN'T BE SERIOUS!?
BUT OUR CUSTOMERS ALWAYS EAT OUR MUSHROOMS...
RIGHT...?
FIDGET...
WHY THE TABOO ON MUSHROOMS SPECIFIC-ALLY?
ABOUT 100 YEARS AGO...
THIS AREA SAW A NUMBER OF WITCH HUNTS.
THE PEOPLE FEARED THAT WITCHES WERE USING *PILZE* TO SPREAD FOOD POISONING.
AND *PILZE* WERE TO BLAME.
WITCHES ...

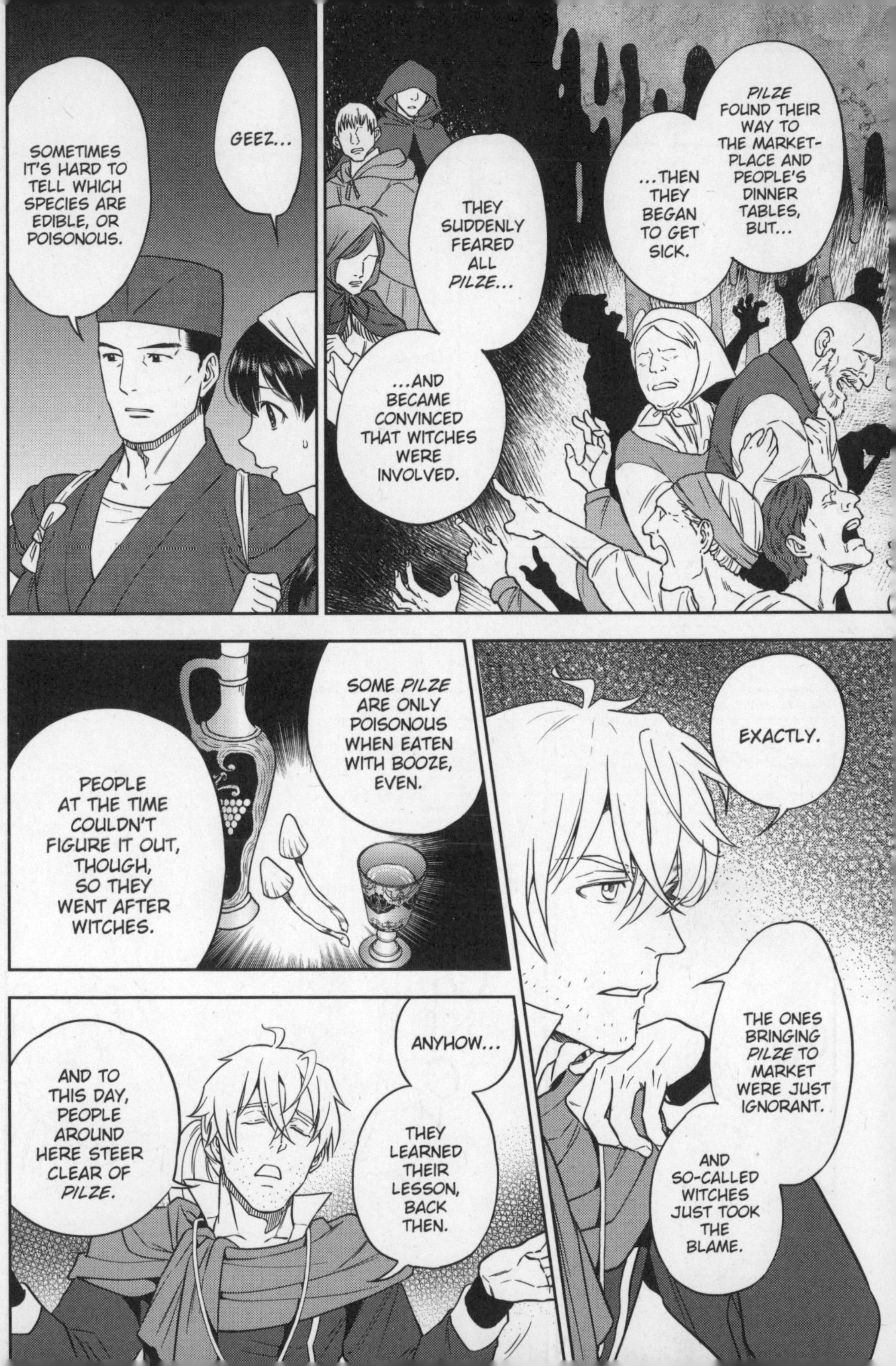
PILZE FOUND THEIR WAY TO THE MARKETPLACE AND PEOPLE'S DINNER TABLES, BUT...
...THEN THEY BEGAN TO GET SICK.
THEY SUDDENLY FEARED ALL *PILZE*...
...AND BECAME CONVINCED THAT WITCHES WERE INVOLVED.
GEEZ...
SOMETIMES IT'S HARD TO TELL WHICH SPECIES ARE EDIBLE, OR POISONOUS.
EXACTLY.
THE ONES BRINGING *PILZE* TO MARKET WERE JUST IGNORANT.
AND SO-CALLED WITCHES JUST TOOK THE BLAME.
SOME *PILZE* ARE ONLY POISONOUS WHEN EATEN WITH BOOZE, EVEN.
PEOPLE AT THE TIME COULDN'T FIGURE IT OUT, THOUGH, SO THEY WENT AFTER WITCHES.
ANYHOW...
THEY LEARNED THEIR LESSON, BACK THEN.
AND TO THIS DAY, PEOPLE AROUND HERE STEER CLEAR OF *PILZE*.

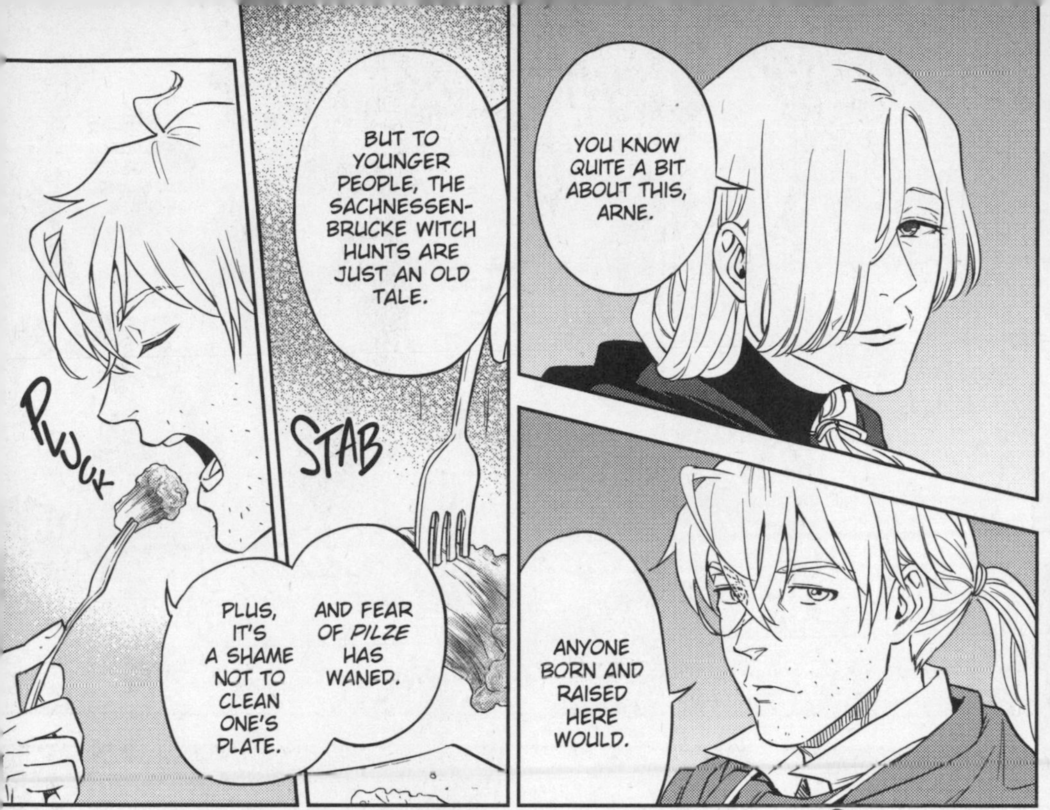
YOU KNOW QUITE A BIT ABOUT THIS, ARNE.
ANYONE BORN AND RAISED HERE WOULD.
BUT TO YOUNGER PEOPLE, THE SACHNESSEN-BRUCKE WITCH HUNTS ARE JUST AN OLD TALE.
STAB
AND FEAR OF *PILZE* HAS WANED.
PLUS, IT'S A SHAME NOT TO CLEAN ONE'S PLATE.

*MAITAKE IS JAPANESE FOR HEN-OF-THE-WOODS MUSHROOM

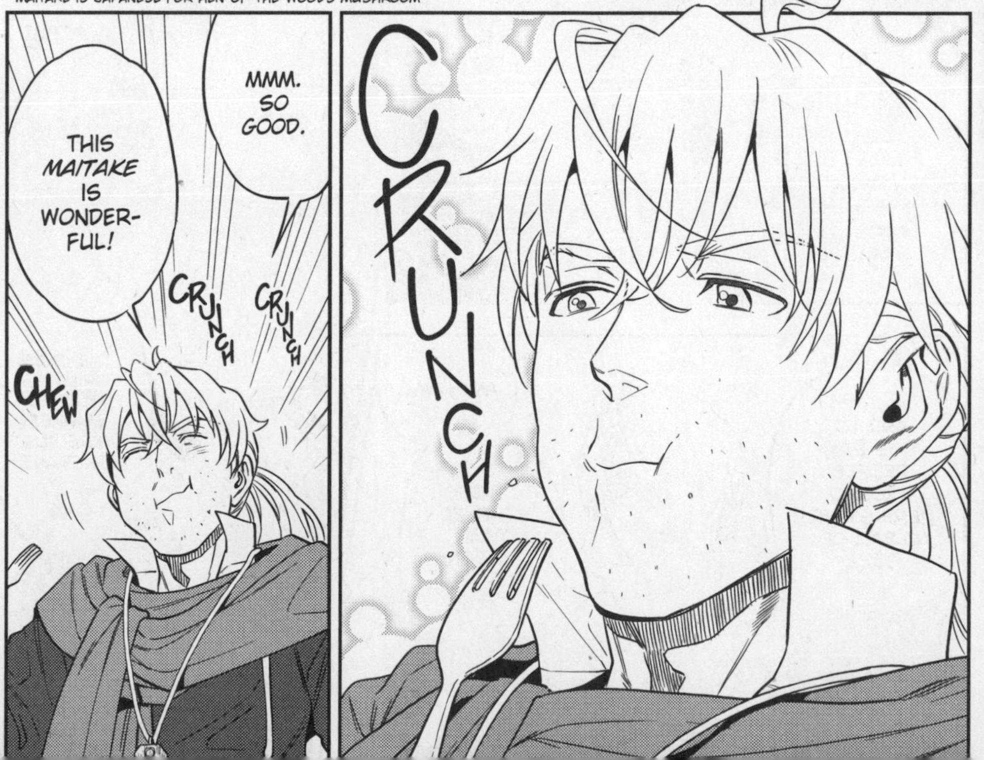
CRUNCH
MMM. SO GOOD.
THIS *MAITAKE* IS WONDERFUL!
CRUNCH
CRUNCH
CHEW

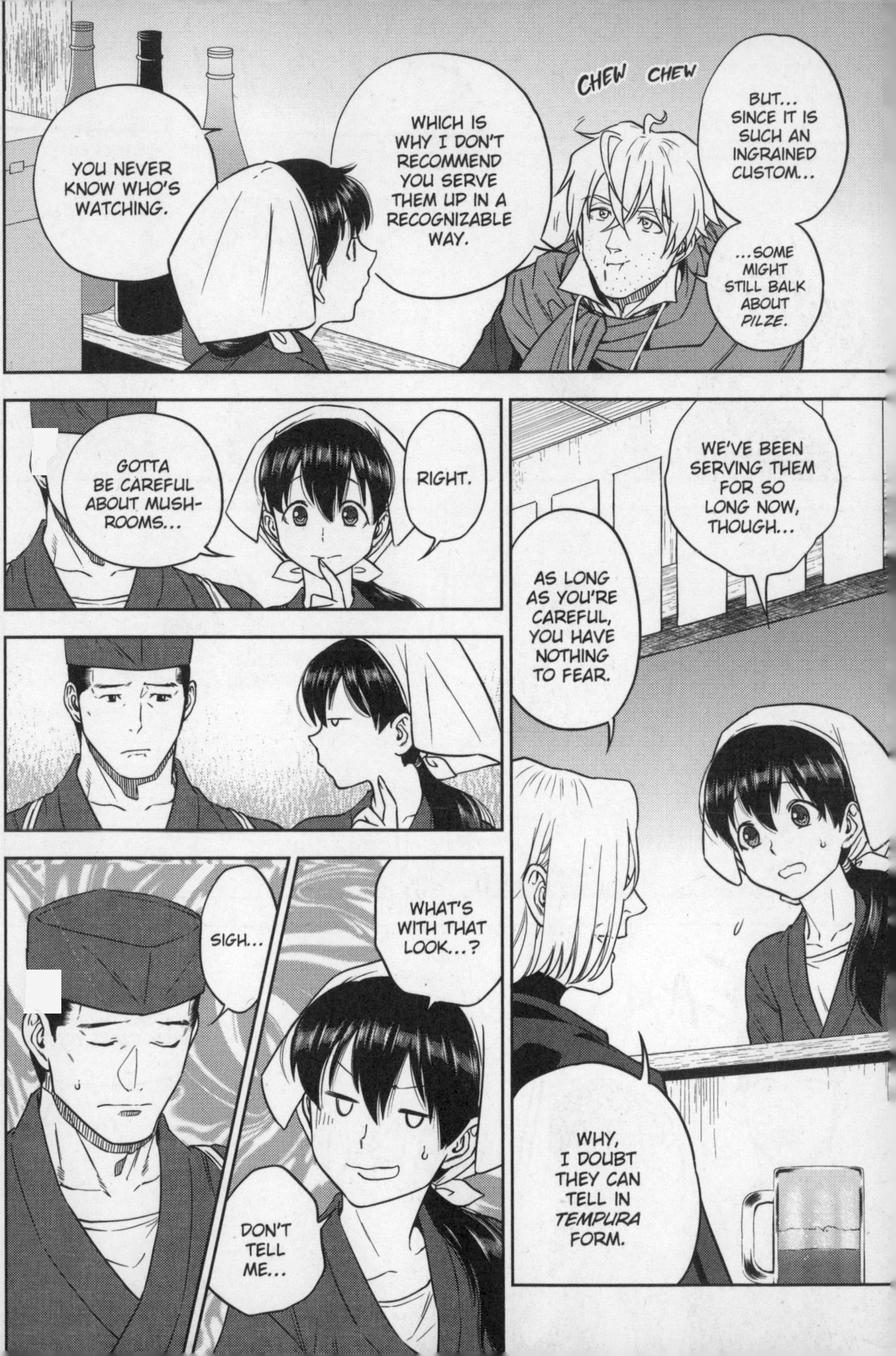
CHEW CHEW
BUT... SINCE IT IS SUCH AN INGRAINED CUSTOM...
...SOME MIGHT STILL BALK ABOUT *PILZE*.
WHICH IS WHY I DON'T RECOMMEND YOU SERVE THEM UP IN A RECOGNIZABLE WAY.
YOU NEVER KNOW WHO'S WATCHING.
WE'VE BEEN SERVING THEM FOR SO LONG NOW, THOUGH...
AS LONG AS YOU'RE CAREFUL, YOU HAVE NOTHING TO FEAR.
WHY, I DOUBT THEY CAN TELL IN *TEMPURA* FORM.
RIGHT.
GOTTA BE CAREFUL ABOUT MUSH-ROOMS...
WHAT'S WITH THAT LOOK...?
DON'T TELL ME...
SIGH...

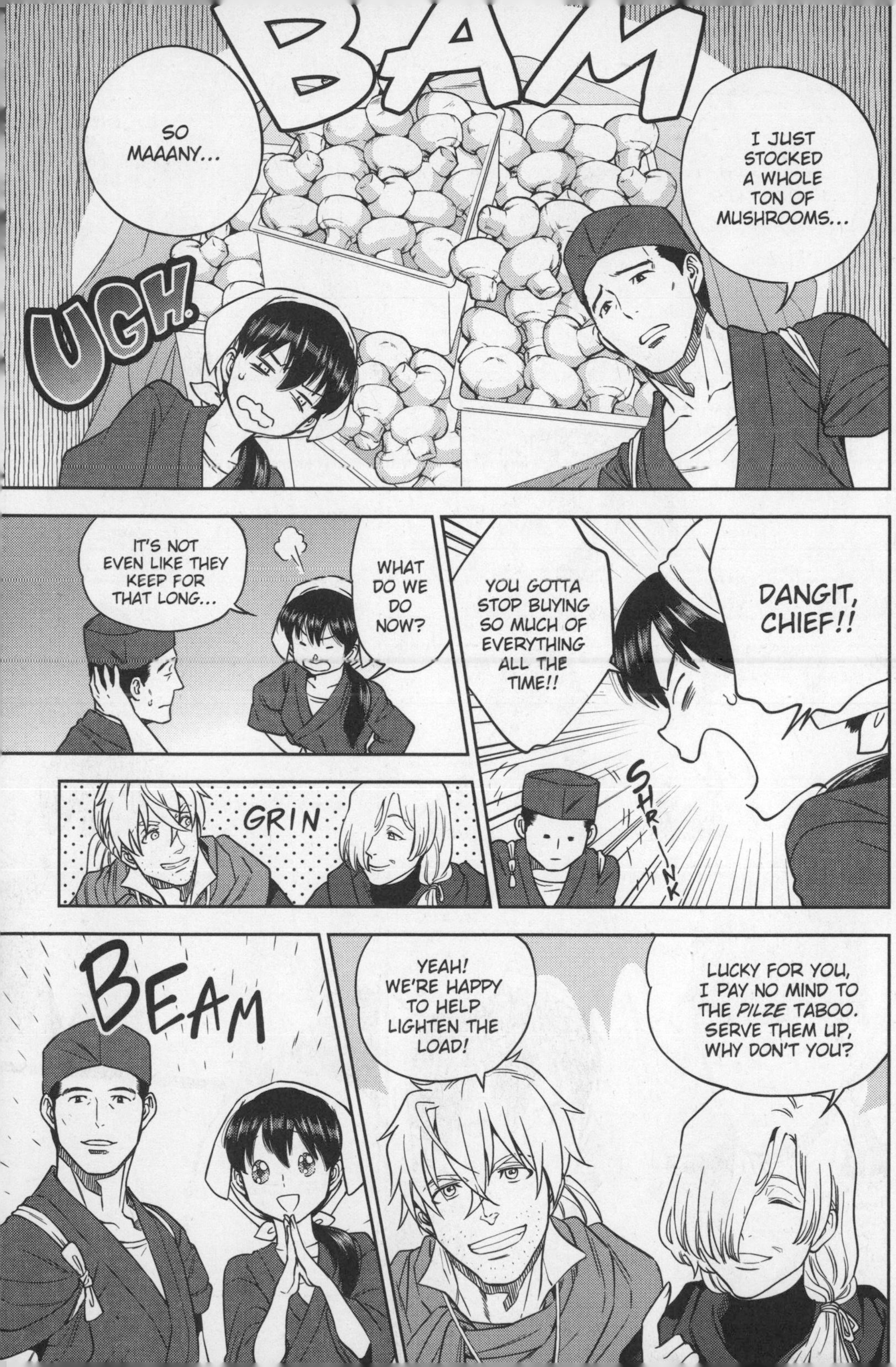
BAM
I JUST STOCKED A WHOLE TON OF MUSHROOMS...
SO MAAANY...
UGH.
DANGIT, CHIEF!!
YOU GOTTA STOP BUYING SO MUCH OF EVERYTHING ALL THE TIME!!
SHRINK
WHAT DO WE DO NOW?
IT'S NOT EVEN LIKE THEY KEEP FOR THAT LONG...
GRIN
LUCKY FOR YOU, I PAY NO MIND TO THE *PILZE* TABOO. SERVE THEM UP, WHY DON'T YOU?
YEAH! WE'RE HAPPY TO HELP LIGHTEN THE LOAD!
BEAM

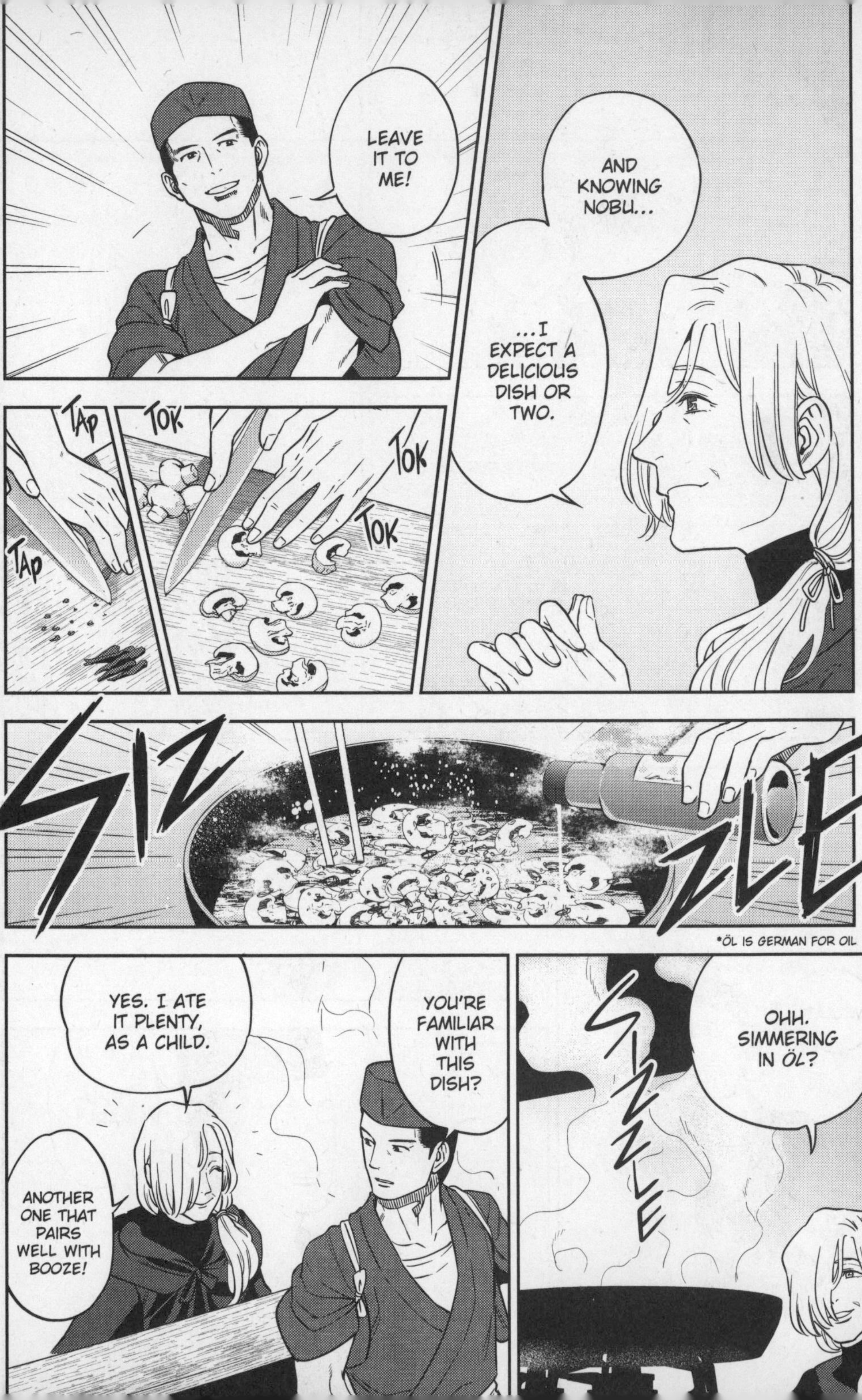
AND KNOWING NOBU...
...I EXPECT A DELICIOUS DISH OR TWO.
LEAVE IT TO ME!
TOK
TOK
TOK
TAP
TAP
SIZZLE
*ÖL IS GERMAN FOR OIL
OHH. SIMMERING IN ÖL?
SIZZLE
YOU'RE FAMILIAR WITH THIS DISH?
YES. I ATE IT PLENTY, AS A CHILD.
ANOTHER ONE THAT PAIRS WELL WITH BOOZE!

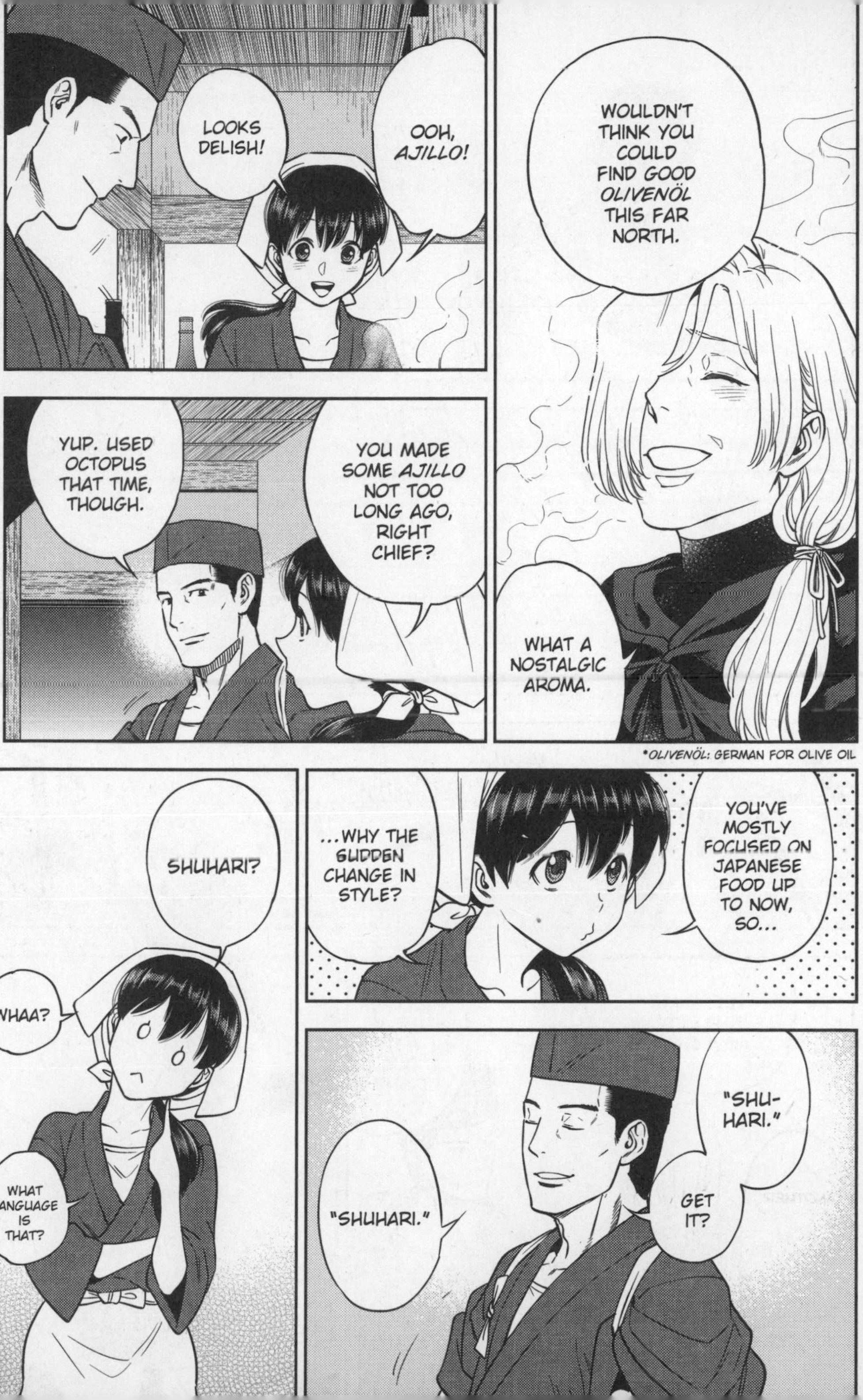
WOULDN'T THINK YOU COULD FIND GOOD *OLIVENÖL* THIS FAR NORTH.
WHAT A NOSTALGIC AROMA.
OOH, *AJILLO!*
LOOKS DELISH!
YOU MADE SOME *AJILLO* NOT TOO LONG AGO, RIGHT CHIEF?
YUP. USED OCTOPUS THAT TIME, THOUGH.
YOU'VE MOSTLY FOCUSED ON JAPANESE FOOD UP TO NOW, SO...
...WHY THE SUDDEN CHANGE IN STYLE?
"SHU-HARI."
GET IT?
"SHUHARI."
SHUHARI?
WHAA?
WHAT LANGUAGE IS THAT?

*OLIVENÖL: GERMAN FOR OLIVE OIL

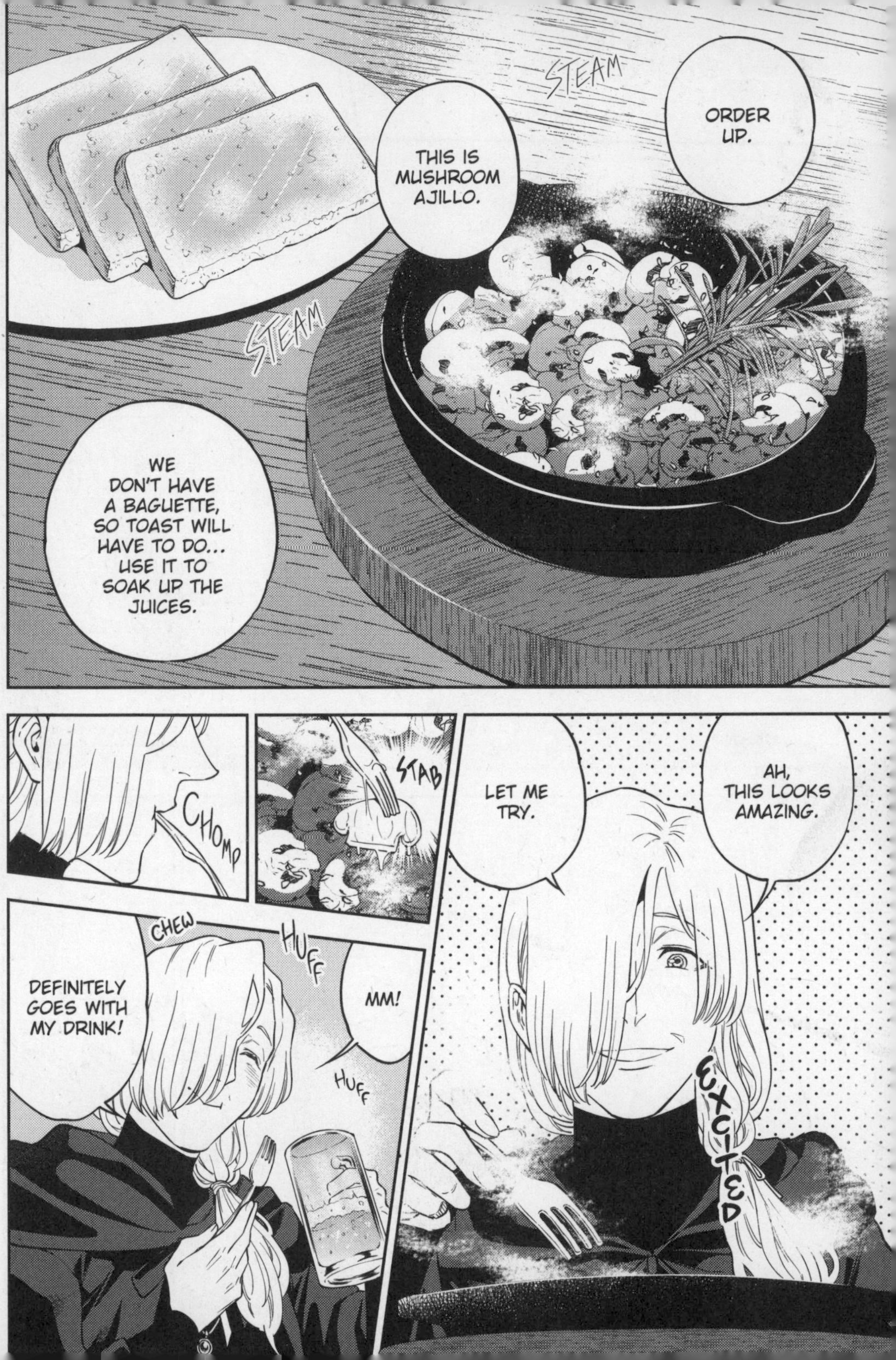
ORDER UP.
STEAM
THIS IS MUSHROOM AJILLO.
STEAM
WE DON'T HAVE A BAGUETTE, SO TOAST WILL HAVE TO DO... USE IT TO SOAK UP THE JUICES.
AH, THIS LOOKS AMAZING.
LET ME TRY.
EXCITED
STAB
CHOMP
MM!
HUFF
HUFF
CHEW
DEFINITELY GOES WITH MY DRINK!

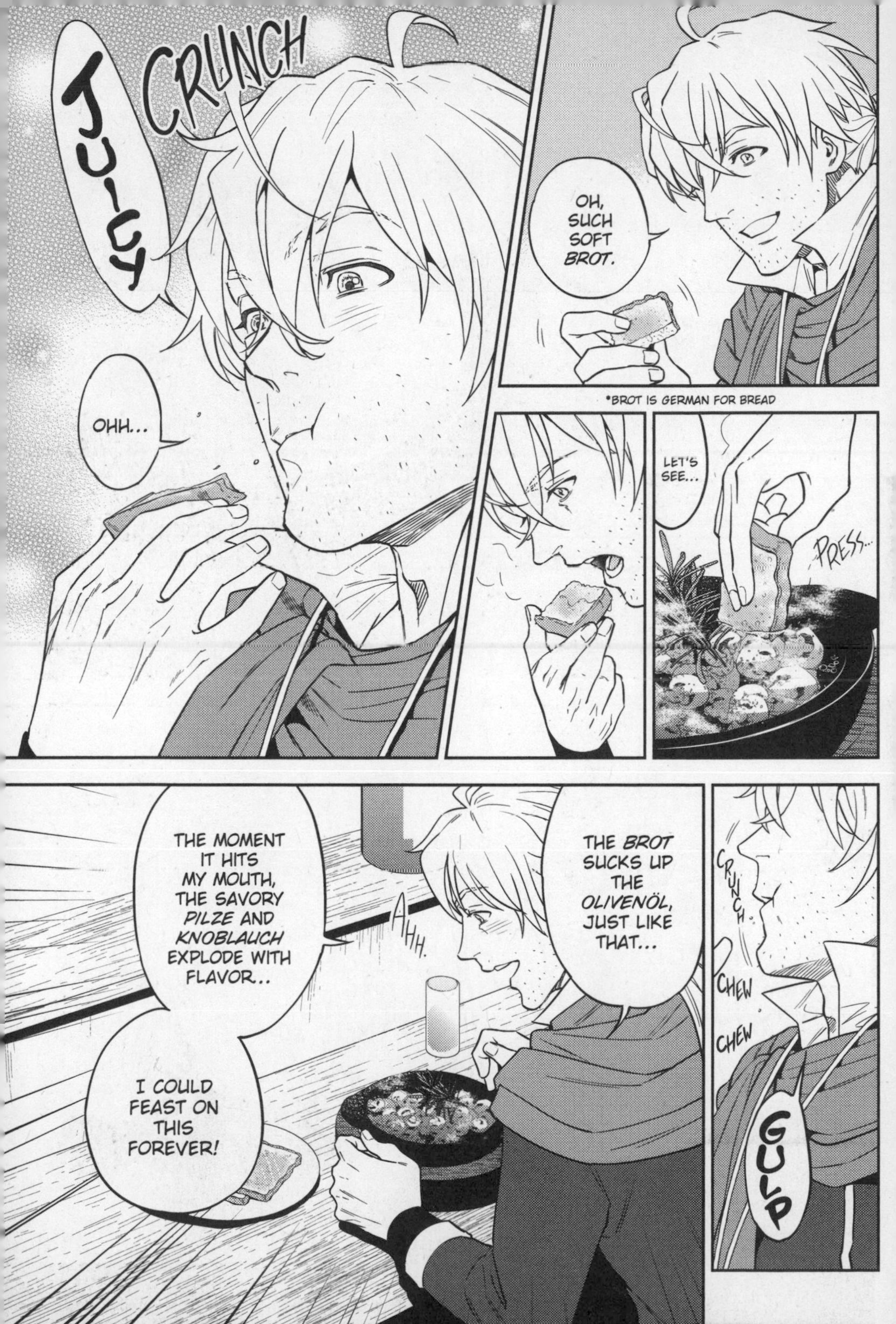
OH, SUCH SOFT BROT.
*BROT IS GERMAN FOR BREAD
LET'S SEE...
PRESS...
CRUNCH
JUICY
OHH...
CRUNCH
CHEW CHEW
GULP
THE BROT SUCKS UP THE OLIVENÖL, JUST LIKE THAT...
AHH.
THE MOMENT IT HITS MY MOUTH, THE SAVORY PILZE AND KNOBLAUCH EXPLODE WITH FLAVOR...
I COULD FEAST ON THIS FOREVER!

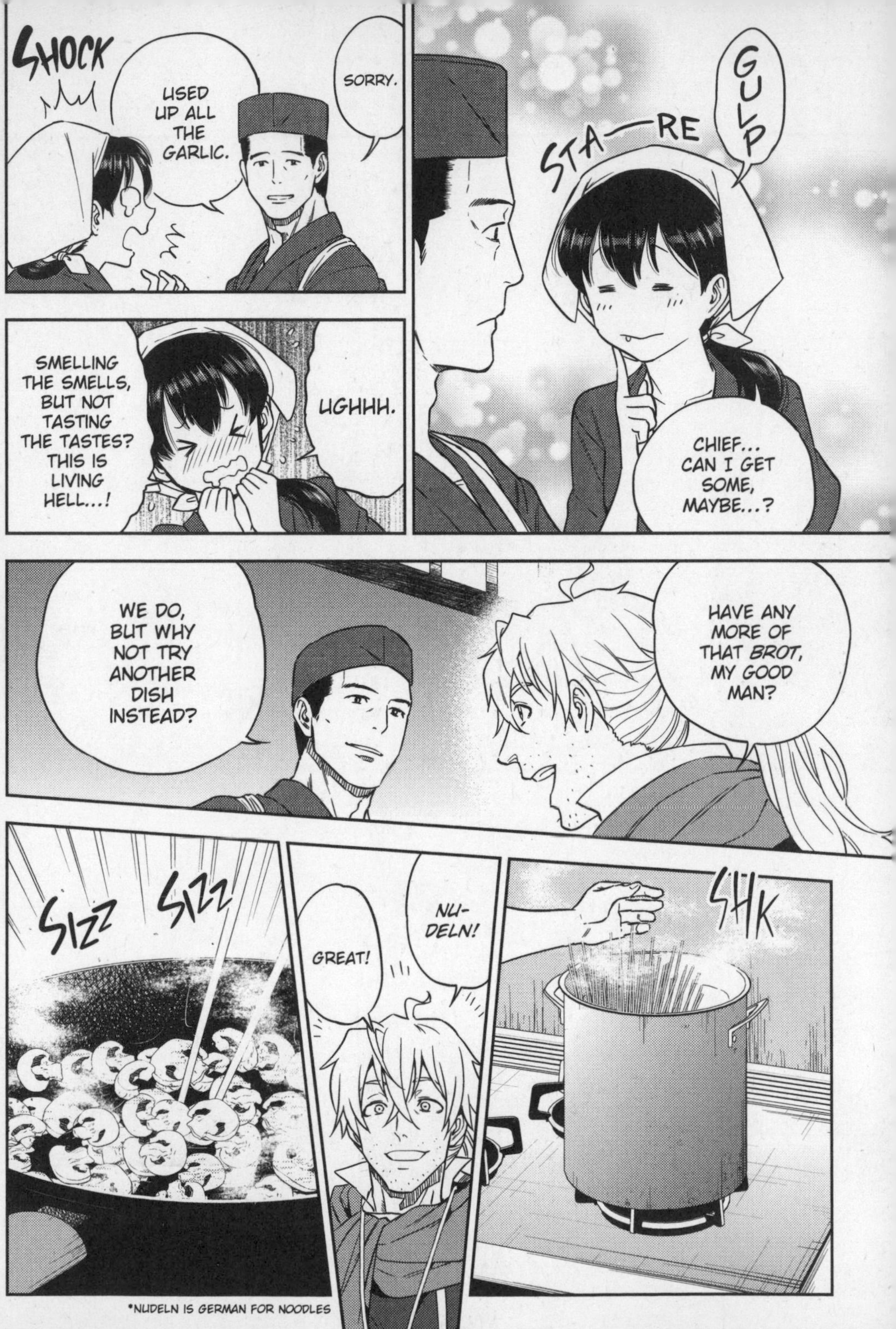

GULP
STA—RE
CHIEF... CAN I GET SOME, MAYBE...?
SORRY.
USED UP ALL THE GARLIC.
SHOCK
UGHHH.
SMELLING THE SMELLS, BUT NOT TASTING THE TASTES? THIS IS LIVING HELL...!
HAVE ANY MORE OF THAT *BROT*, MY GOOD MAN?
WE DO, BUT WHY NOT TRY ANOTHER DISH INSTEAD?
SHK
NU-DELN!
GREAT!
SIZZ
SIZZ

*NUDELN IS GERMAN FOR NOODLES

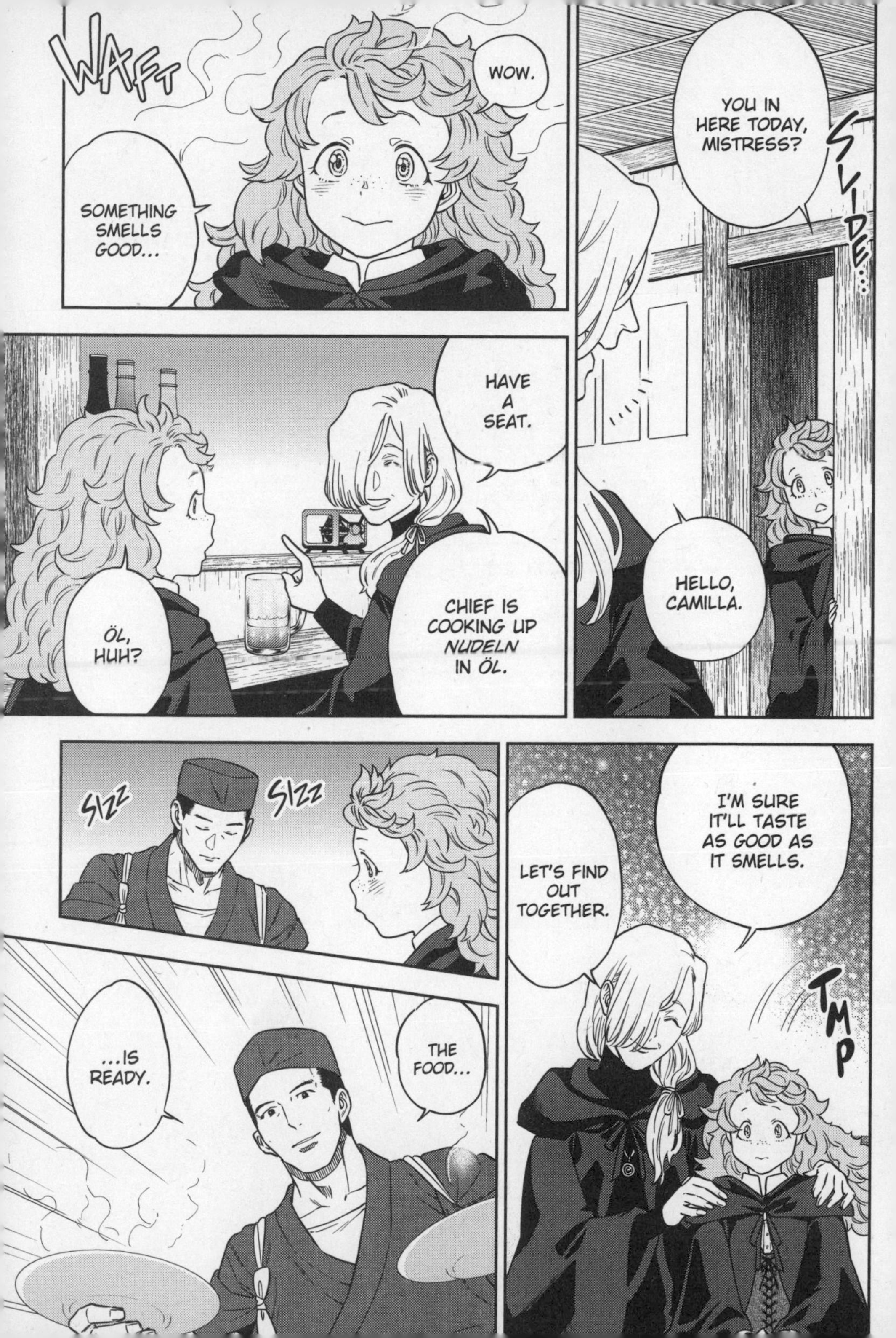
YOU IN HERE TODAY, MISTRESS?
SLIDE...
HELLO, CAMILLA.
WOW.
WAFT
SOMETHING SMELLS GOOD...
HAVE A SEAT.
CHIEF IS COOKING UP *NUDELN* IN ÖL.
ÖL, HUH?
I'M SURE IT'LL TASTE AS GOOD AS IT SMELLS.
LET'S FIND OUT TOGETHER.
TMP
SIZZ
SIZZ
THE FOOD...
...IS READY.

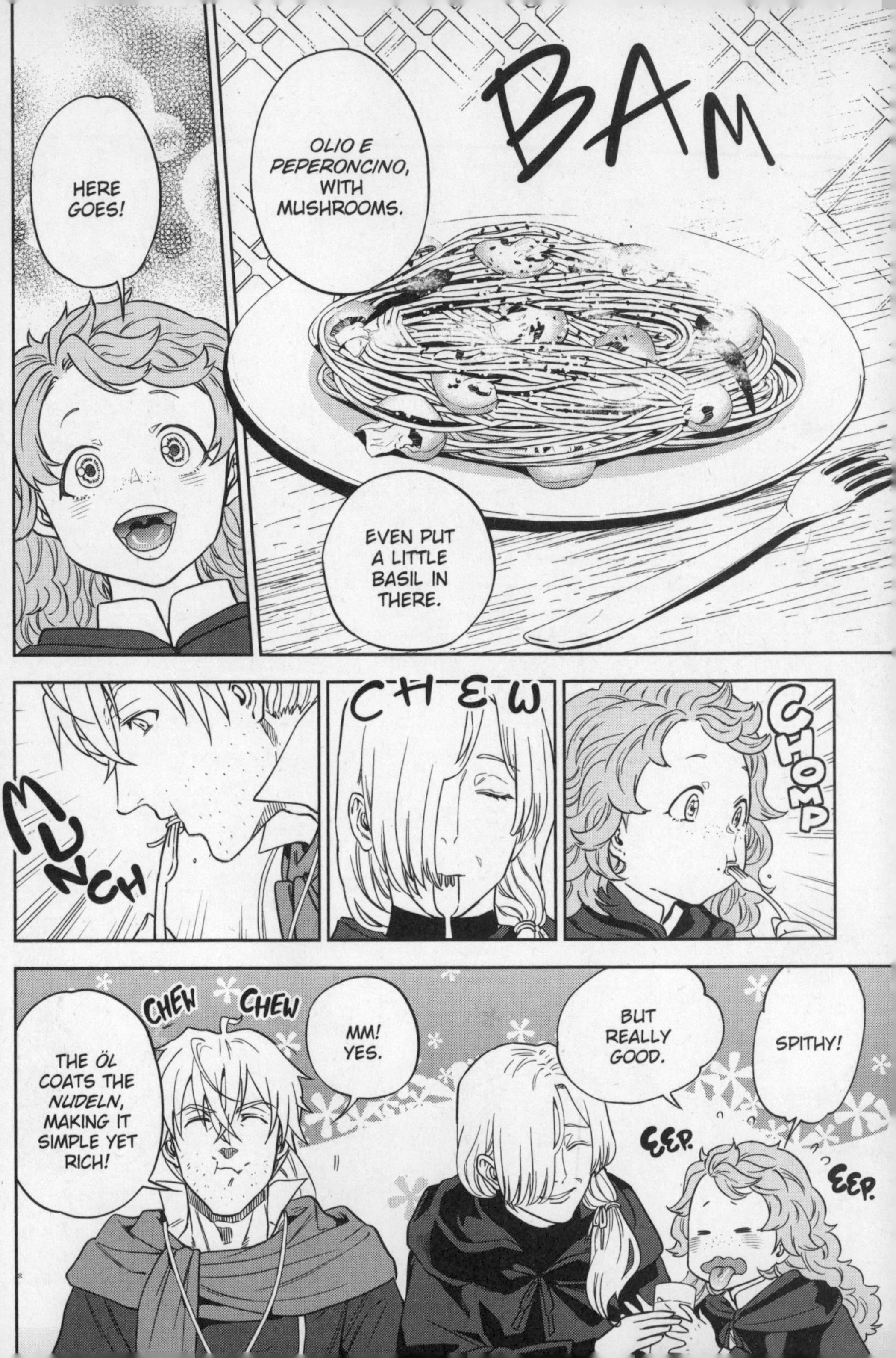
BAM
OLIO E PEPERONCINO, WITH MUSHROOMS.
EVEN PUT A LITTLE BASIL IN THERE.
HERE GOES!
CHOMP
CHEW
MUNCH
SPITHY!
EEP.
EEP.
BUT REALLY GOOD.
MM! YES.
CHEW CHEW
THE ÖL COATS THE *NUDELN*, MAKING IT SIMPLE YET RICH!

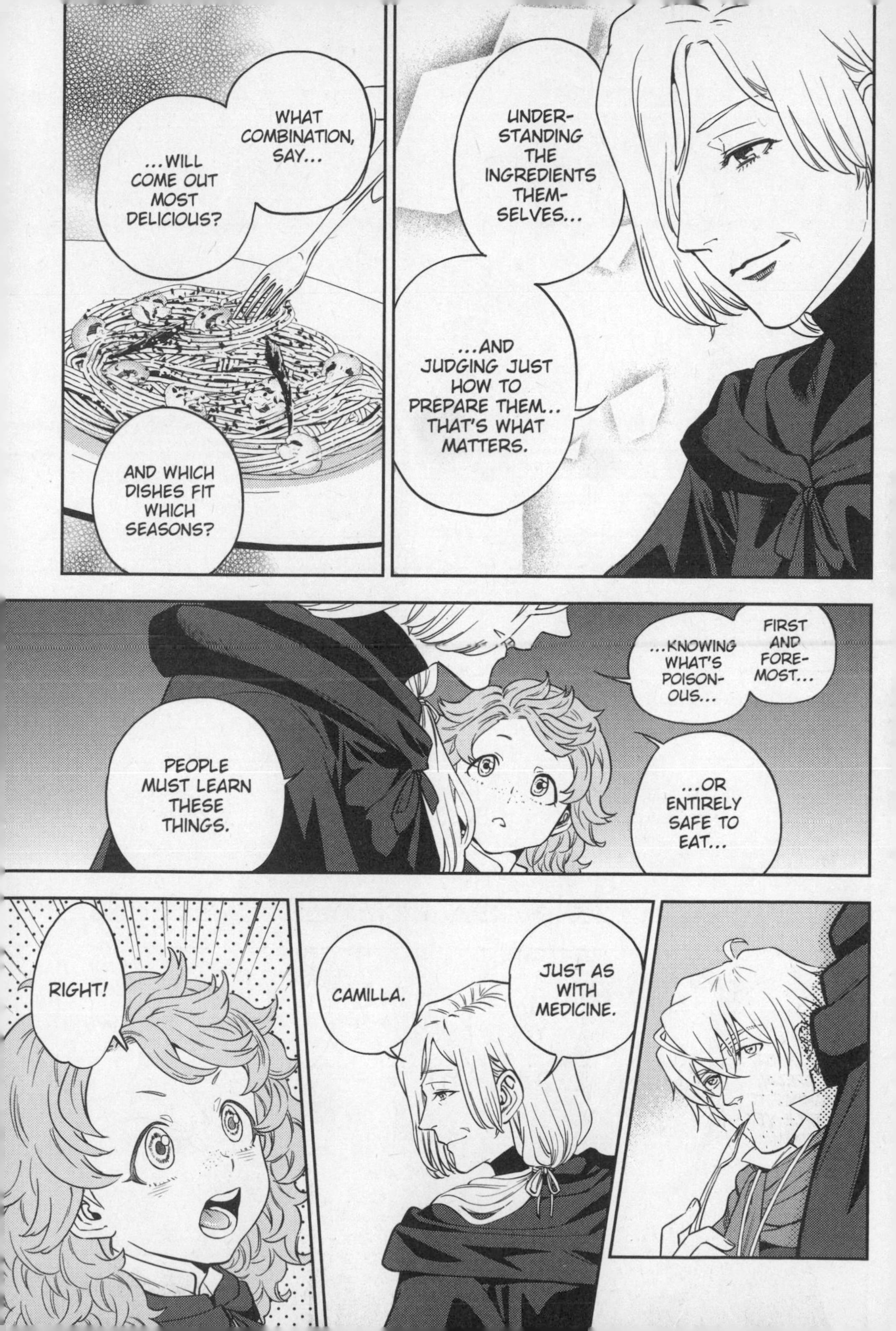
UNDER-STANDING THE INGREDIENTS THEM-SELVES...
...AND JUDGING JUST HOW TO PREPARE THEM... THAT'S WHAT MATTERS.
WHAT COMBINATION, SAY...
...WILL COME OUT MOST DELICIOUS?
AND WHICH DISHES FIT WHICH SEASONS?
FIRST AND FORE-MOST...
...KNOWING WHAT'S POISON-OUS...
...OR ENTIRELY SAFE TO EAT...
PEOPLE MUST LEARN THESE THINGS.
JUST AS WITH MEDICINE.
CAMILLA.
RIGHT!

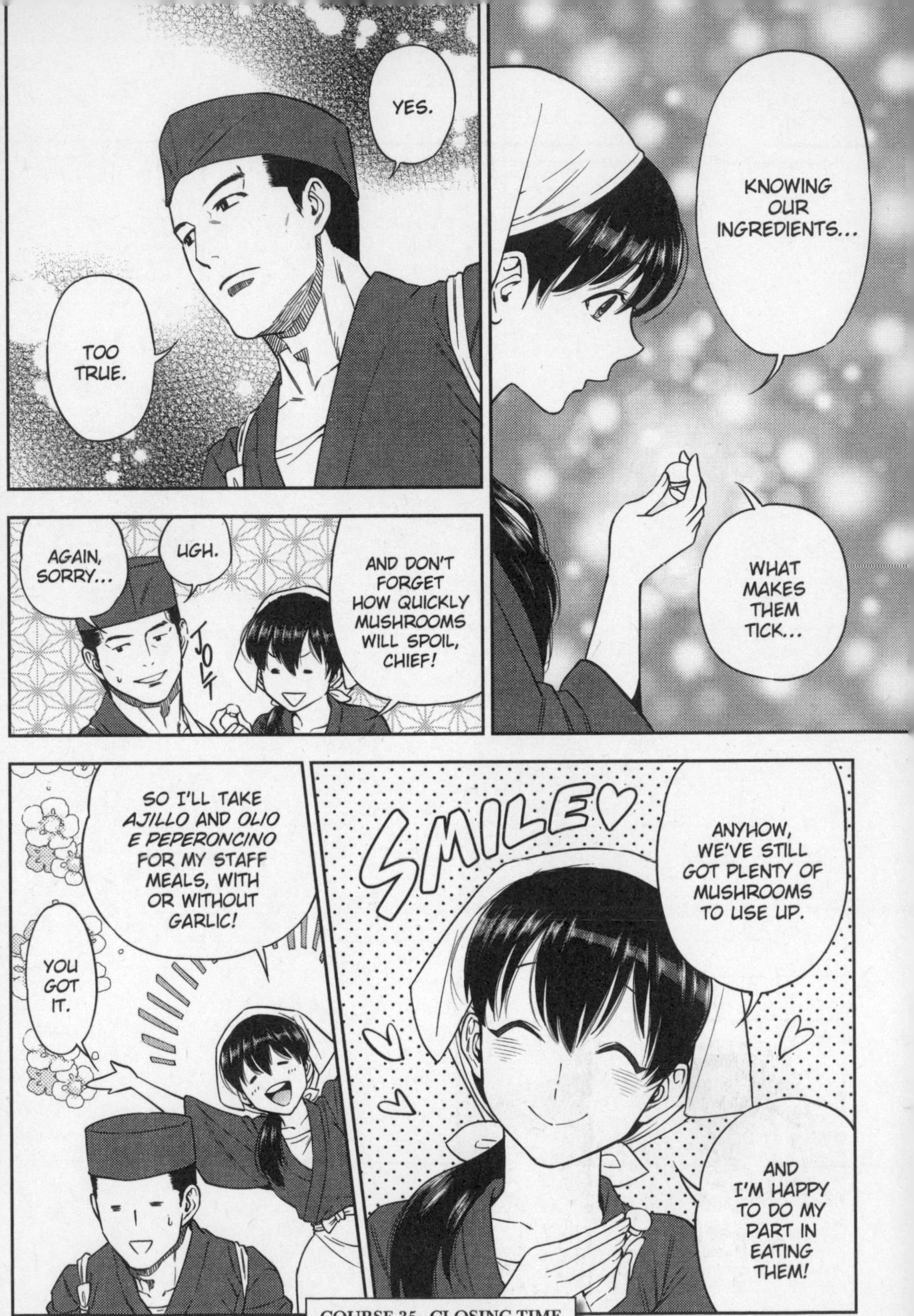
KNOWING OUR INGREDIENTS...
WHAT MAKES THEM TICK...
YES.
TOO TRUE.
AND DON'T FORGET HOW QUICKLY MUSHROOMS WILL SPOIL, CHIEF!
UGH.
JOLT
AGAIN, SORRY...
SMILE
ANYHOW, WE'VE STILL GOT PLENTY OF MUSHROOMS TO USE UP.
AND I'M HAPPY TO DO MY PART IN EATING THEM!
SO I'LL TAKE *AJILLO* AND *OLIO E PEPERONCINO* FOR MY STAFF MEALS, WITH OR WITHOUT GARLIC!
YOU GOT IT.

COURSE 35 - CLOSING TIME

Mushroom Ajillo

OTHERWORLDLY IZAKAYA

NOBU

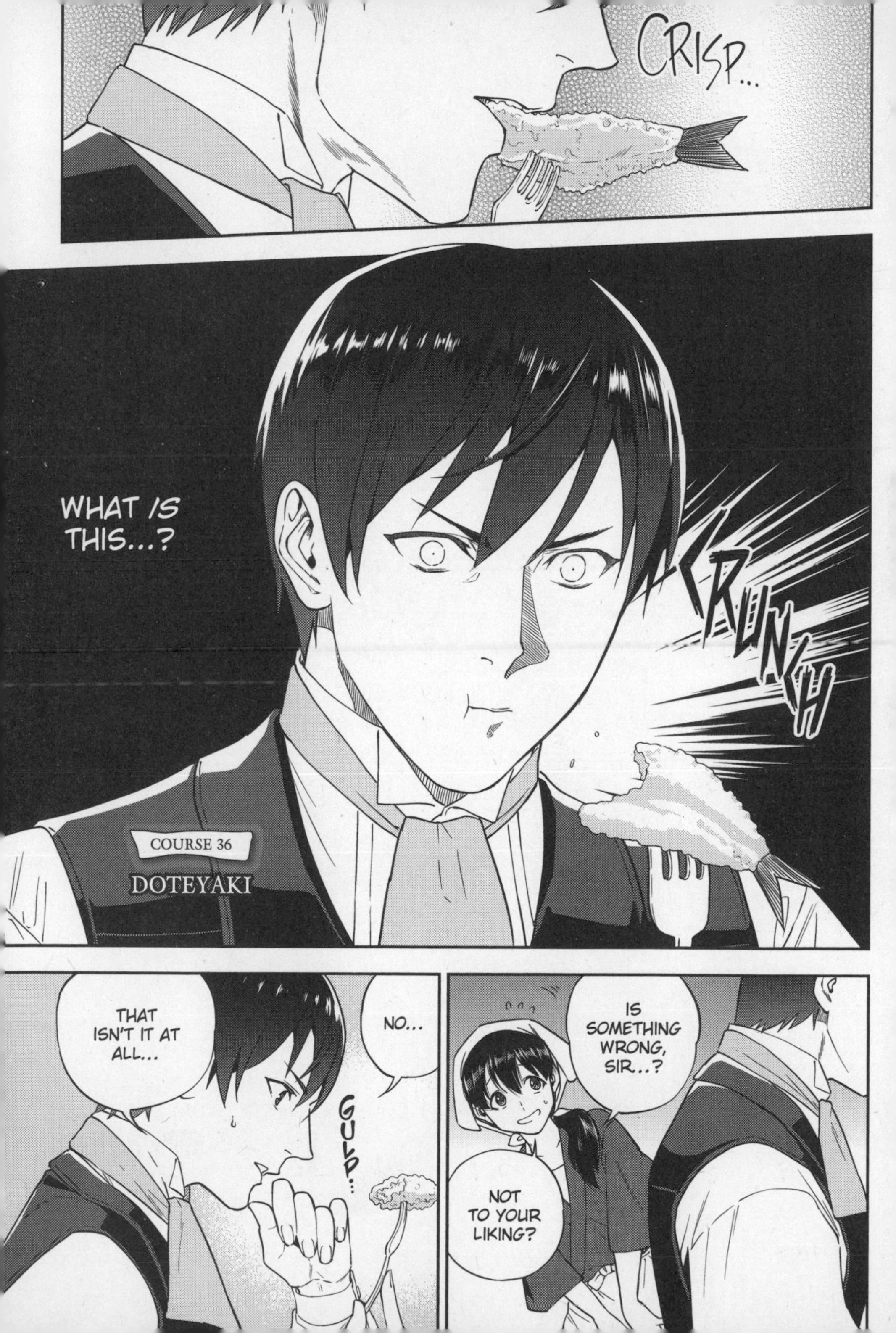
CRISP...
WHAT IS THIS...?
CRUNCH
COURSE 36
DOTEYAKI
IS SOMETHING WRONG, SIR...?
NOT TO YOUR LIKING?
NO...
THAT ISN'T IT AT ALL...
GULP...

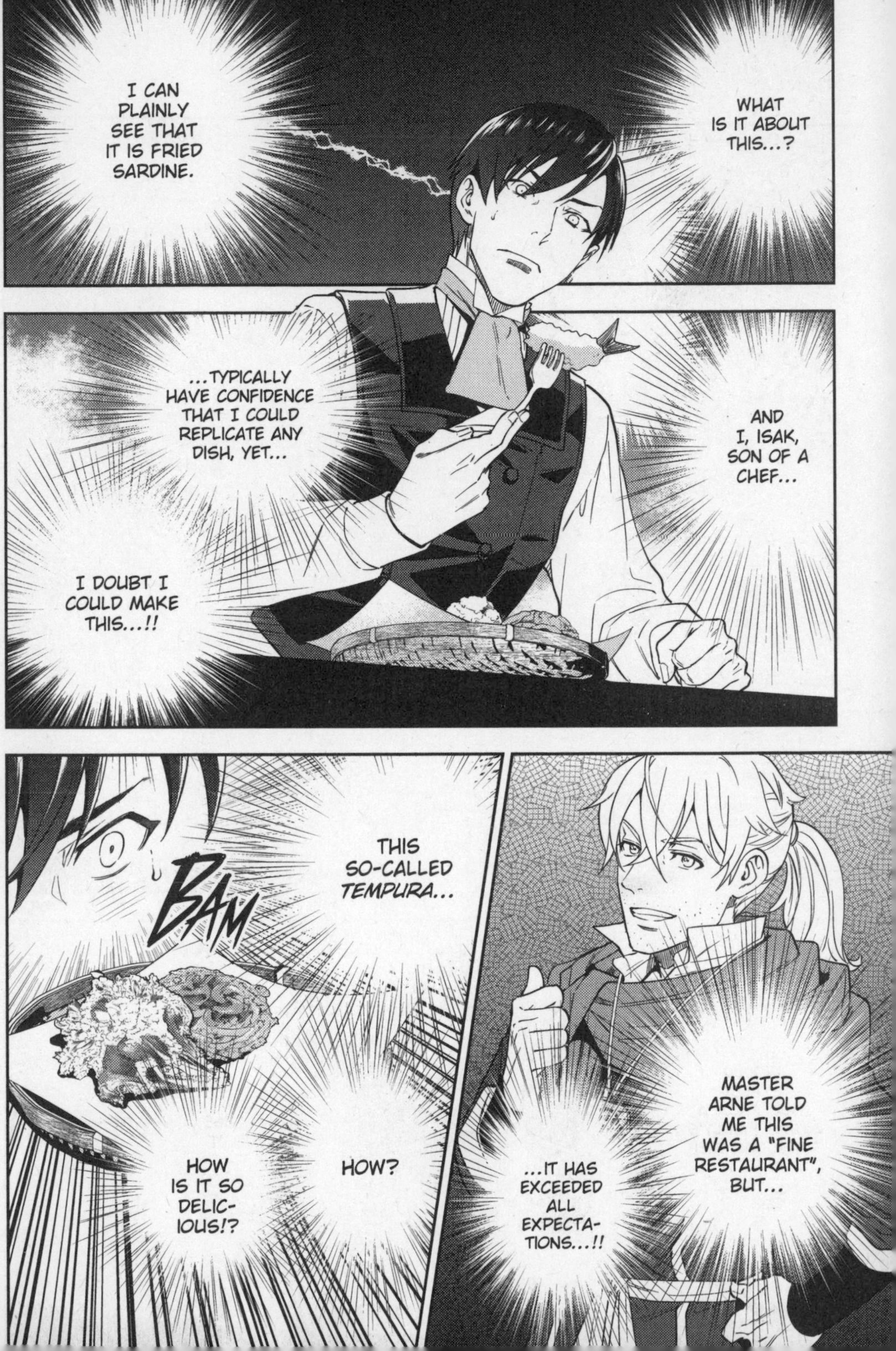
WHAT IS IT ABOUT THIS...?
I CAN PLAINLY SEE THAT IT IS FRIED SARDINE.
AND I, ISAK, SON OF A CHEF...
...TYPICALLY HAVE CONFIDENCE THAT I COULD REPLICATE ANY DISH, YET...
I DOUBT I COULD MAKE THIS...!!
MASTER ARNE TOLD ME THIS WAS A "FINE RESTAURANT", BUT...
...IT HAS EXCEEDED ALL EXPECTA- TIONS...!!
THIS SO-CALLED TEMPURA...
BAM
HOW?
HOW IS IT SO DELIC- IOUS!?

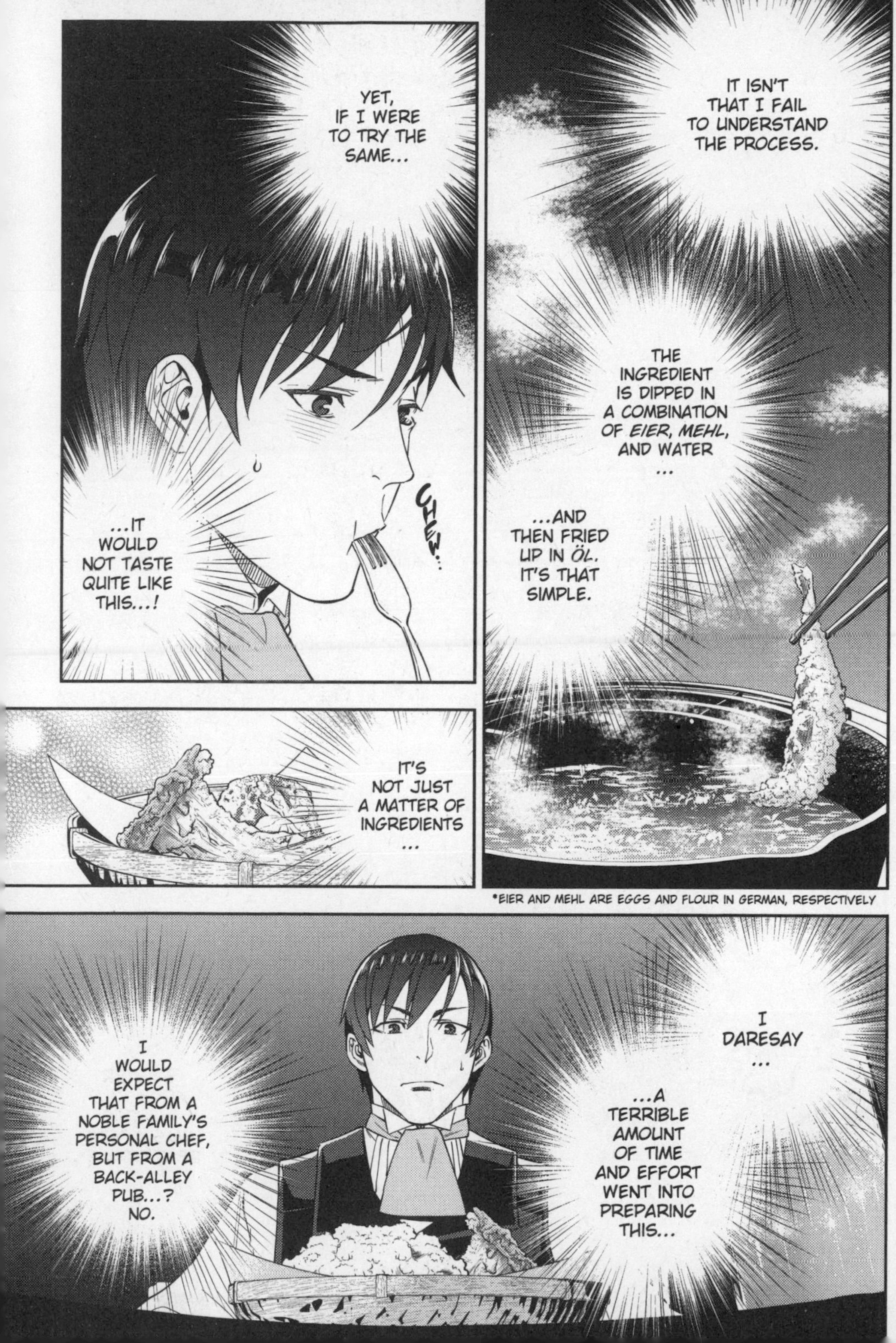
IT ISN'T THAT I FAIL TO UNDERSTAND THE PROCESS.
THE INGREDIENT IS DIPPED IN A COMBINATION OF *EIER, MEHL,* AND WATER ...
...AND THEN FRIED UP IN *ÖL.* IT'S THAT SIMPLE.
YET, IF I WERE TO TRY THE SAME...
CHEW...
...IT WOULD NOT TASTE QUITE LIKE THIS...!
IT'S NOT JUST A MATTER OF INGREDIENTS ...
I DARESAY ...
...A TERRIBLE AMOUNT OF TIME AND EFFORT WENT INTO PREPARING THIS...
I WOULD EXPECT THAT FROM A NOBLE FAMILY'S PERSONAL CHEF, BUT FROM A BACK-ALLEY PUB...? NO.
*EIER AND MEHL ARE EGGS AND FLOUR IN GERMAN, RESPECTIVELY

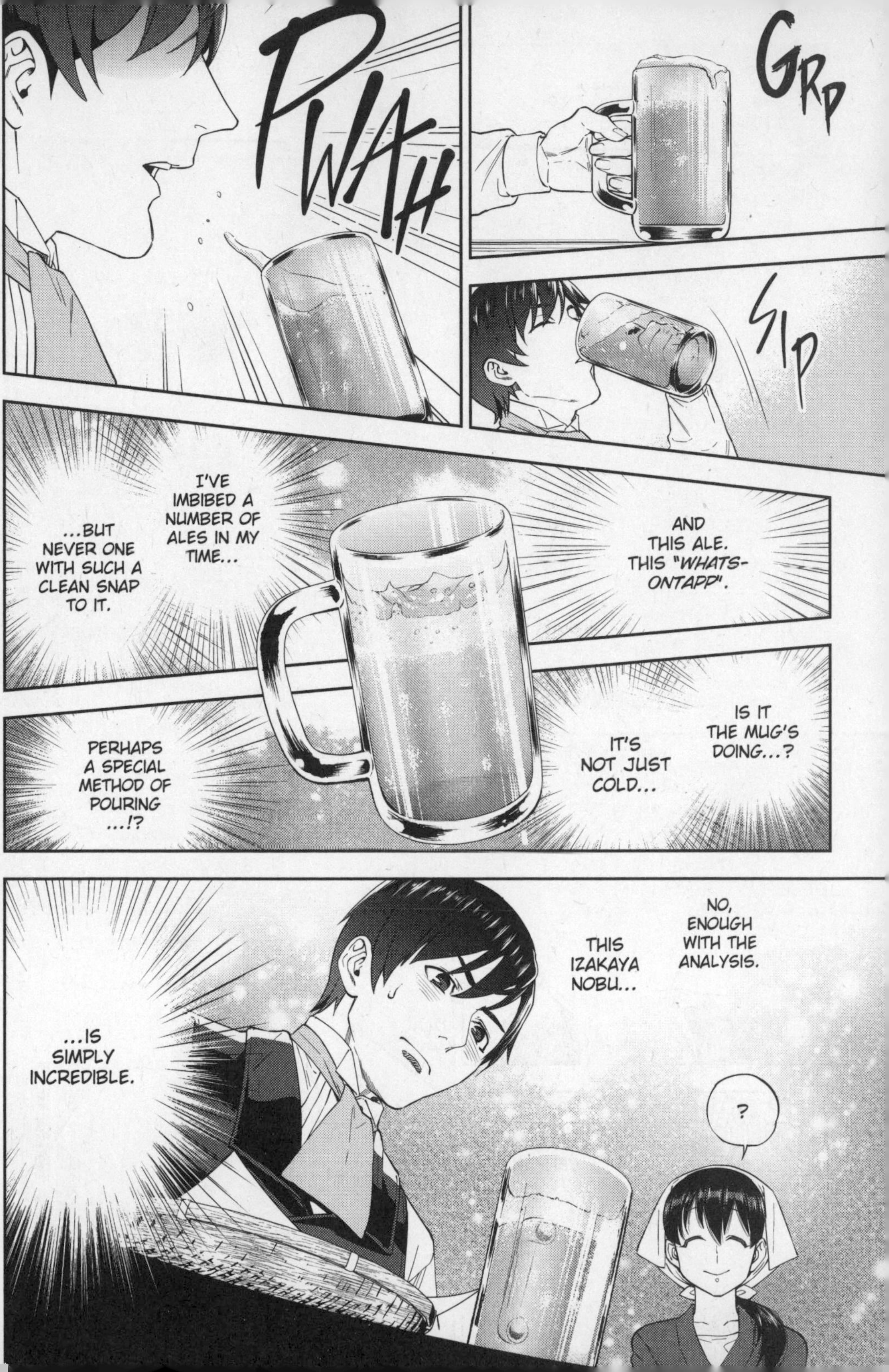
GRP
SIP
PWAH
AND THIS ALE. THIS "WHATS-ONTAPP".
I'VE IMBIBED A NUMBER OF ALES IN MY TIME...
...BUT NEVER ONE WITH SUCH A CLEAN SNAP TO IT.
IS IT THE MUG'S DOING...?
IT'S NOT JUST COLD...
PERHAPS A SPECIAL METHOD OF POURING ...!?
NO, ENOUGH WITH THE ANALYSIS.
THIS IZAKAYA NOBU...
...IS SIMPLY INCREDIBLE.
?

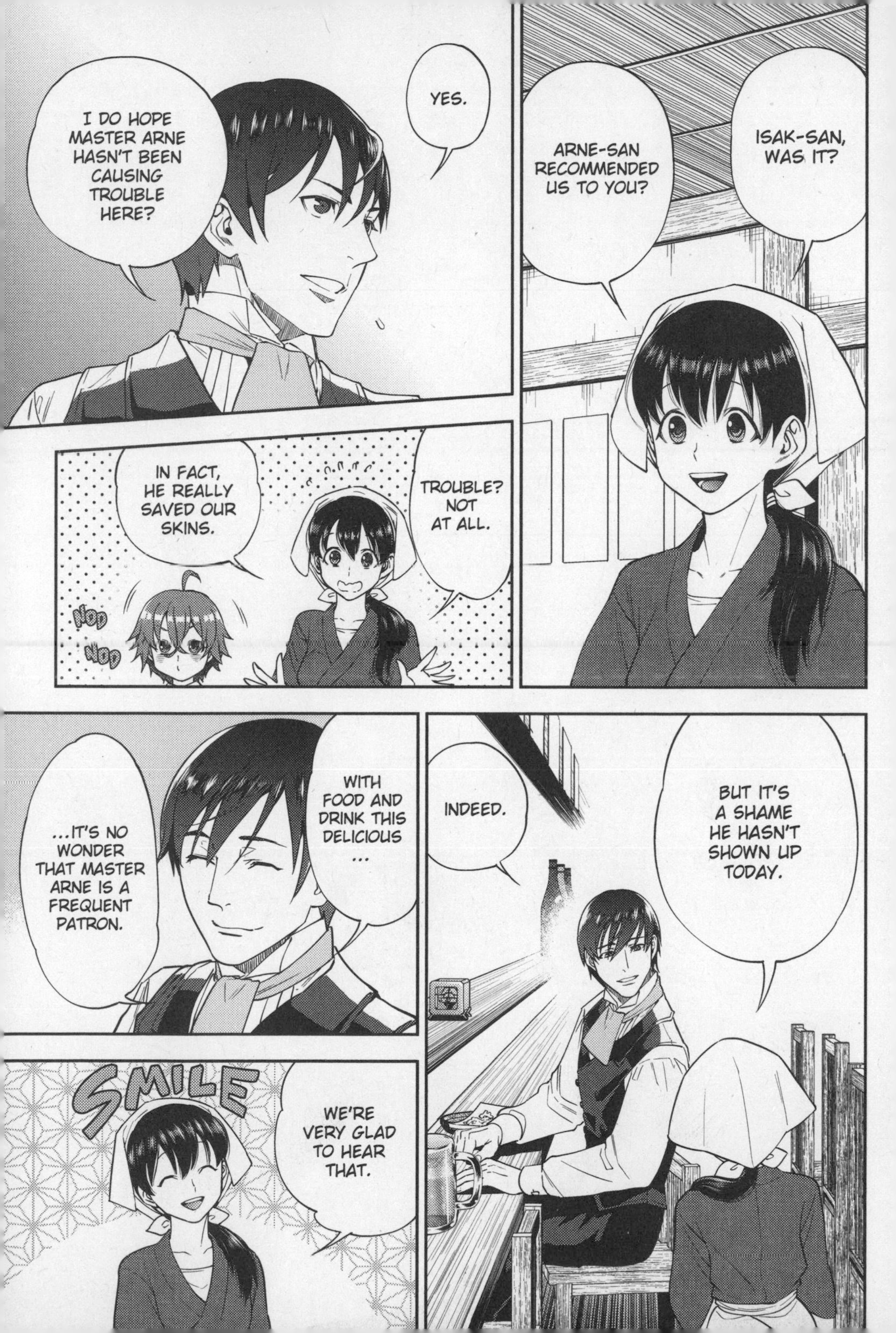
ISAK-SAN, WAS IT?
ARNE-SAN RECOMMENDED US TO YOU?
YES.
I DO HOPE MASTER ARNE HASN'T BEEN CAUSING TROUBLE HERE?
TROUBLE? NOT AT ALL.
IN FACT, HE REALLY SAVED OUR SKINS.
NOD
NOD
BUT IT'S A SHAME HE HASN'T SHOWN UP TODAY.
INDEED.
WITH FOOD AND DRINK THIS DELICIOUS ...
...IT'S NO WONDER THAT MASTER ARNE IS A FREQUENT PATRON.
SMILE
WE'RE VERY GLAD TO HEAR THAT.

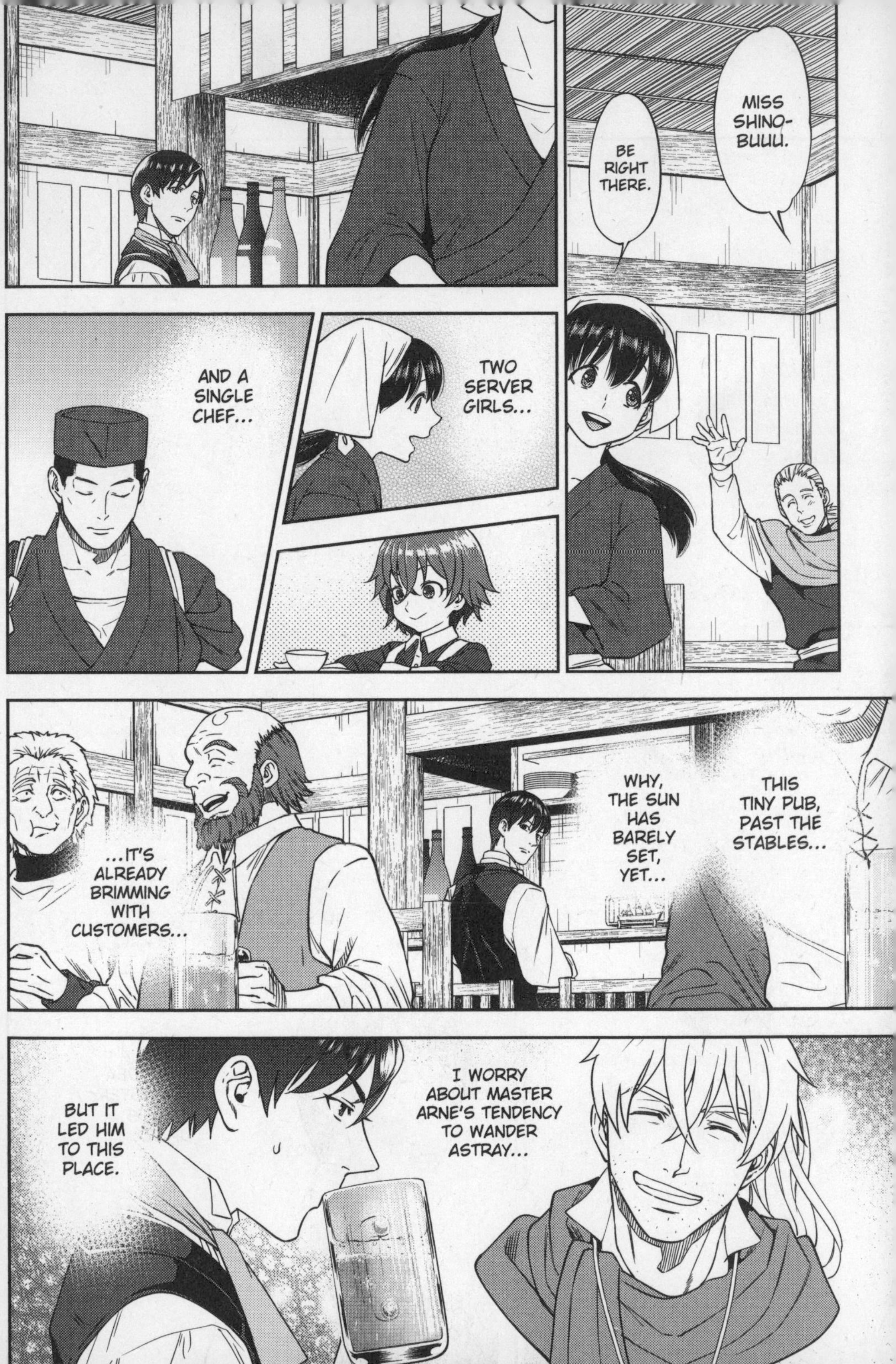
MISS SHINO-BUUU.
BE RIGHT THERE.
TWO SERVER GIRLS...
AND A SINGLE CHEF...
THIS TINY PUB, PAST THE STABLES...
WHY, THE SUN HAS BARELY SET, YET...
...IT'S ALREADY BRIMMING WITH CUSTOMERS...
I WORRY ABOUT MASTER ARNE'S TENDENCY TO WANDER ASTRAY...
BUT IT LED HIM TO THIS PLACE.

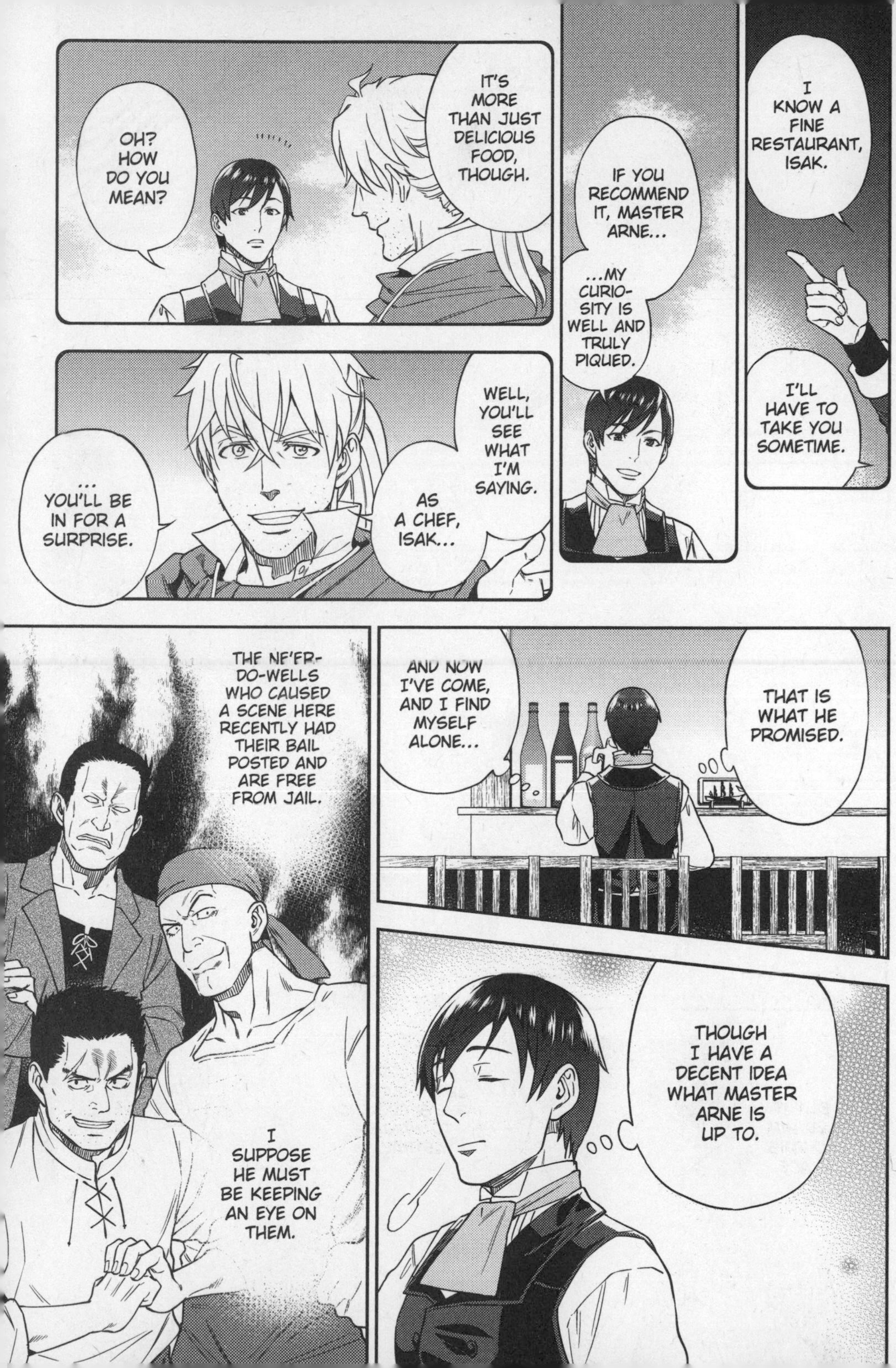
I KNOW A FINE RESTAURANT, ISAK.
I'LL HAVE TO TAKE YOU SOMETIME.
IF YOU RECOMMEND IT, MASTER ARNE...
...MY CURIOSITY IS WELL AND TRULY PIQUED.
IT'S MORE THAN JUST DELICIOUS FOOD, THOUGH.
OH? HOW DO YOU MEAN?
WELL, YOU'LL SEE WHAT I'M SAYING.
AS A CHEF, ISAK...
... YOU'LL BE IN FOR A SURPRISE.
THAT IS WHAT HE PROMISED.
AND NOW I'VE COME, AND I FIND MYSELF ALONE...
THOUGH I HAVE A DECENT IDEA WHAT MASTER ARNE IS UP TO.
THE NE'ER-DO-WELLS WHO CAUSED A SCENE HERE RECENTLY HAD THEIR BAIL POSTED AND ARE FREE FROM JAIL.
I SUPPOSE HE MUST BE KEEPING AN EYE ON THEM.

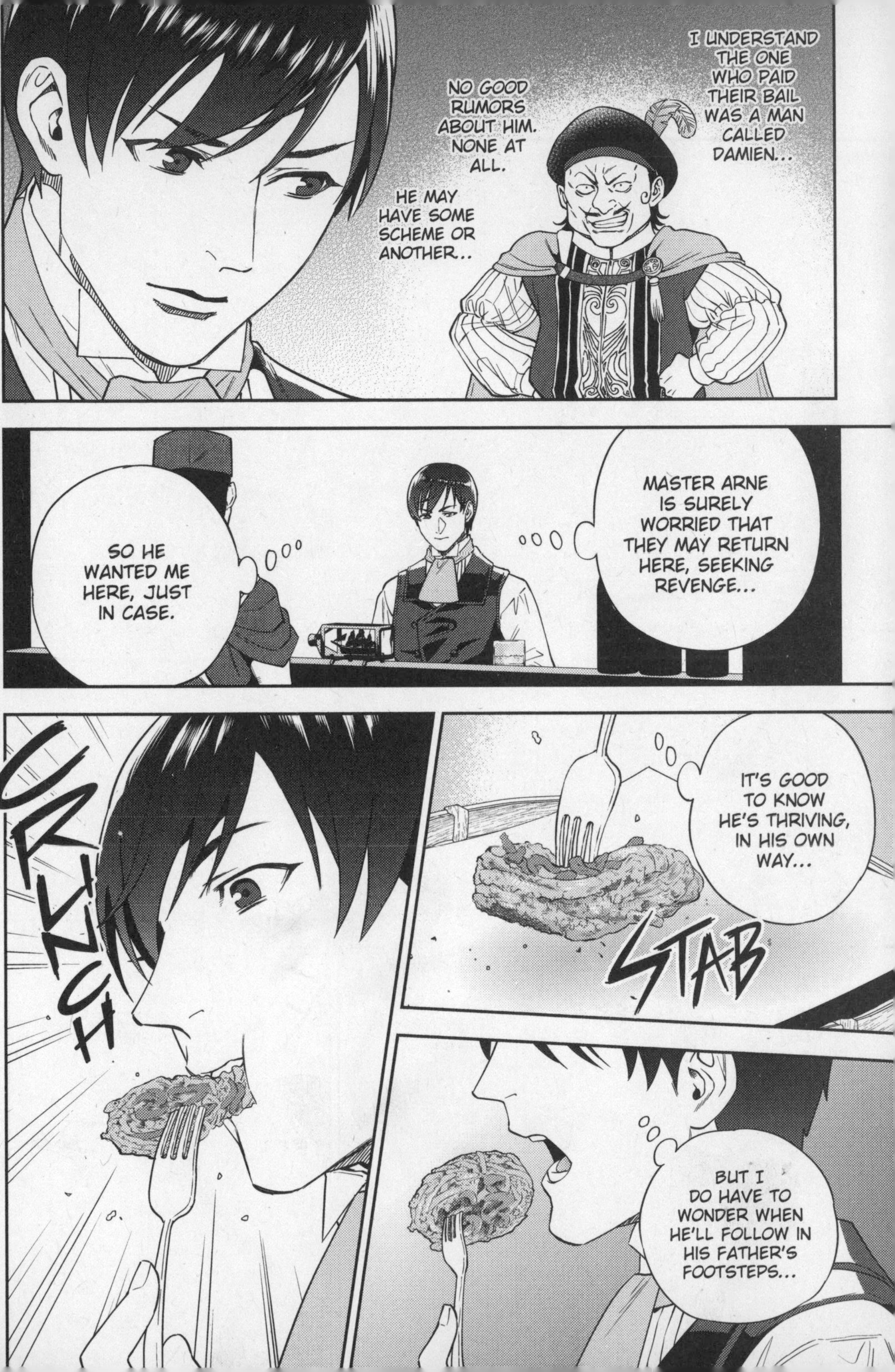
I UNDERSTAND THE ONE WHO PAID THEIR BAIL WAS A MAN CALLED DAMIEN...
NO GOOD RUMORS ABOUT HIM. NONE AT ALL.
HE MAY HAVE SOME SCHEME OR ANOTHER...
MASTER ARNE IS SURELY WORRIED THAT THEY MAY RETURN HERE, SEEKING REVENGE...
SO HE WANTED ME HERE, JUST IN CASE.
IT'S GOOD TO KNOW HE'S THRIVING, IN HIS OWN WAY...
STAB
BUT I DO HAVE TO WONDER WHEN HE'LL FOLLOW IN HIS FATHER'S FOOTSTEPS...
CRUNCH

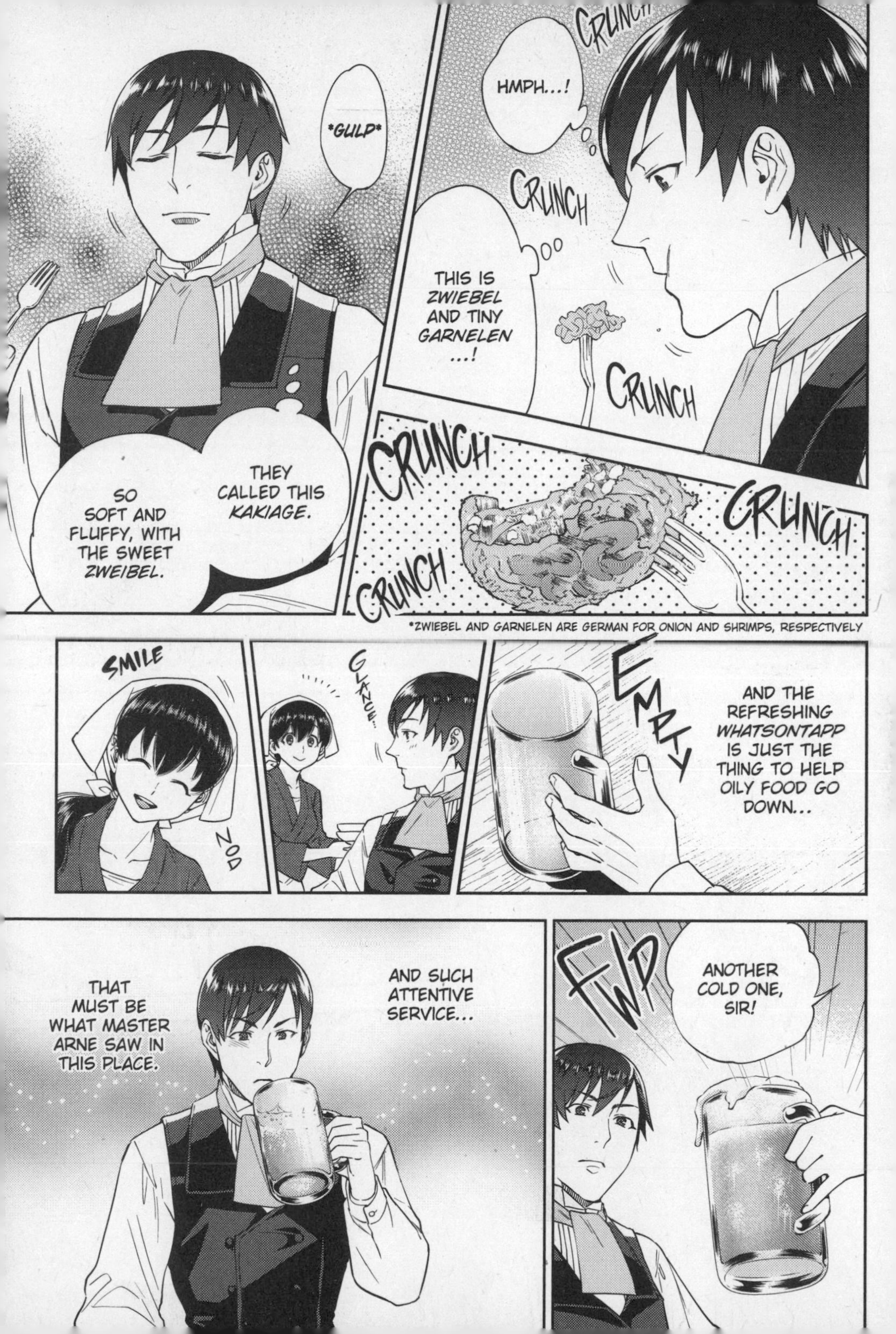
CRUNCH
HMPH...!
CRUNCH
THIS IS ZWIEBEL AND TINY GARNELEN ...!
CRUNCH
CRUNCH
CRUNCH
CRUNCH
GULP
THEY CALLED THIS KAKIAGE.
SO SOFT AND FLUFFY, WITH THE SWEET ZWEIBEL.
*ZWIEBEL AND GARNELEN ARE GERMAN FOR ONION AND SHRIMPS, RESPECTIVELY
EMPTY
AND THE REFRESHING WHATSONTAPP IS JUST THE THING TO HELP OILY FOOD GO DOWN...
GLANCE...
SMILE
NOD
FWP
ANOTHER COLD ONE, SIR!
AND SUCH ATTENTIVE SERVICE...
THAT MUST BE WHAT MASTER ARNE SAW IN THIS PLACE.

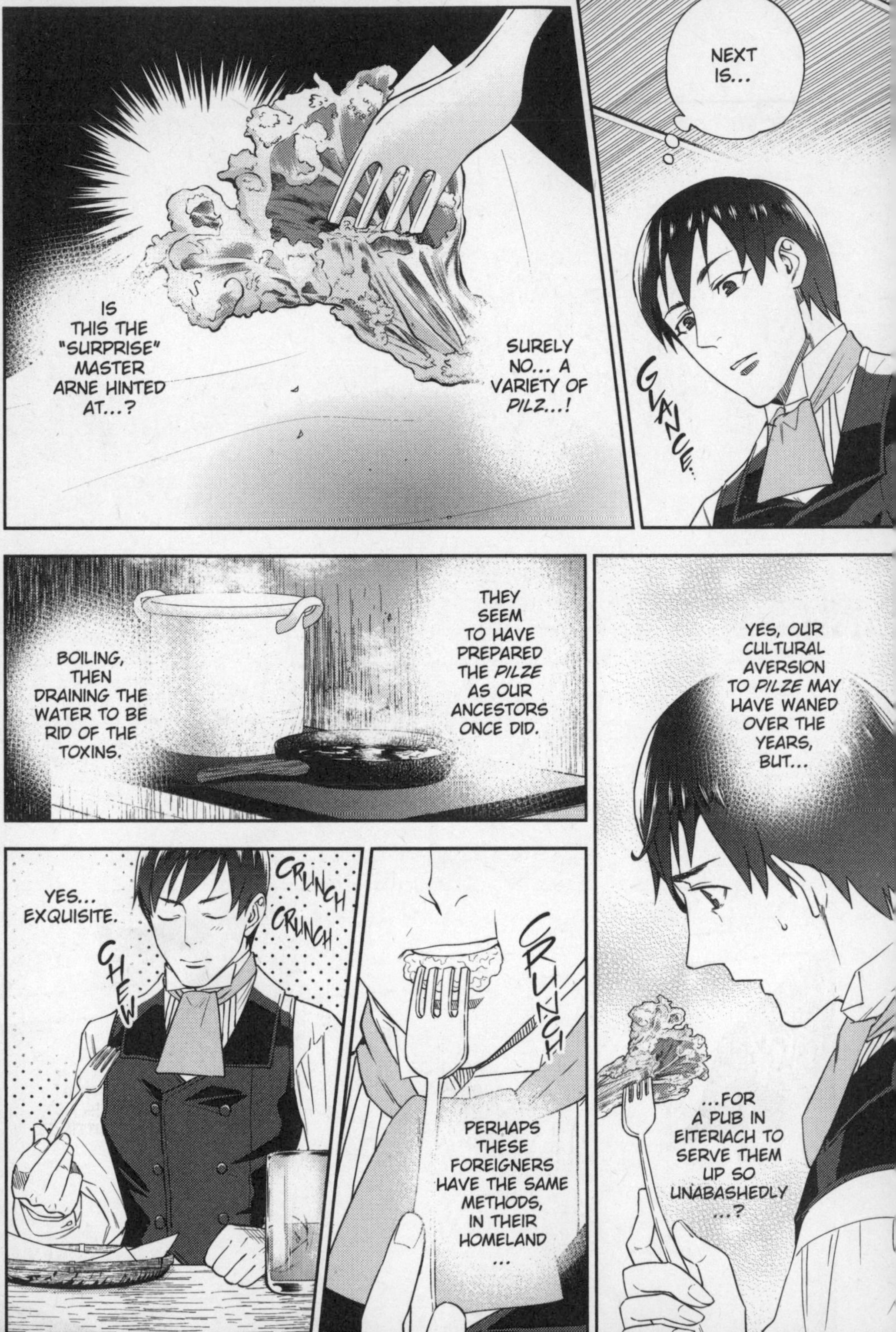
NEXT IS...
GLANCE...
SURELY NO... A VARIETY OF *PILZ*...!
IS THIS THE "SURPRISE" MASTER ARNE HINTED AT...?
YES, OUR CULTURAL AVERSION TO *PILZE* MAY HAVE WANED OVER THE YEARS, BUT...
...FOR A PUB IN EITERIACH TO SERVE THEM UP SO UNABASHEDLY ...?
THEY SEEM TO HAVE PREPARED THE *PILZE* AS OUR ANCESTORS ONCE DID.
BOILING, THEN DRAINING THE WATER TO BE RID OF THE TOXINS.
CRUNCH
PERHAPS THESE FOREIGNERS HAVE THE SAME METHODS, IN THEIR HOMELAND ...
CRUNCH CRUNCH
YES... EXQUISITE.
CHEW

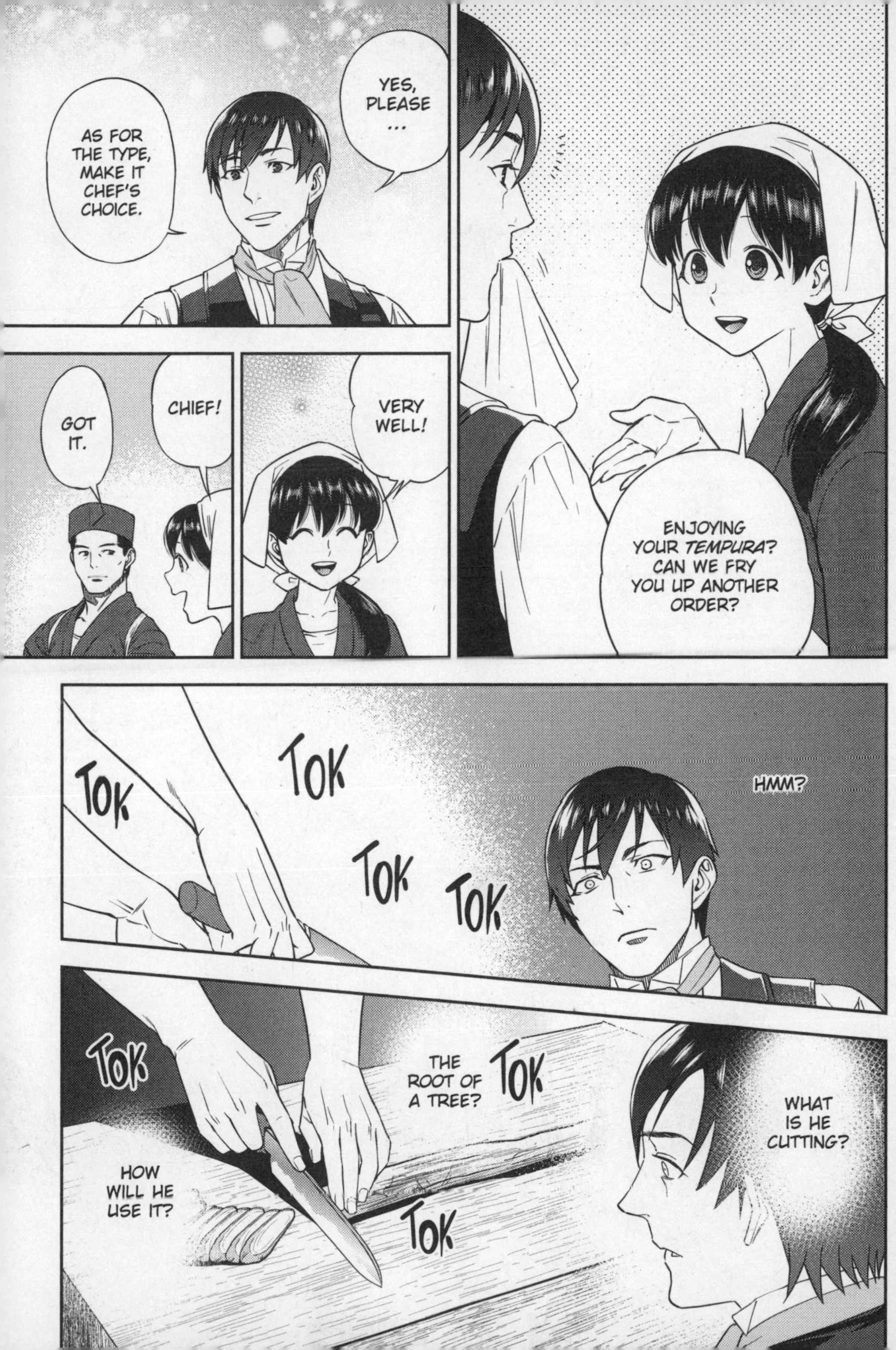
ENJOYING YOUR *TEMPURA*? CAN WE FRY YOU UP ANOTHER ORDER?
YES, PLEASE ...
AS FOR THE TYPE, MAKE IT CHEF'S CHOICE.
VERY WELL!
CHIEF!
GOT IT.
HMM?
TOK
TOK
TOK
TOK
WHAT IS HE CUTTING?
TOK
THE ROOT OF A TREE?
TOK
TOK
HOW WILL HE USE IT?

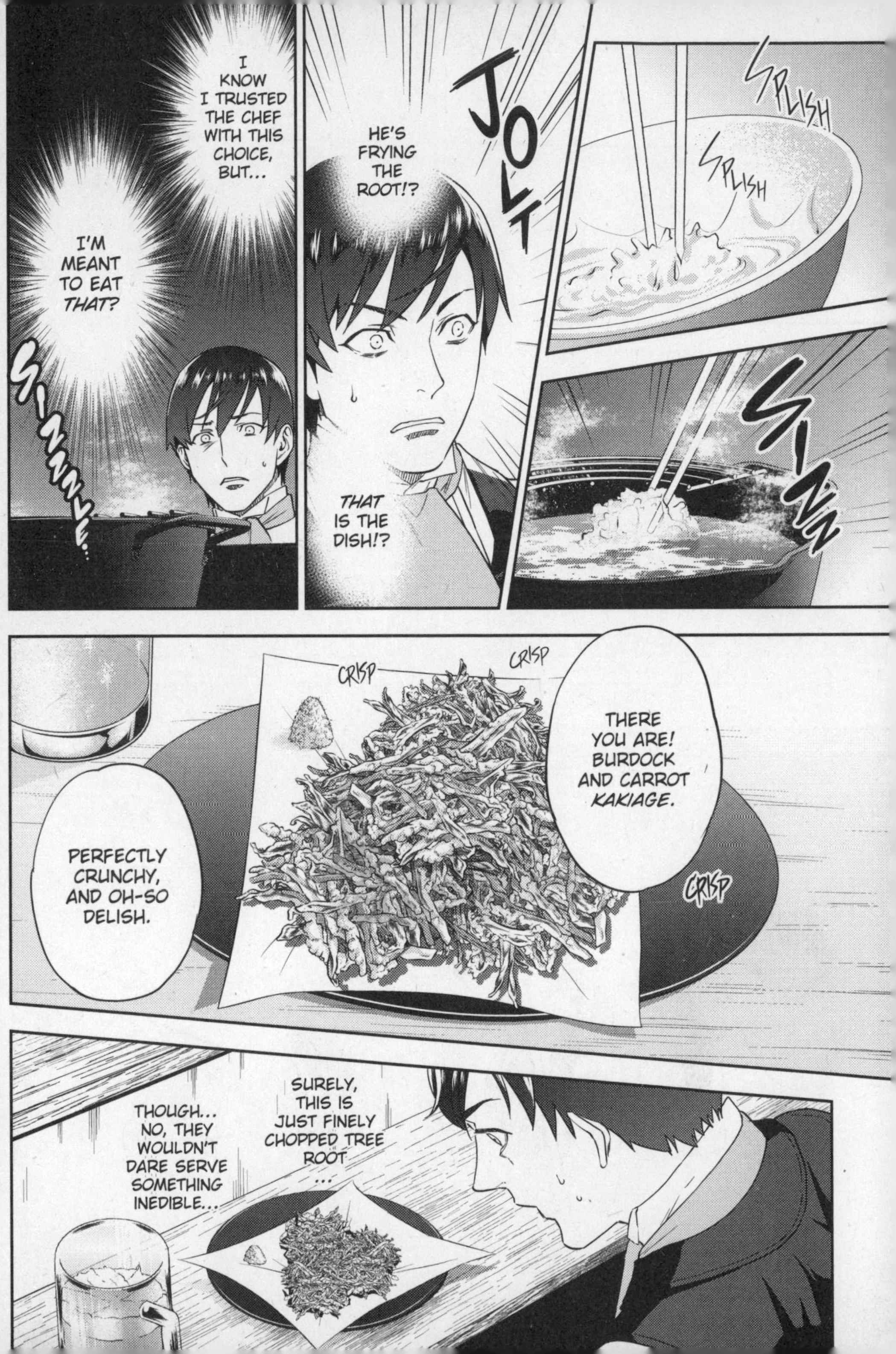
SPLISH
SPLISH
JOLT
HE'S FRYING THE ROOT!?
THAT IS THE DISH!?
I KNOW I TRUSTED THE CHEF WITH THIS CHOICE, BUT...
I'M MEANT TO EAT *THAT?*
THERE YOU ARE! BURDOCK AND CARROT *KAKIAGE.*
CRISP
CRISP
CRISP
PERFECTLY CRUNCHY, AND OH-SO DELISH.
SURELY, THIS IS JUST FINELY CHOPPED TREE ROOT ...
THOUGH... NO, THEY WOULDN'T DARE SERVE SOMETHING INEDIBLE...

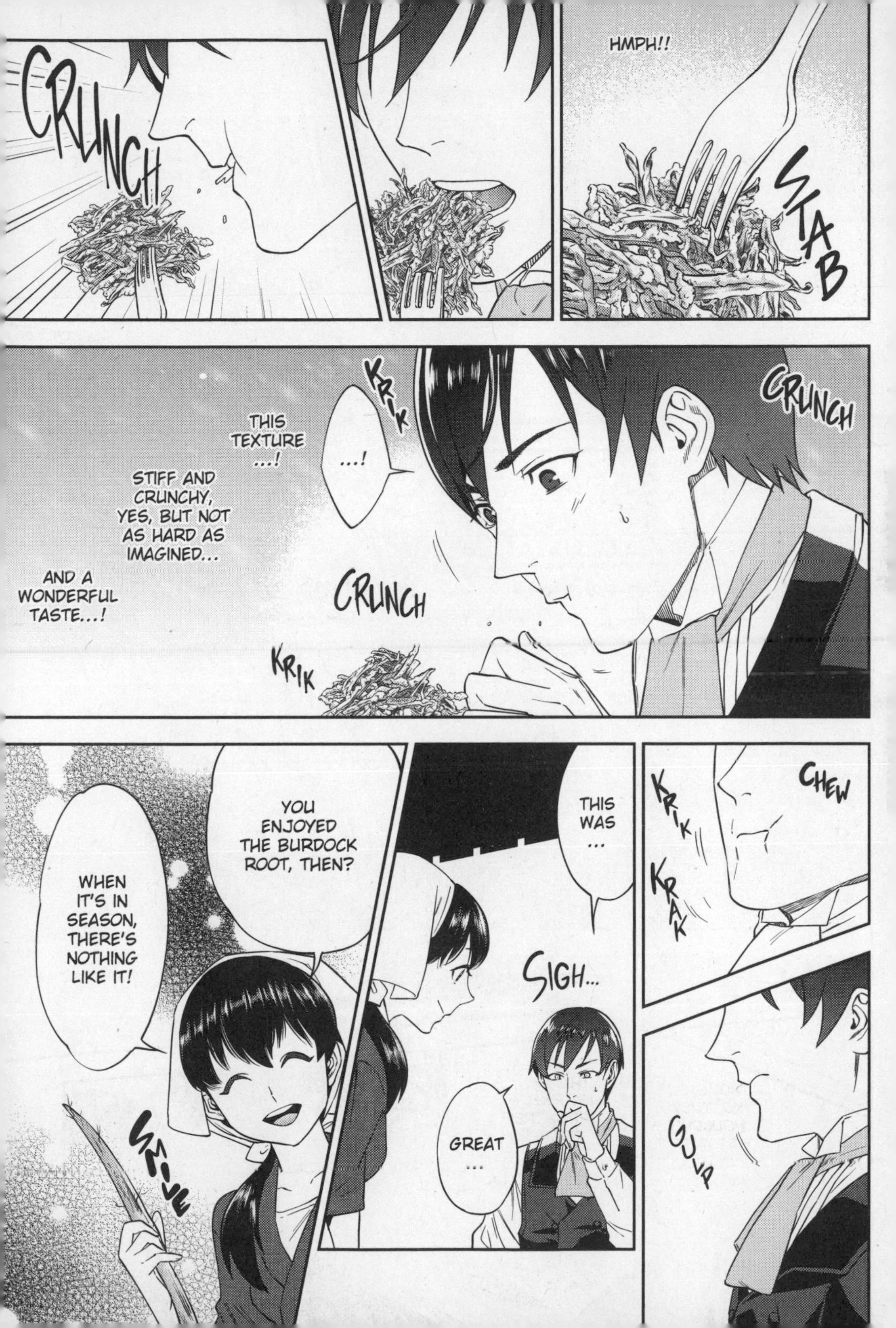
HMPH!!
STAB
CRUNCH
CRUNCH
KRIK
...!
THIS TEXTURE ...!
STIFF AND CRUNCHY, YES, BUT NOT AS HARD AS IMAGINED...
CRUNCH
AND A WONDERFUL TASTE...!
KRIK
CHEW
KRIK
KRAK
GULP
THIS WAS ...
SIGH...
GREAT ...
YOU ENJOYED THE BURDOCK ROOT, THEN?
WHEN IT'S IN SEASON, THERE'S NOTHING LIKE IT!
SMILE

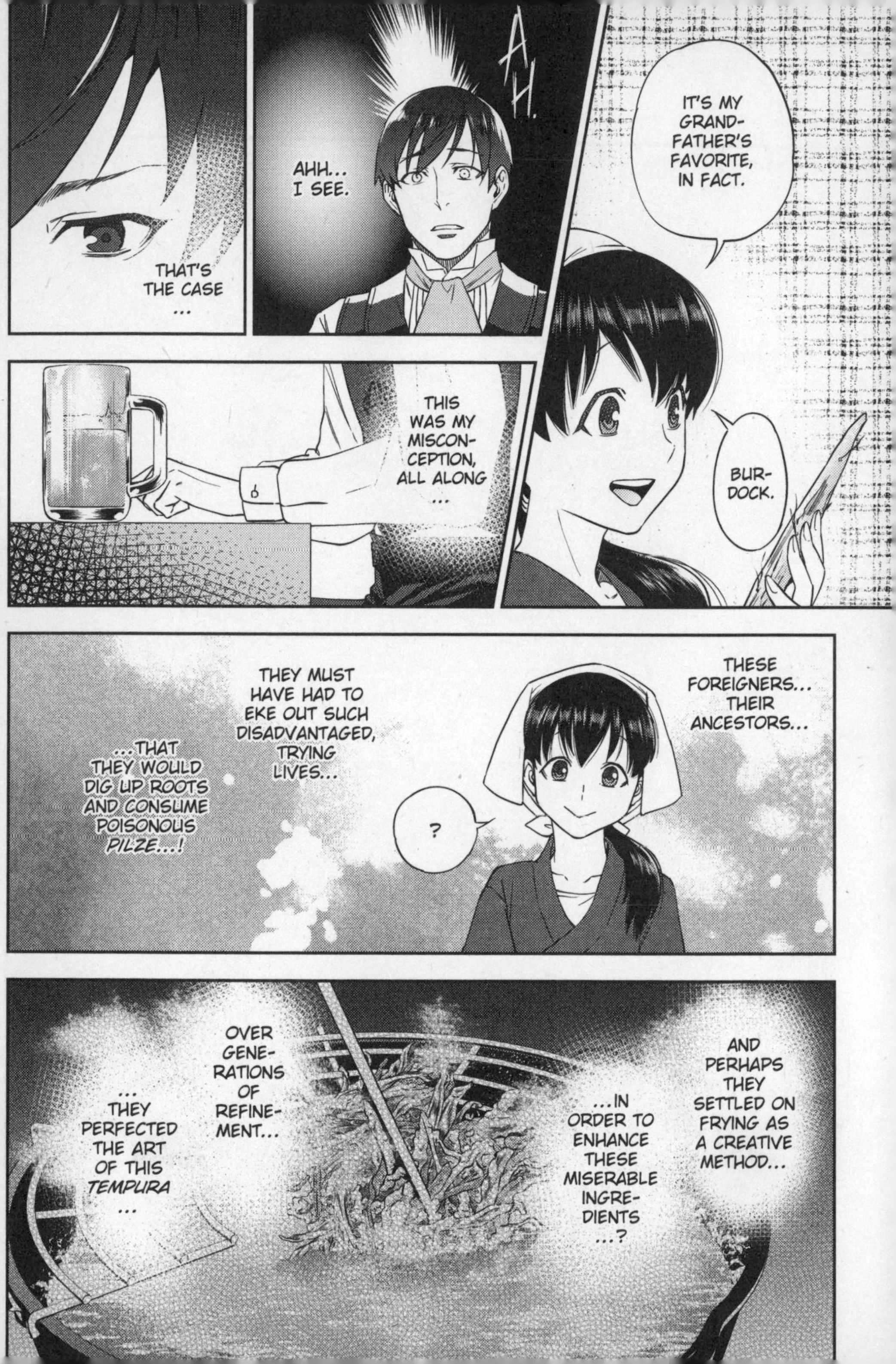
IT'S MY GRAND-FATHER'S FAVORITE, IN FACT.
BUR-DOCK.
AH.
AHH... I SEE.
THAT'S THE CASE ...
THIS WAS MY MISCON-CEPTION, ALL ALONG ...
THESE FOREIGNERS... THEIR ANCESTORS...
?
THEY MUST HAVE HAD TO EKE OUT SUCH DISADVANTAGED, TRYING LIVES...
...THAT THEY WOULD DIG UP ROOTS AND CONSUME POISONOUS *PILZE*...!
AND PERHAPS THEY SETTLED ON FRYING AS A CREATIVE METHOD...
...IN ORDER TO ENHANCE THESE MISERABLE INGRE-DIENTS ...?
OVER GENE-RATIONS OF REFINE-MENT...
... THEY PERFECTED THE ART OF THIS *TEMPURA* ...

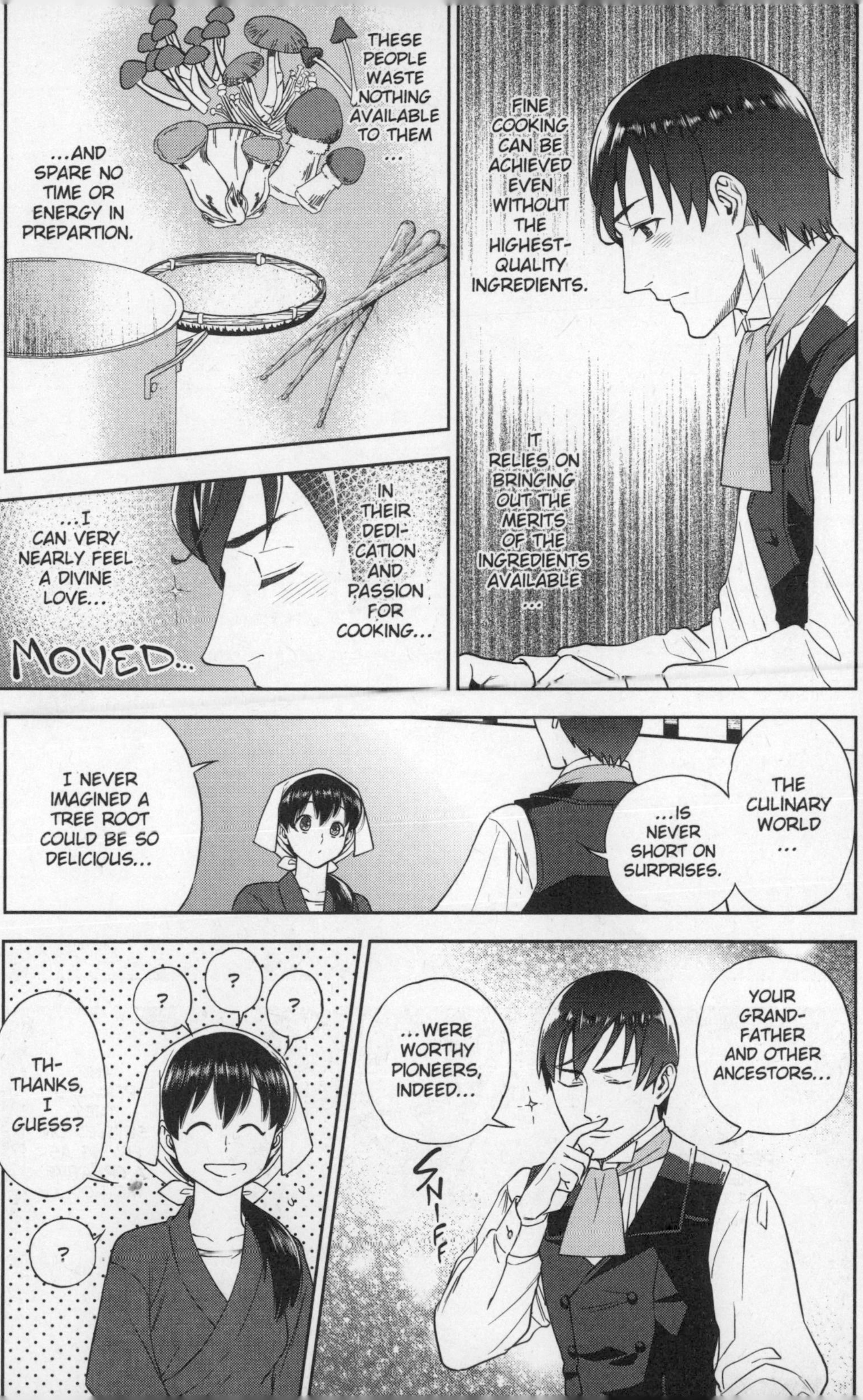
FINE COOKING CAN BE ACHIEVED EVEN WITHOUT THE HIGHEST-QUALITY INGREDIENTS.
IT RELIES ON BRINGING OUT THE MERITS OF THE INGREDIENTS AVAILABLE ...
THESE PEOPLE WASTE NOTHING AVAILABLE TO THEM ...
...AND SPARE NO TIME OR ENERGY IN PREPARTION.
IN THEIR DEDICATION AND PASSION FOR COOKING...
...I CAN VERY NEARLY FEEL A DIVINE LOVE...
MOVED...
THE CULINARY WORLD ...
...IS NEVER SHORT ON SURPRISES.
I NEVER IMAGINED A TREE ROOT COULD BE SO DELICIOUS...
YOUR GRANDFATHER AND OTHER ANCESTORS...
...WERE WORTHY PIONEERS, INDEED...
SNIFF
?
?
?
TH-THANKS, I GUESS?
?

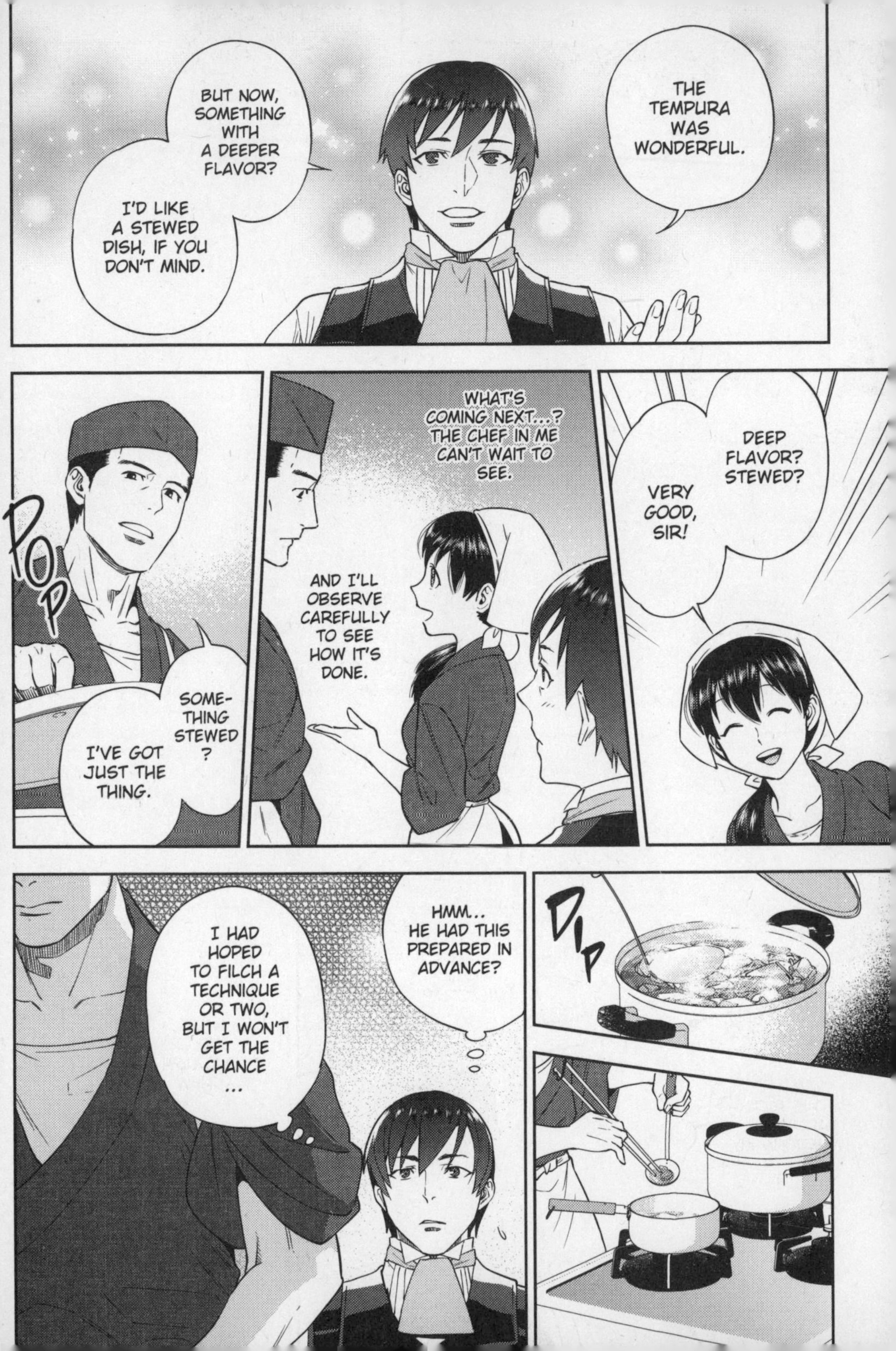
THE TEMPURA WAS WONDERFUL.
BUT NOW, SOMETHING WITH A DEEPER FLAVOR?
I'D LIKE A STEWED DISH, IF YOU DON'T MIND.
DEEP FLAVOR? STEWED?
VERY GOOD, SIR!
WHAT'S COMING NEXT...? THE CHEF IN ME CAN'T WAIT TO SEE.
AND I'LL OBSERVE CAREFULLY TO SEE HOW IT'S DONE.
POP
SOME-THING STEWED?
I'VE GOT JUST THE THING.
DIP
HMM.. HE HAD THIS PREPARED IN ADVANCE?
I HAD HOPED TO FILCH A TECHNIQUE OR TWO, BUT I WON'T GET THE CHANCE ...

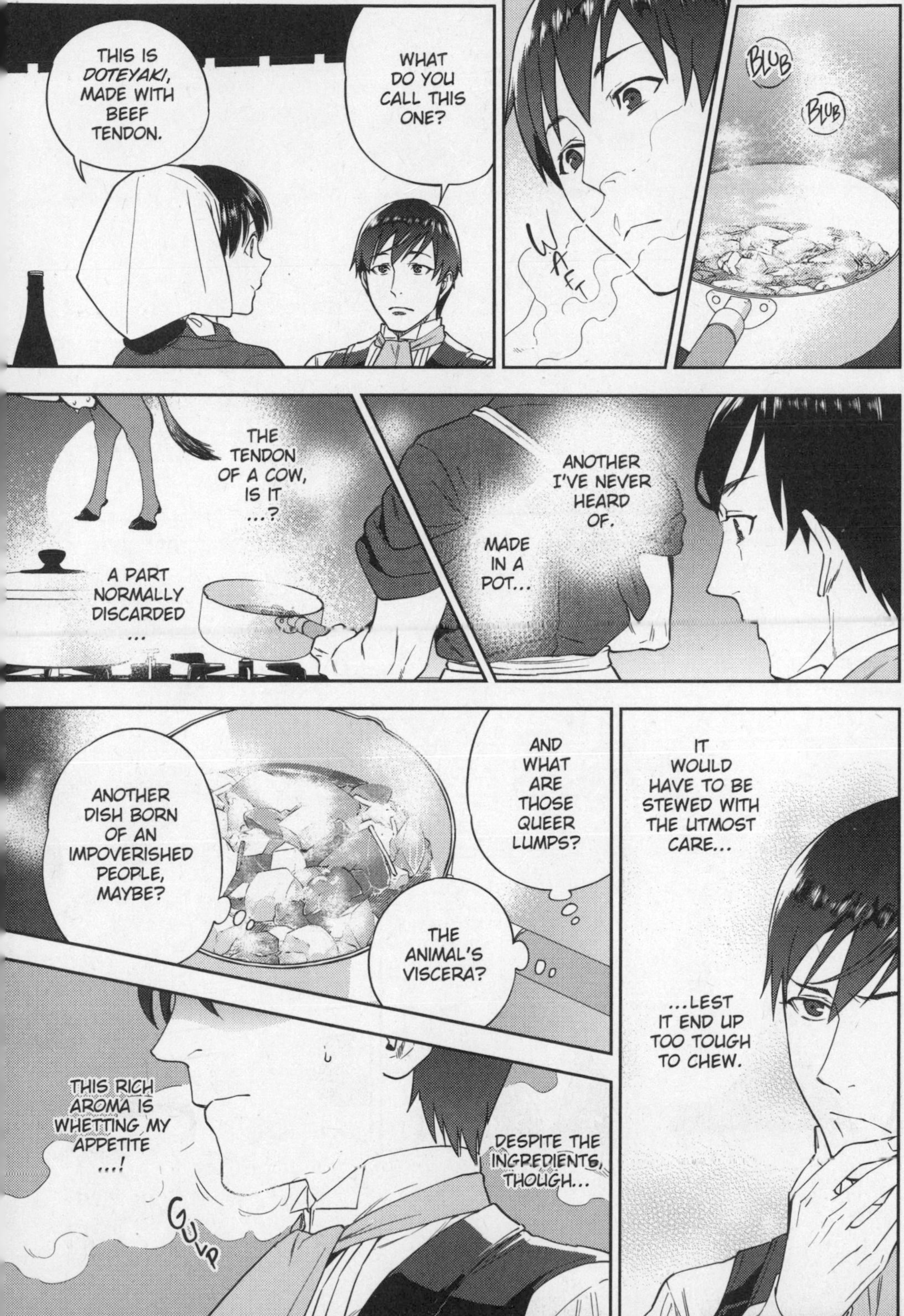

BLUB
BLUB
WAFT
WHAT DO YOU CALL THIS ONE?
THIS IS *DOTEYAKI*, MADE WITH BEEF TENDON.
ANOTHER I'VE NEVER HEARD OF.
MADE IN A POT...
THE TENDON OF A COW, IS IT ...?
A PART NORMALLY DISCARDED ...
IT WOULD HAVE TO BE STEWED WITH THE UTMOST CARE...
...LEST IT END UP TOO TOUGH TO CHEW.
AND WHAT ARE THOSE QUEER LUMPS?
ANOTHER DISH BORN OF AN IMPOVERISHED PEOPLE, MAYBE?
THE ANIMAL'S VISCERA?
DESPITE THE INGREDIENTS, THOUGH...
THIS RICH AROMA IS WHETTING MY APPETITE ...!
GULP

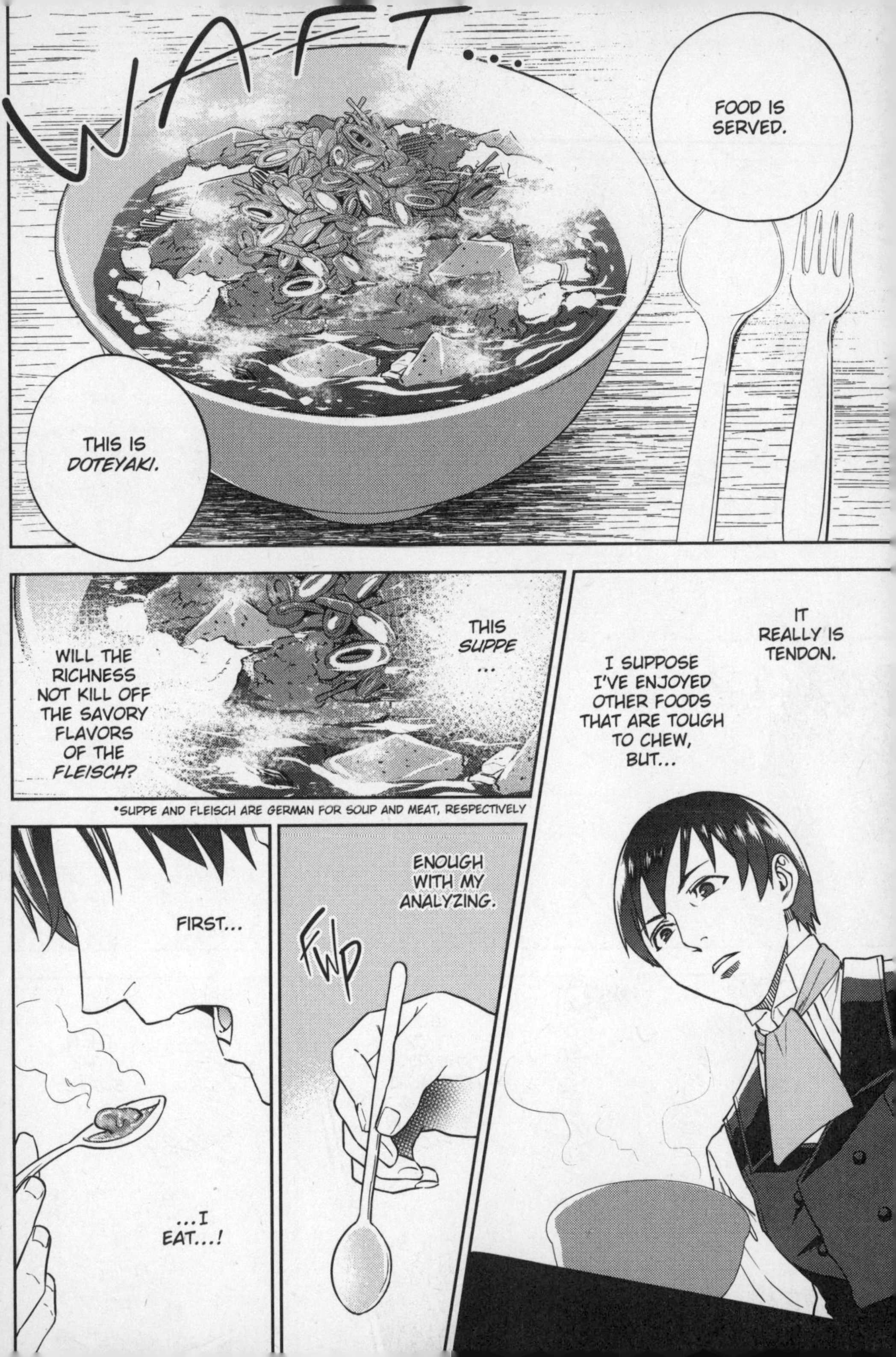
FOOD IS SERVED.
WAFT...
THIS IS DOTEYAKI.
IT REALLY IS TENDON.
I SUPPOSE I'VE ENJOYED OTHER FOODS THAT ARE TOUGH TO CHEW, BUT...
THIS SUPPE...
WILL THE RICHNESS NOT KILL OFF THE SAVORY FLAVORS OF THE FLEISCH?
*SUPPE AND FLEISCH ARE GERMAN FOR SOUP AND MEAT, RESPECTIVELY
ENOUGH WITH MY ANALYZING.
Fwp
FIRST...
...I EAT...!

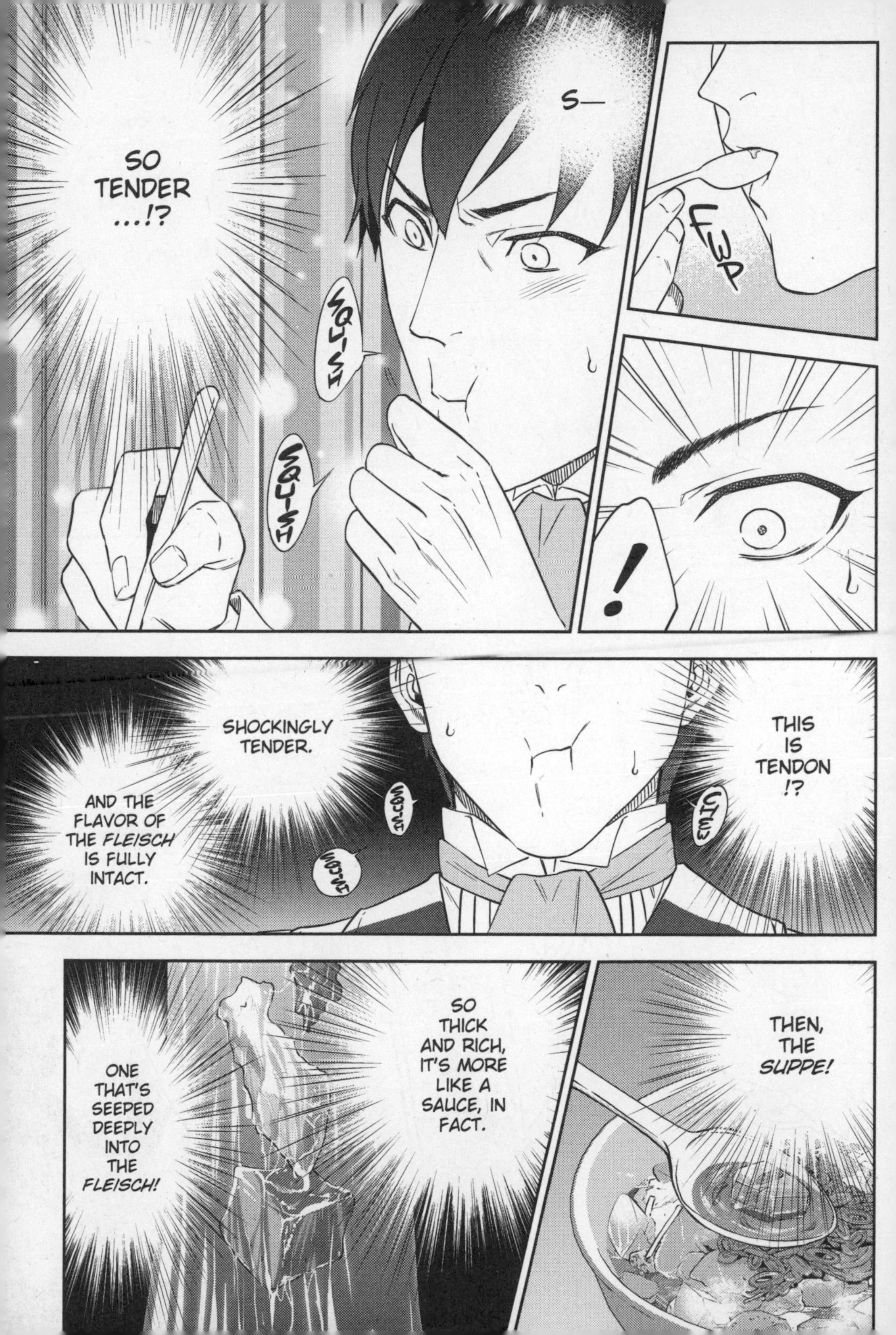

FWP
!
S—
SQUISH
SQUISH
SO TENDER ...!?
THIS IS TENDON !?
CHEW
SQUISH
SQUISH
SHOCKINGLY TENDER.
AND THE FLAVOR OF THE *FLEISCH* IS FULLY INTACT.
THEN, THE *SUPPE!*
SO THICK AND RICH, IT'S MORE LIKE A SAUCE, IN FACT.
ONE THAT'S SEEPED DEEPLY INTO THE *FLEISCH!*

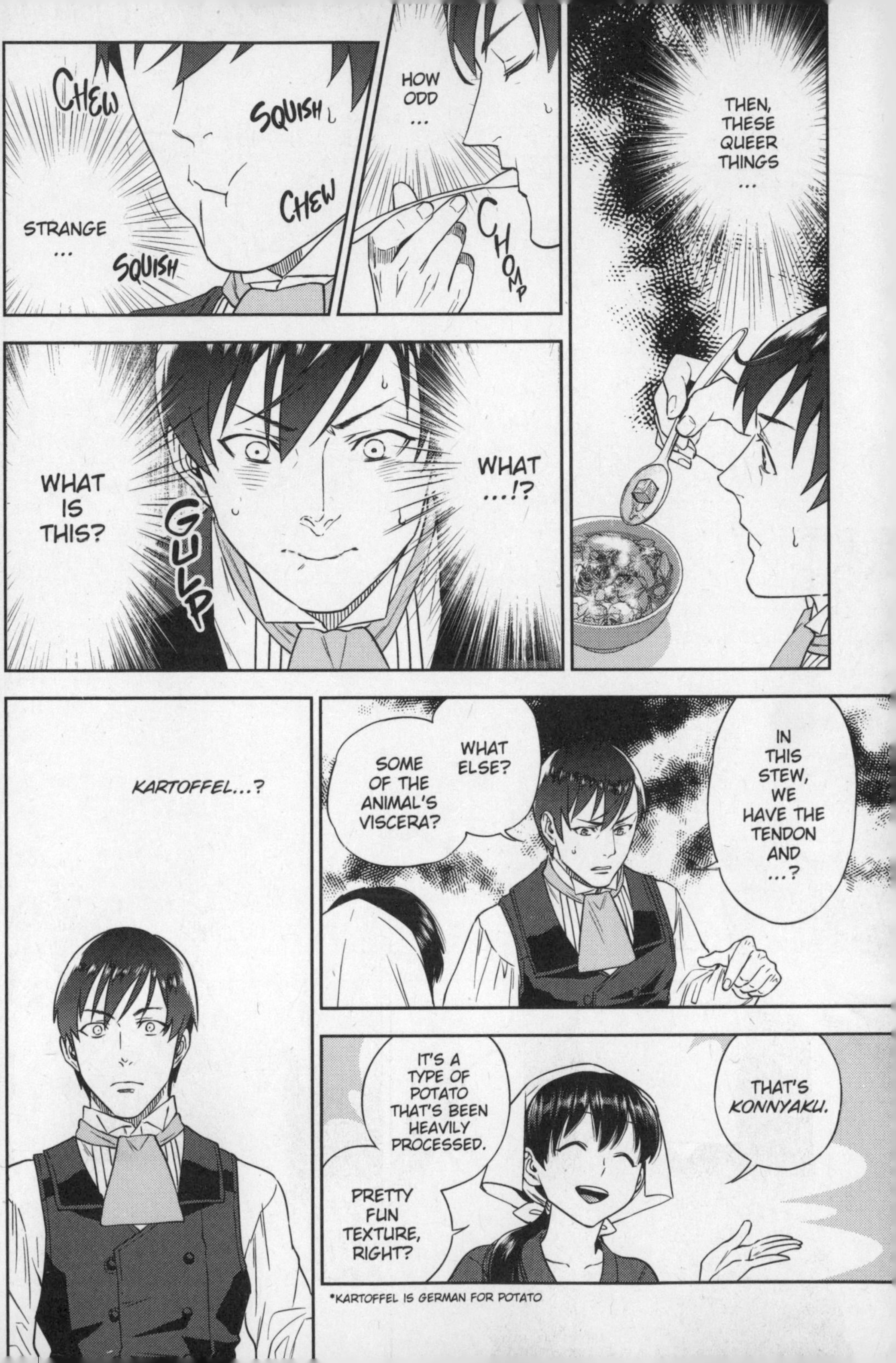
THEN, THESE QUEER THINGS ...
HOW ODD ...
CHOMP
CHEW
SQUISH
CHEW
STRANGE ...
SQUISH
WHAT ...!?
GULP
WHAT IS THIS?
IN THIS STEW, WE HAVE THE TENDON AND ...?
WHAT ELSE?
SOME OF THE ANIMAL'S VISCERA?
THAT'S KONNYAKU.
IT'S A TYPE OF POTATO THAT'S BEEN HEAVILY PROCESSED.
PRETTY FUN TEXTURE, RIGHT?
KARTOFFEL...?

*KARTOFFEL IS GERMAN FOR POTATO

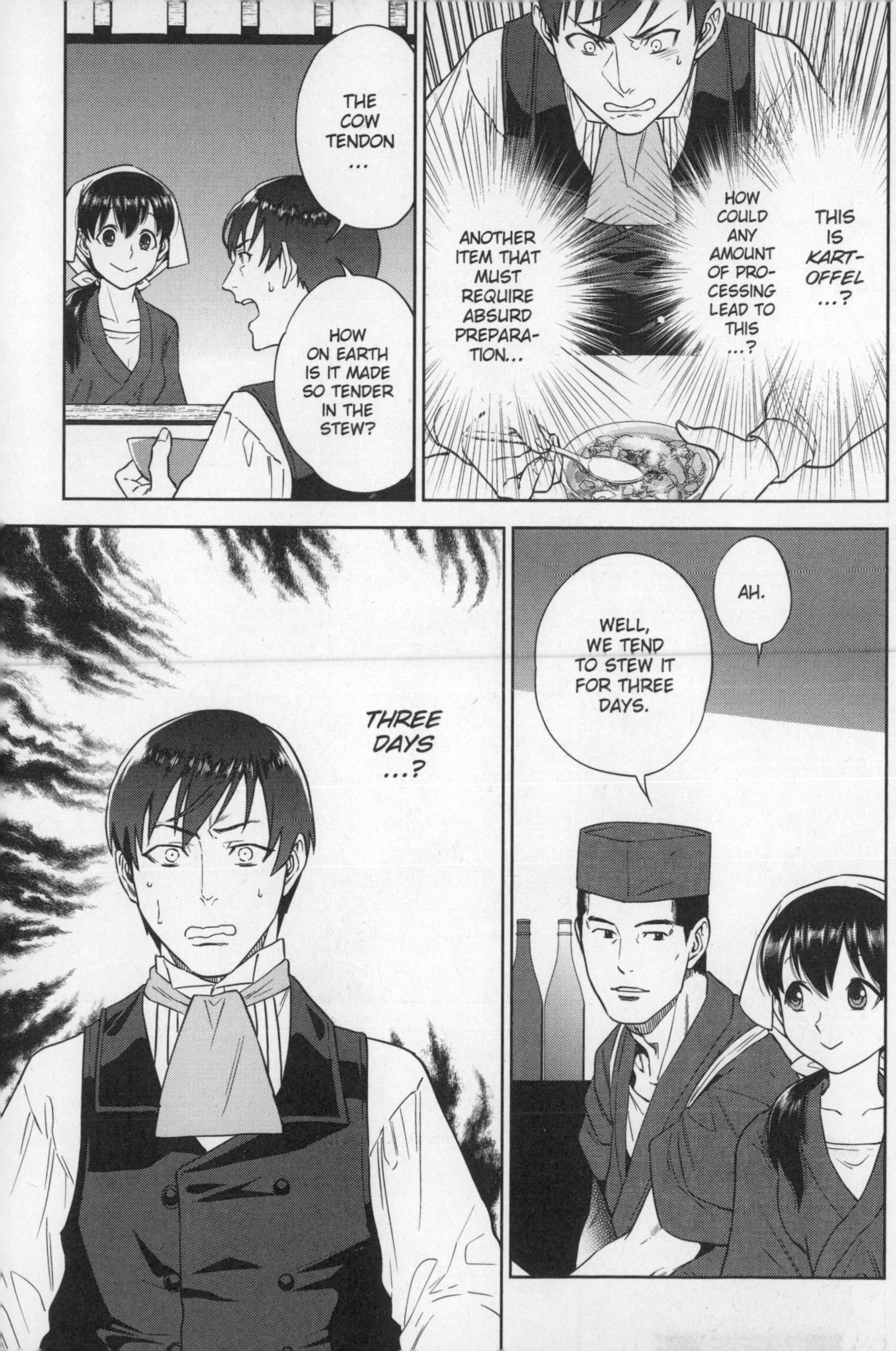
THIS IS KART-OFFEL ...?
HOW COULD ANY AMOUNT OF PRO-CESSING LEAD TO THIS ...?
ANOTHER ITEM THAT MUST REQUIRE ABSURD PREPARA-TION...
THE COW TENDON ...
HOW ON EARTH IS IT MADE SO TENDER IN THE STEW?
AH.
WELL, WE TEND TO STEW IT FOR THREE DAYS.
THREE DAYS ...?

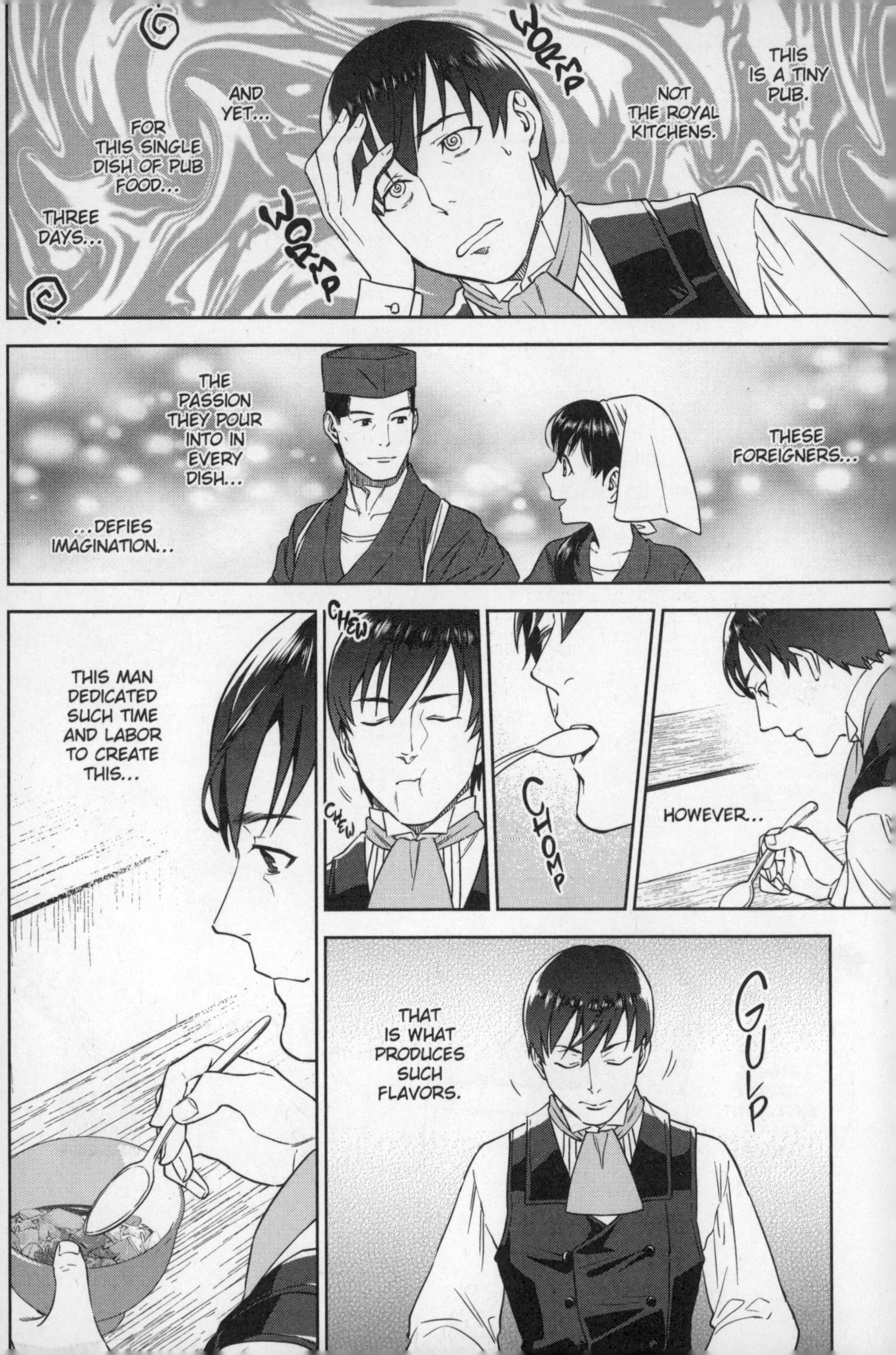
THIS IS A TINY PUB.
NOT THE ROYAL KITCHENS.
WORRP
AND YET...
FOR THIS SINGLE DISH OF PUB FOOD...
WORRP
THREE DAYS...
THESE FOREIGNERS...
THE PASSION THEY POUR INTO IN EVERY DISH...
...DEFIES IMAGINATION...
HOWEVER...
CHOMP
CHEW
CHEW
GULP
THAT IS WHAT PRODUCES SUCH FLAVORS.
THIS MAN DEDICATED SUCH TIME AND LABOR TO CREATE THIS...

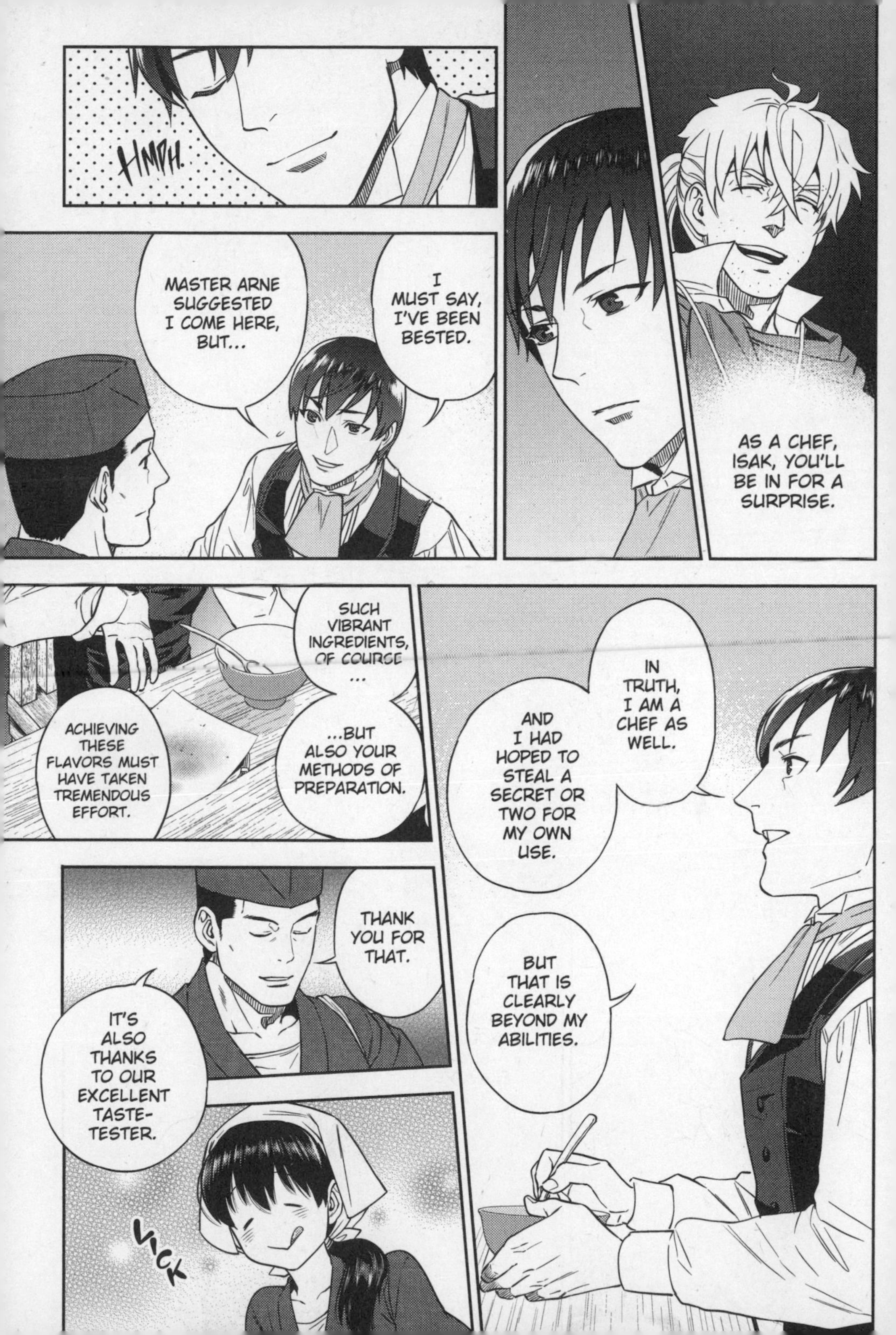

AS A CHEF, ISAK, YOU'LL BE IN FOR A SURPRISE.
HMPH.
I MUST SAY, I'VE BEEN BESTED.
MASTER ARNE SUGGESTED I COME HERE, BUT...
IN TRUTH, I AM A CHEF AS WELL.
AND I HAD HOPED TO STEAL A SECRET OR TWO FOR MY OWN USE.
BUT THAT IS CLEARLY BEYOND MY ABILITIES.
SUCH VIBRANT INGREDIENTS, OF COURSE...
...BUT ALSO YOUR METHODS OF PREPARATION.
ACHIEVING THESE FLAVORS MUST HAVE TAKEN TREMENDOUS EFFORT.
THANK YOU FOR THAT.
IT'S ALSO THANKS TO OUR EXCELLENT TASTE-TESTER.
LICK

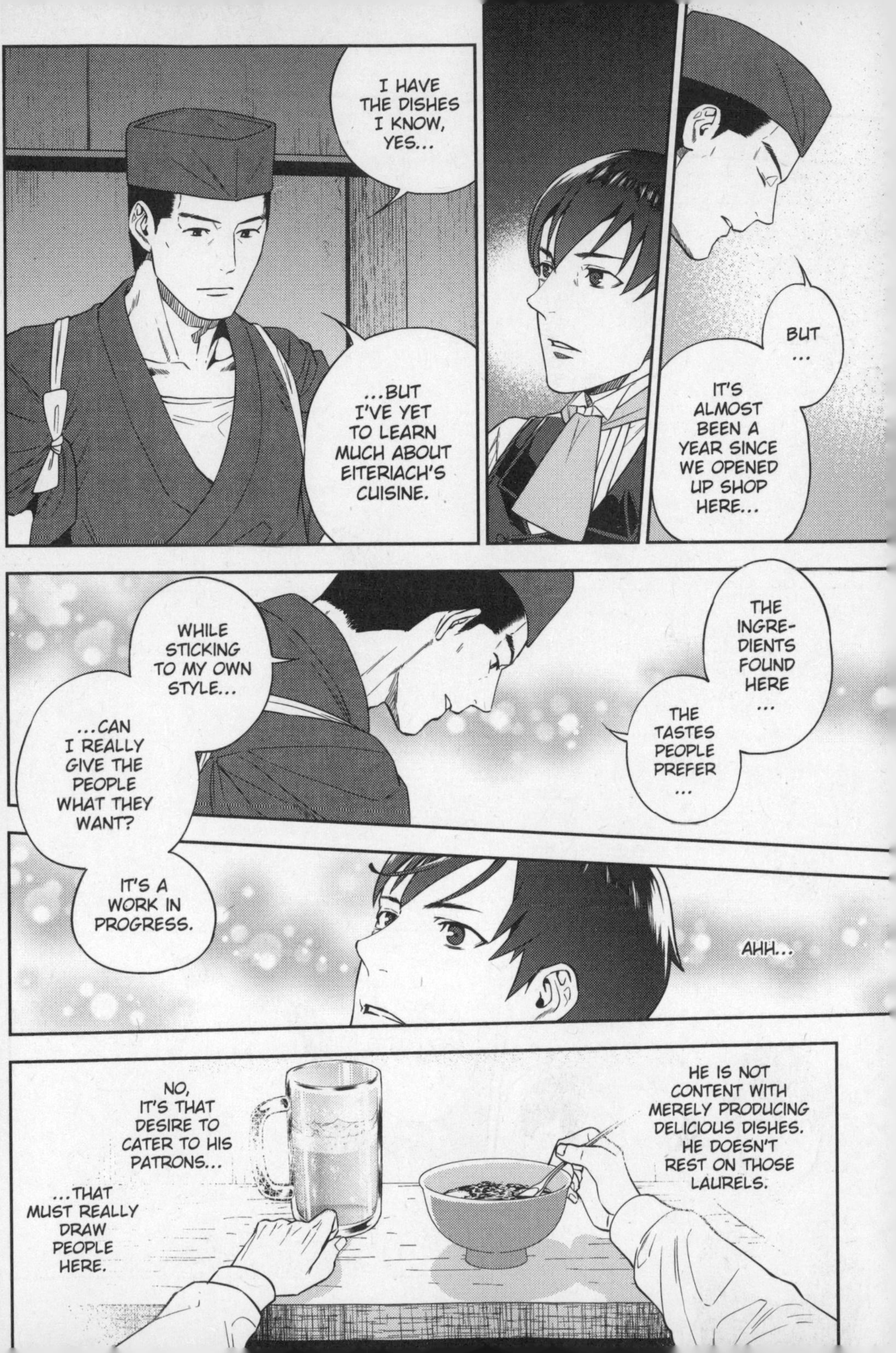
BUT...
IT'S ALMOST BEEN A YEAR SINCE WE OPENED UP SHOP HERE...
I HAVE THE DISHES I KNOW, YES...
...BUT I'VE YET TO LEARN MUCH ABOUT EITERIACH'S CUISINE.
THE INGREDIENTS FOUND HERE...
THE TASTES PEOPLE PREFER...
WHILE STICKING TO MY OWN STYLE...
...CAN I REALLY GIVE THE PEOPLE WHAT THEY WANT?
IT'S A WORK IN PROGRESS.
AHH...
HE IS NOT CONTENT WITH MERELY PRODUCING DELICIOUS DISHES. HE DOESN'T REST ON THOSE LAURELS.
NO, IT'S THAT DESIRE TO CATER TO HIS PATRONS...
...THAT MUST REALLY DRAW PEOPLE HERE.

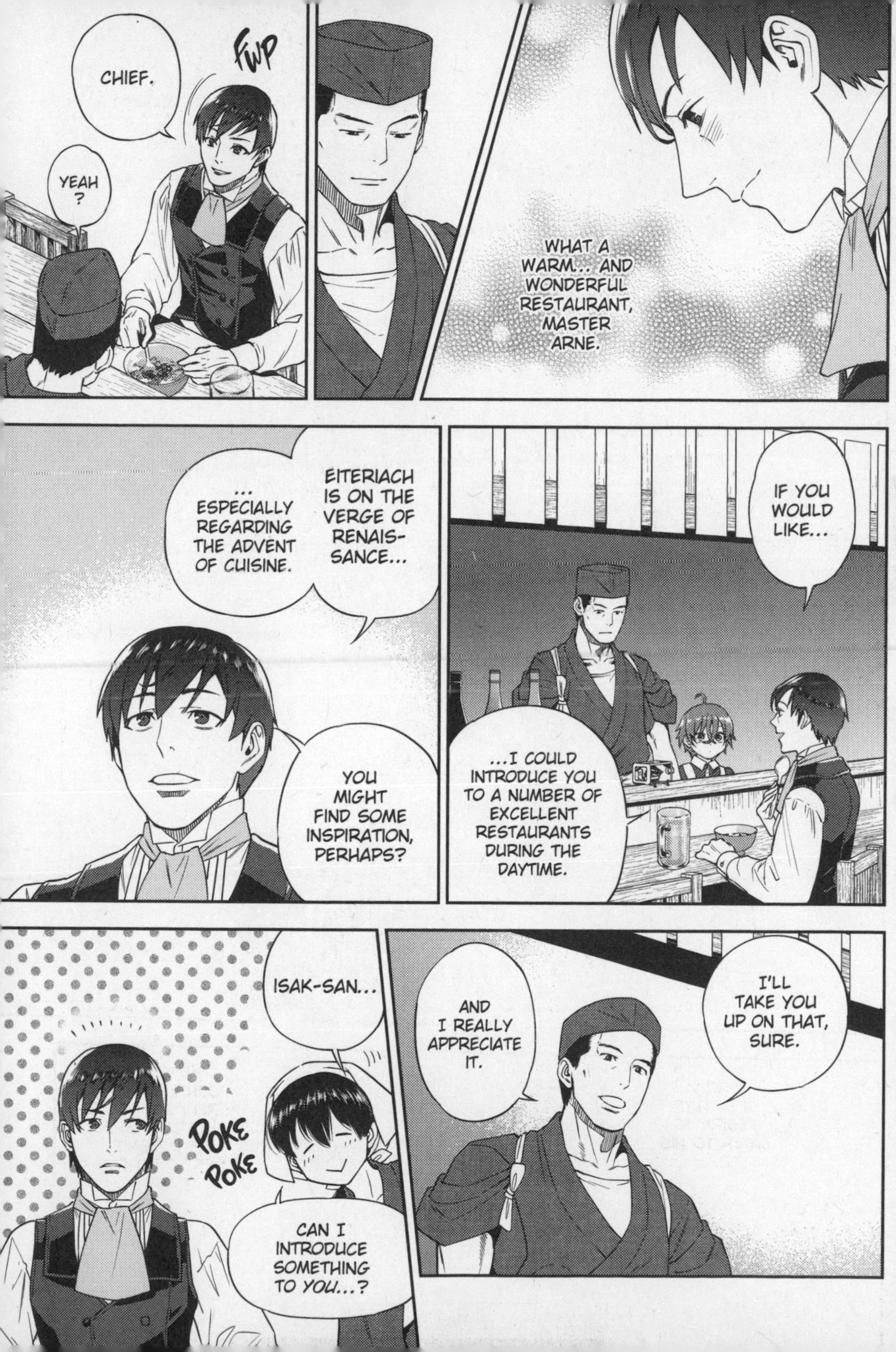
WHAT A WARM... AND WONDERFUL RESTAURANT, MASTER ARNE.
FWP
CHIEF.
YEAH?
IF YOU WOULD LIKE...
...I COULD INTRODUCE YOU TO A NUMBER OF EXCELLENT RESTAURANTS DURING THE DAYTIME.
EITERIACH IS ON THE VERGE OF RENAIS-SANCE...
...ESPECIALLY REGARDING THE ADVENT OF CUISINE.
YOU MIGHT FIND SOME INSPIRATION, PERHAPS?
I'LL TAKE YOU UP ON THAT, SURE.
AND I REALLY APPRECIATE IT.
ISAK-SAN...
POKE POKE
CAN I INTRODUCE SOMETHING TO YOU...?

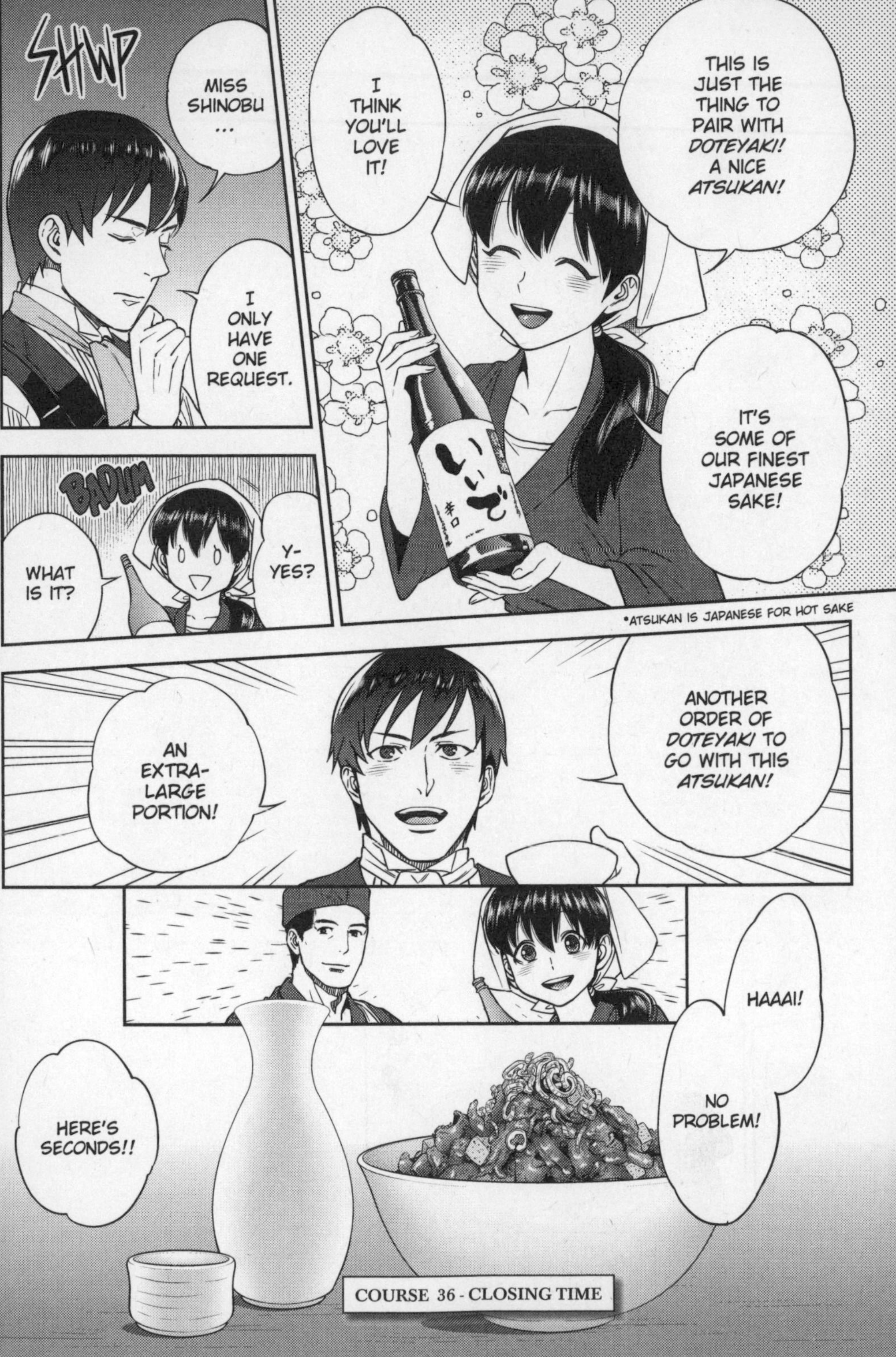
THIS IS JUST THE THING TO PAIR WITH *DOTEYAKI!* A NICE *ATSUKAN!*
I THINK YOU'LL LOVE IT!
IT'S SOME OF OUR FINEST JAPANESE SAKE!
SHWP
MISS SHINOBU ...
I ONLY HAVE ONE REQUEST.
BADUM
Y-YES?
WHAT IS IT?
*ATSUKAN IS JAPANESE FOR HOT SAKE
ANOTHER ORDER OF *DOTEYAKI* TO GO WITH THIS *ATSUKAN!*
AN EXTRA-LARGE PORTION!
HAAAI!
NO PROBLEM!
HERE'S SECONDS!!
COURSE 36 - CLOSING TIME

Doteyaki

OTHERWORLDLY IZAKAYA

NOBU

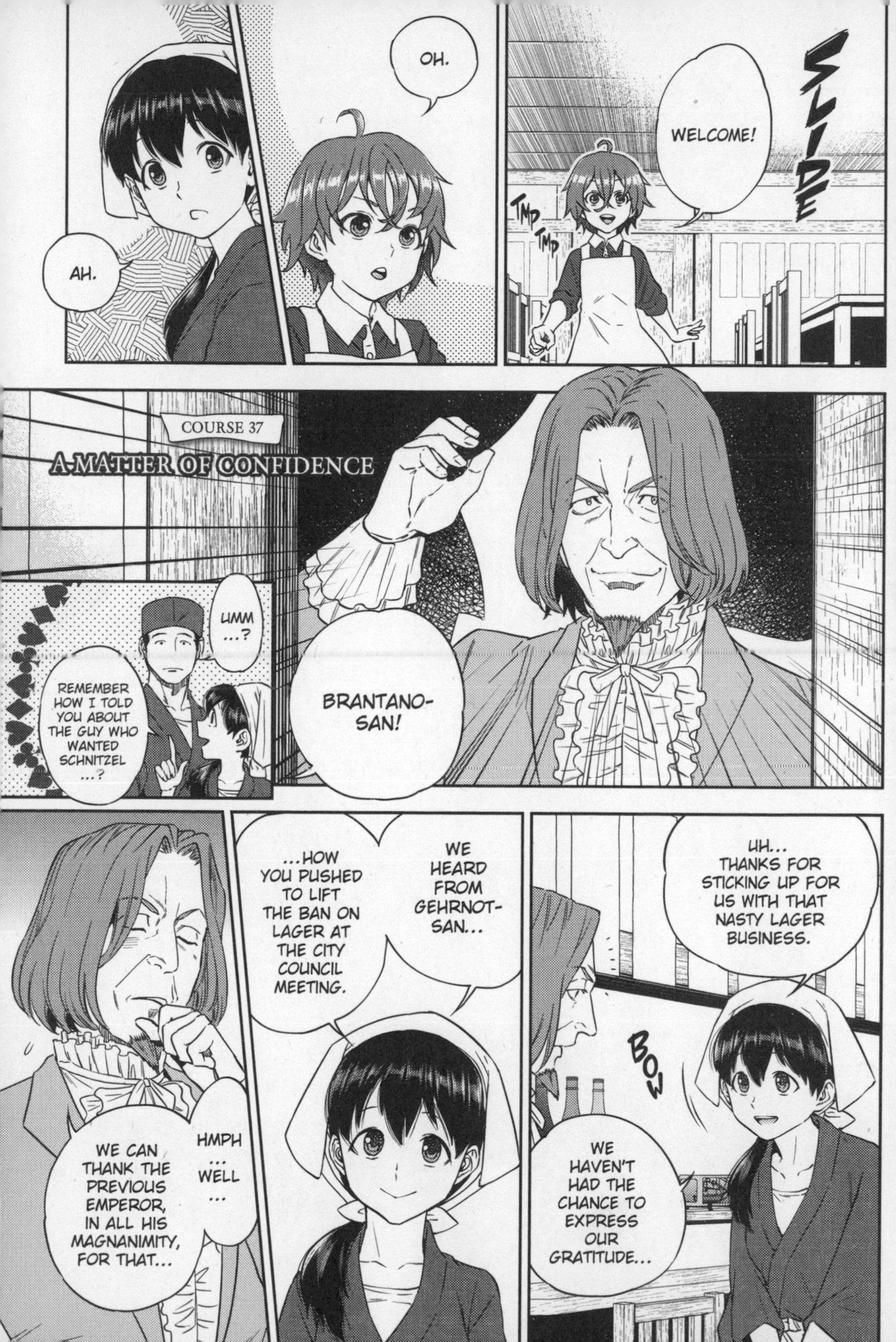
SLIDE
WELCOME!
TMP TMP
OH.
AH.
COURSE 37
A MATTER OF CONFIDENCE
BRANTANO-SAN!
UMM ...?
REMEMBER HOW I TOLD YOU ABOUT THE GUY WHO WANTED SCHNITZEL ...?
UH... THANKS FOR STICKING UP FOR US WITH THAT NASTY LAGER BUSINESS.
BOW
WE HAVEN'T HAD THE CHANCE TO EXPRESS OUR GRATITUDE...
WE HEARD FROM GEHRNOT-SAN...
...HOW YOU PUSHED TO LIFT THE BAN ON LAGER AT THE CITY COUNCIL MEETING.
HMPH ... WELL ...
WE CAN THANK THE PREVIOUS EMPEROR, IN ALL HIS MAGNANIMITY, FOR THAT...

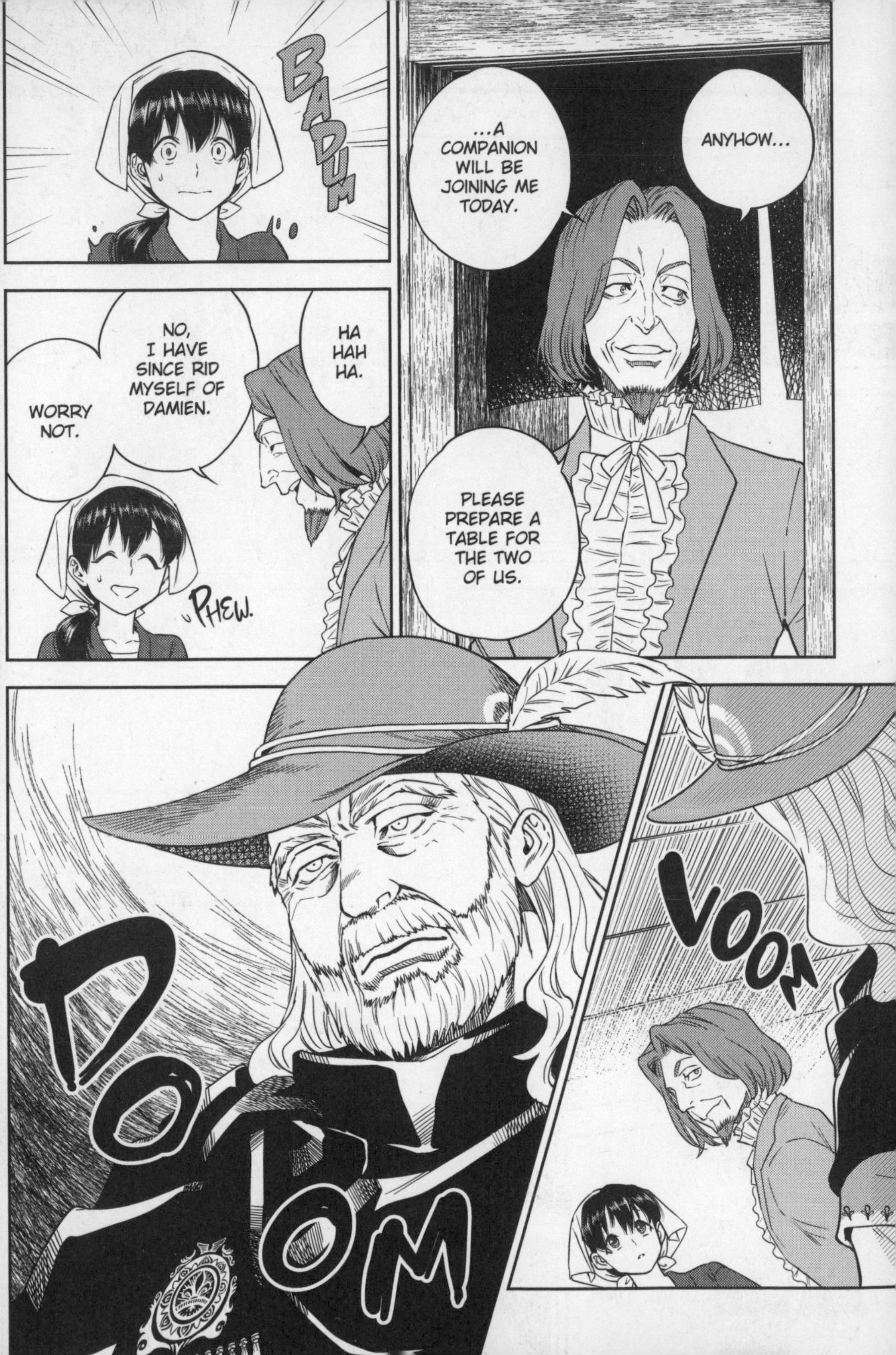
ANYHOW...
...A COMPANION WILL BE JOINING ME TODAY.
PLEASE PREPARE A TABLE FOR THE TWO OF US.
BADUM
HA HAH HA.
NO, I HAVE SINCE RID MYSELF OF DAMIEN.
WORRY NOT.
PHEW.
VOOM
DOOM

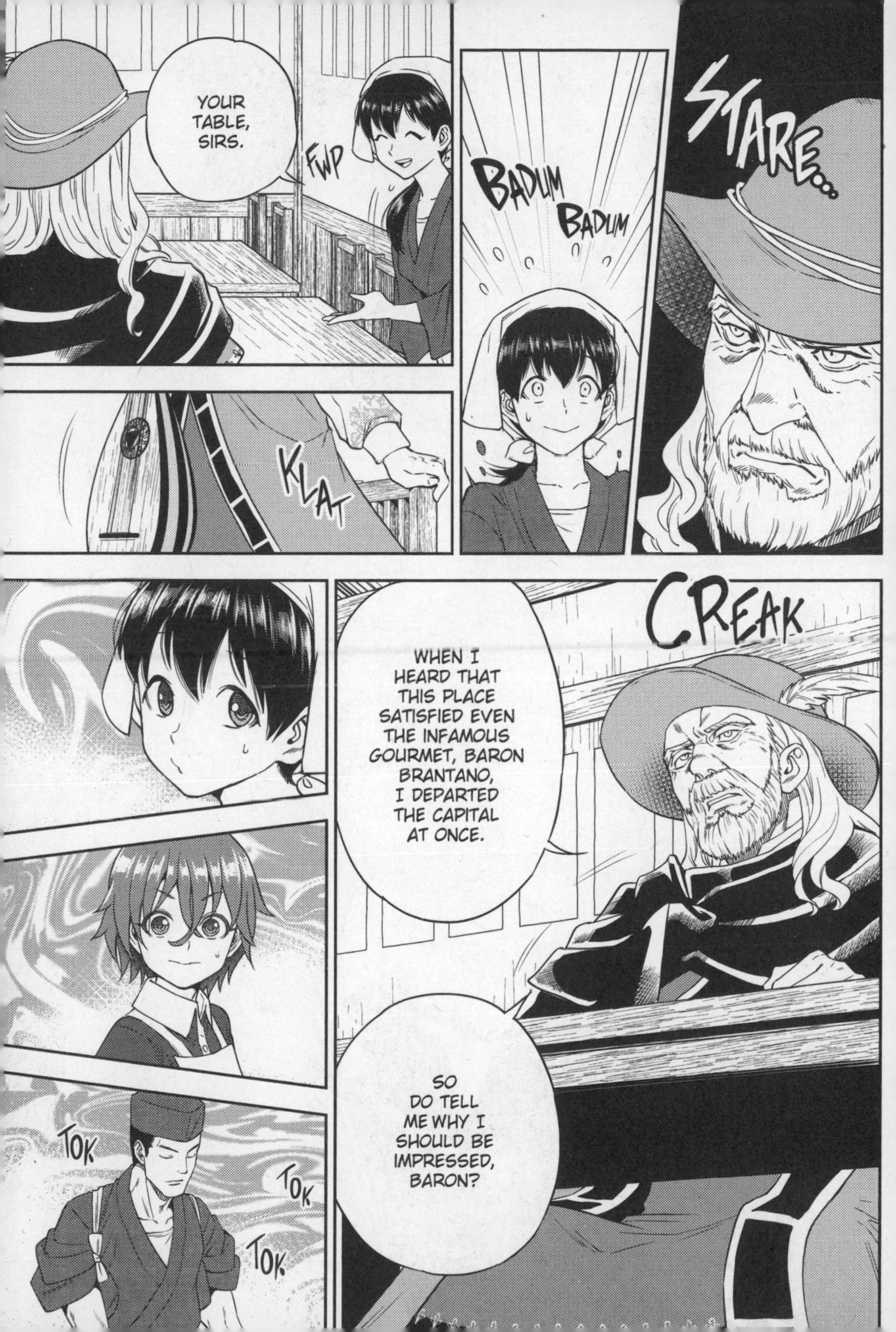
STARE...
BADUM
BADUM
YOUR TABLE, SIRS.
FWP
KLAT
CREAK
WHEN I HEARD THAT THIS PLACE SATISFIED EVEN THE INFAMOUS GOURMET, BARON BRANTANO, I DEPARTED THE CAPITAL AT ONCE.
SO DO TELL ME WHY I SHOULD BE IMPRESSED, BARON?
TOK
TOK
TOK

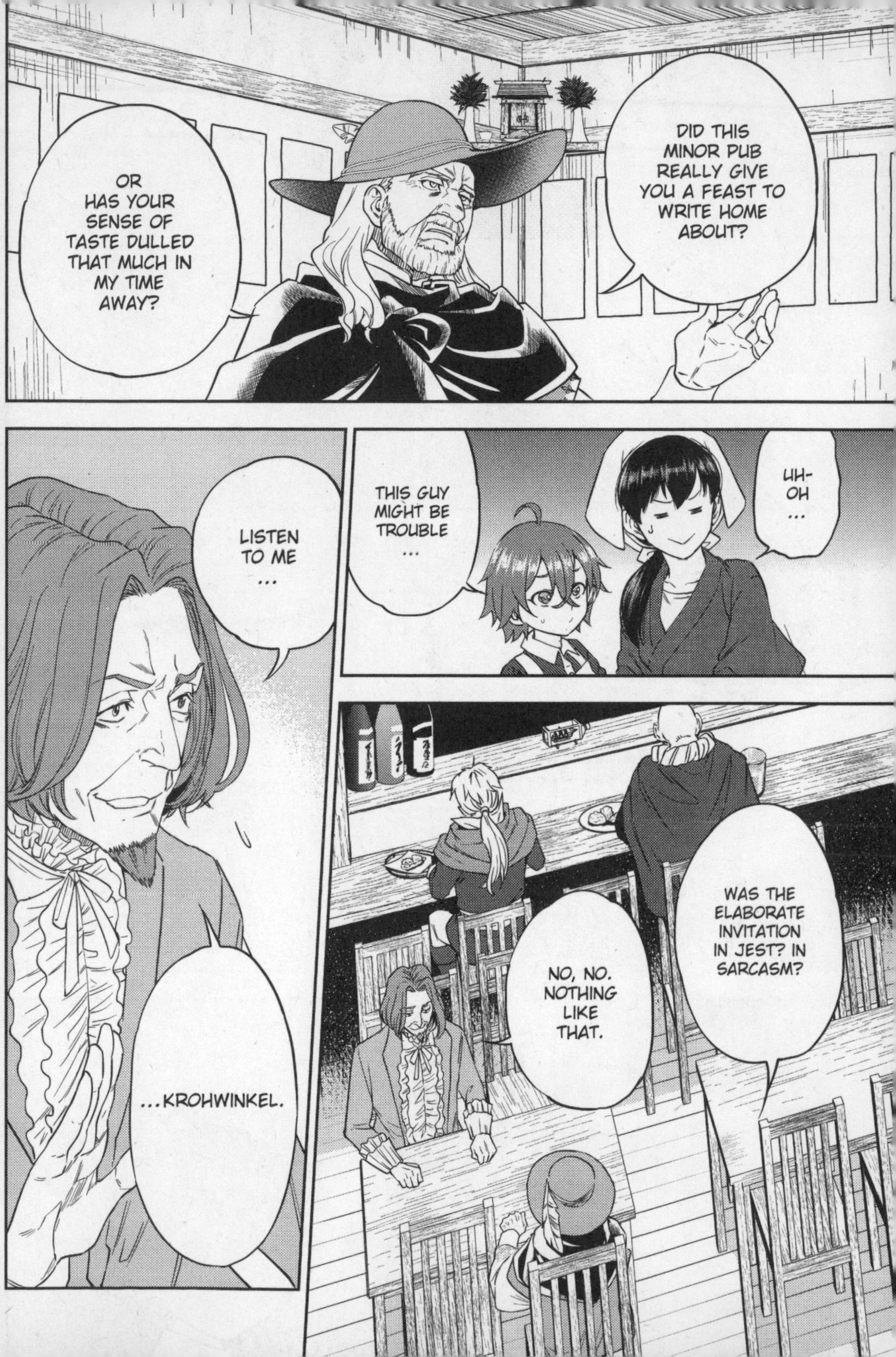
DID THIS MINOR PUB REALLY GIVE YOU A FEAST TO WRITE HOME ABOUT?
OR HAS YOUR SENSE OF TASTE DULLED THAT MUCH IN MY TIME AWAY?
UH-OH ...
THIS GUY MIGHT BE TROUBLE ...
WAS THE ELABORATE INVITATION IN JEST? IN SARCASM?
NO, NO. NOTHING LIKE THAT.
LISTEN TO ME ...
...KROHWINKEL.

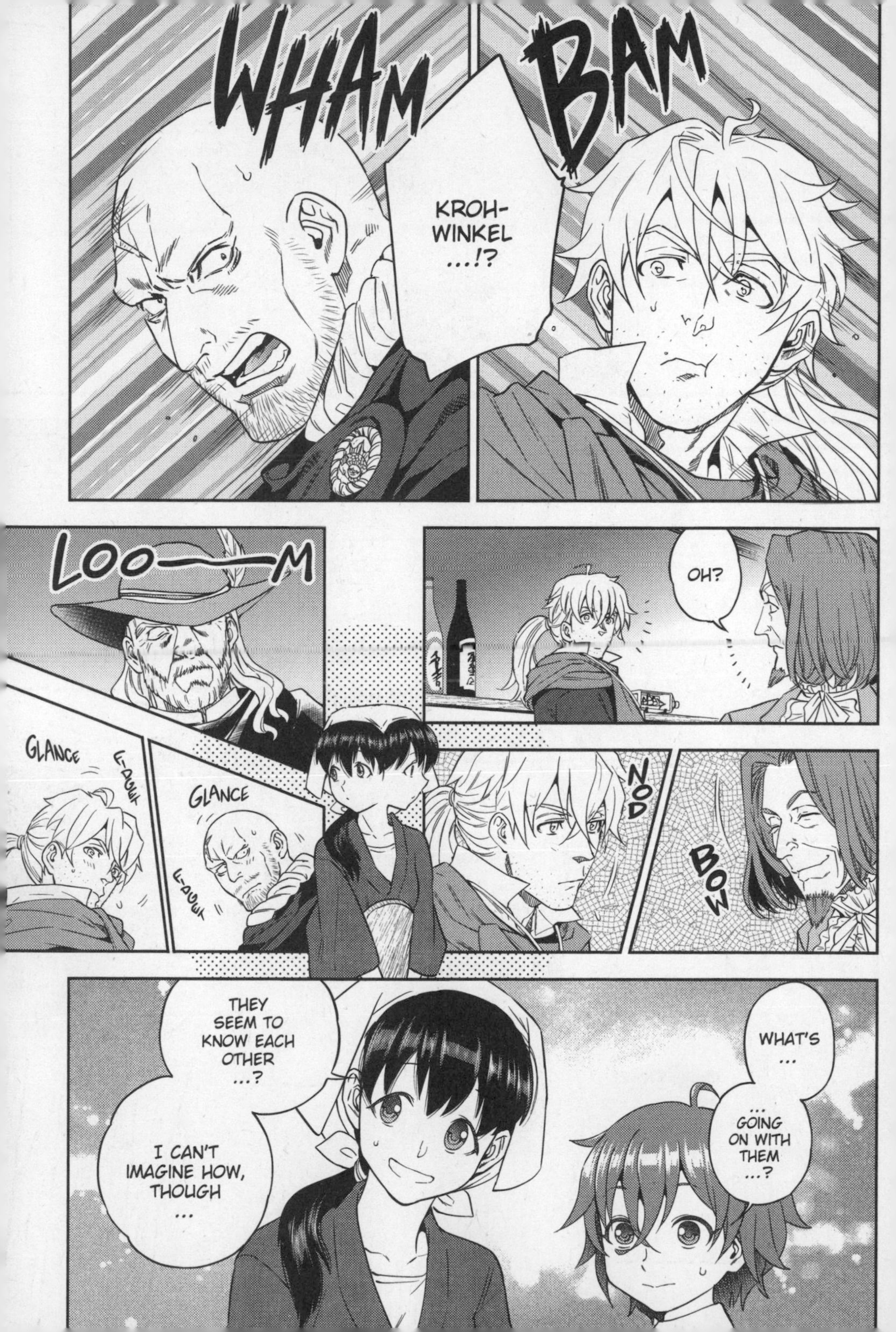
BAM
WHAM
KROH-WINKEL ...!?
OH?
LOO——M
BOW
NOD
GLANCE
FIDGET
GLANCE
FIDGET
WHAT'S ...
... GOING ON WITH THEM ...?
THEY SEEM TO KNOW EACH OTHER ...?
I CAN'T IMAGINE HOW, THOUGH ...

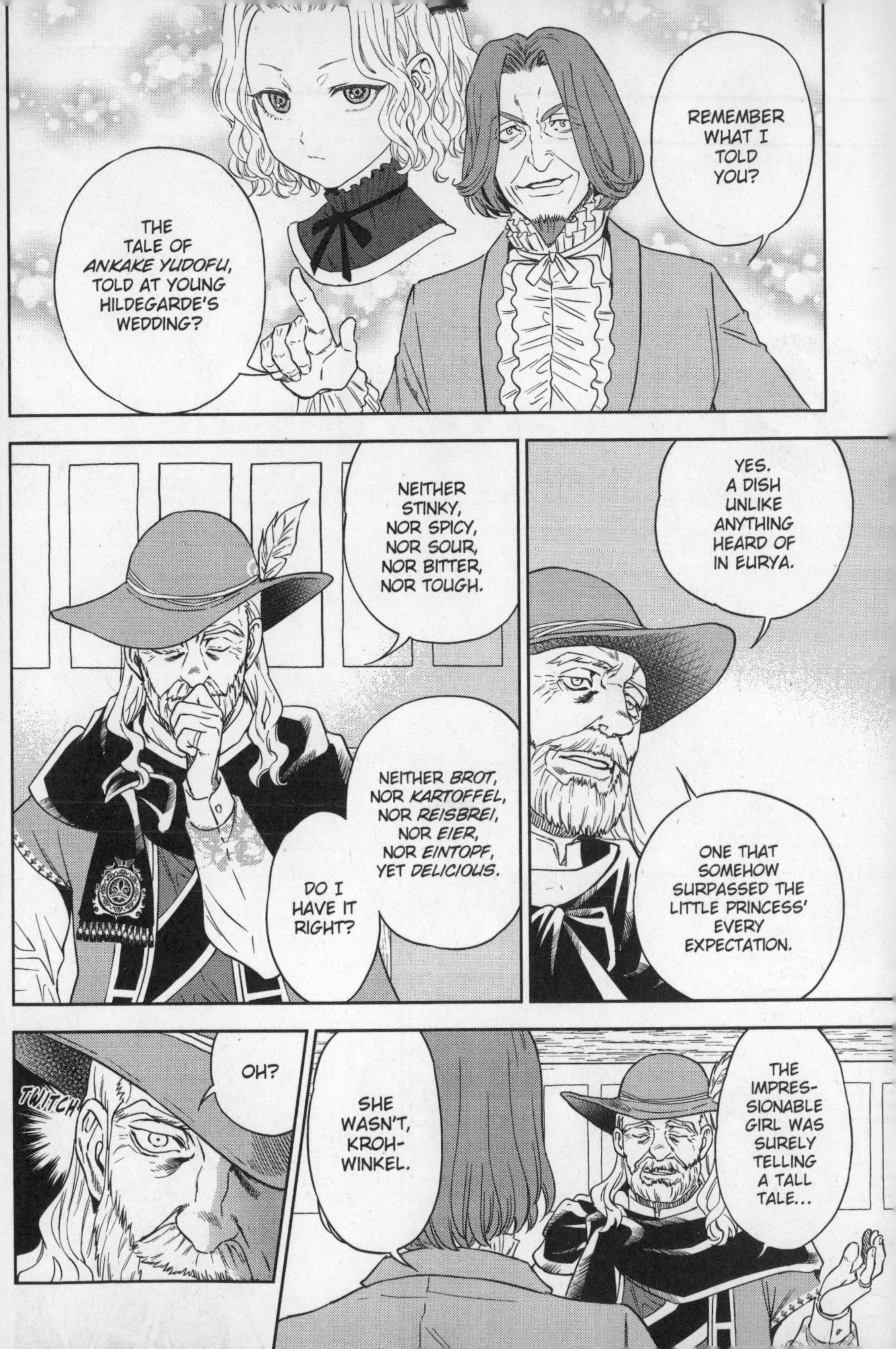
REMEMBER WHAT I TOLD YOU?
THE TALE OF *ANKAKE YUDOFU*, TOLD AT YOUNG HILDEGARDE'S WEDDING?
YES. A DISH UNLIKE ANYTHING HEARD OF IN EURYA.
ONE THAT SOMEHOW SURPASSED THE LITTLE PRINCESS' EVERY EXPECTATION.
NEITHER STINKY, NOR SPICY, NOR SOUR, NOR BITTER, NOR TOUGH.
NEITHER *BROT*, NOR *KARTOFFEL*, NOR *REISBREI*, NOR *EIER*, NOR *EINTOPF*, YET *DELICIOUS*.
DO I HAVE IT RIGHT?
THE IMPRESSIONABLE GIRL WAS SURELY TELLING A TALL TALE...
SHE WASN'T, KROH-WINKEL.
OH?
TWITCH

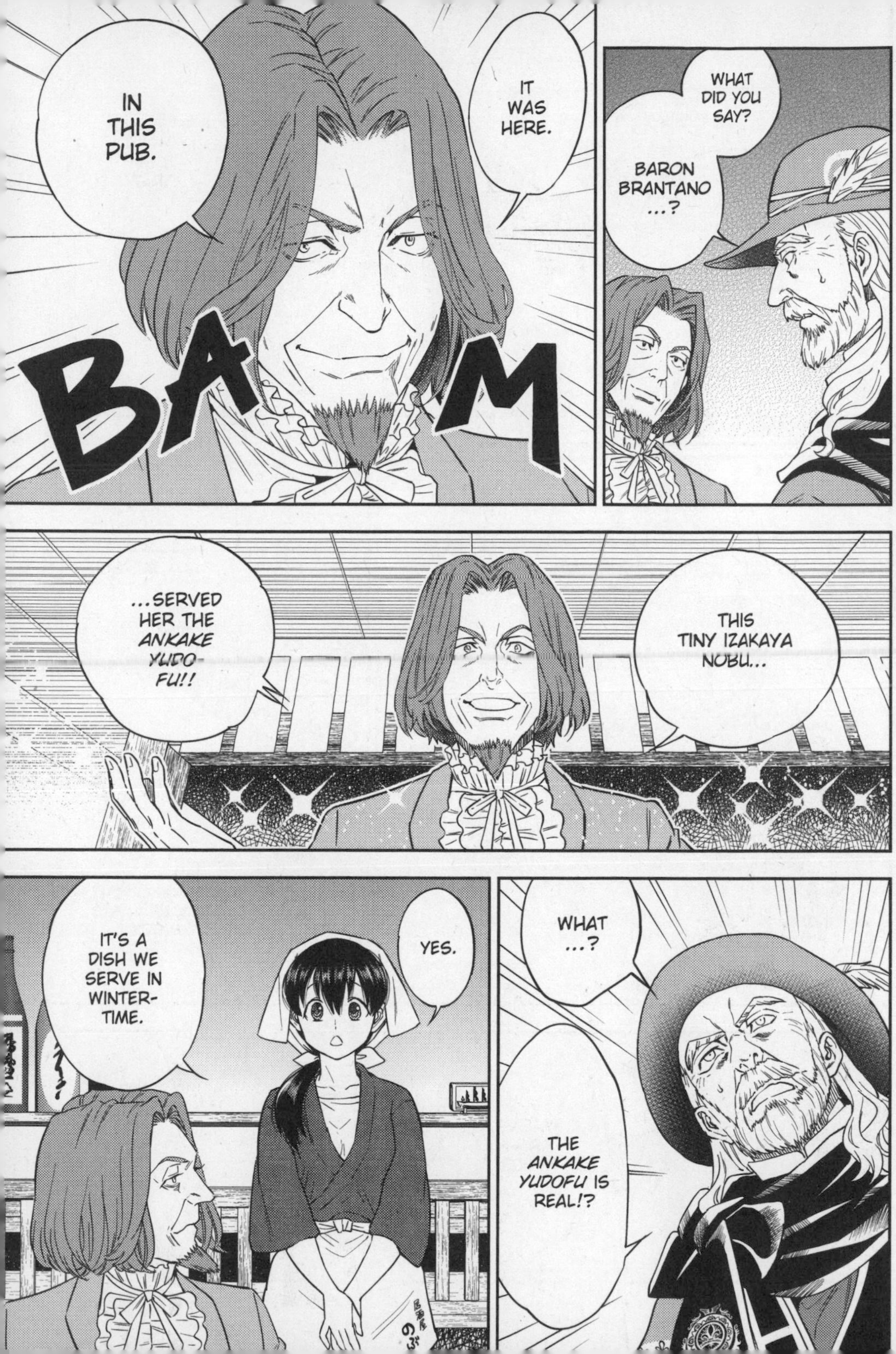
WHAT DID YOU SAY?
BARON BRANTANO ...?
IT WAS HERE.
IN THIS PUB.
BAM
THIS TINY IZAKAYA NOBU...
...SERVED HER THE *ANKAKE YUDOFU*!!
WHAT ...?
THE *ANKAKE YUDOFU* IS REAL!?
YES.
IT'S A DISH WE SERVE IN WINTER-TIME.
居酒屋 のぶ

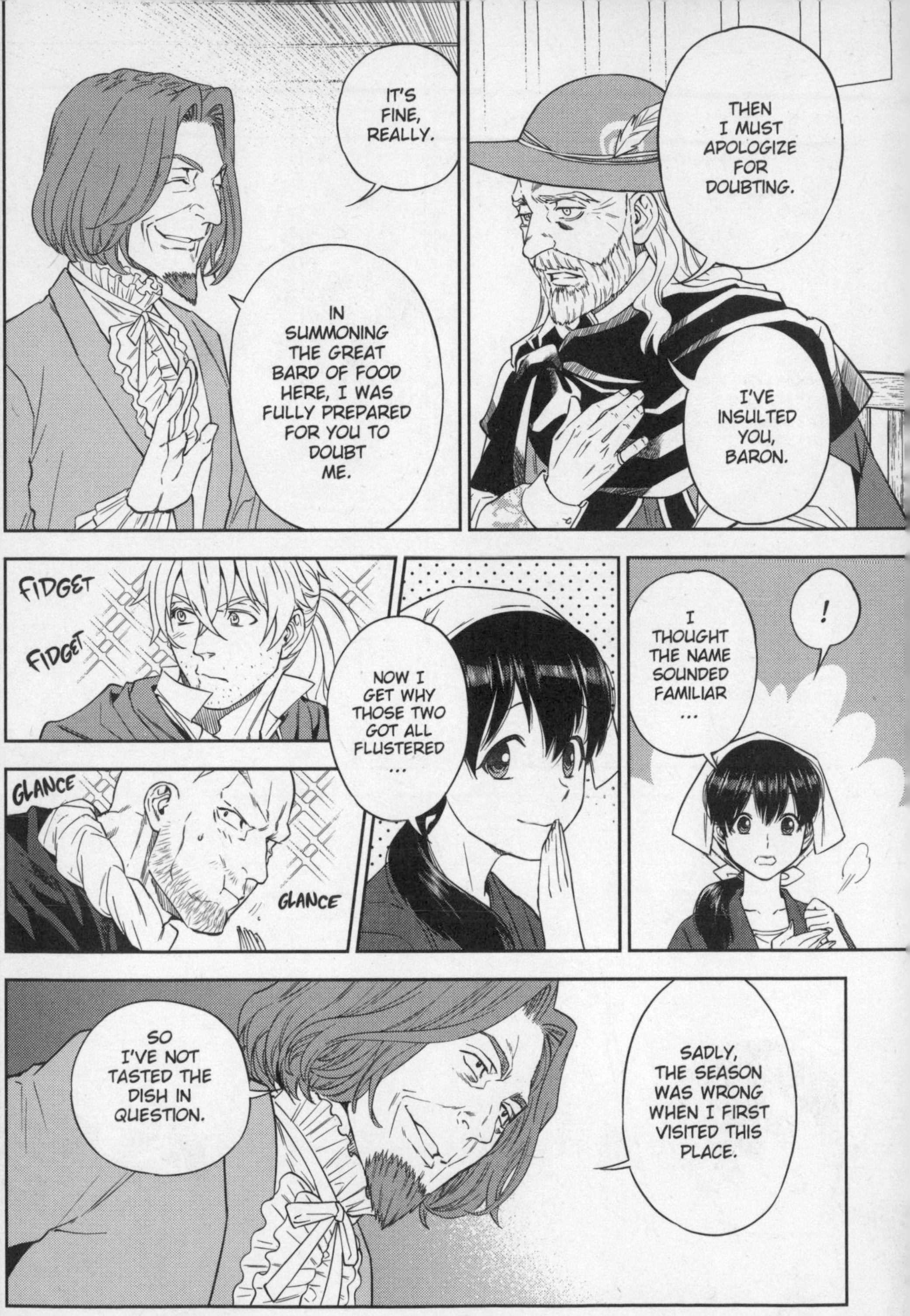
THEN I MUST APOLOGIZE FOR DOUBTING.
I'VE INSULTED YOU, BARON.
IT'S FINE, REALLY.
IN SUMMONING THE GREAT BARD OF FOOD HERE, I WAS FULLY PREPARED FOR YOU TO DOUBT ME.
!
I THOUGHT THE NAME SOUNDED FAMILIAR...
NOW I GET WHY THOSE TWO GOT ALL FLUSTERED...
FIDGET
FIDGET
GLANCE
GLANCE
SADLY, THE SEASON WAS WRONG WHEN I FIRST VISITED THIS PLACE.
SO I'VE NOT TASTED THE DISH IN QUESTION.

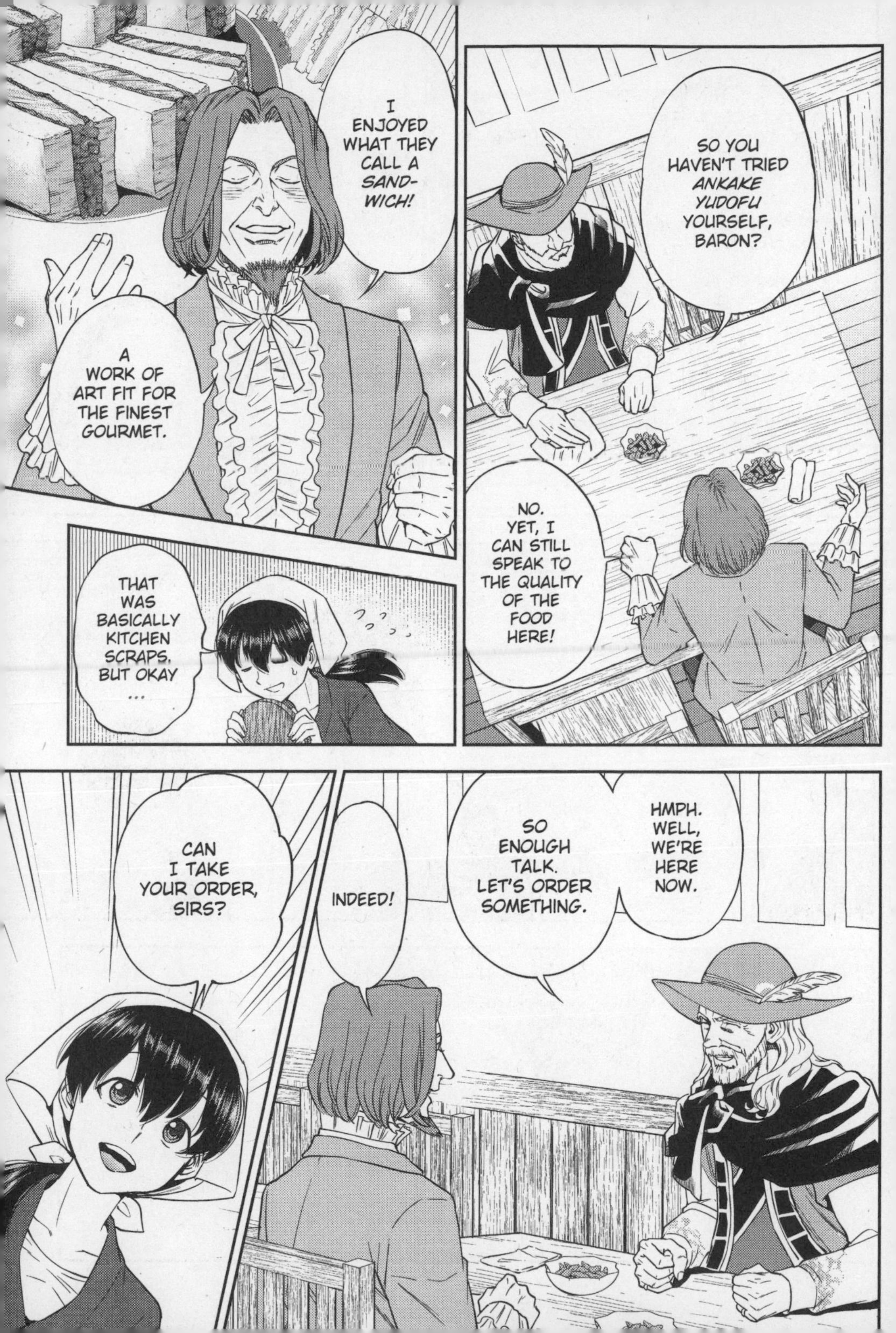

SO YOU HAVEN'T TRIED *ANKAKE YUDOFU* YOURSELF, BARON?
NO. YET, I CAN STILL SPEAK TO THE QUALITY OF THE FOOD HERE!
I ENJOYED WHAT THEY CALL A *SAND-WICH!*
A WORK OF ART FIT FOR THE FINEST GOURMET.
THAT WAS BASICALLY KITCHEN SCRAPS, BUT OKAY ...
HMPH. WELL, WE'RE HERE NOW.
SO ENOUGH TALK. LET'S ORDER SOMETHING.
INDEED!
CAN I TAKE YOUR ORDER, SIRS?

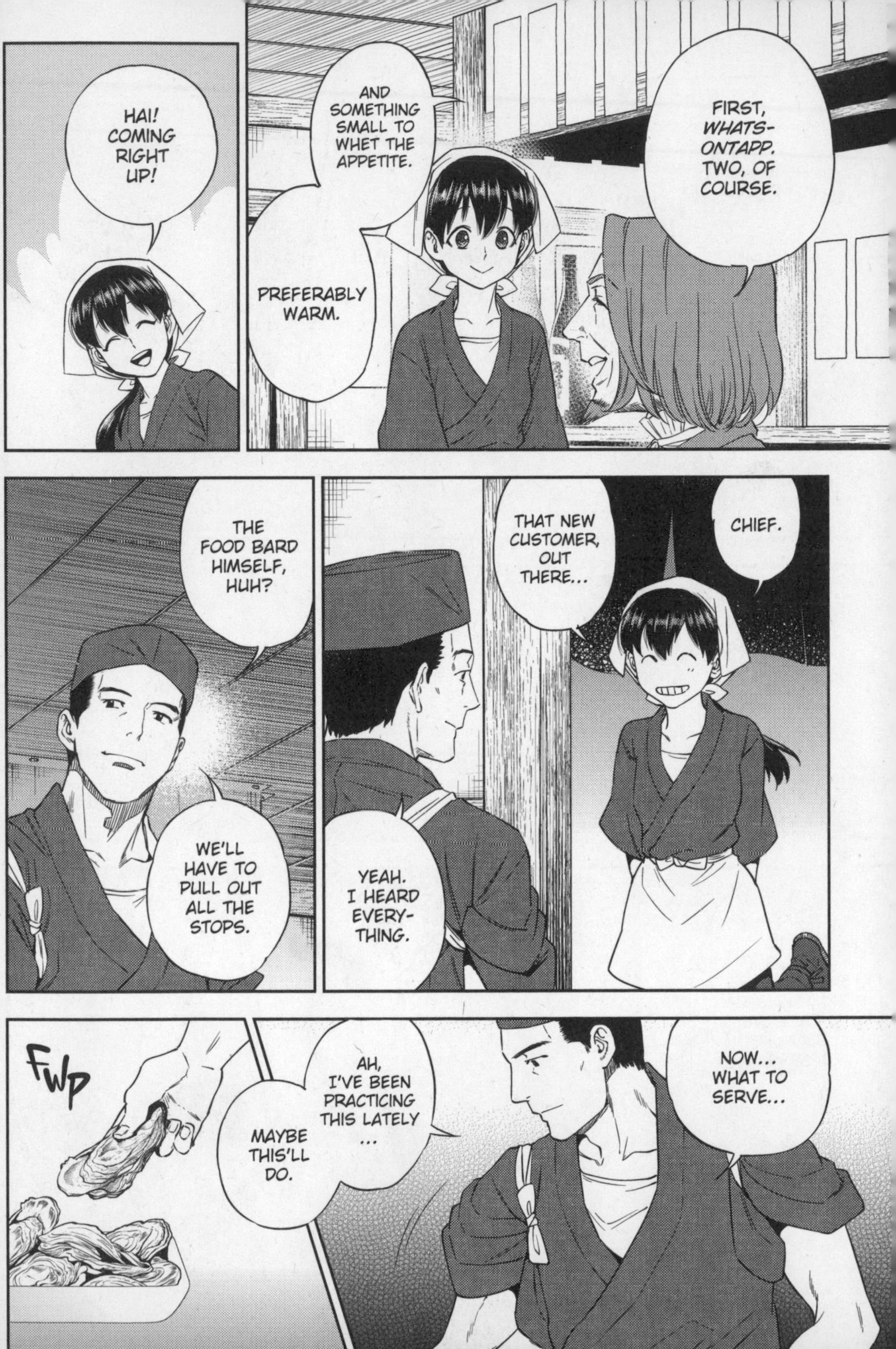
FIRST, WHATS-ONTAPP. TWO, OF COURSE.
AND SOMETHING SMALL TO WHET THE APPETITE.
PREFERABLY WARM.
HAI! COMING RIGHT UP!
CHIEF.
THAT NEW CUSTOMER, OUT THERE...
YEAH. I HEARD EVERY-THING.
THE FOOD BARD HIMSELF, HUH?
WE'LL HAVE TO PULL OUT ALL THE STOPS.
NOW... WHAT TO SERVE...
AH, I'VE BEEN PRACTICING THIS LATELY ...
MAYBE THIS'LL DO.
FWP

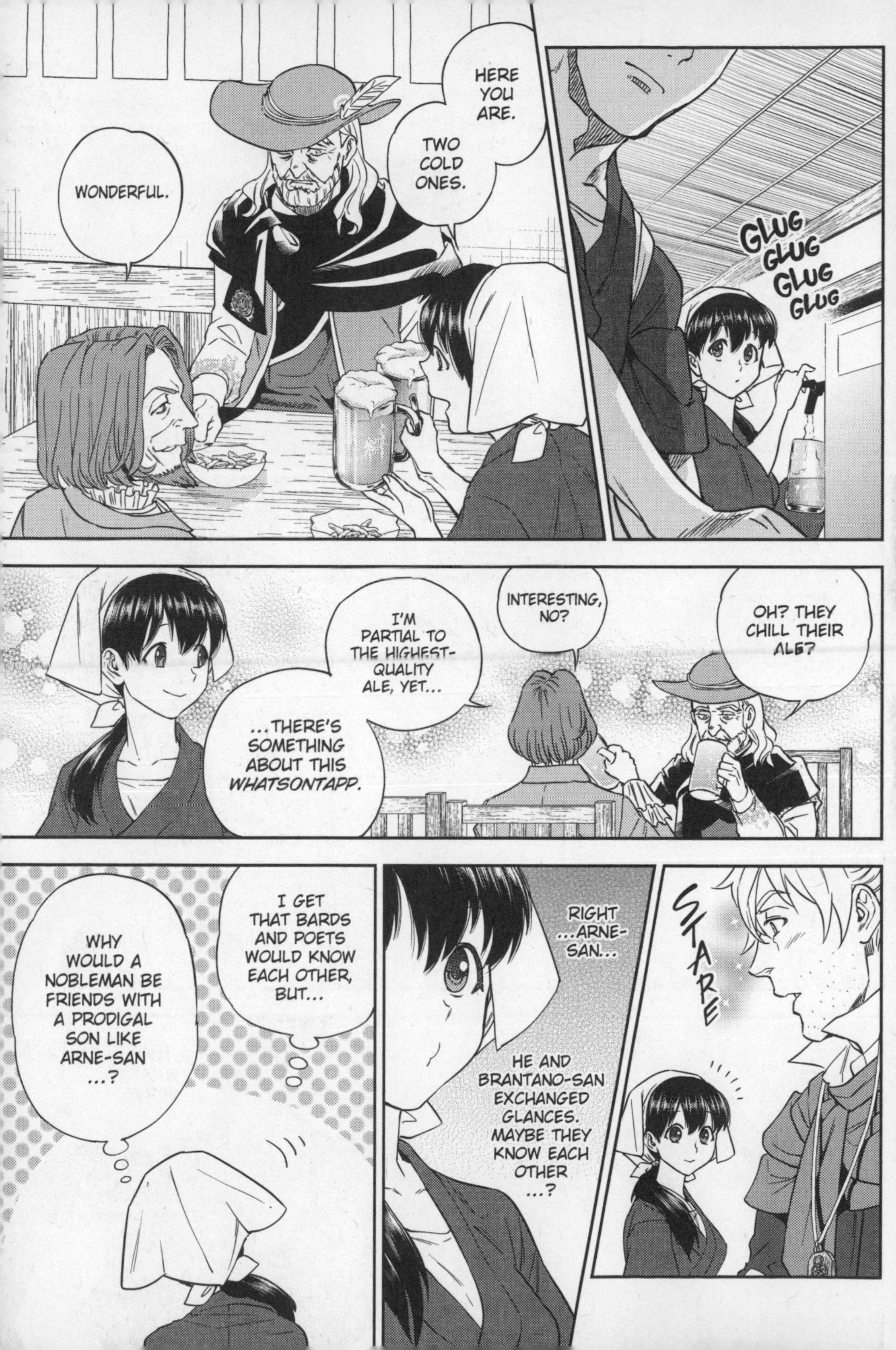
GLUG GLUG GLUG GLUG
HERE YOU ARE.
TWO COLD ONES.
WONDERFUL.
OH? THEY CHILL THEIR ALE?
INTERESTING, NO?
I'M PARTIAL TO THE HIGHEST-QUALITY ALE, YET...
...THERE'S SOMETHING ABOUT THIS *WHATSONTAPP*.
STARE
RIGHT ...ARNE-SAN...
HE AND BRANTANO-SAN EXCHANGED GLANCES. MAYBE THEY KNOW EACH OTHER ...?
I GET THAT BARDS AND POETS WOULD KNOW EACH OTHER, BUT...
WHY WOULD A NOBLEMAN BE FRIENDS WITH A PRODIGAL SON LIKE ARNE-SAN ...?

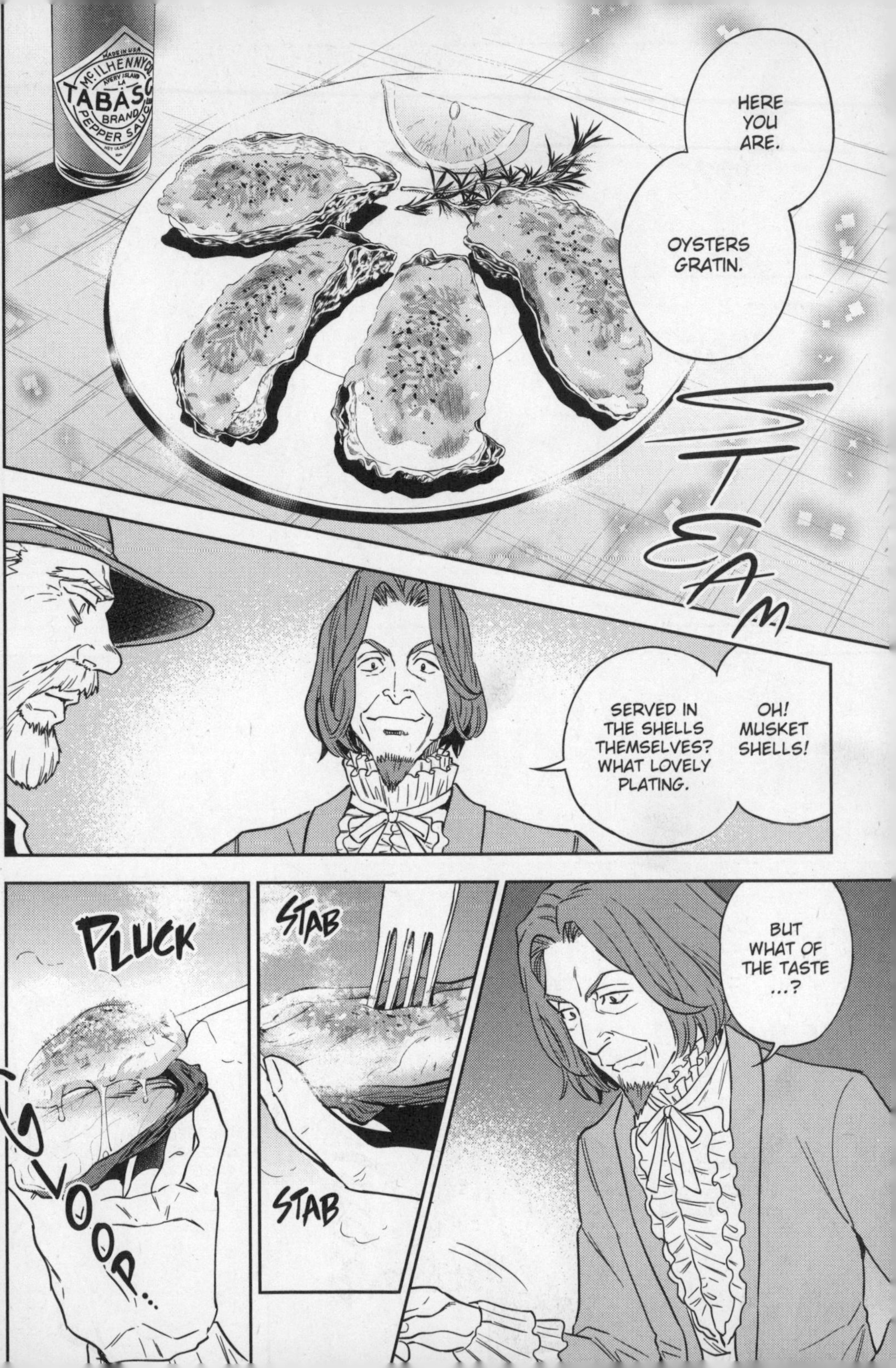
TABASC
BRAND
PEPPER SAUC
HERE YOU ARE.
OYSTERS GRATIN.
STEAM
OH! MUSKET SHELLS!
SERVED IN THE SHELLS THEMSELVES? WHAT LOVELY PLATING.
BUT WHAT OF THE TASTE ...?
STAB
STAB
PLUCK
GLOOP...

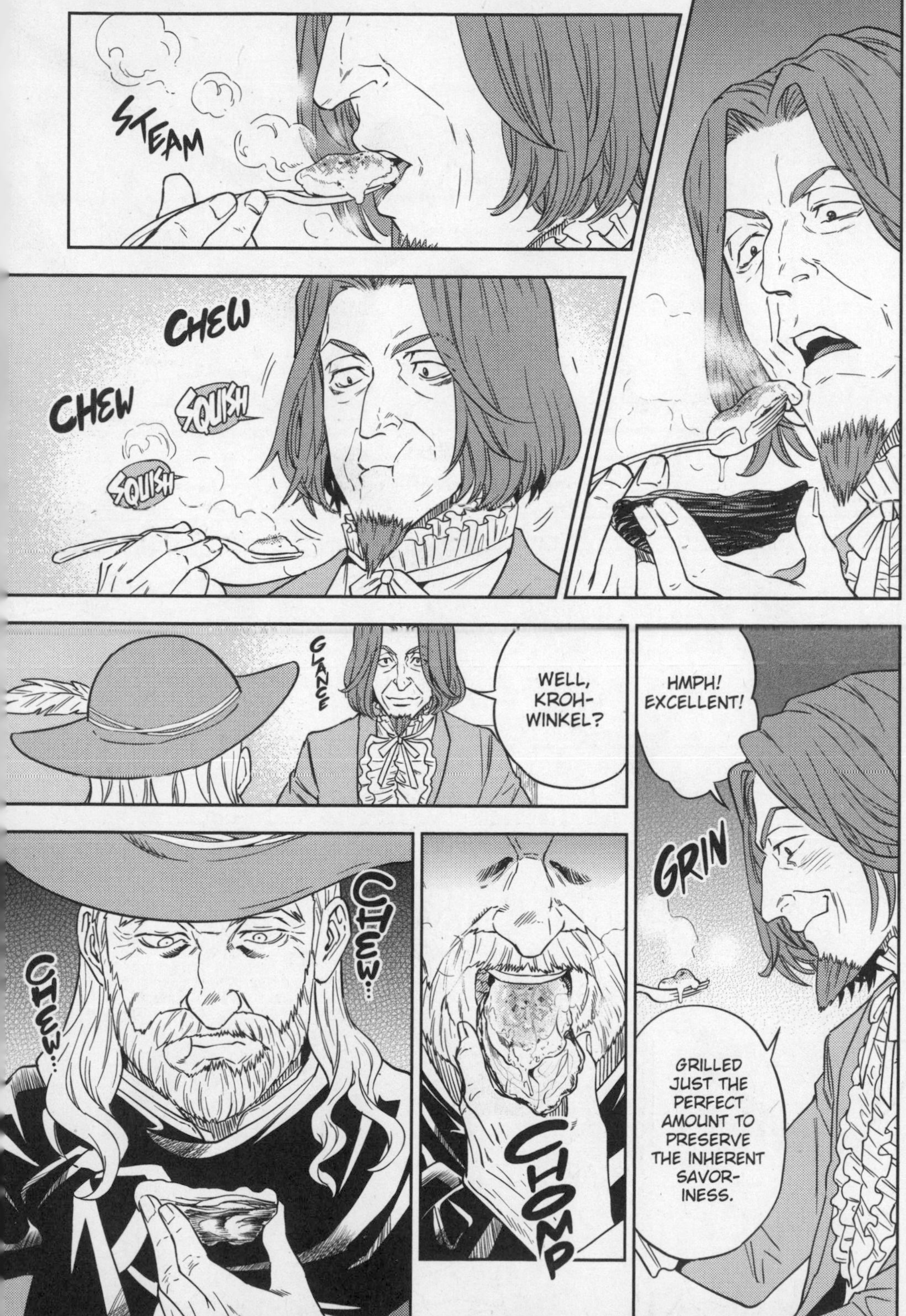
STEAM
CHEW
CHEW
SQUISH
SQUISH
HMPH! EXCELLENT!
GRIN
GRILLED JUST THE PERFECT AMOUNT TO PRESERVE THE INHERENT SAVOR-INESS.
WELL, KROH-WINKEL?
GLANCE
CHOMP
CHEW...
CHEW...

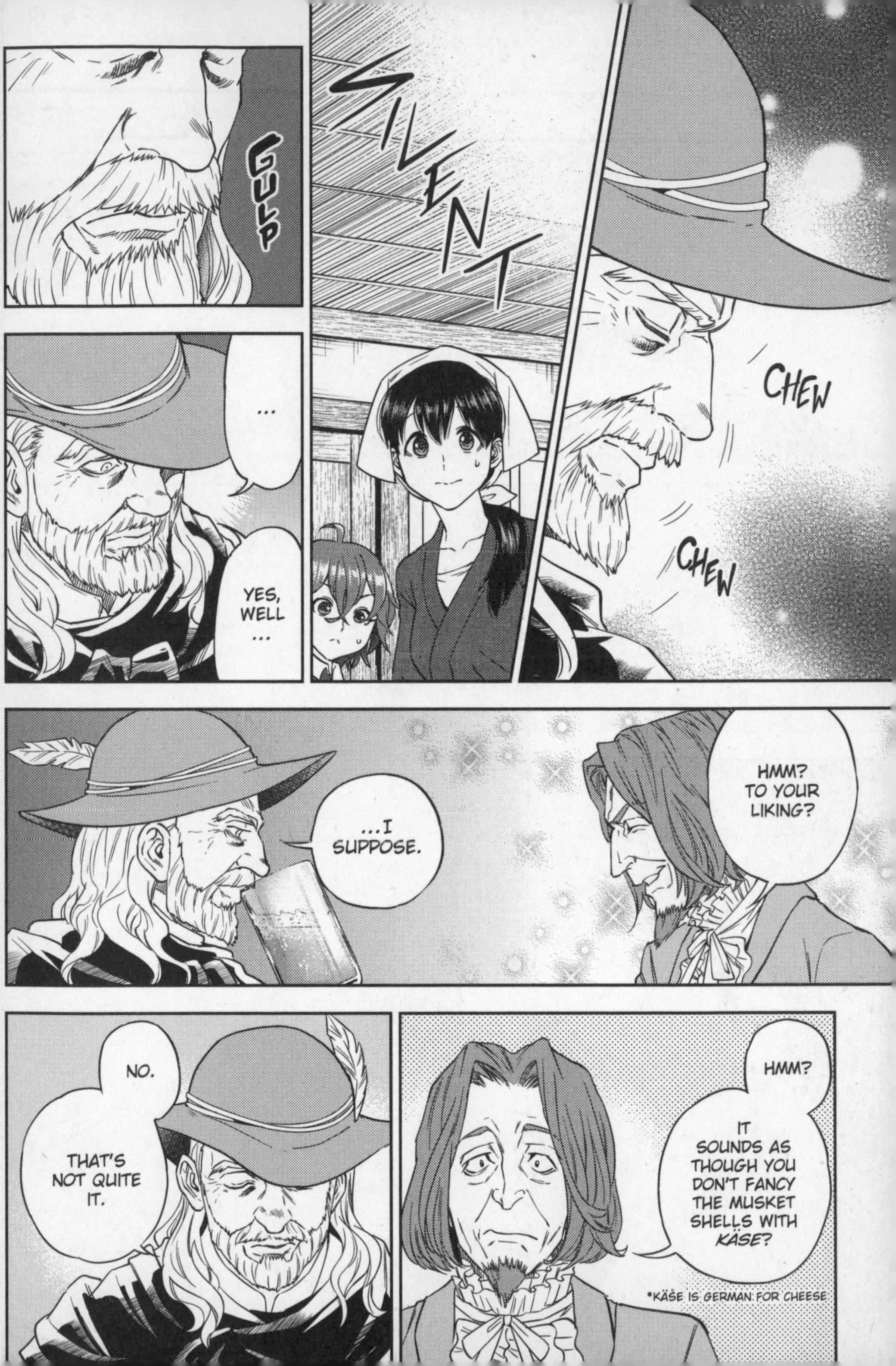
CHEW
CHEW
SILENT
GULP
...
YES, WELL ...
HMM? TO YOUR LIKING?
...I SUPPOSE.
HMM?
IT SOUNDS AS THOUGH YOU DON'T FANCY THE MUSKET SHELLS WITH *KÄSE*?
*KÄSE IS GERMAN FOR CHEESE
NO.
THAT'S NOT QUITE IT.

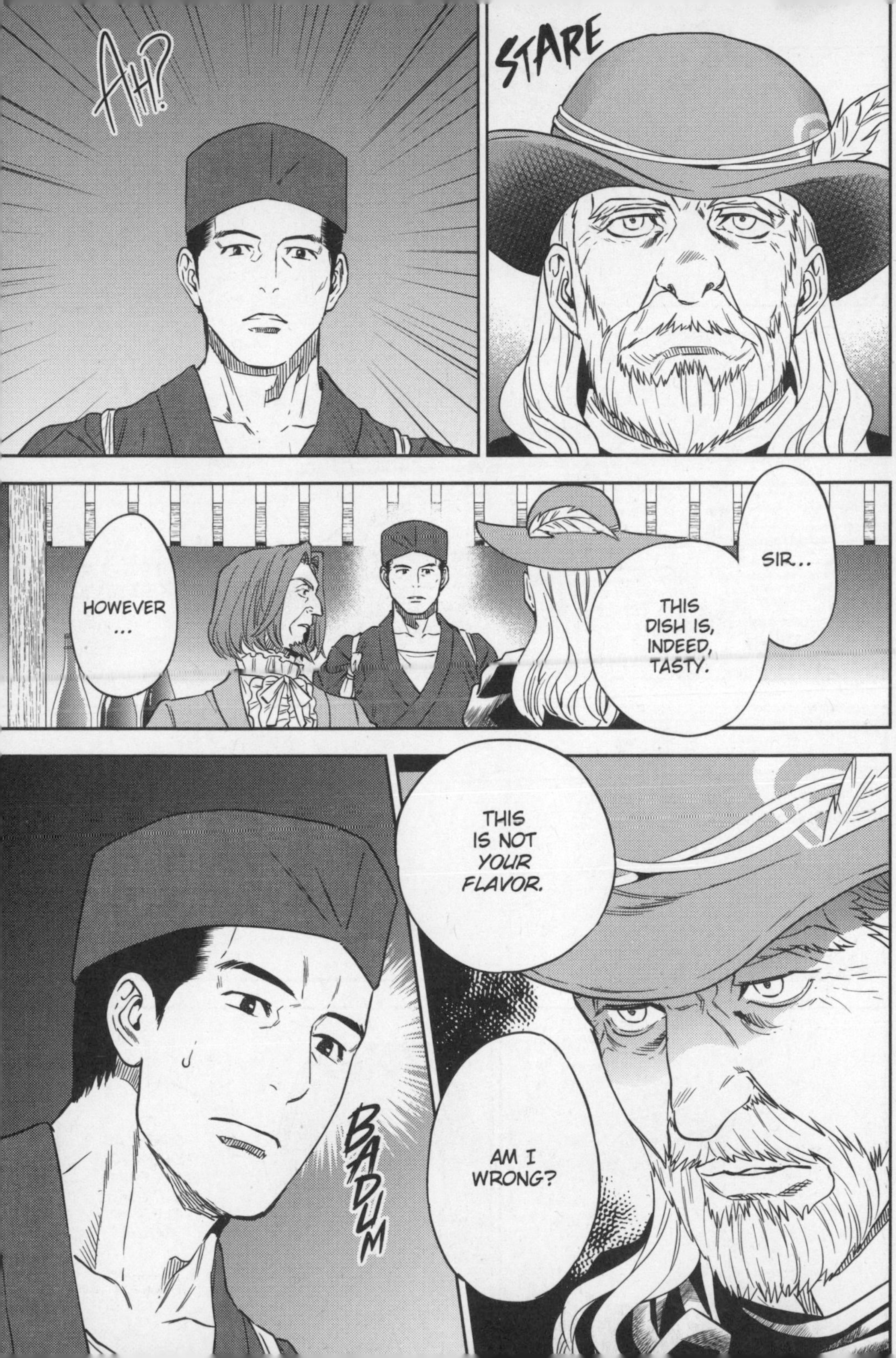
STARE
AH?
SIR..
THIS DISH IS, INDEED, TASTY.
HOWEVER ...
THIS IS NOT YOUR FLAVOR.
AM I WRONG?
BADUM

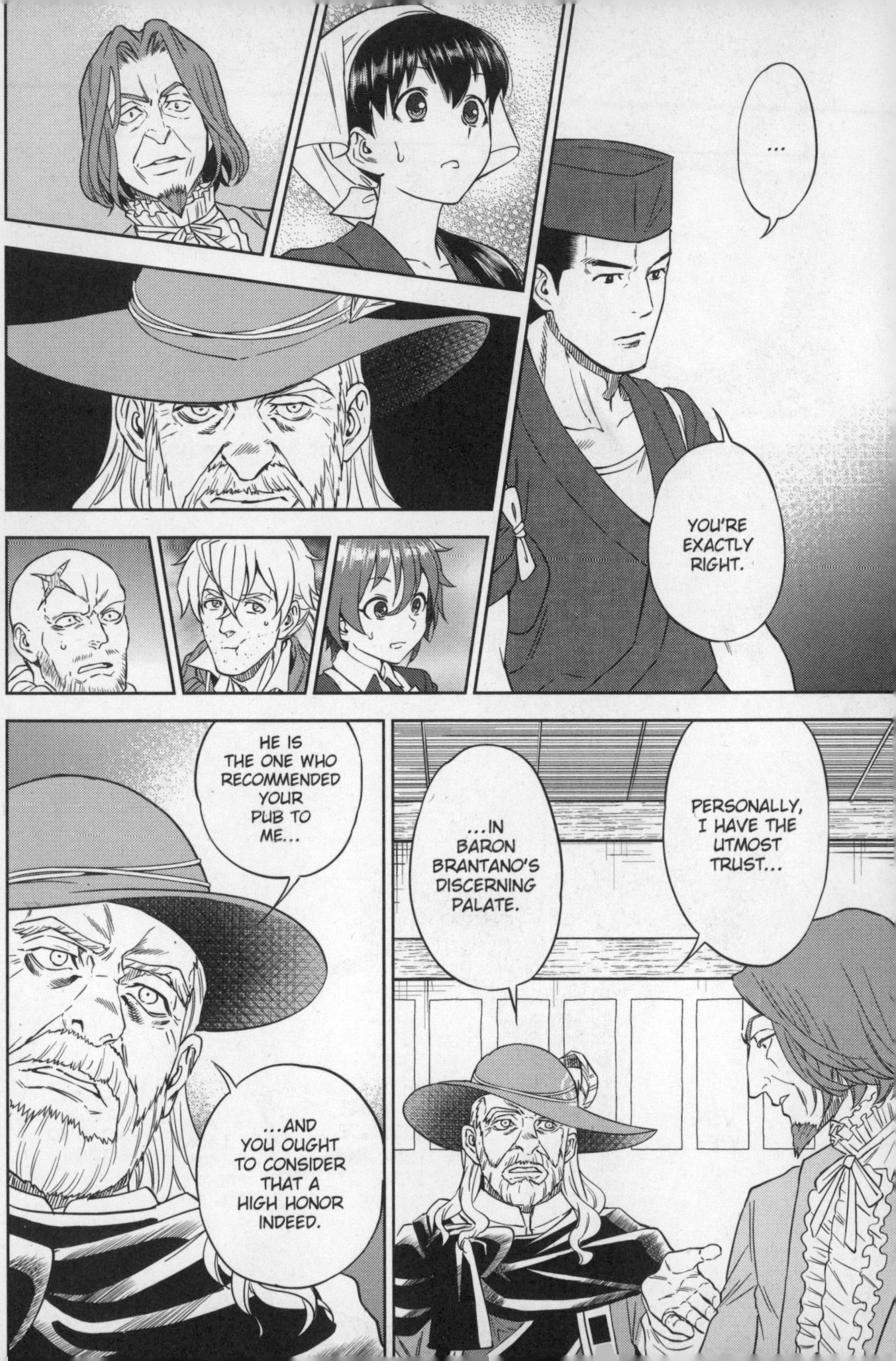
...
YOU'RE EXACTLY RIGHT.
PERSONALLY, I HAVE THE UTMOST TRUST...
...IN BARON BRANTANO'S DISCERNING PALATE.
HE IS THE ONE WHO RECOMMENDED YOUR PUB TO ME...
...AND YOU OUGHT TO CONSIDER THAT A HIGH HONOR INDEED.

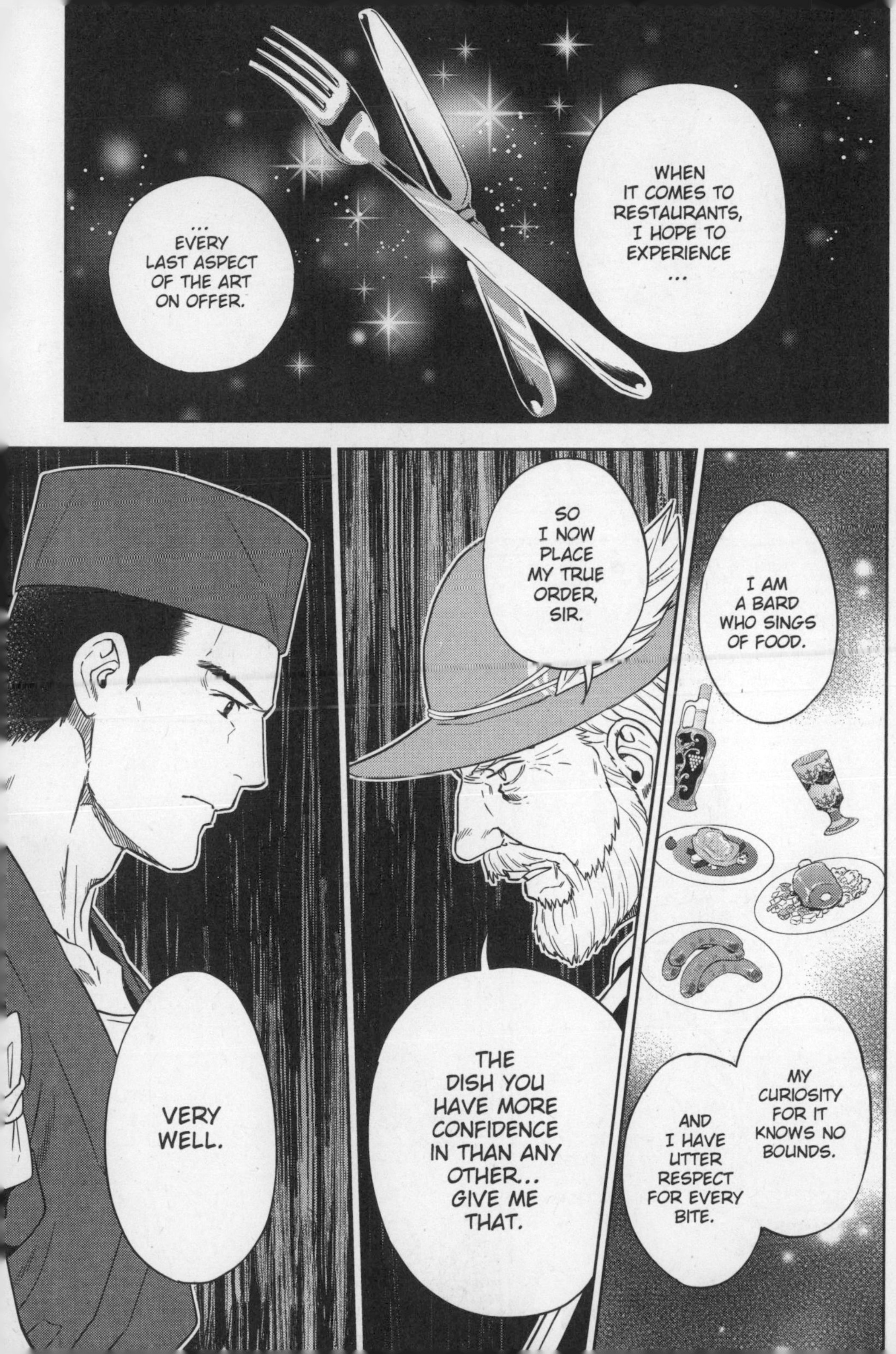
WHEN IT COMES TO RESTAURANTS, I HOPE TO EXPERIENCE ...
... EVERY LAST ASPECT OF THE ART ON OFFER.
I AM A BARD WHO SINGS OF FOOD.
MY CURIOSITY FOR IT KNOWS NO BOUNDS.
AND I HAVE UTTER RESPECT FOR EVERY BITE.
SO I NOW PLACE MY TRUE ORDER, SIR.
THE DISH YOU HAVE MORE CONFIDENCE IN THAN ANY OTHER.. GIVE ME THAT.
VERY WELL.

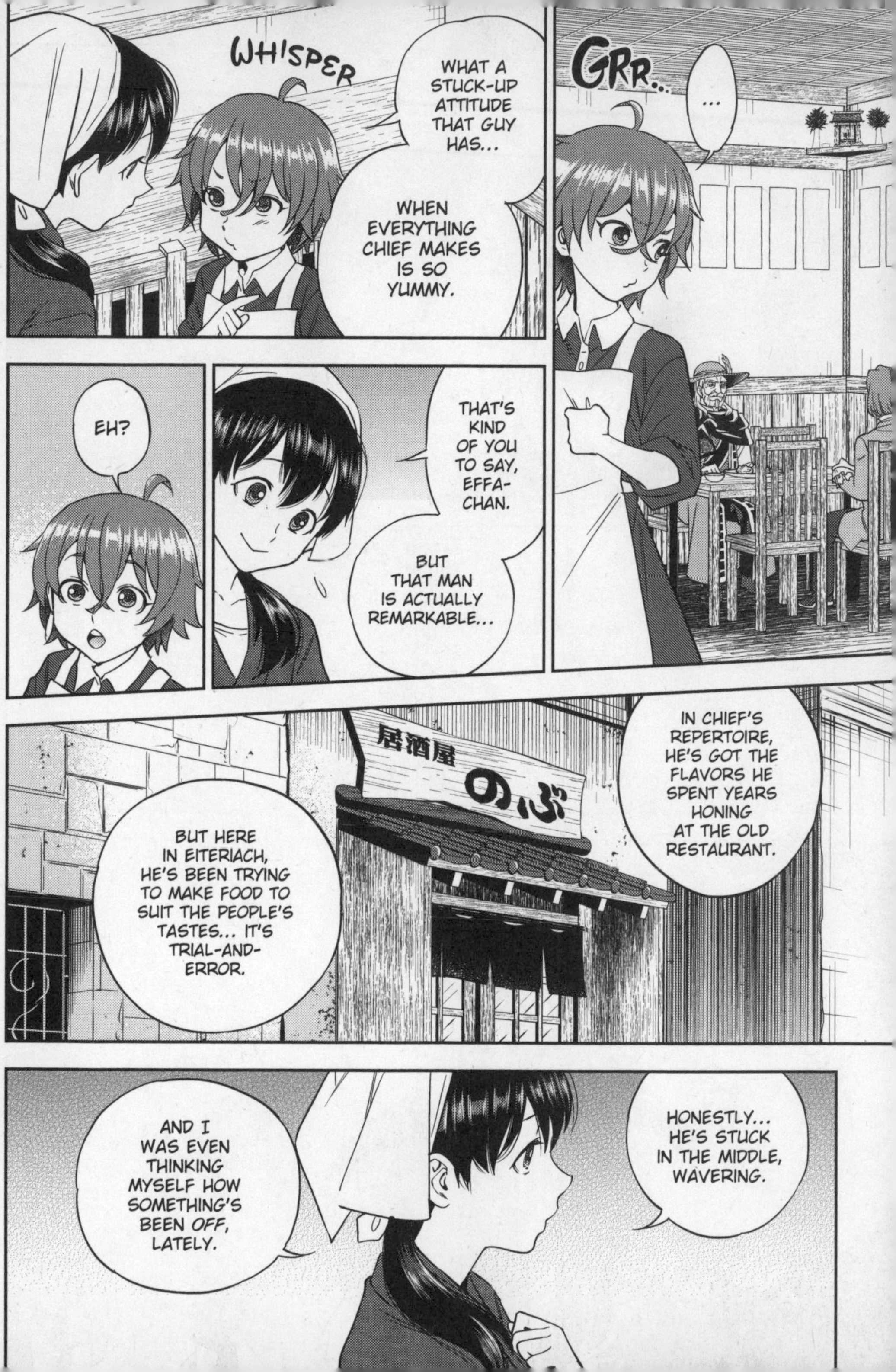
GRR...
...
WHISPER
WHAT A STUCK-UP ATTITUDE THAT GUY HAS...
WHEN EVERYTHING CHIEF MAKES IS SO YUMMY.
THAT'S KIND OF YOU TO SAY, EFFA-CHAN.
BUT THAT MAN IS ACTUALLY REMARKABLE...
EH?
居酒屋
のぶ
IN CHIEF'S REPERTOIRE, HE'S GOT THE FLAVORS HE SPENT YEARS HONING AT THE OLD RESTAURANT.
BUT HERE IN EITERIACH, HE'S BEEN TRYING TO MAKE FOOD TO SUIT THE PEOPLE'S TASTES... IT'S TRIAL-AND-ERROR.
HONESTLY... HE'S STUCK IN THE MIDDLE, WAVERING.
AND I WAS EVEN THINKING MYSELF HOW SOMETHING'S BEEN OFF, LATELY.

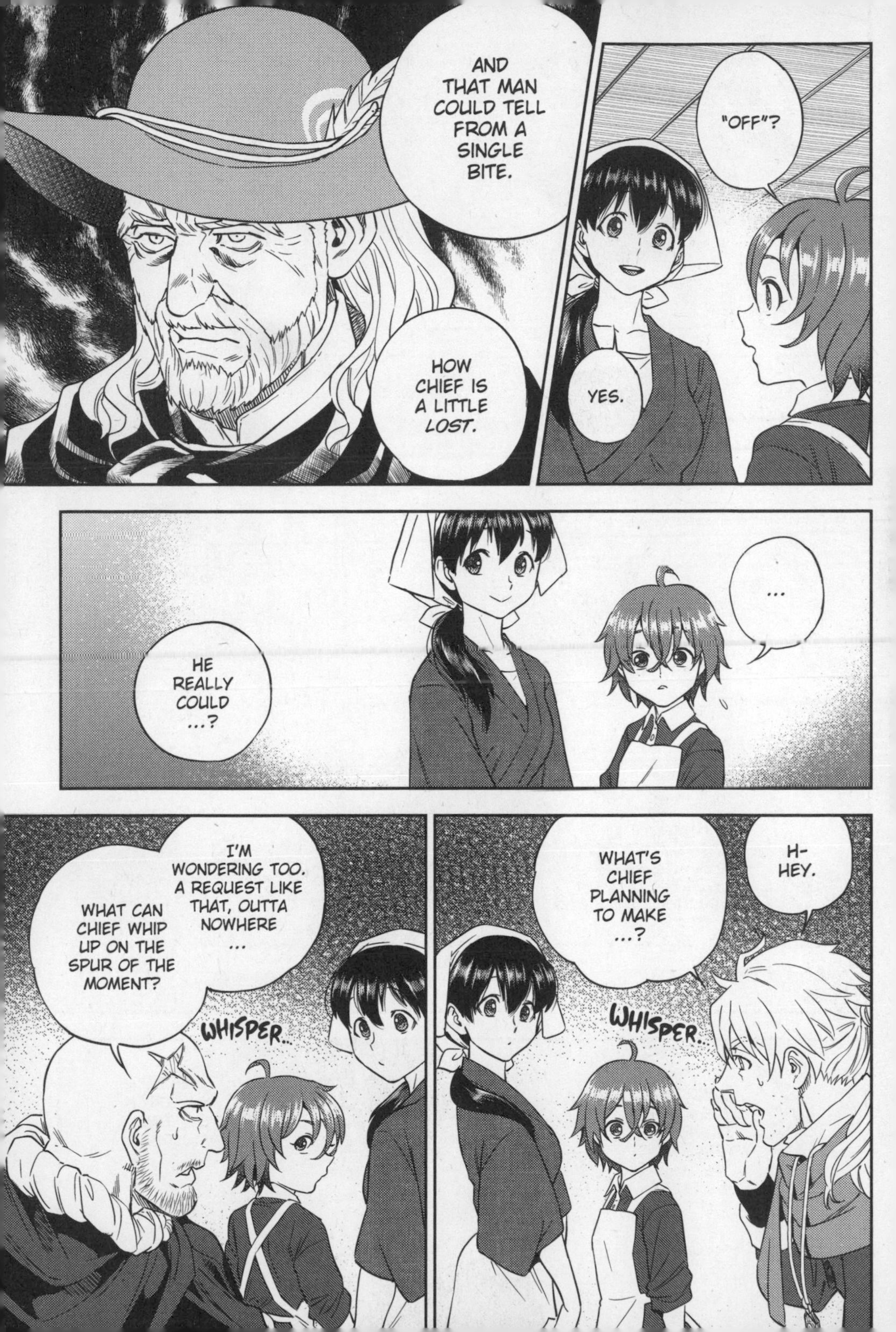
"OFF"?
YES.
AND THAT MAN COULD TELL FROM A SINGLE BITE.
HOW CHIEF IS A LITTLE *LOST*.
...
HE REALLY COULD ...?
H- HEY.
WHAT'S CHIEF PLANNING TO MAKE ...?
WHISPER...
I'M WONDERING TOO. A REQUEST LIKE THAT, OUTTA NOWHERE ...
WHAT CAN CHIEF WHIP UP ON THE SPUR OF THE MOMENT?
WHISPER...

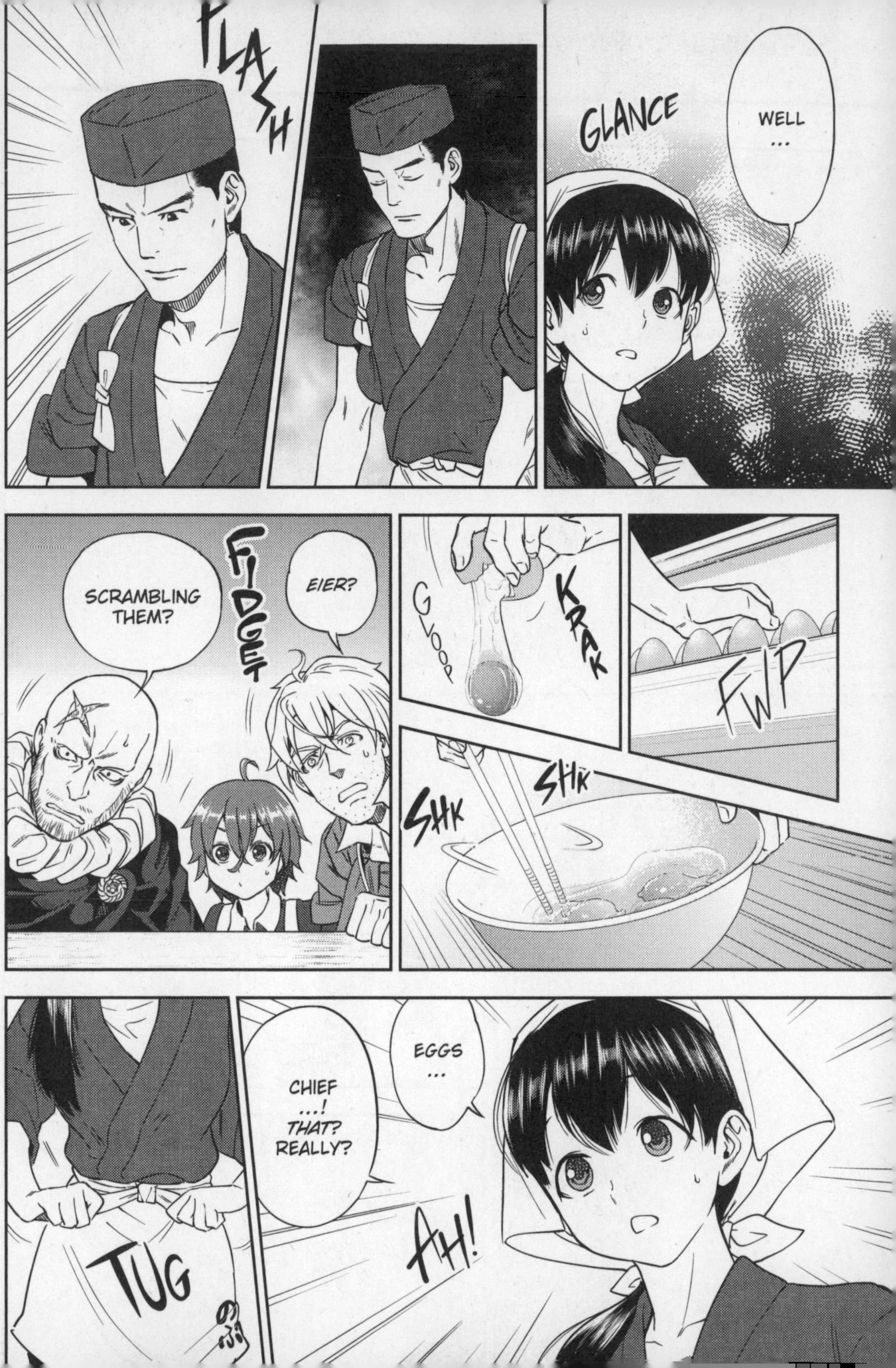
WELL ...
GLANCE
FLASH
FWP
KRAK
GVOOP
SHK
SHK
EIER?
FIDGET
SCRAMBLING THEM?
AH!
EGGS ...
CHIEF ...! THAT? REALLY?
TUG

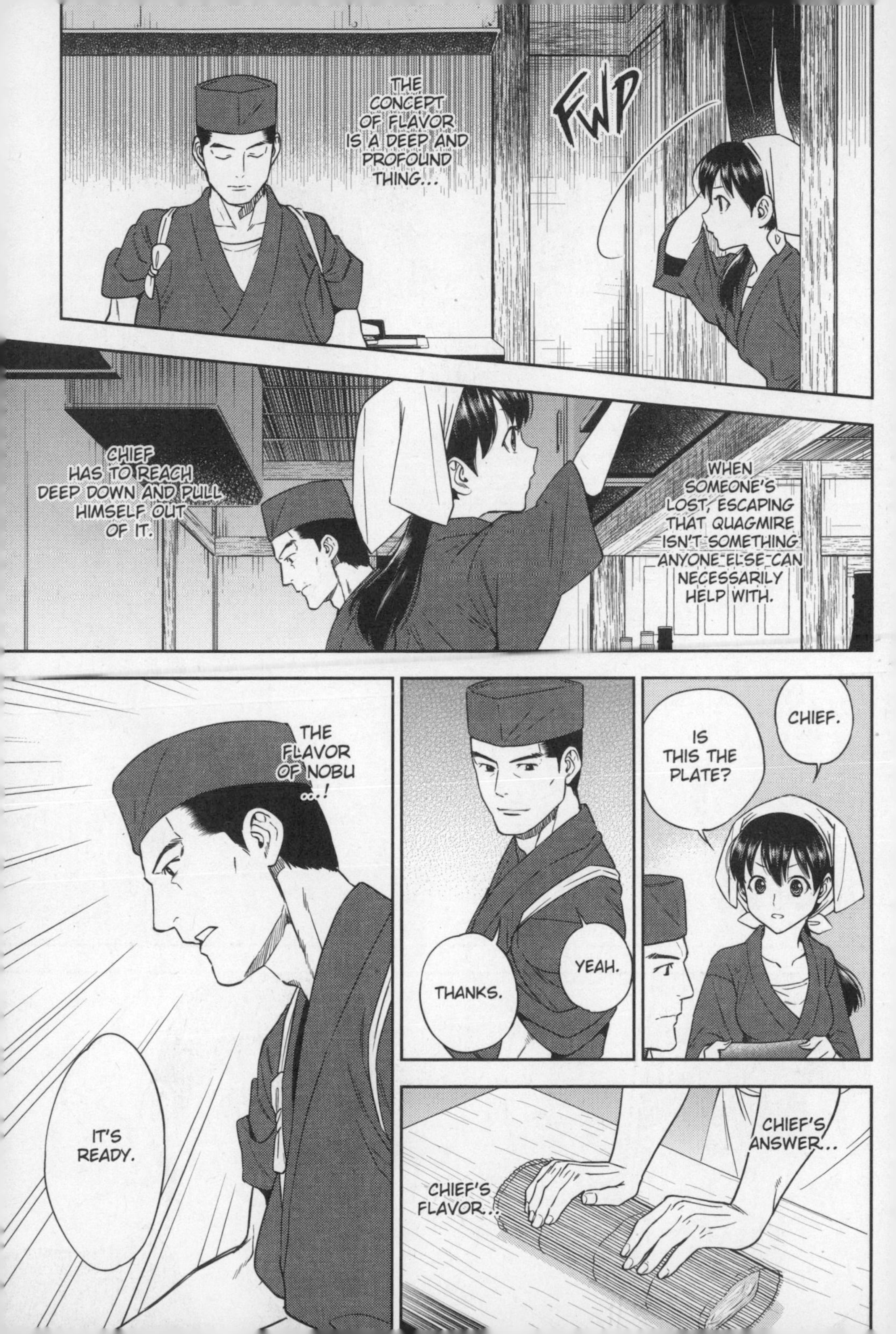
FWP
THE CONCEPT OF FLAVOR IS A DEEP AND PROFOUND THING...
WHEN SOMEONE'S LOST, ESCAPING THAT QUAGMIRE ISN'T SOMETHING ANYONE ELSE CAN NECESSARILY HELP WITH.
CHIEF HAS TO REACH DEEP DOWN AND PULL HIMSELF OUT OF IT.
CHIEF.
IS THIS THE PLATE?
YEAH.
THANKS.
CHIEF'S ANSWER...
CHIEF'S FLAVOR...
THE FLAVOR OF NOBU ...!
IT'S READY.

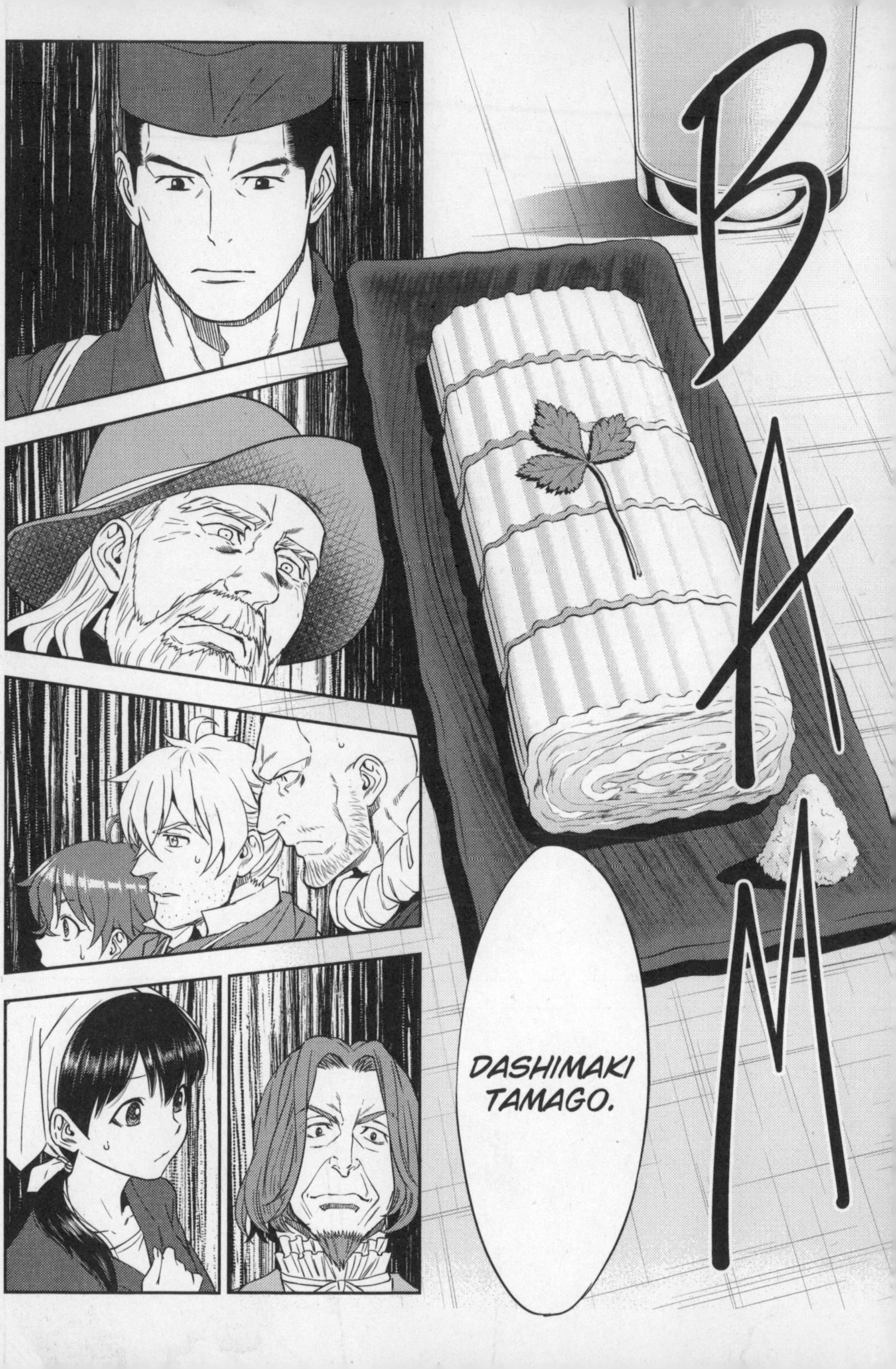
BAM
DASHIMAKI TAMAGO.

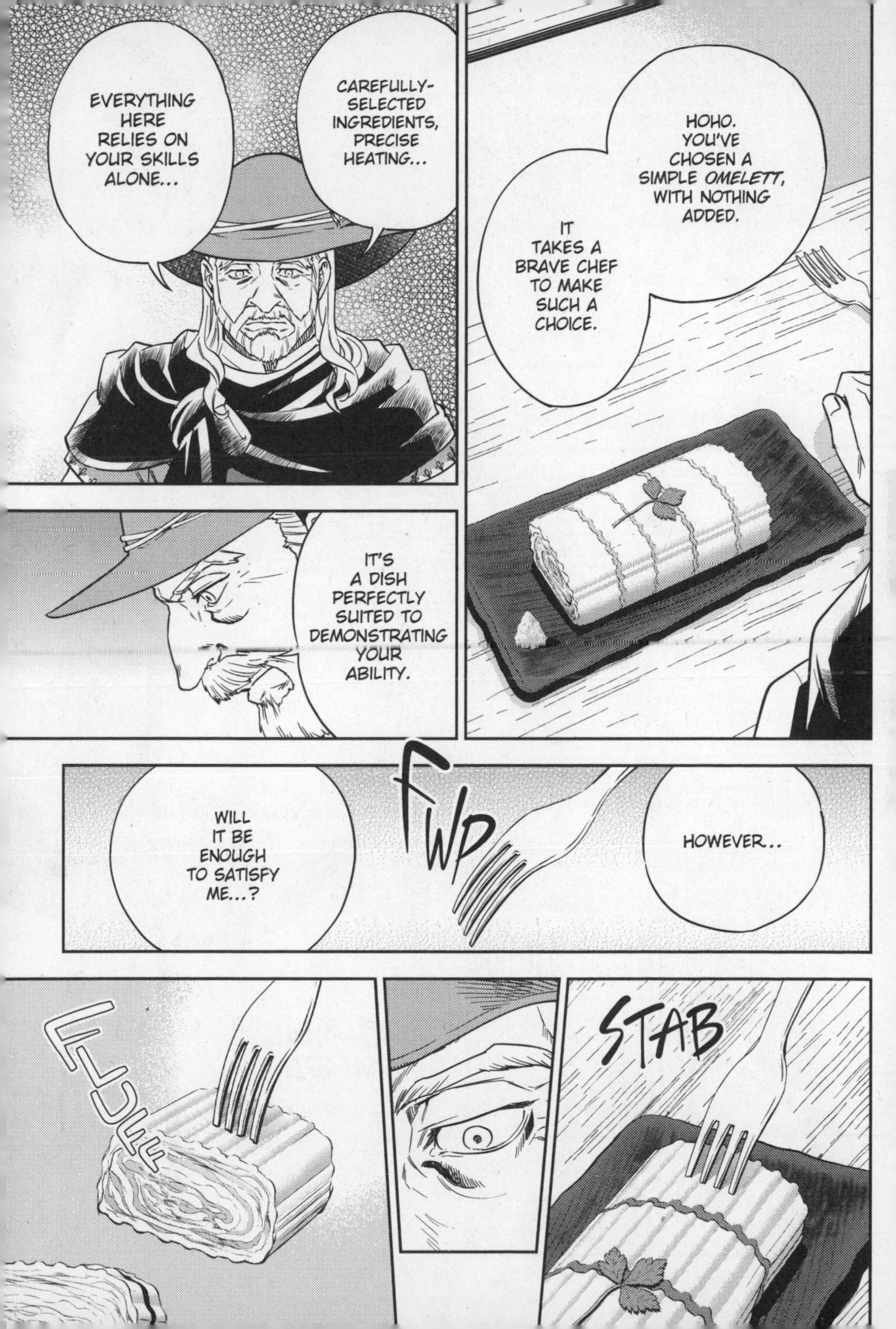
HOHO. YOU'VE CHOSEN A SIMPLE *OMELETT*, WITH NOTHING ADDED.
IT TAKES A BRAVE CHEF TO MAKE SUCH A CHOICE.
CAREFULLY-SELECTED INGREDIENTS, PRECISE HEATING...
EVERYTHING HERE RELIES ON YOUR SKILLS ALONE...
IT'S A DISH PERFECTLY SUITED TO DEMONSTRATING YOUR ABILITY.
HOWEVER...
FWP
WILL IT BE ENOUGH TO SATISFY ME...?
STAB
FLUFF

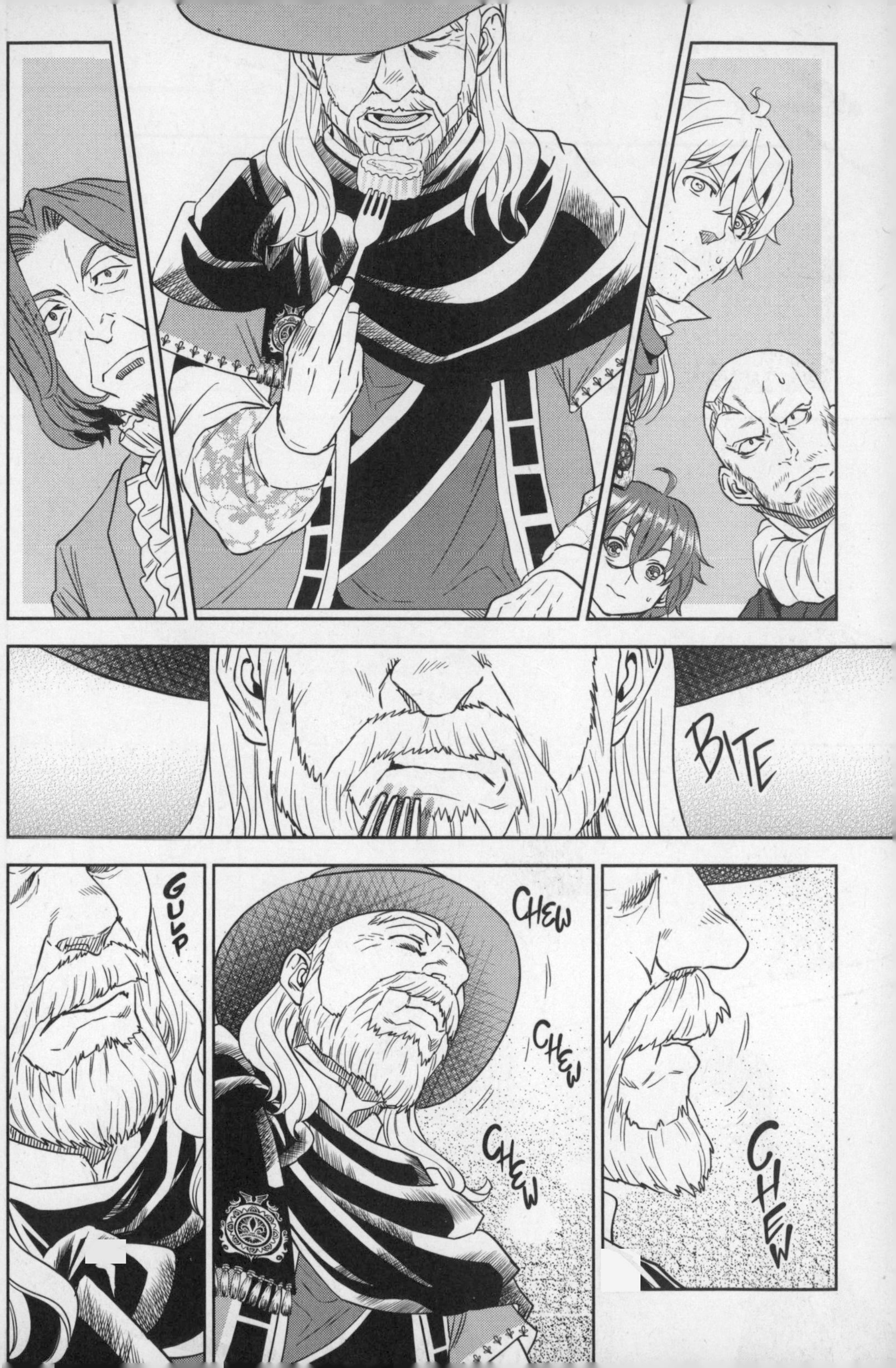
BITE
CHEW
CHEW
CHEW
CHEW
GULP

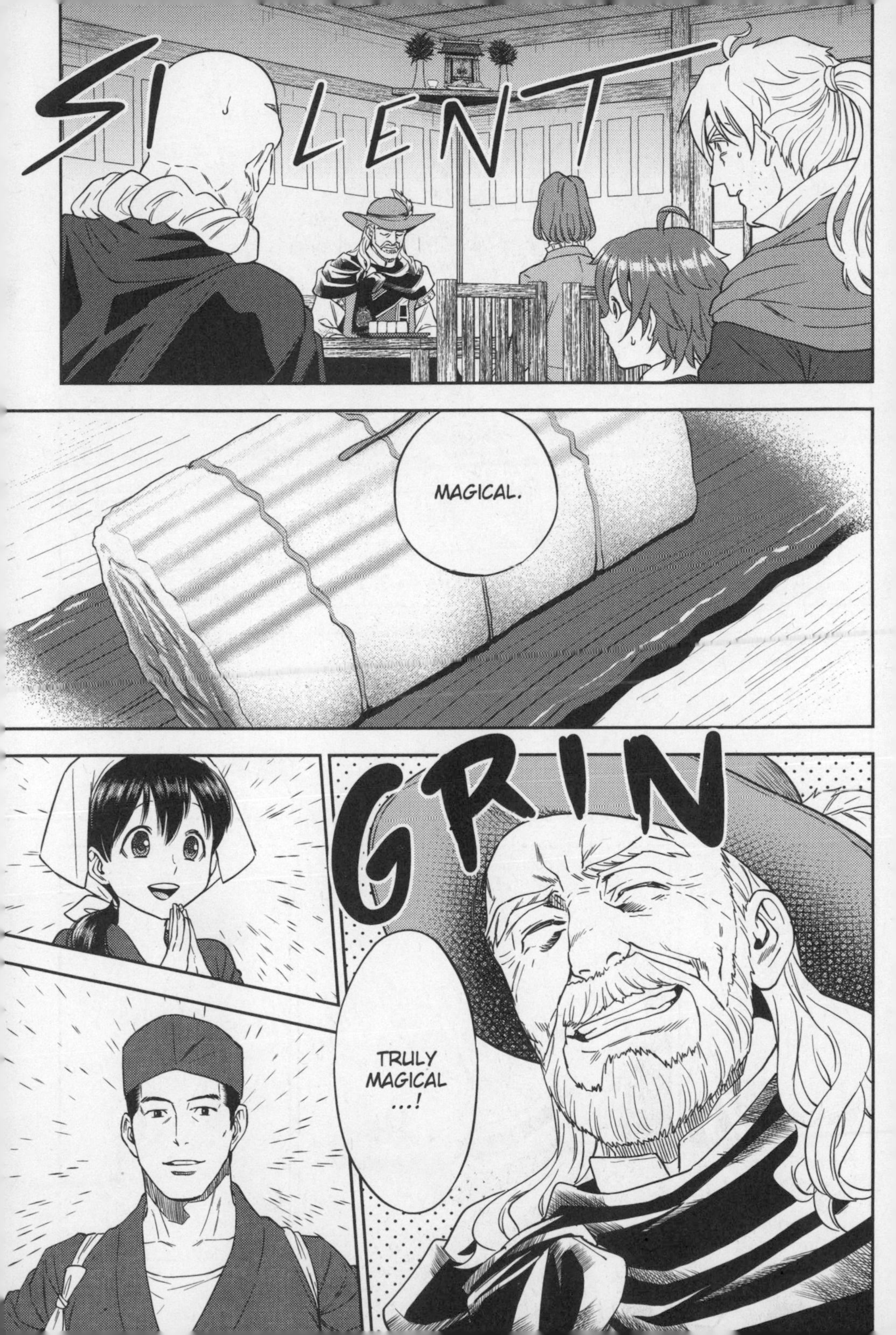
SILENT
MAGICAL.
GRIN
TRULY MAGICAL ...!

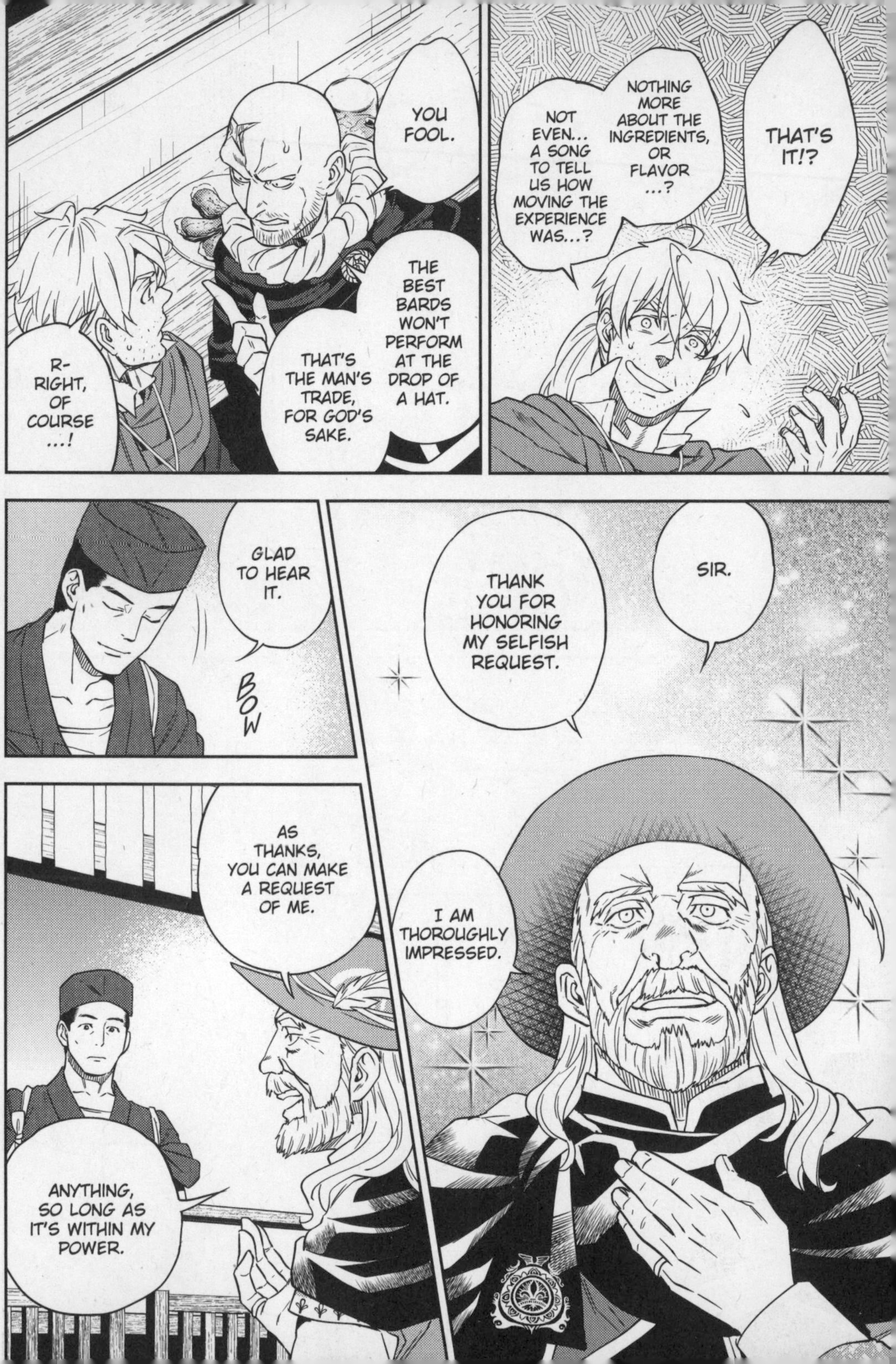
THAT'S IT!?
NOTHING MORE ABOUT THE INGREDIENTS, OR FLAVOR ...?
NOT EVEN... A SONG TO TELL US HOW MOVING THE EXPERIENCE WAS...?
YOU FOOL.
THE BEST BARDS WON'T PERFORM AT THE DROP OF A HAT.
THAT'S THE MAN'S TRADE, FOR GOD'S SAKE.
R-RIGHT, OF COURSE ...!
SIR.
THANK YOU FOR HONORING MY SELFISH REQUEST.
I AM THOROUGHLY IMPRESSED.
GLAD TO HEAR IT.
BOW
AS THANKS, YOU CAN MAKE A REQUEST OF ME.
ANYTHING, SO LONG AS IT'S WITHIN MY POWER.

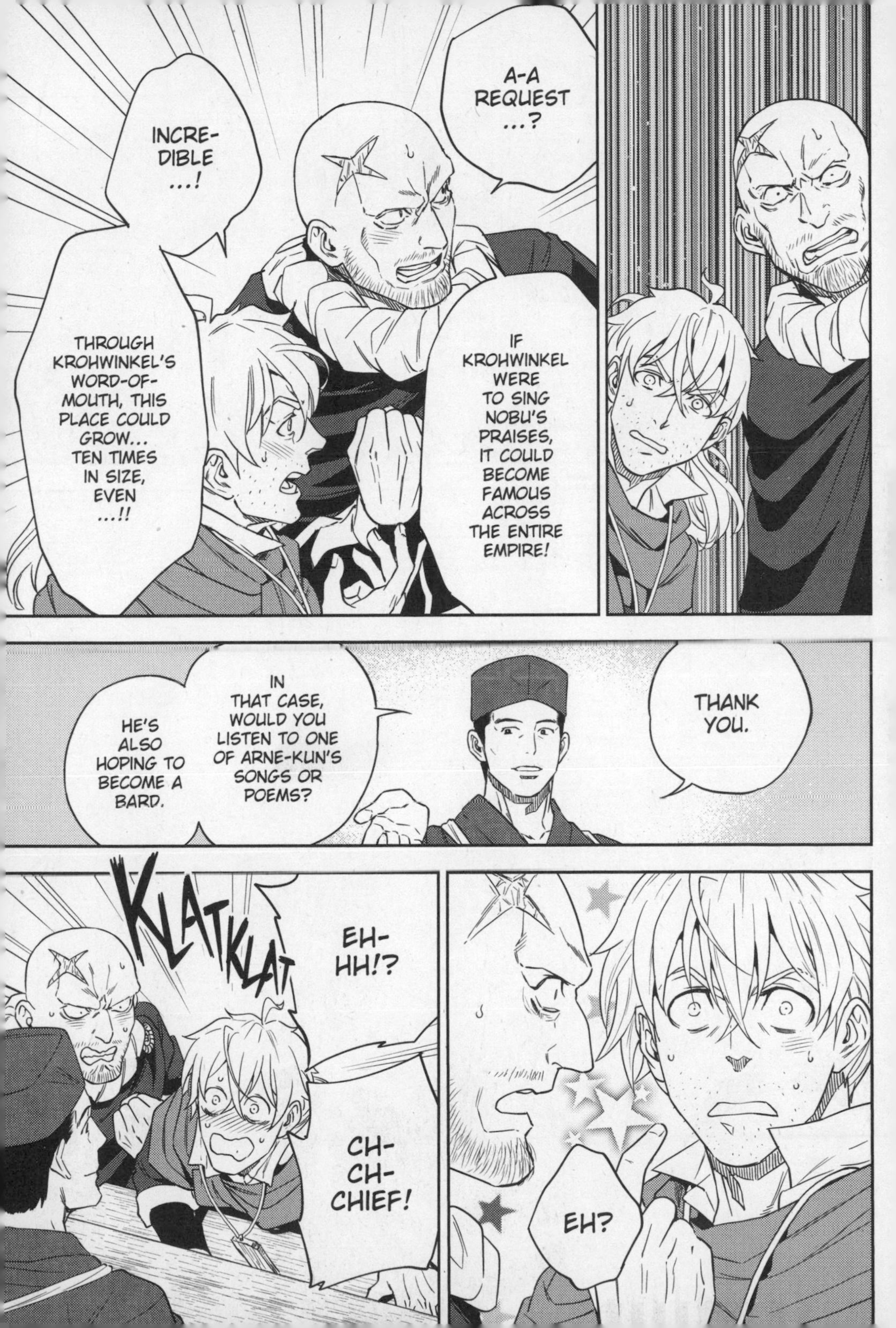
A-A REQUEST ...?
INCRE-DIBLE ...!
IF KROHWINKEL WERE TO SING NOBU'S PRAISES, IT COULD BECOME FAMOUS ACROSS THE ENTIRE EMPIRE!
THROUGH KROHWINKEL'S WORD-OF-MOUTH, THIS PLACE COULD GROW... TEN TIMES IN SIZE, EVEN ...!!
THANK YOU.
IN THAT CASE, WOULD YOU LISTEN TO ONE OF ARNE-KUN'S SONGS OR POEMS?
HE'S ALSO HOPING TO BECOME A BARD.
EH?
KLATKLAT
EH-HH!?
CH-CH-CHIEF!

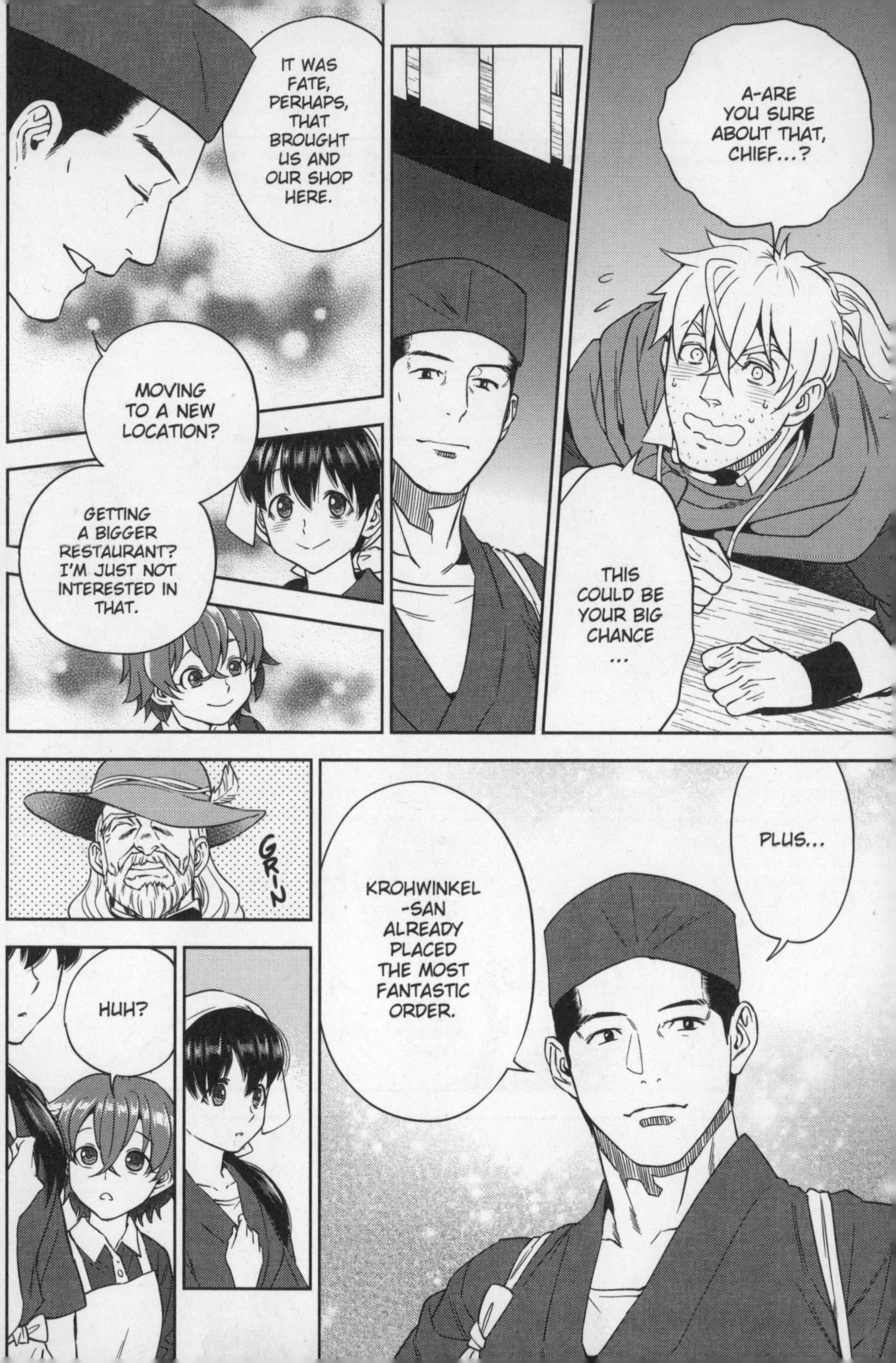
A-ARE YOU SURE ABOUT THAT, CHIEF...?
THIS COULD BE YOUR BIG CHANCE ...
IT WAS FATE, PERHAPS, THAT BROUGHT US AND OUR SHOP HERE.
MOVING TO A NEW LOCATION?
GETTING A BIGGER RESTAURANT? I'M JUST NOT INTERESTED IN THAT.
PLUS...
KROHWINKEL-SAN ALREADY PLACED THE MOST FANTASTIC ORDER.
GRIN
HUH?

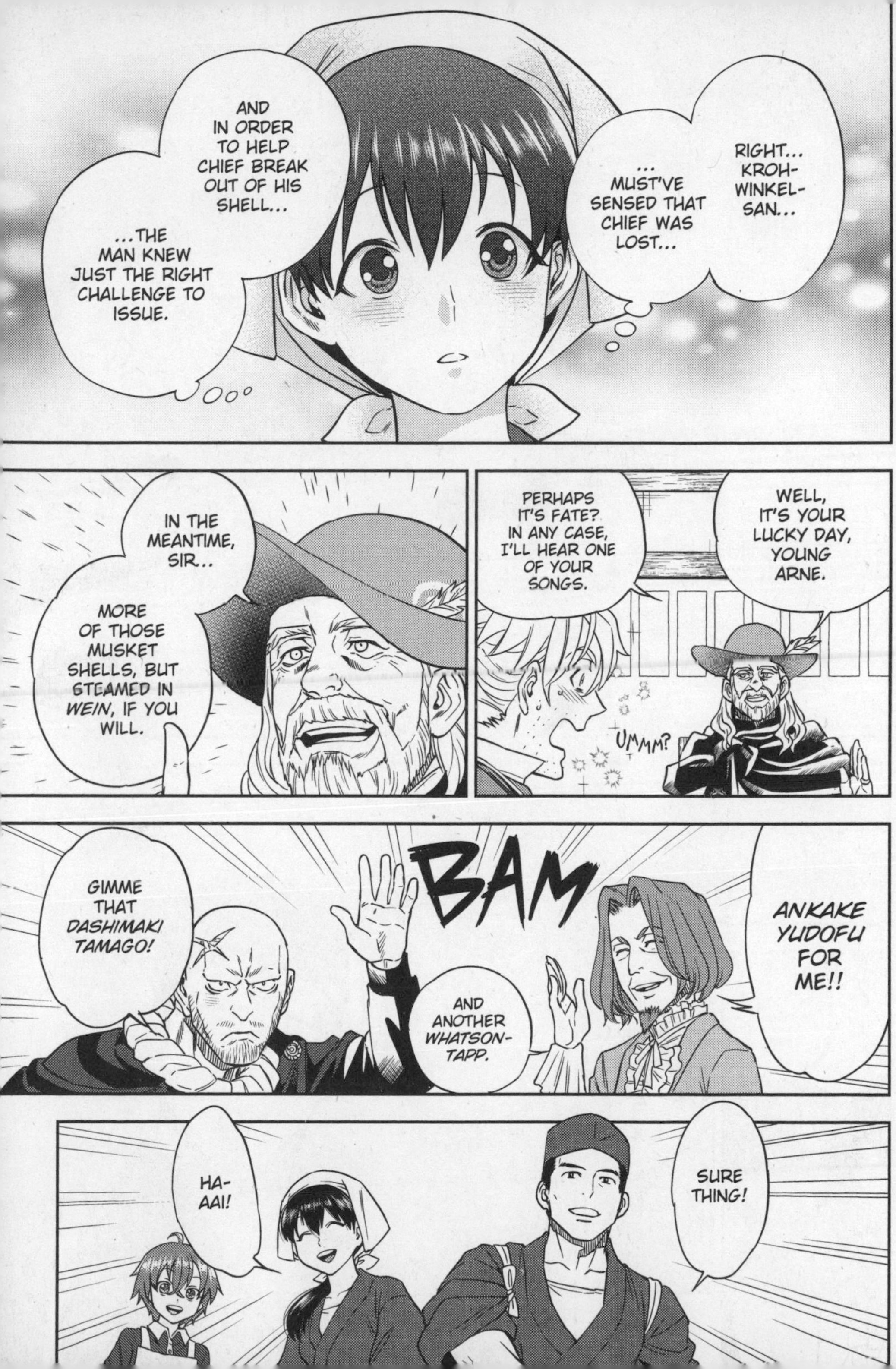
RIGHT... KROH-WINKEL-SAN...
... MUST'VE SENSED THAT CHIEF WAS LOST...
AND IN ORDER TO HELP CHIEF BREAK OUT OF HIS SHELL...
...THE MAN KNEW JUST THE RIGHT CHALLENGE TO ISSUE.
WELL, IT'S YOUR LUCKY DAY, YOUNG ARNE.
PERHAPS IT'S FATE? IN ANY CASE, I'LL HEAR ONE OF YOUR SONGS.
UMMM?
IN THE MEANTIME, SIR...
MORE OF THOSE MUSKET SHELLS, BUT STEAMED IN *WEIN*, IF YOU WILL.
ANKAKE YUDOFU FOR ME!!
BAM
AND ANOTHER *WHATSON-TAPP*.
GIMME THAT *DASHIMAKI TAMAGO*!
SURE THING!
HA-AAI!

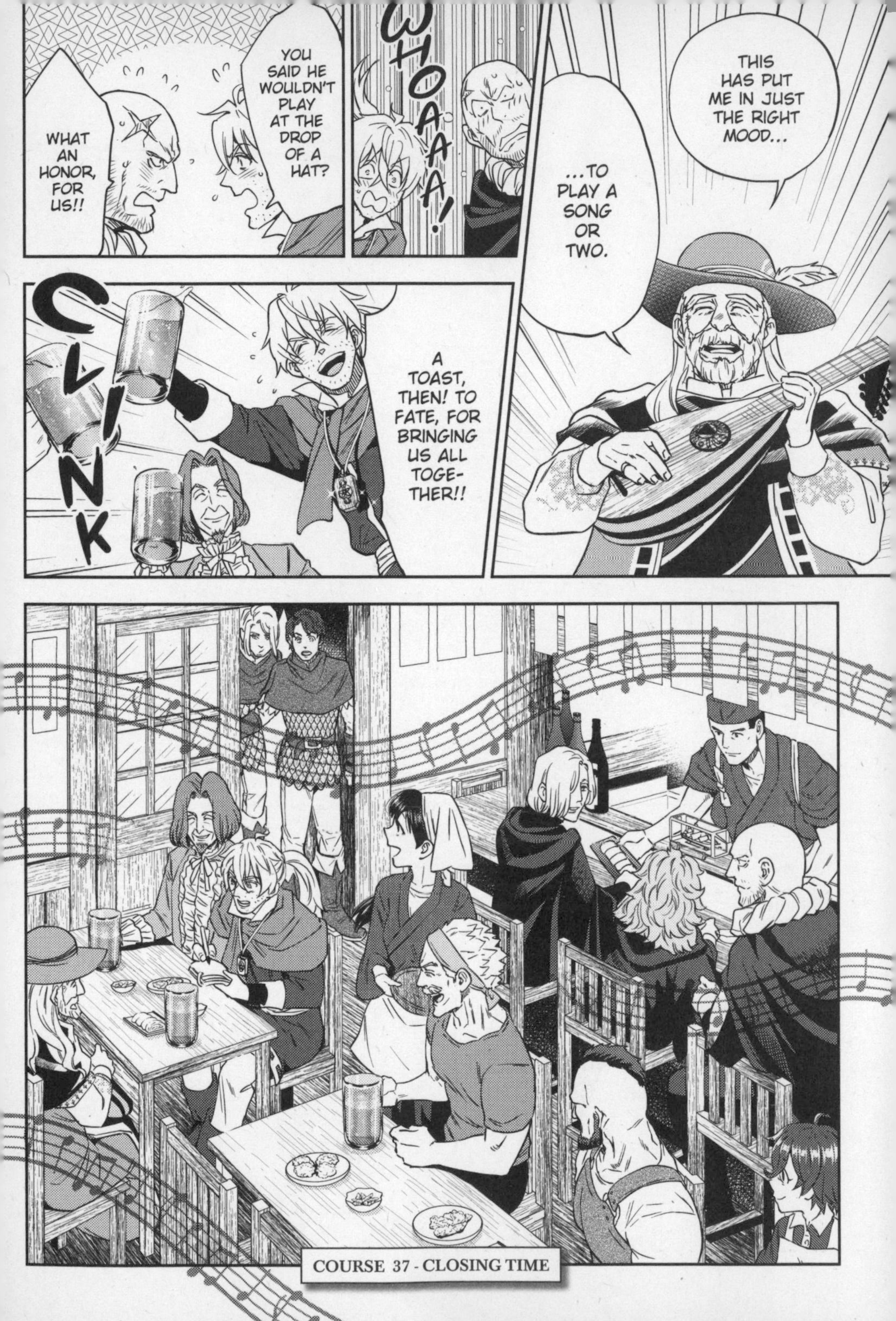
THIS HAS PUT ME IN JUST THE RIGHT MOOD...
...TO PLAY A SONG OR TWO.
WHOAAAA!
YOU SAID HE WOULDN'T PLAY AT THE DROP OF A HAT?
WHAT AN HONOR, FOR US!!
A TOAST, THEN! TO FATE, FOR BRINGING US ALL TOGE-THER!!
CLINK

COURSE 37 - CLOSING TIME

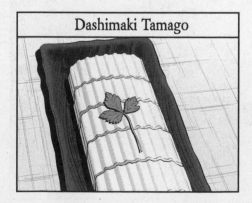

Dashimaki Tamago

OTHERWORLDLY IZAKAYA

NOBU

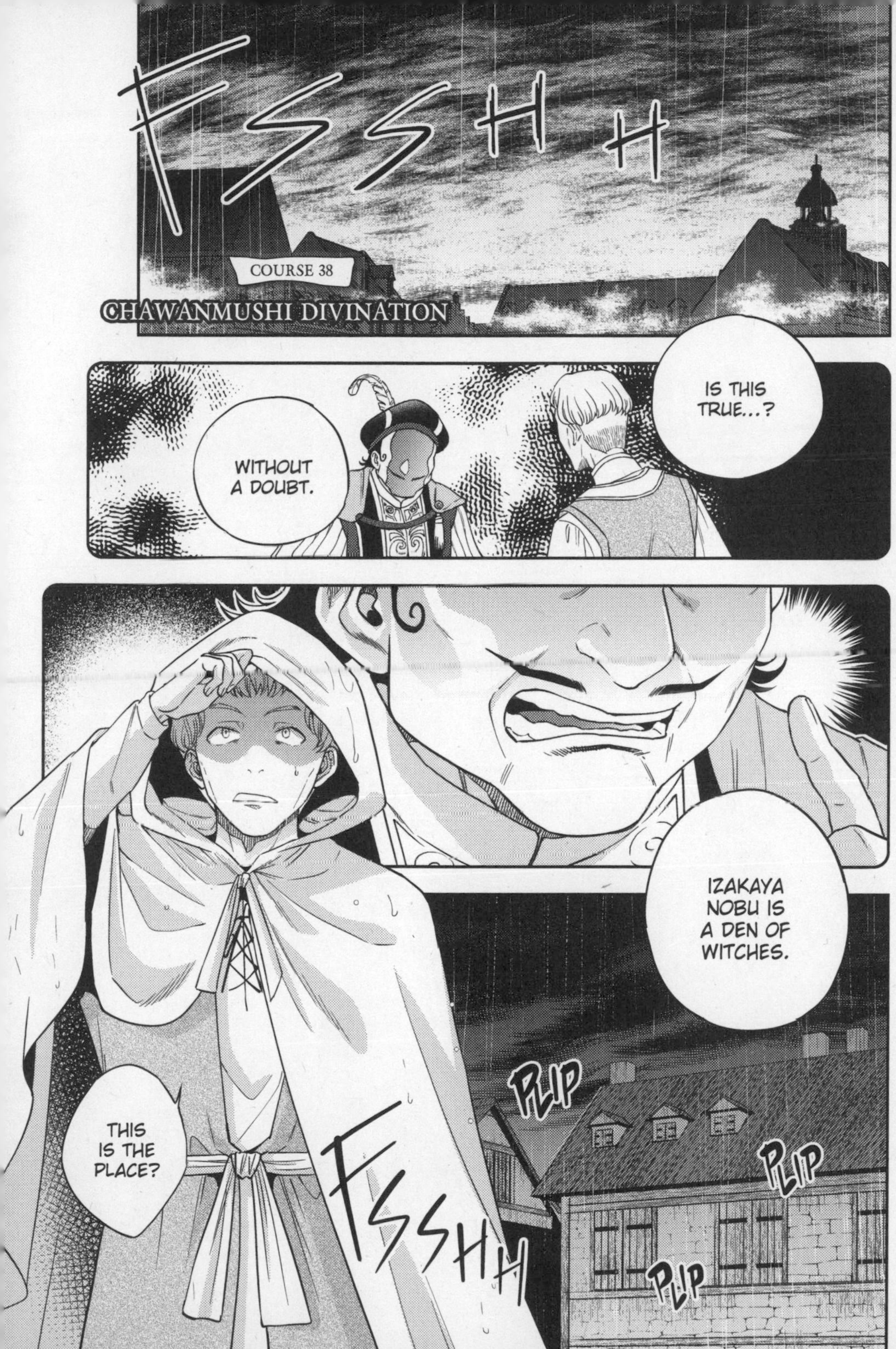
FSSHH
COURSE 38
CHAWANMUSHI DIVINATION
IS THIS TRUE...?
WITHOUT A DOUBT.
IZAKAYA NOBU IS A DEN OF WITCHES.
PLIP
PLIP
FSSHH
THIS IS THE PLACE?
PLIP

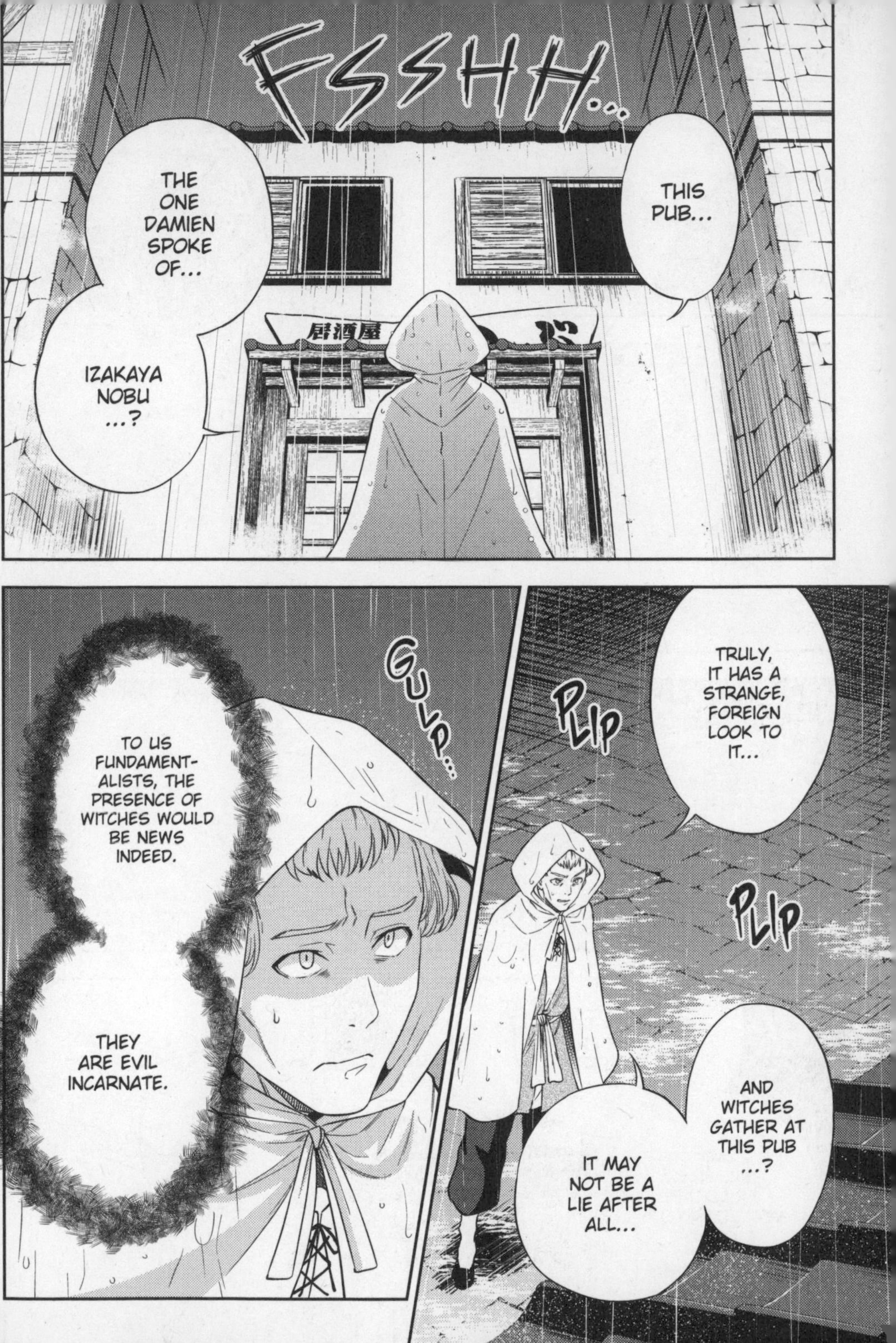
FSSHH...
THIS PUB...
THE ONE DAMIEN SPOKE OF...
IZAKAYA NOBU ...?
居酒屋
TRULY, IT HAS A STRANGE, FOREIGN LOOK TO IT...
PLIP
PLIP
AND WITCHES GATHER AT THIS PUB ...?
IT MAY NOT BE A LIE AFTER ALL...
GULP...
TO US FUNDAMENT-ALISTS, THE PRESENCE OF WITCHES WOULD BE NEWS INDEED.
THEY ARE EVIL INCARNATE.

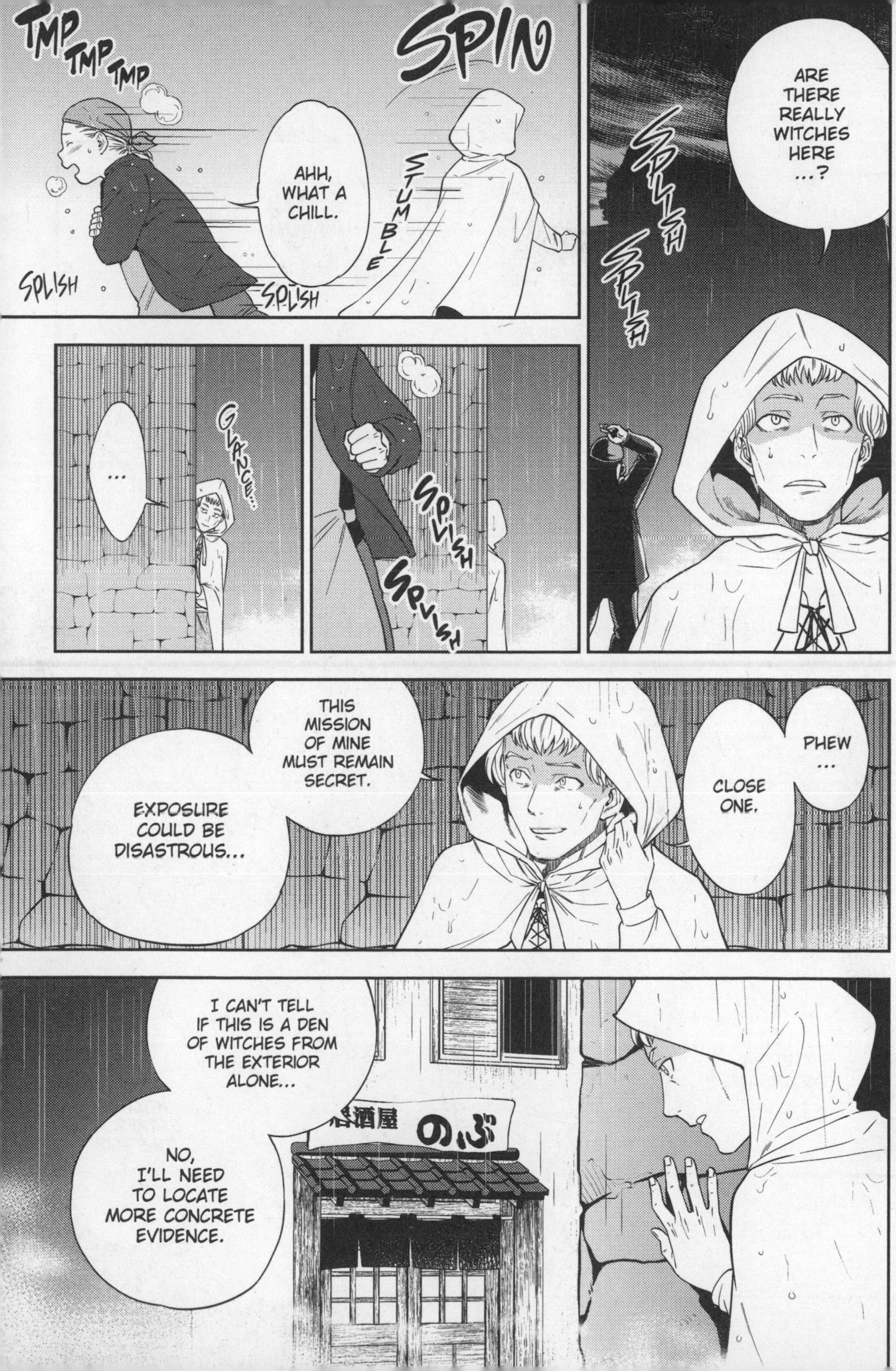
ARE THERE REALLY WITCHES HERE ...?
SPLISH
SPLISH
TMP TMP TMP
SPIN
AHH, WHAT A CHILL.
STUMBLE
SPLISH
SPLISH
SPLISH
SPLISH
GLANCE...
...
PHEW ...
CLOSE ONE.
THIS MISSION OF MINE MUST REMAIN SECRET.
EXPOSURE COULD BE DISASTROUS...
I CAN'T TELL IF THIS IS A DEN OF WITCHES FROM THE EXTERIOR ALONE...
NO, I'LL NEED TO LOCATE MORE CONCRETE EVIDENCE.
居酒屋 のぶ

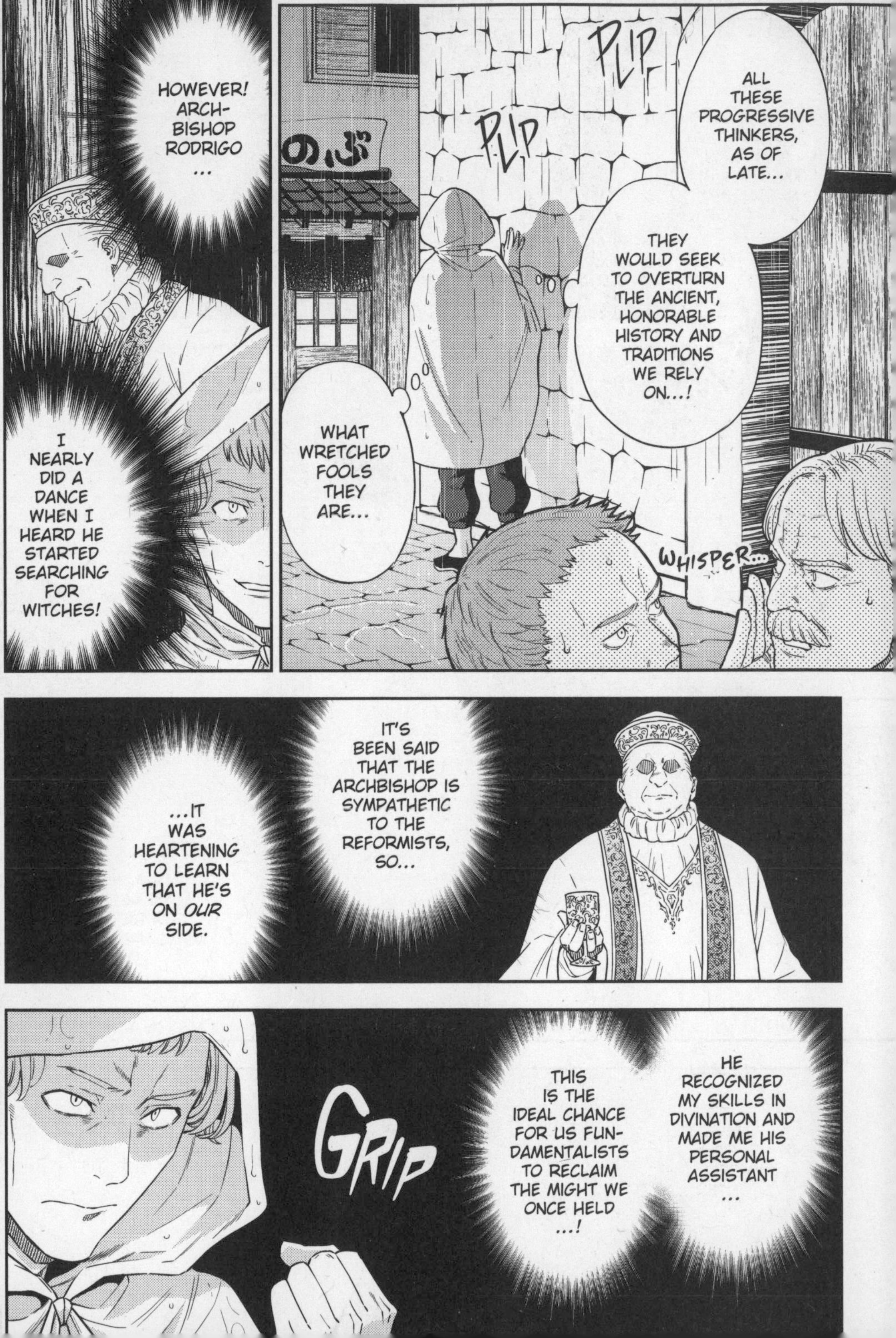
PLIP
ALL THESE PROGRESSIVE THINKERS, AS OF LATE...
PLIP
THEY WOULD SEEK TO OVERTURN THE ANCIENT, HONORABLE HISTORY AND TRADITIONS WE RELY ON...!
のぶ
WHAT WRETCHED FOOLS THEY ARE...
WHISPER...
HOWEVER! ARCH-BISHOP RODRIGO ...
I NEARLY DID A DANCE WHEN I HEARD HE STARTED SEARCHING FOR WITCHES!
IT'S BEEN SAID THAT THE ARCHBISHOP IS SYMPATHETIC TO THE REFORMISTS, SO...
...IT WAS HEARTENING TO LEARN THAT HE'S ON *OUR* SIDE.
HE RECOGNIZED MY SKILLS IN DIVINATION AND MADE ME HIS PERSONAL ASSISTANT ...
THIS IS THE IDEAL CHANCE FOR US FUN-DAMENTALISTS TO RECLAIM THE MIGHT WE ONCE HELD ...!
GRIP

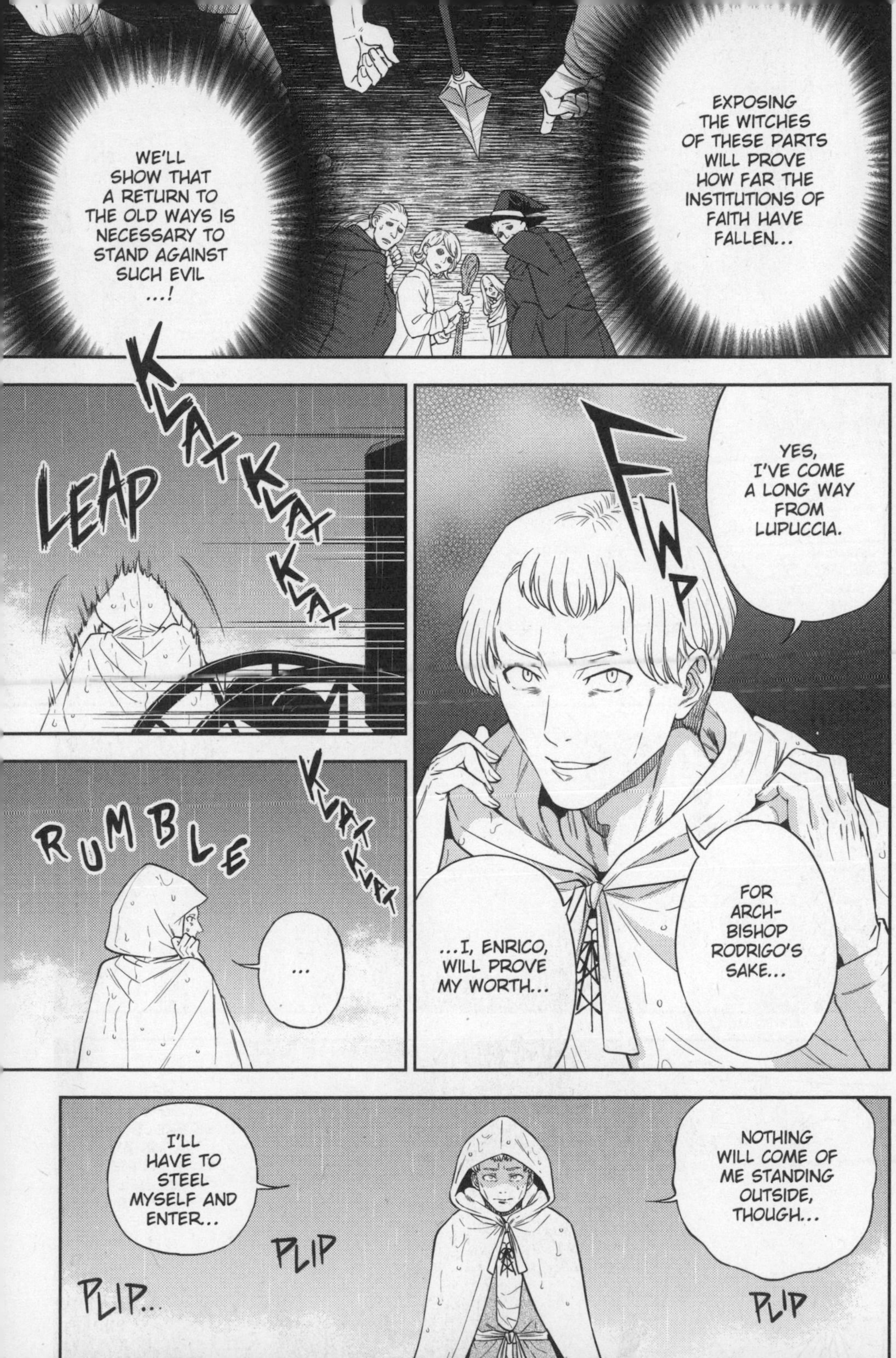
EXPOSING THE WITCHES OF THESE PARTS WILL PROVE HOW FAR THE INSTITUTIONS OF FAITH HAVE FALLEN...
WE'LL SHOW THAT A RETURN TO THE OLD WAYS IS NECESSARY TO STAND AGAINST SUCH EVIL ...!
FWP
YES, I'VE COME A LONG WAY FROM LUPUCCIA.
FOR ARCH-BISHOP RODRIGO'S SAKE...
...I, ENRICO, WILL PROVE MY WORTH...
KLAK KLAK KLAK KLAK
LEAP
KLAK KLAK
RUMBLE
...
NOTHING WILL COME OF ME STANDING OUTSIDE, THOUGH...
PLIP
I'LL HAVE TO STEEL MYSELF AND ENTER...
PLIP
PLIP...

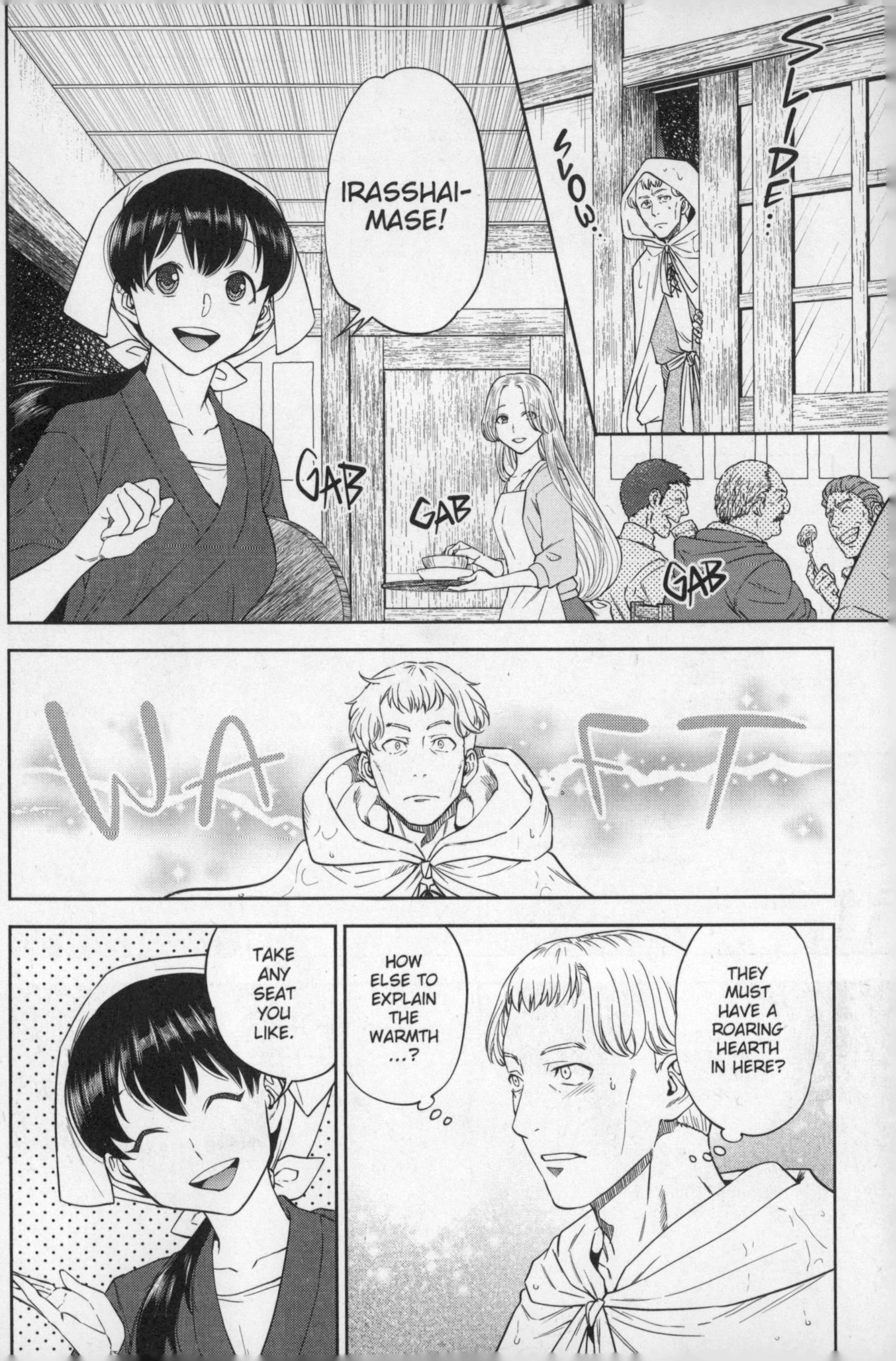
SLIDE...
IRASSHAI-MASE!
GAB
GAB
GAB
WAFT
THEY MUST HAVE A ROARING HEARTH IN HERE?
HOW ELSE TO EXPLAIN THE WARMTH ...?
TAKE ANY SEAT YOU LIKE.

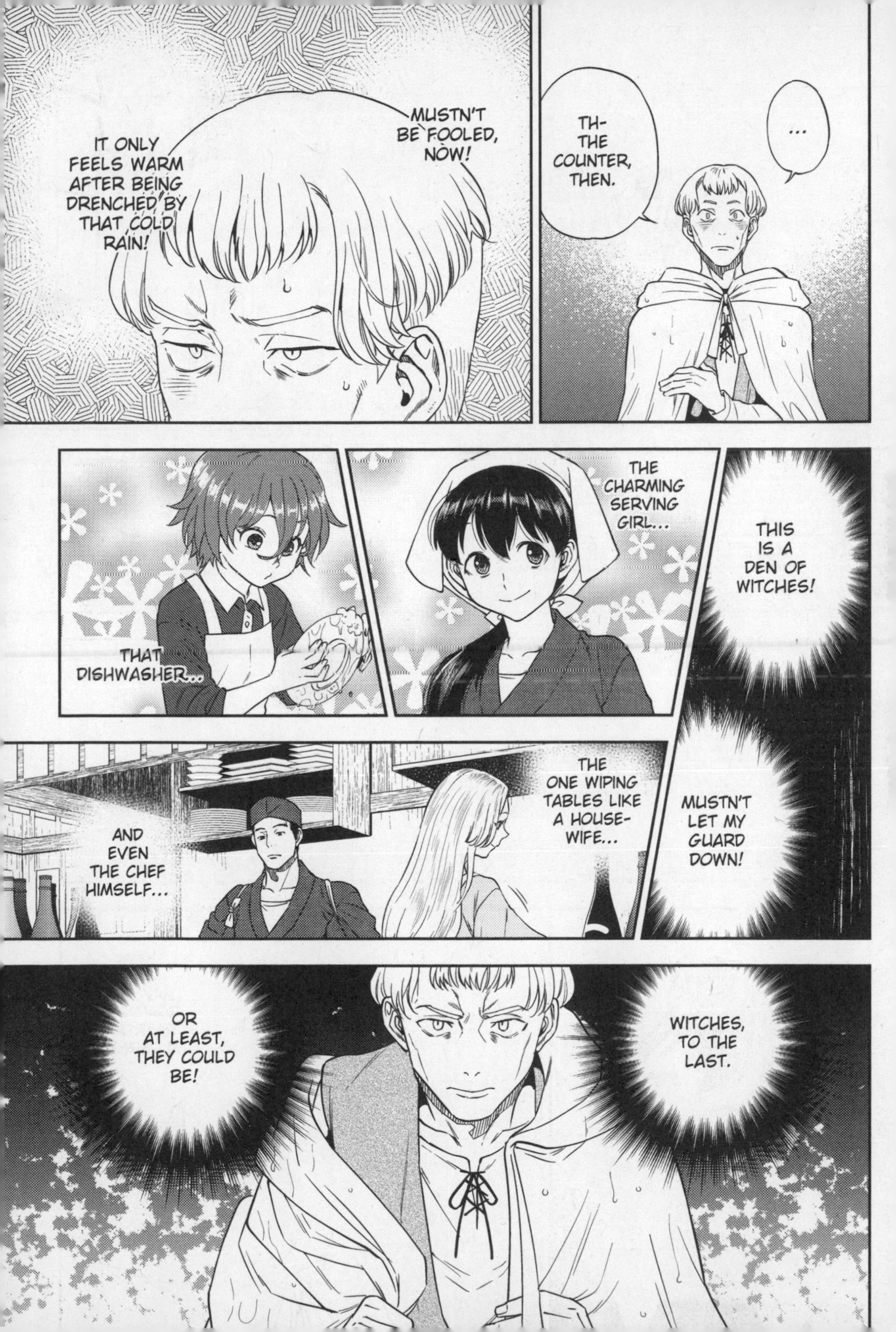
...
TH- THE COUNTER, THEN.
MUSTN'T BE FOOLED, NOW!
IT ONLY FEELS WARM AFTER BEING DRENCHED BY THAT COLD RAIN!
THIS IS A DEN OF WITCHES!
MUSTN'T LET MY GUARD DOWN!
THE CHARMING SERVING GIRL...
THAT DISHWASHER...
THE ONE WIPING TABLES LIKE A HOUSE-WIFE...
AND EVEN THE CHEF HIMSELF...
WITCHES, TO THE LAST.
OR AT LEAST, THEY COULD BE!

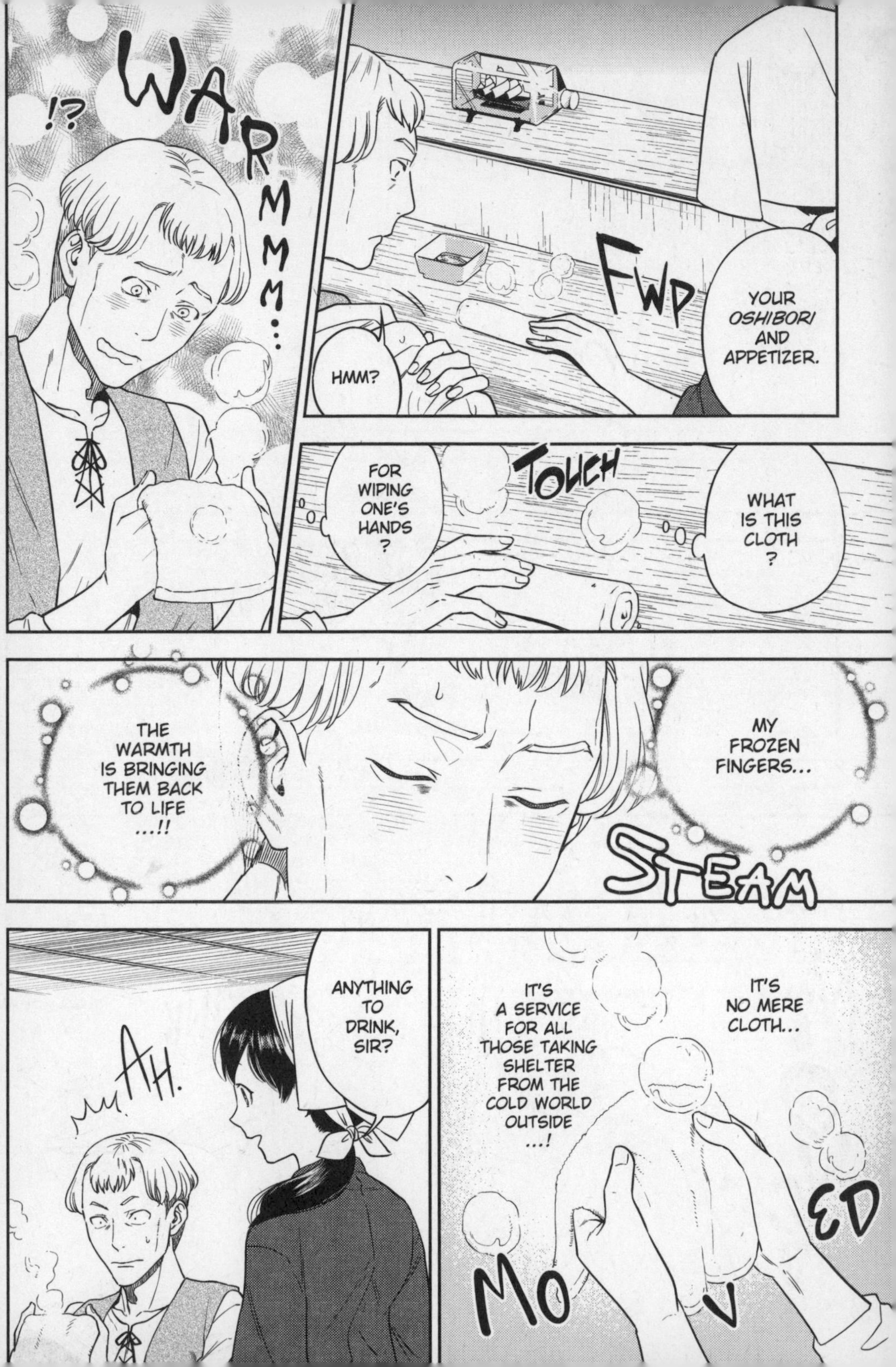
YOUR OSHIBORI AND APPETIZER.
FWP
HMM?
WHAT IS THIS CLOTH?
FOR WIPING ONE'S HANDS?
TOUCH
WARMMMM...
!?
MY FROZEN FINGERS...
THE WARMTH IS BRINGING THEM BACK TO LIFE...!!
STEAM
IT'S NO MERE CLOTH...
IT'S A SERVICE FOR ALL THOSE TAKING SHELTER FROM THE COLD WORLD OUTSIDE...!
MOVED
ANYTHING TO DRINK, SIR?
AH.

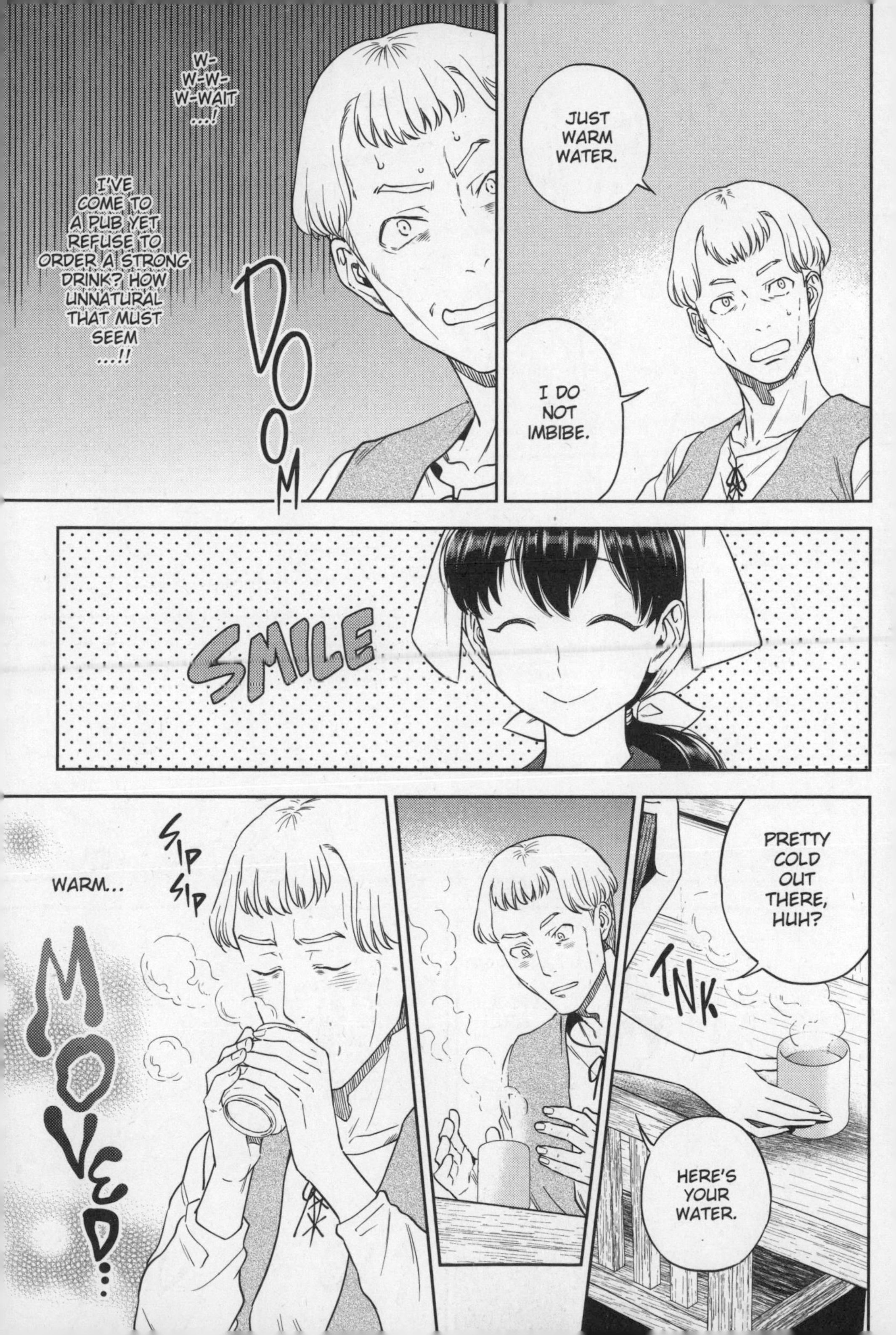
JUST WARM WATER.
I DO NOT IMBIBE.
W-W-W-W-WAIT ...!
I'VE COME TO A PUB YET REFUSE TO ORDER A STRONG DRINK? HOW UNNATURAL THAT MUST SEEM ...!!
DOOM
SMILE
PRETTY COLD OUT THERE, HUH?
TNK
HERE'S YOUR WATER.
SIP SIP
WARM...
MOVED...

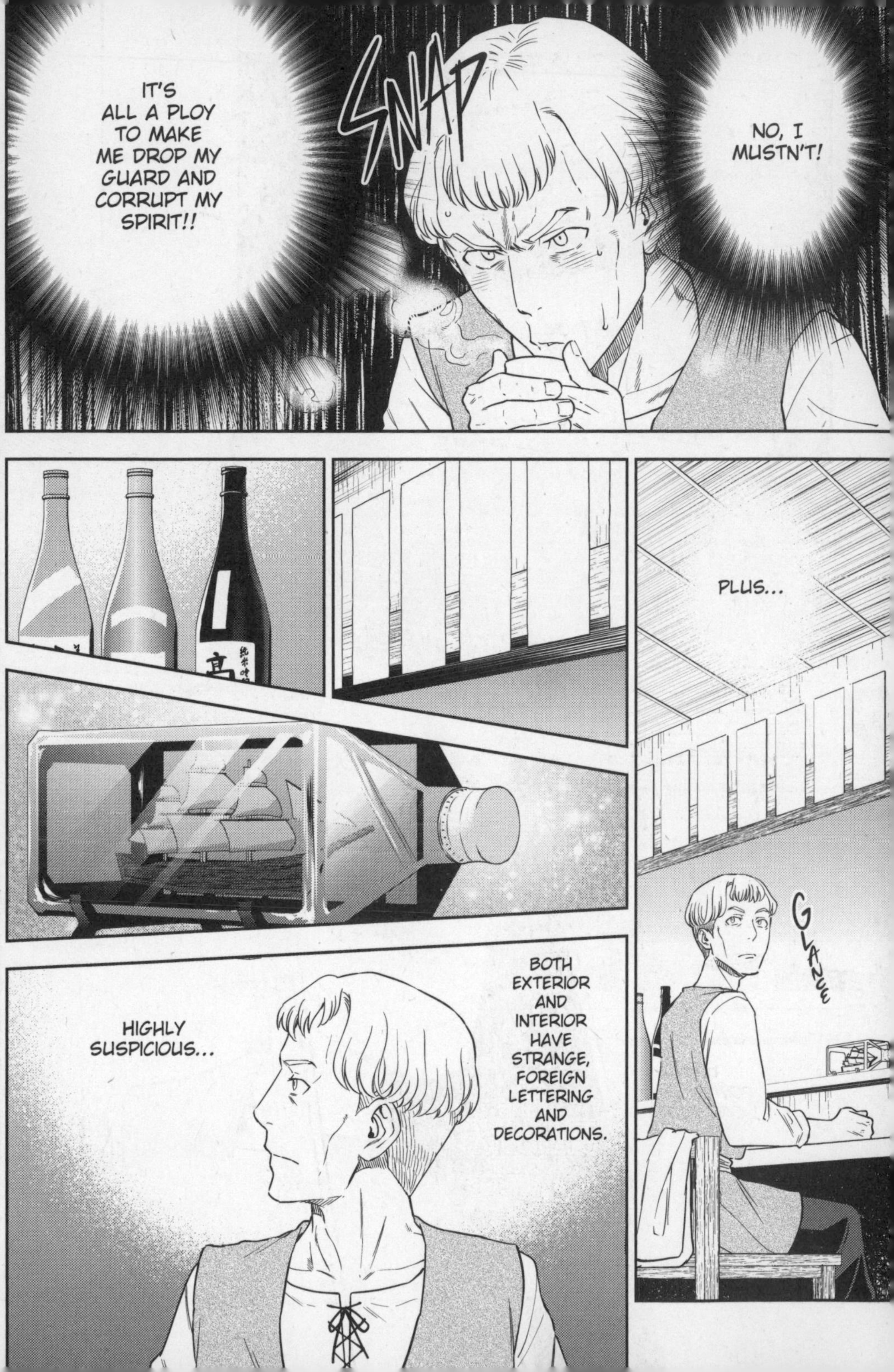
NO, I MUSTN'T!
SNAP
IT'S ALL A PLOY TO MAKE ME DROP MY GUARD AND CORRUPT MY SPIRIT!!
PLUS...
GLANCE
BOTH EXTERIOR AND INTERIOR HAVE STRANGE, FOREIGN LETTERING AND DECORATIONS.
HIGHLY SUSPICIOUS...

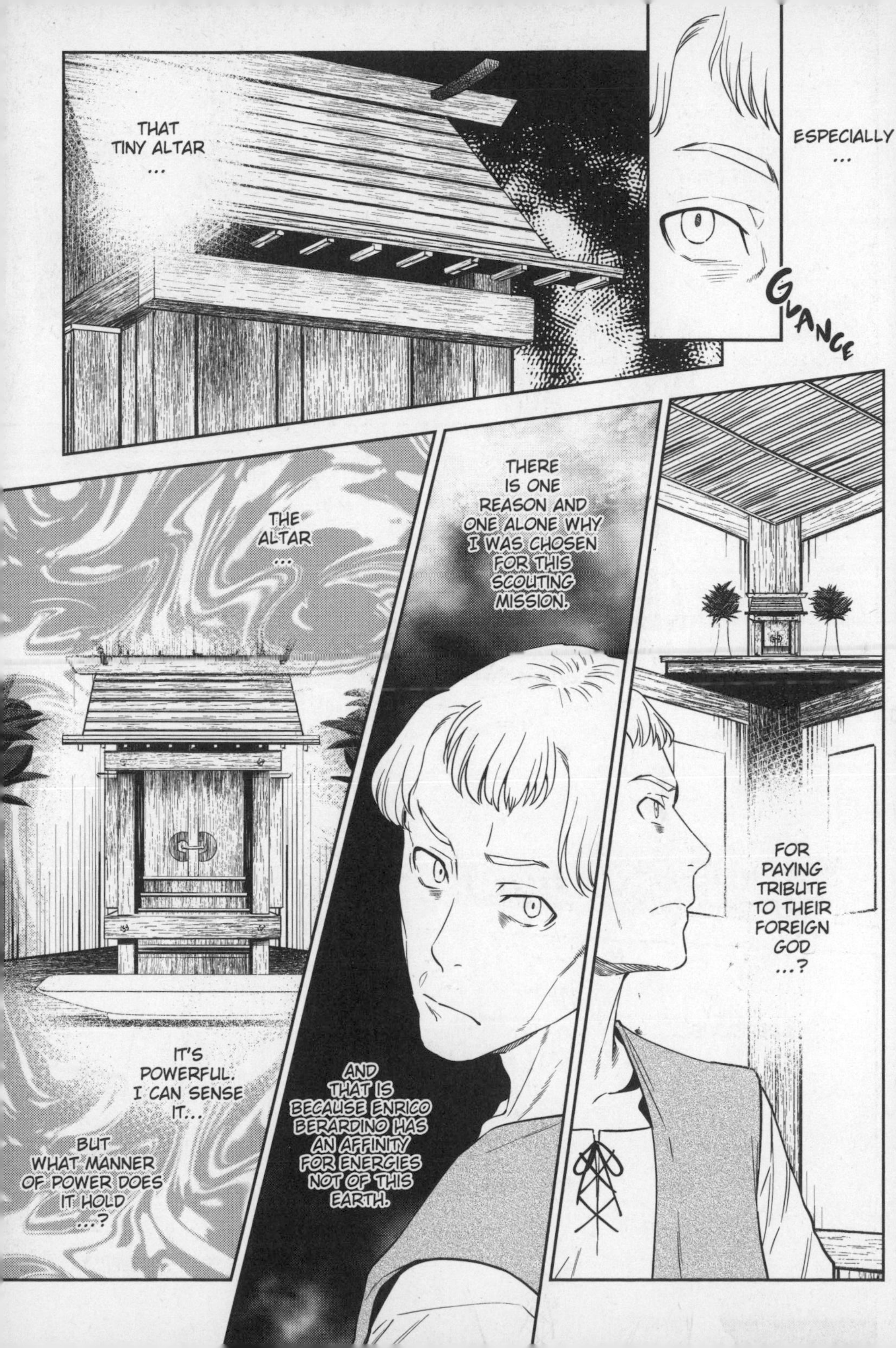

ESPECIALLY ...
GLANCE
THAT TINY ALTAR ...
FOR PAYING TRIBUTE TO THEIR FOREIGN GOD ...?
THERE IS ONE REASON AND ONE ALONE WHY I WAS CHOSEN FOR THIS SCOUTING MISSION.
AND THAT IS BECAUSE ENRICO BERARDINO HAS AN AFFINITY FOR ENERGIES NOT OF THIS EARTH.
THE ALTAR ...
IT'S POWERFUL. I CAN SENSE IT...
BUT WHAT MANNER OF POWER DOES IT HOLD ...?

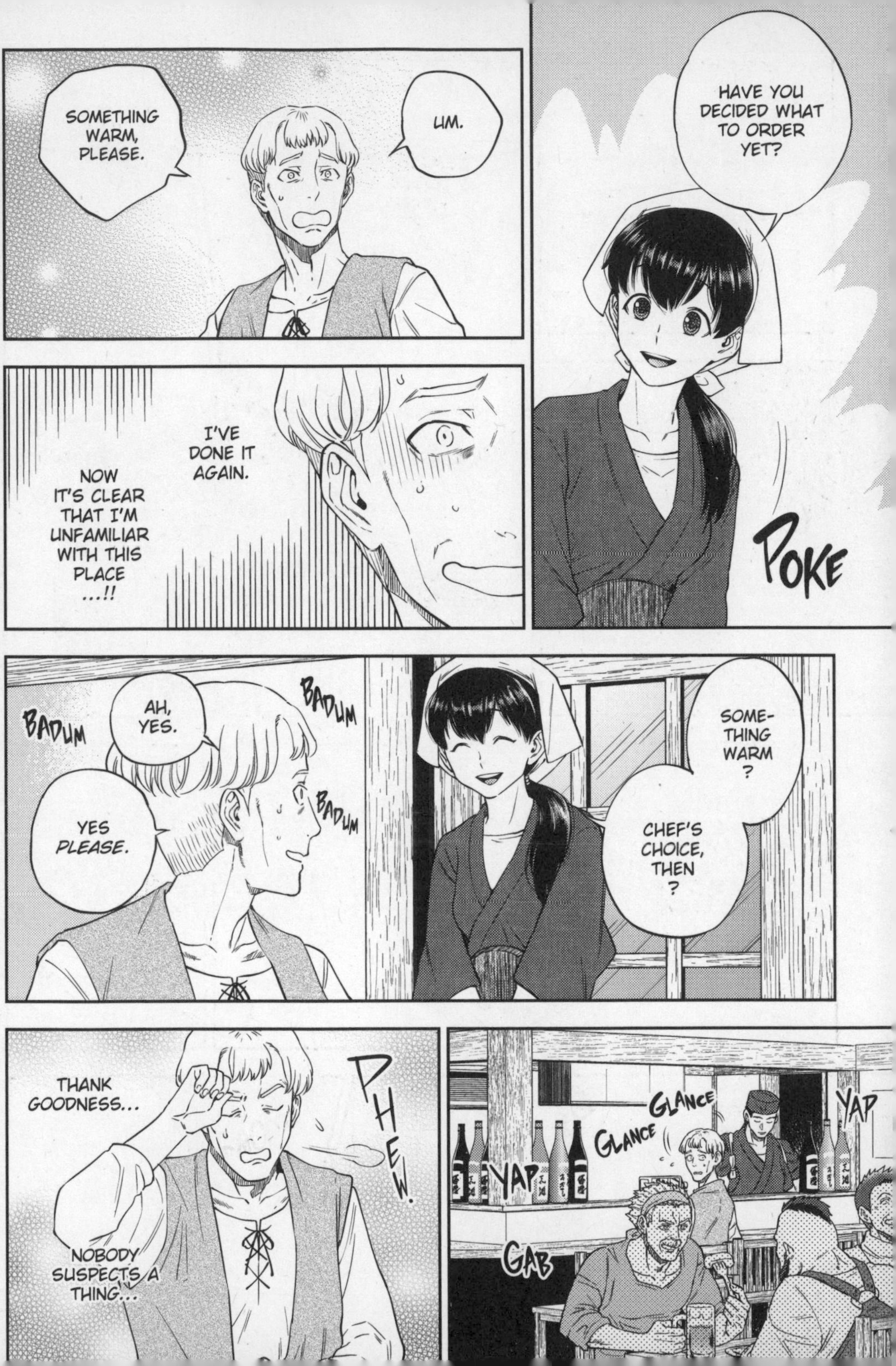
HAVE YOU DECIDED WHAT TO ORDER YET?
POKE
UM.
SOMETHING WARM, PLEASE.
I'VE DONE IT AGAIN.
NOW IT'S CLEAR THAT I'M UNFAMILIAR WITH THIS PLACE ...!!
SOME-THING WARM?
CHEF'S CHOICE, THEN?
BADUM
BADUM
BADUM
AH, YES.
YES PLEASE.
YAP
GLANCE
GLANCE
YAP
GAB
PHEW.
THANK GOODNESS...
NOBODY SUSPECTS A THING...

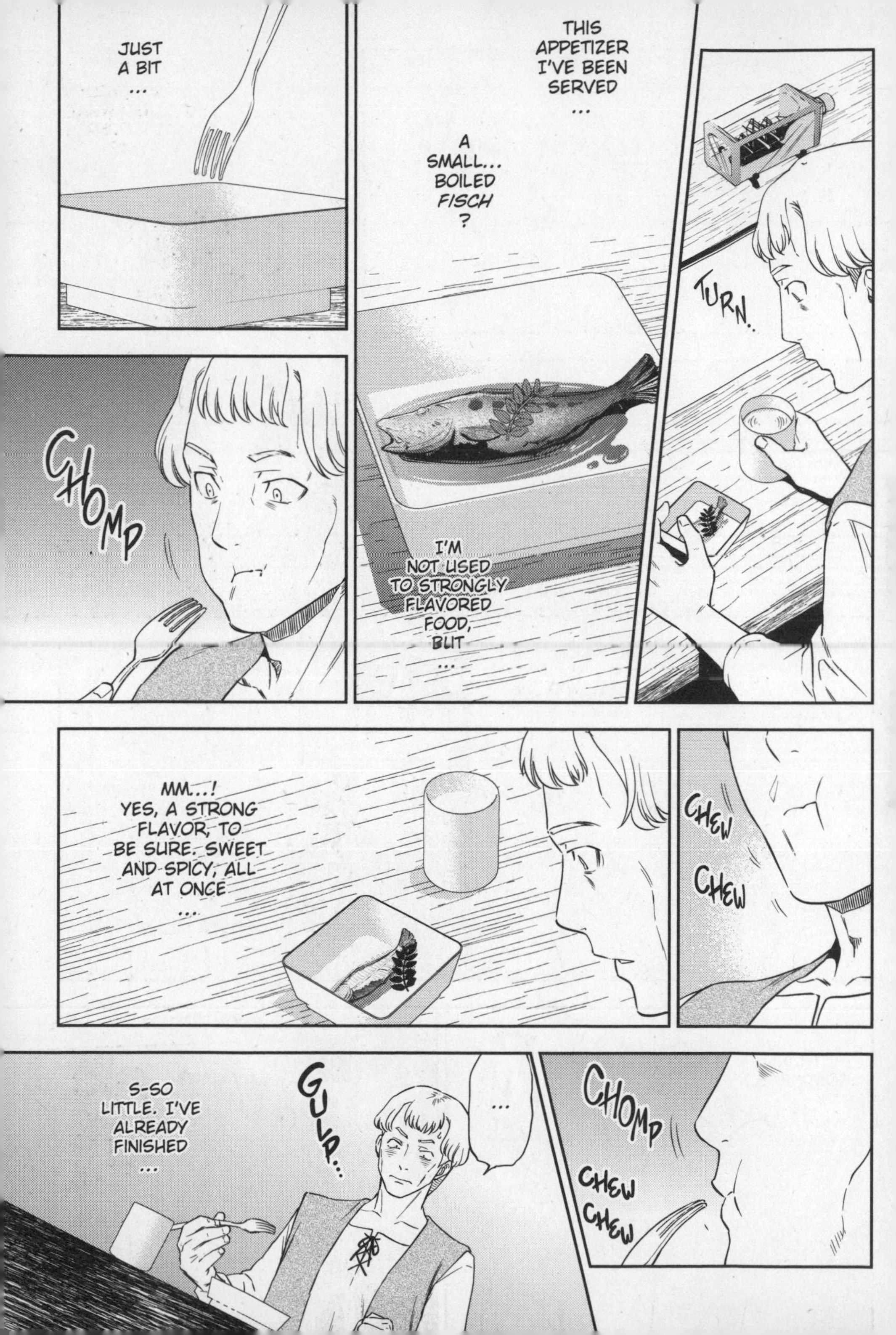
TURN..
THIS APPETIZER I'VE BEEN SERVED ...
A SMALL... BOILED *FISCH* ?
I'M NOT USED TO STRONGLY FLAVORED FOOD, BUT ...
JUST A BIT ...
CHOMP
CHEW
CHEW
MM...! YES, A STRONG FLAVOR, TO BE SURE. SWEET AND SPICY, ALL AT ONCE ...
CHOMP
CHEW
CHEW
...
GULP...
S-SO LITTLE. I'VE ALREADY FINISHED ...

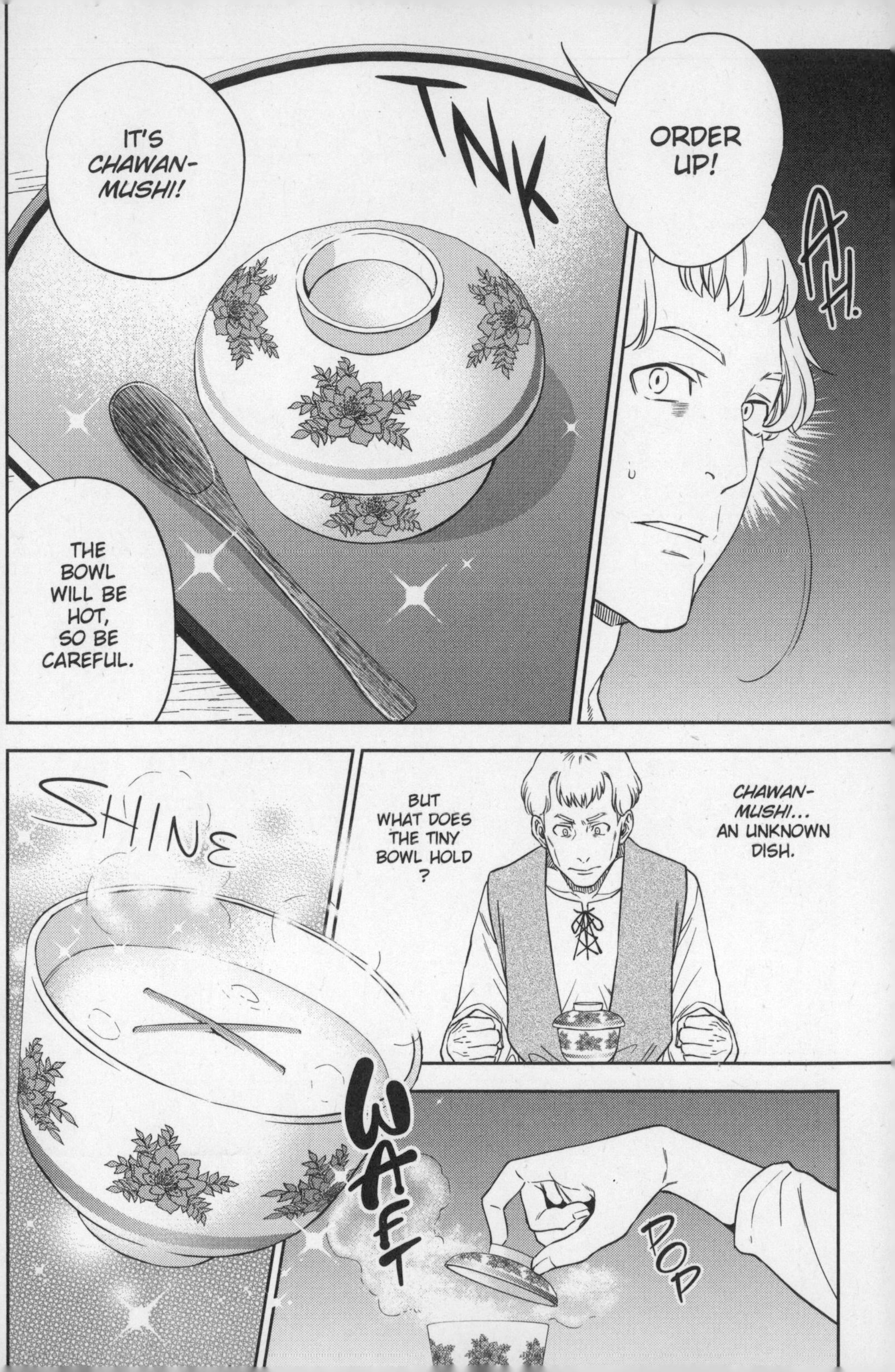
ORDER UP!
AH.
TNK
IT'S CHAWAN-MUSHI!
THE BOWL WILL BE HOT, SO BE CAREFUL.
CHAWAN-MUSHI... AN UNKNOWN DISH.
BUT WHAT DOES THE TINY BOWL HOLD ?
POP
WAFT
SHINE

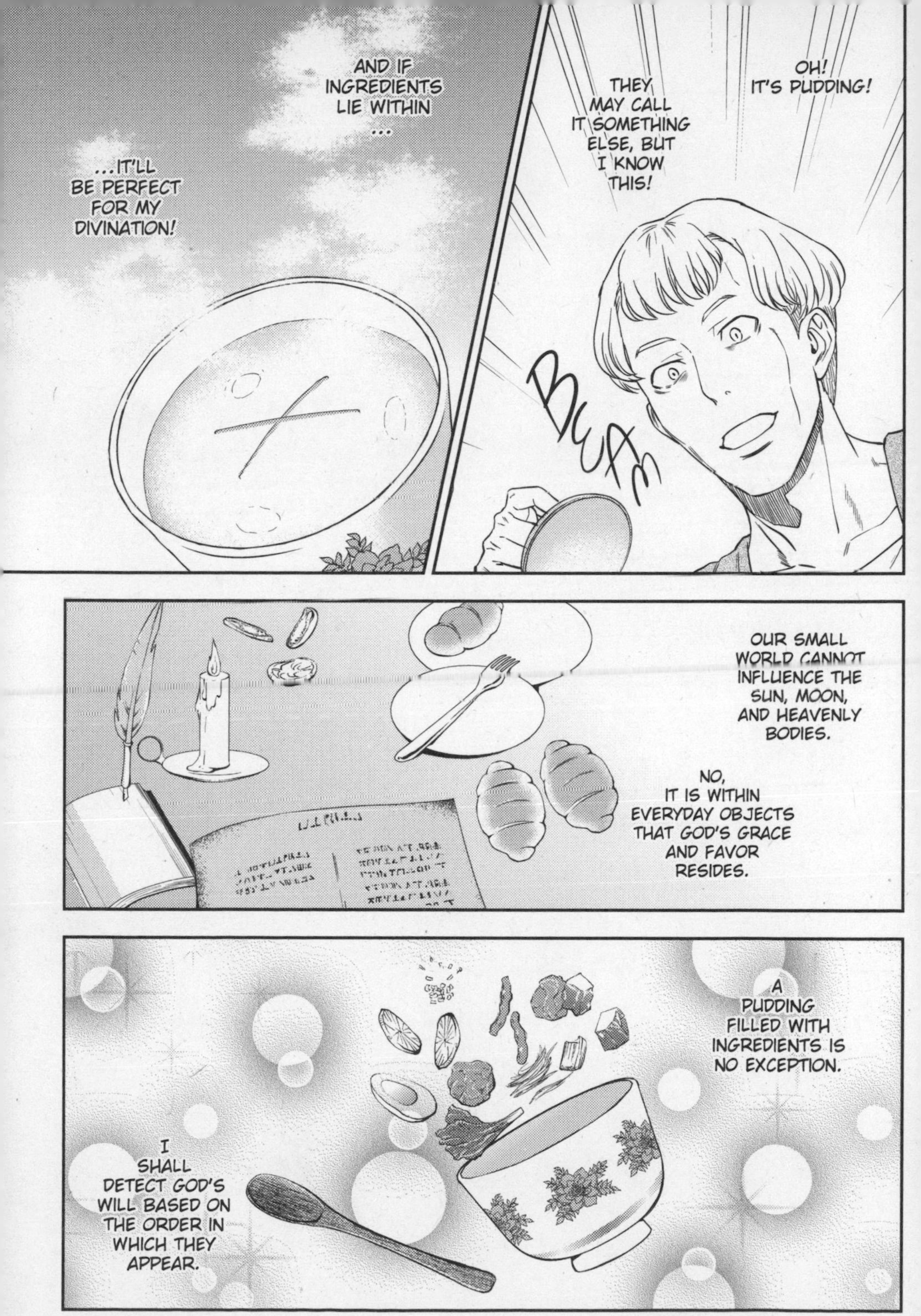
OH! IT'S PUDDING!
THEY MAY CALL IT SOMETHING ELSE, BUT I KNOW THIS!
BWAH
AND IF INGREDIENTS LIE WITHIN ...
...IT'LL BE PERFECT FOR MY DIVINATION!
OUR SMALL WORLD CANNOT INFLUENCE THE SUN, MOON, AND HEAVENLY BODIES.
NO, IT IS WITHIN EVERYDAY OBJECTS THAT GOD'S GRACE AND FAVOR RESIDES.
A PUDDING FILLED WITH INGREDIENTS IS NO EXCEPTION.
I SHALL DETECT GOD'S WILL BASED ON THE ORDER IN WHICH THEY APPEAR.

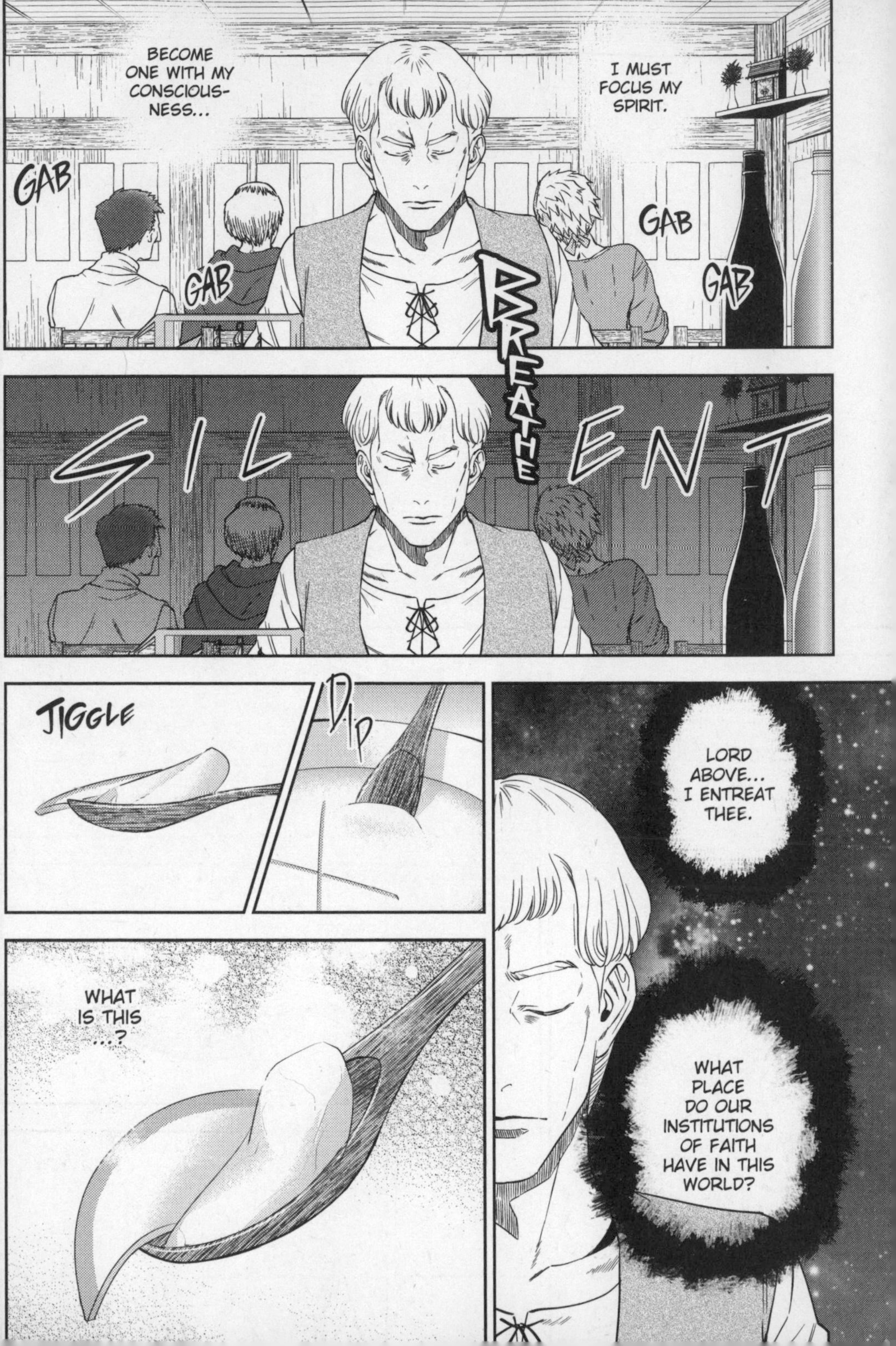
I MUST FOCUS MY SPIRIT.
BECOME ONE WITH MY CONSCIOUS-NESS...
GAB
GAB
GAB
GAB
BREATHE
SILENT
LORD ABOVE... I ENTREAT THEE.
WHAT PLACE DO OUR INSTITUTIONS OF FAITH HAVE IN THIS WORLD?
DIP
JIGGLE
WHAT IS THIS ...?

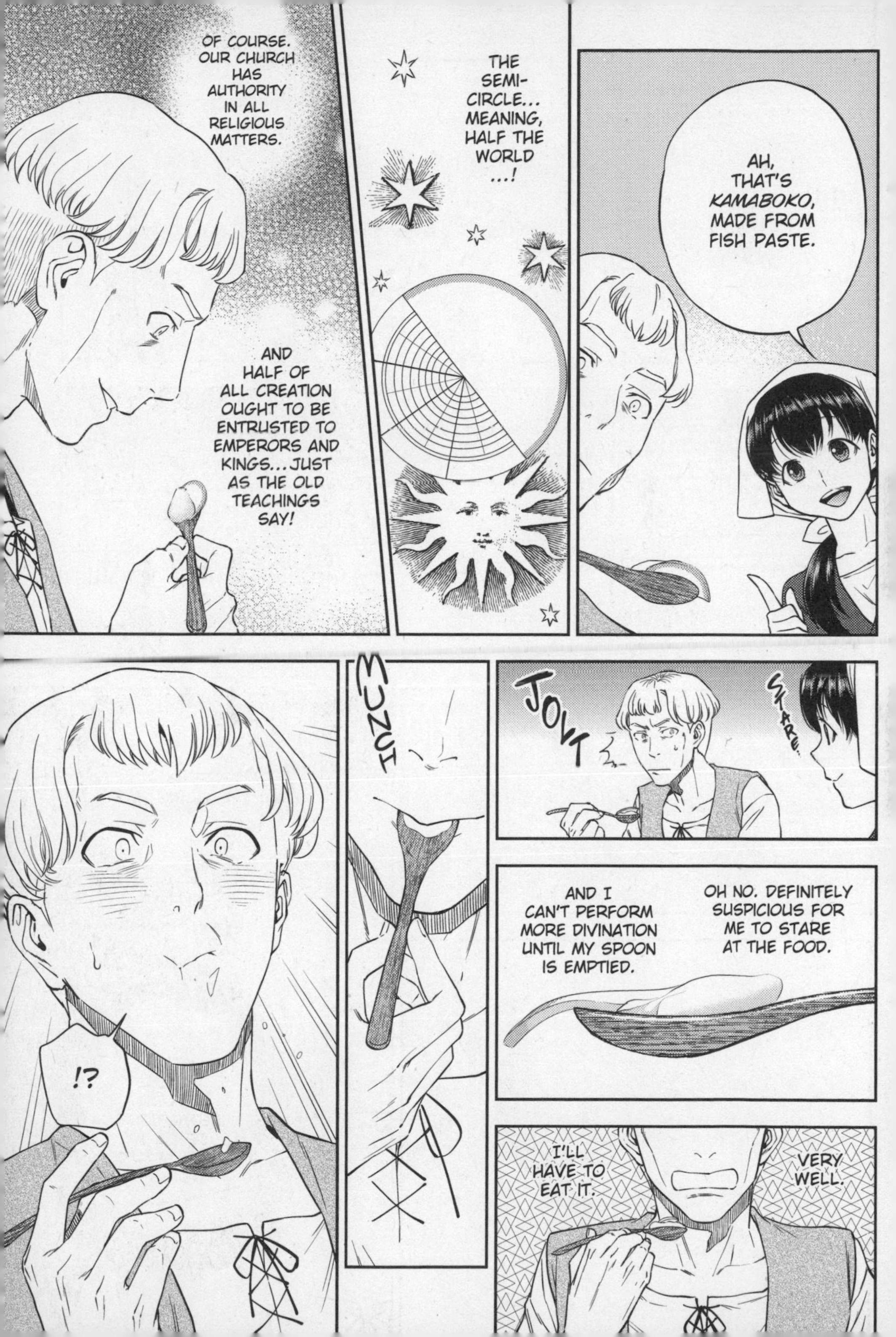

AH, THAT'S *KAMABOKO*, MADE FROM FISH PASTE.
THE SEMI-CIRCLE... MEANING, HALF THE WORLD...!
OF COURSE. OUR CHURCH HAS AUTHORITY IN ALL RELIGIOUS MATTERS.
AND HALF OF ALL CREATION OUGHT TO BE ENTRUSTED TO EMPERORS AND KINGS... JUST AS THE OLD TEACHINGS SAY!
STARE
JOLT
OH NO. DEFINITELY SUSPICIOUS FOR ME TO STARE AT THE FOOD.
AND I CAN'T PERFORM MORE DIVINATION UNTIL MY SPOON IS EMPTIED.
VERY WELL.
I'LL HAVE TO EAT IT.
MUNCH
!?

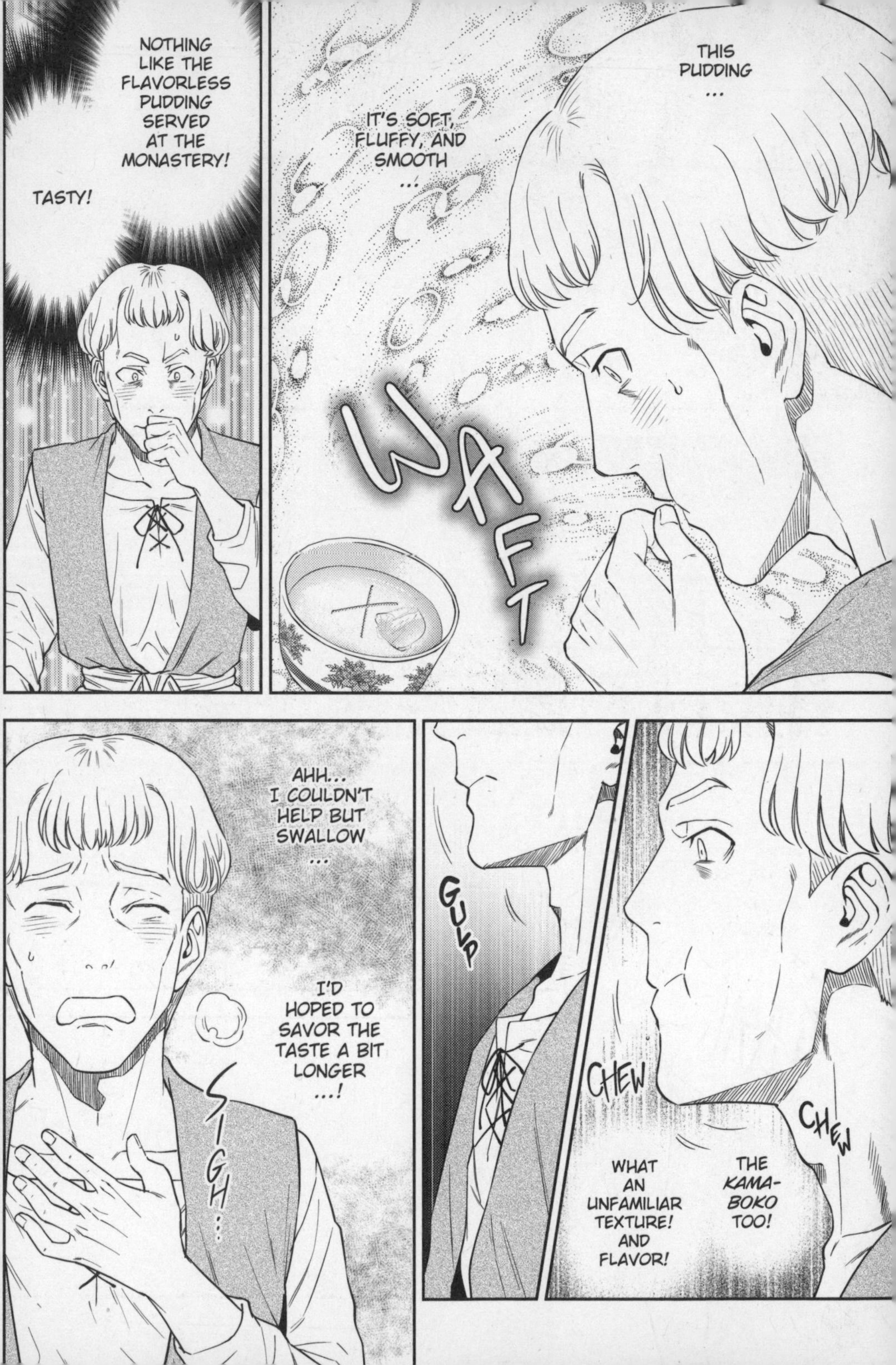
THIS PUDDING ...
IT'S SOFT, FLUFFY, AND SMOOTH ...
WAFT
NOTHING LIKE THE FLAVORLESS PUDDING SERVED AT THE MONASTERY!
TASTY!
CHEW
THE KAMA-BOKO TOO!
CHEW
WHAT AN UNFAMILIAR TEXTURE! AND FLAVOR!
GULP
AHH... I COULDN'T HELP BUT SWALLOW ...
I'D HOPED TO SAVOR THE TASTE A BIT LONGER ...!
SIGH...

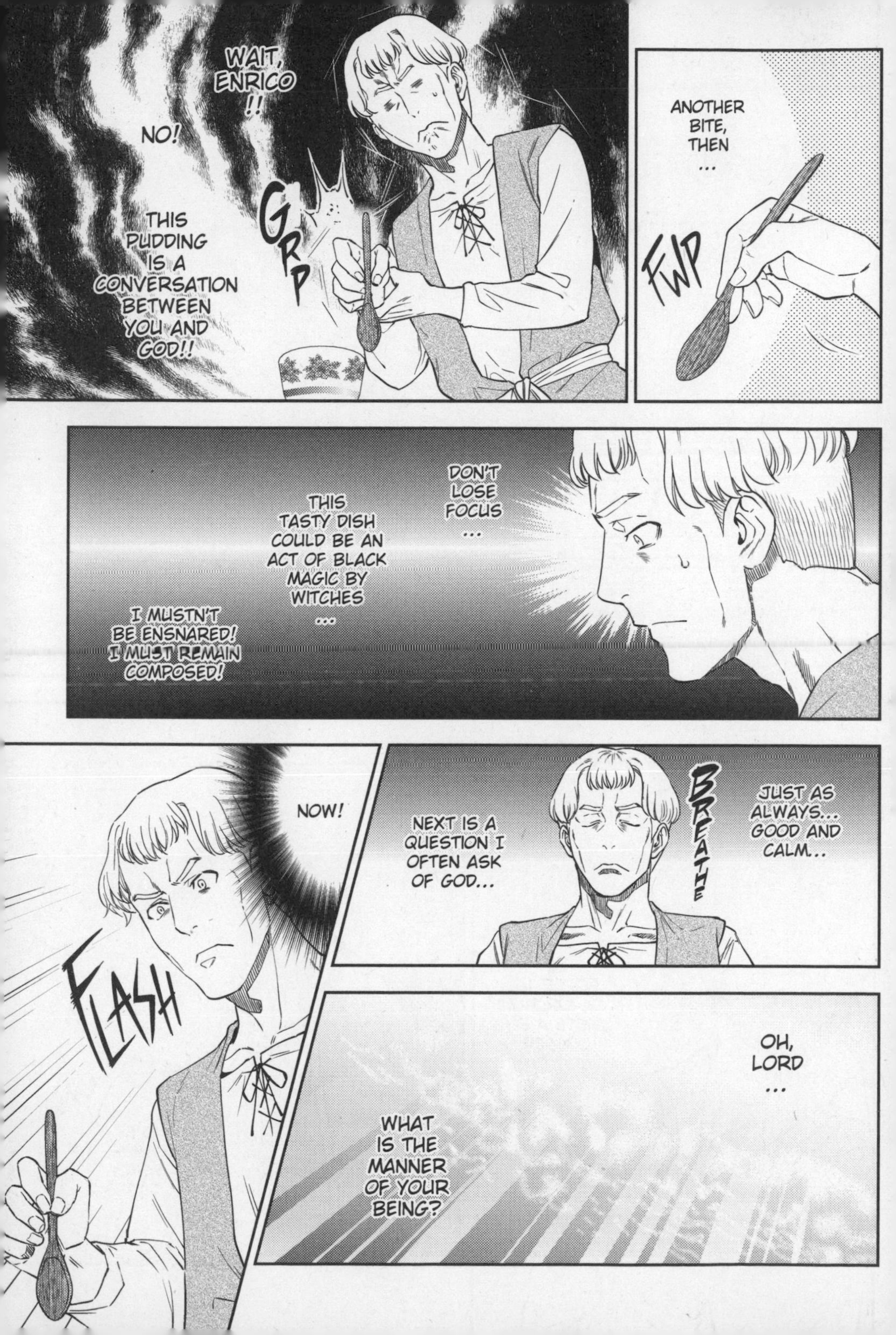
ANOTHER BITE, THEN ...
FWP
WAIT, ENRICO!!
GRP
NO!
THIS PUDDING IS A CONVERSATION BETWEEN YOU AND GOD!!
DON'T LOSE FOCUS ...
THIS TASTY DISH COULD BE AN ACT OF BLACK MAGIC BY WITCHES ...
I MUSTN'T BE ENSNARED! I MUST REMAIN COMPOSED!
JUST AS ALWAYS... GOOD AND CALM...
BREATHE
NEXT IS A QUESTION I OFTEN ASK OF GOD...
OH, LORD ...
WHAT IS THE MANNER OF YOUR BEING?
NOW!
FLASH

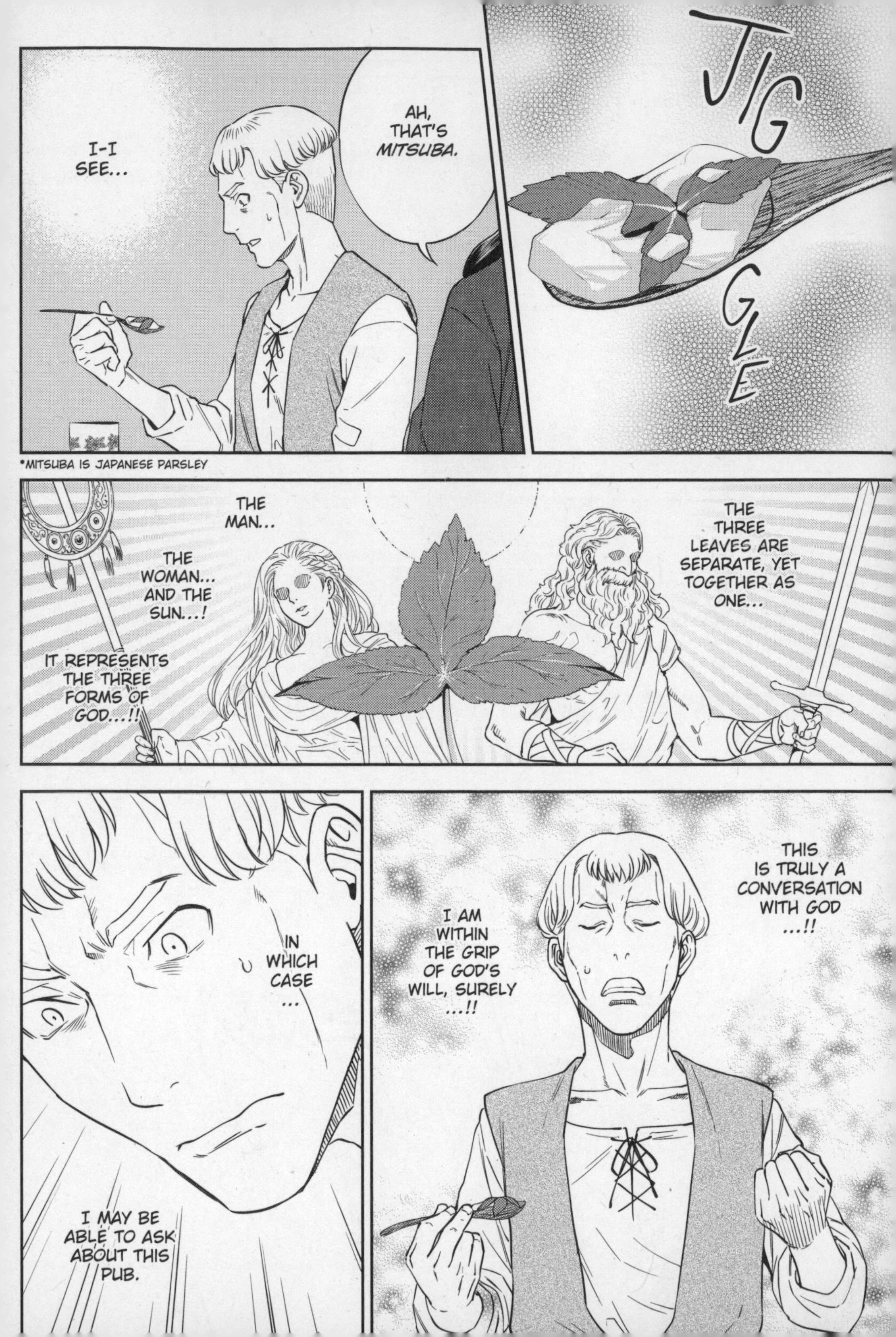
JIGGLE
AH, THAT'S *MITSUBA.*
I-I SEE...
THE THREE LEAVES ARE SEPARATE, YET TOGETHER AS ONE...
THE MAN...
THE WOMAN... AND THE SUN...!
IT REPRESENTS THE THREE FORMS OF GOD...!!
THIS IS TRULY A CONVERSATION WITH GOD ...!!
I AM WITHIN THE GRIP OF GOD'S WILL, SURELY ...!!
IN WHICH CASE ...
I MAY BE ABLE TO ASK ABOUT THIS PUB.

*MITSUBA IS JAPANESE PARSLEY

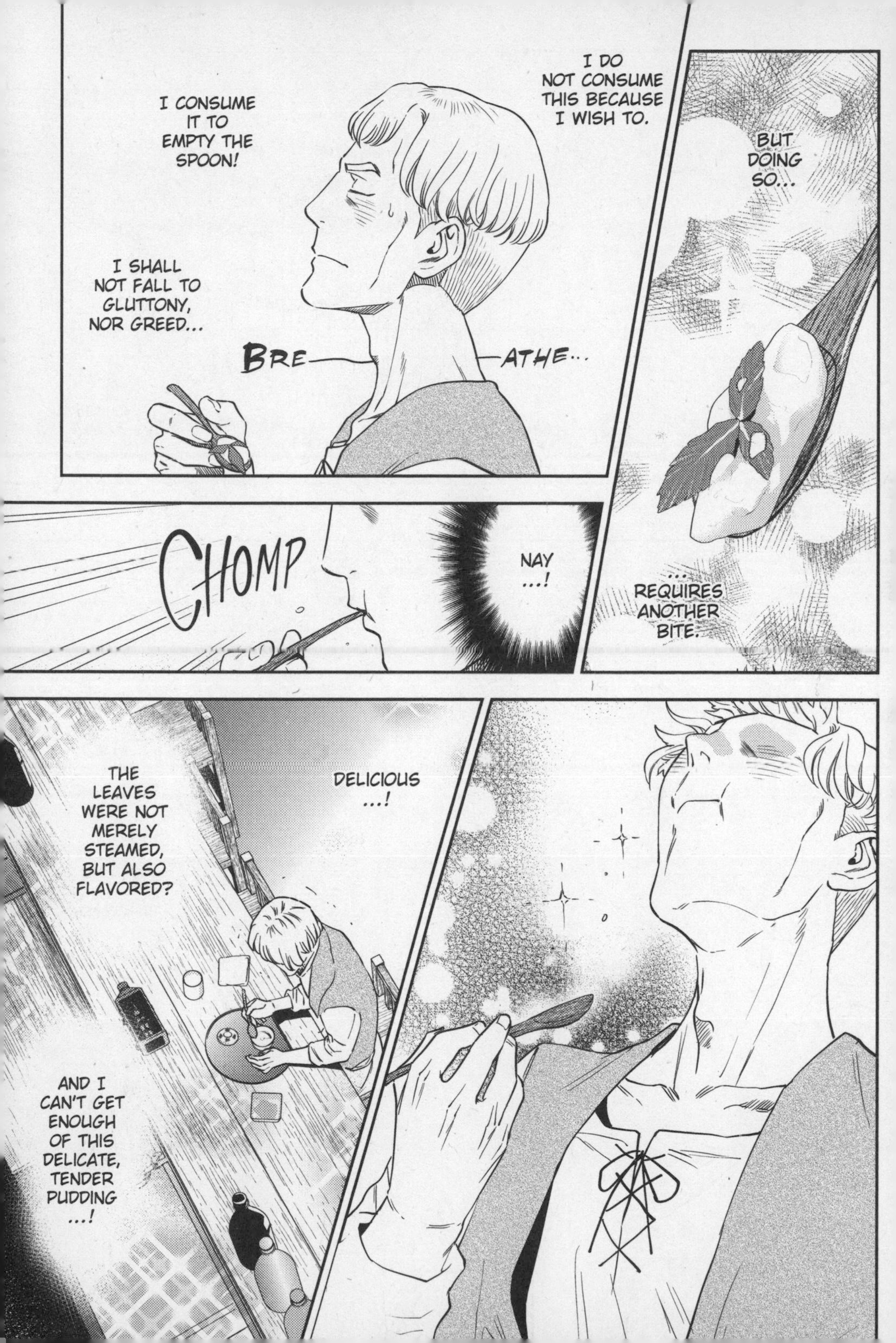

I DO NOT CONSUME THIS BECAUSE I WISH TO.
I CONSUME IT TO EMPTY THE SPOON!
I SHALL NOT FALL TO GLUTTONY, NOR GREED...
BRE— —ATHE...
BUT DOING SO...
...REQUIRES ANOTHER BITE.
NAY ...!
CHOMP
DELICIOUS ...!
THE LEAVES WERE NOT MERELY STEAMED, BUT ALSO FLAVORED?
AND I CAN'T GET ENOUGH OF THIS DELICATE, TENDER PUDDING ...!

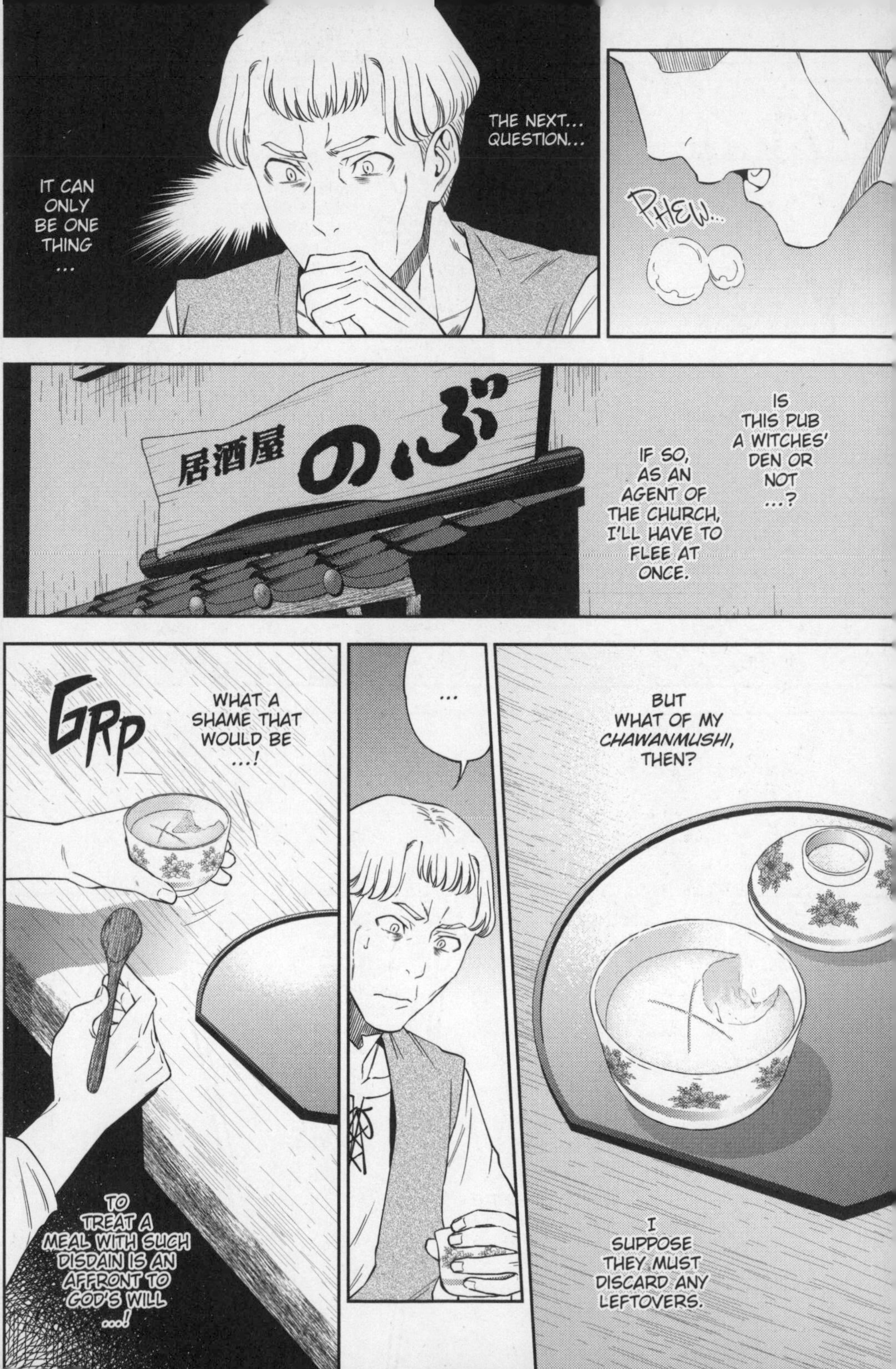
PHEW...
THE NEXT... QUESTION...
IT CAN ONLY BE ONE THING ...
居酒屋 のぶ
IS THIS PUB A WITCHES' DEN OR NOT ...?
IF SO, AS AN AGENT OF THE CHURCH, I'LL HAVE TO FLEE AT ONCE.
BUT WHAT OF MY *CHAWANMUSHI*, THEN?
I SUPPOSE THEY MUST DISCARD ANY LEFTOVERS.
...
GRP
WHAT A SHAME THAT WOULD BE ...!
TO TREAT A MEAL WITH SUCH DISDAIN IS AN AFFRONT TO GOD'S WILL ...!

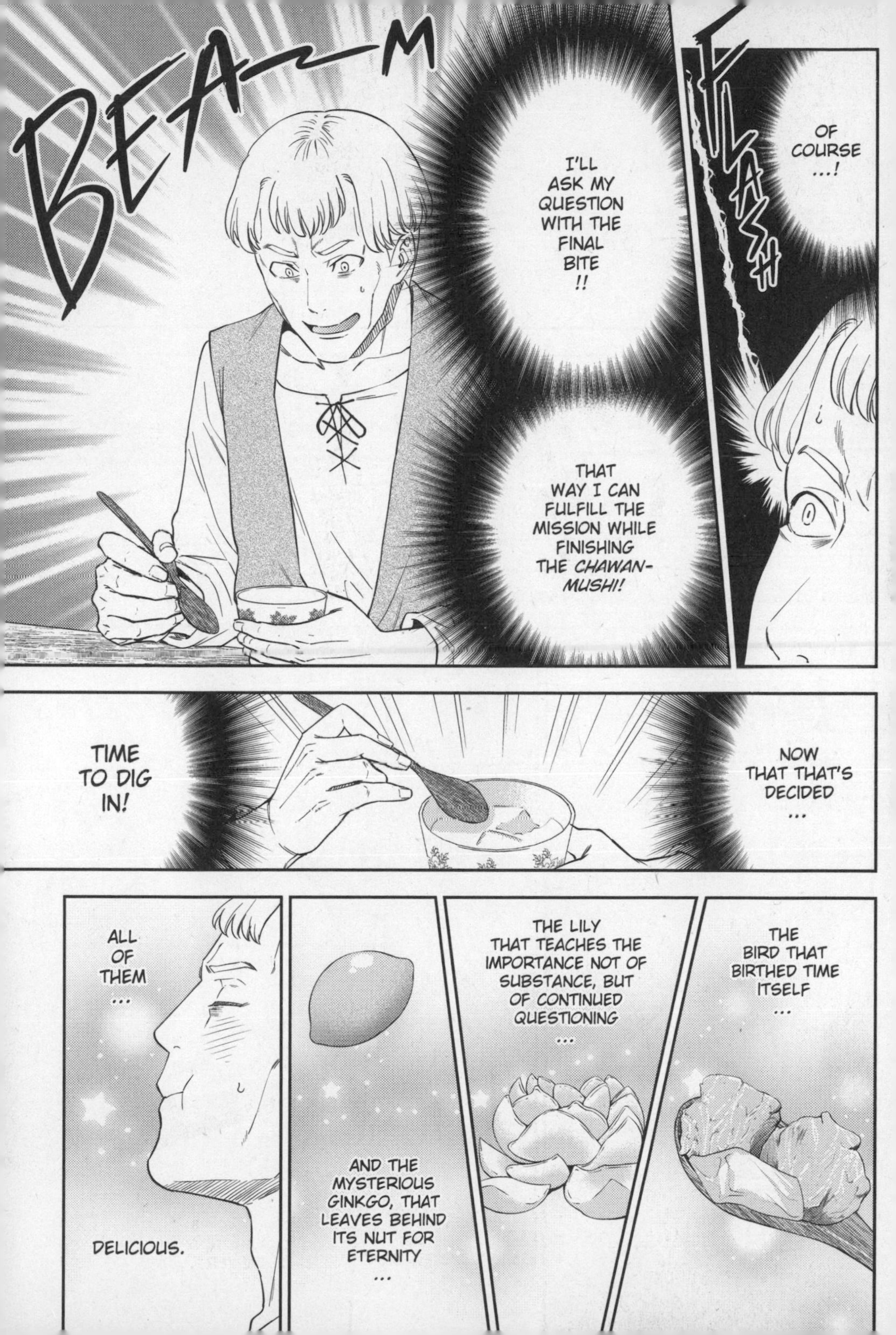
FLASH
OF COURSE ...!
BEA~M
I'LL ASK MY QUESTION WITH THE FINAL BITE !!
THAT WAY I CAN FULFILL THE MISSION WHILE FINISHING THE *CHAWAN-MUSHI!*
NOW THAT THAT'S DECIDED ...
TIME TO DIG IN!
THE BIRD THAT BIRTHED TIME ITSELF ...
THE LILY THAT TEACHES THE IMPORTANCE NOT OF SUBSTANCE, BUT OF CONTINUED QUESTIONING ...
AND THE MYSTERIOUS GINKGO, THAT LEAVES BEHIND ITS NUT FOR ETERNITY ...
ALL OF THEM ...
DELICIOUS.

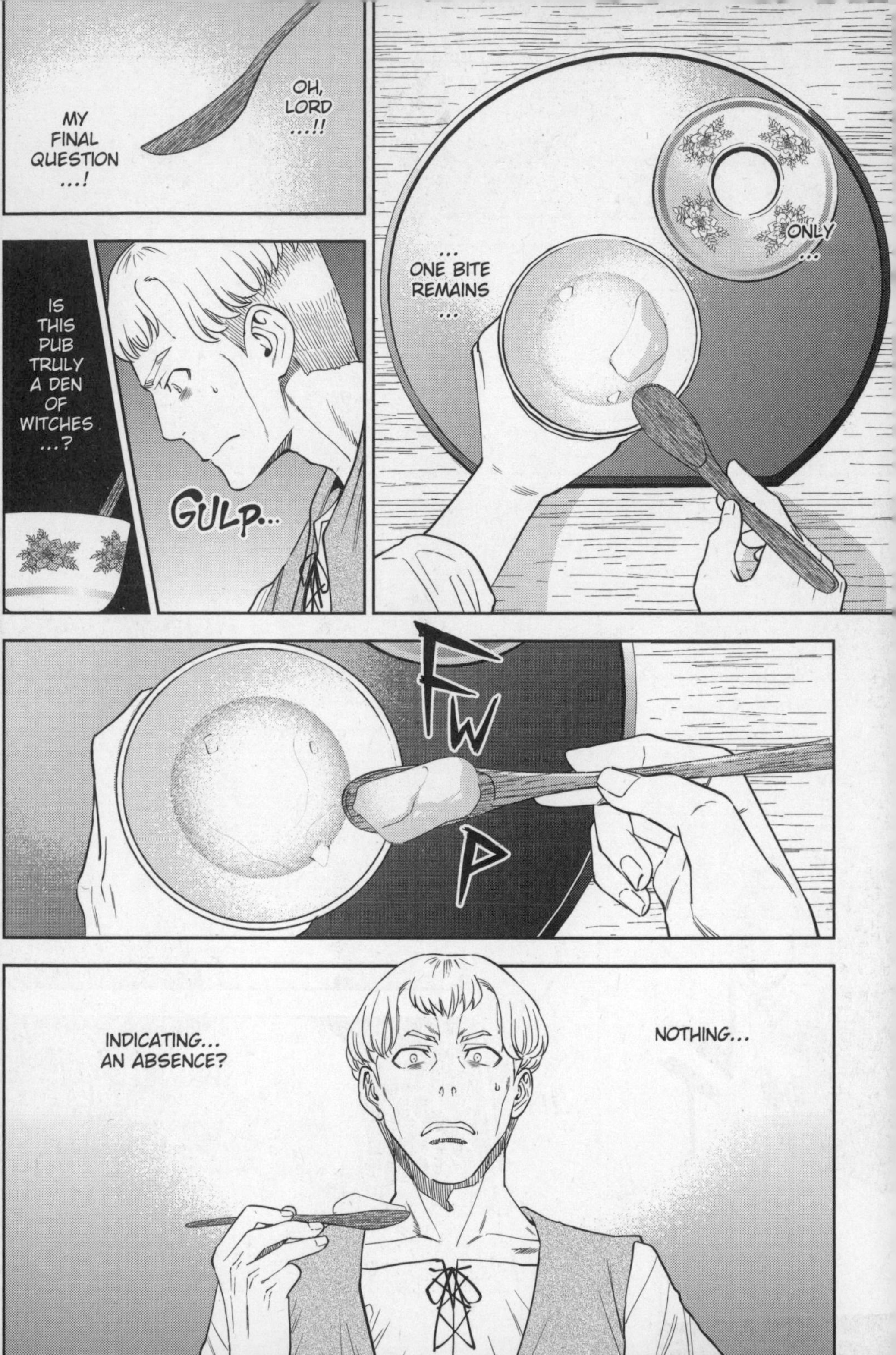
ONLY...
...ONE BITE REMAINS...
OH, LORD...!!
MY FINAL QUESTION...!
IS THIS PUB TRULY A DEN OF WITCHES...?
GULP...
FWP
NOTHING...
INDICATING... AN ABSENCE?

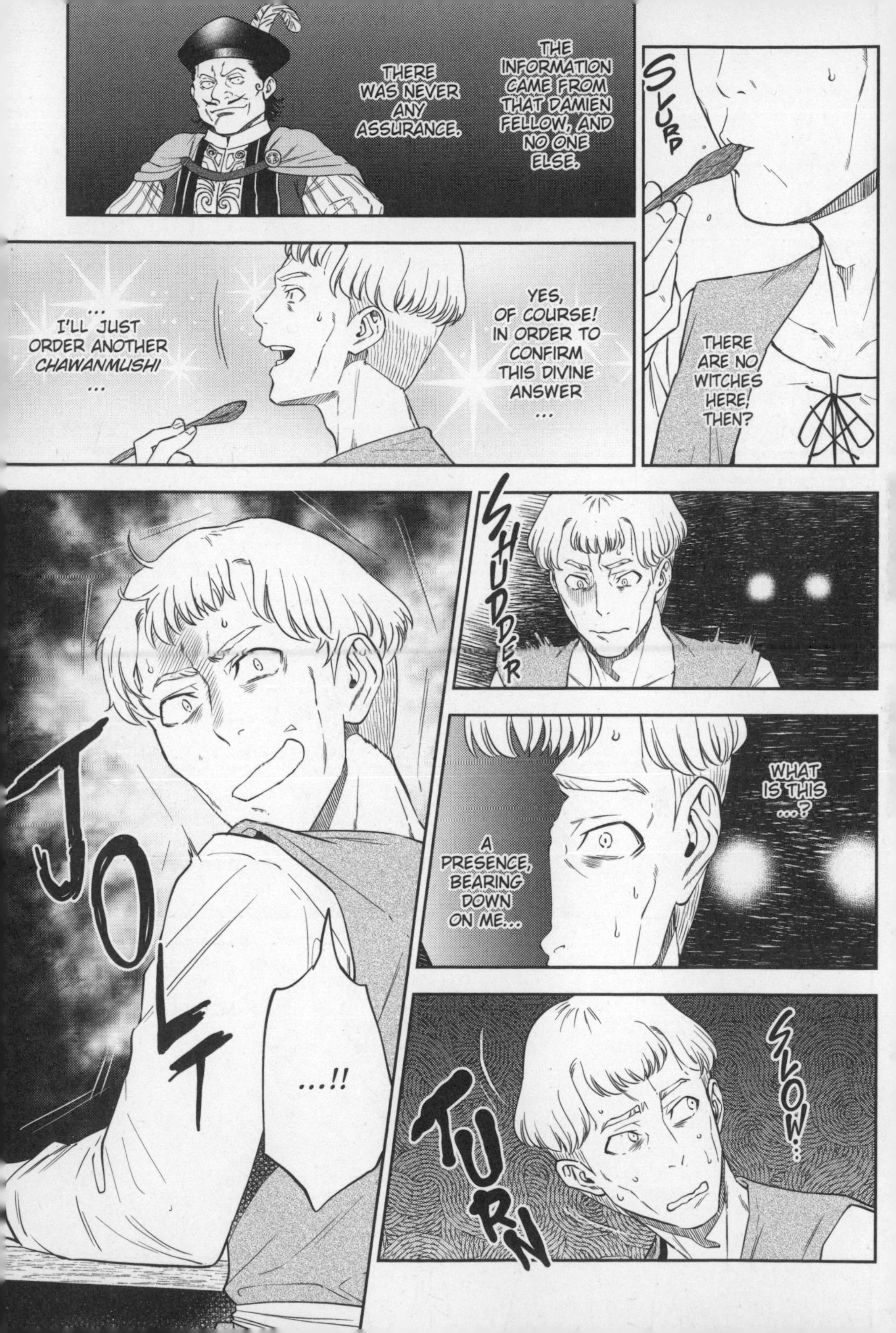
SLURP
THERE ARE NO WITCHES HERE, THEN?
THE INFORMATION CAME FROM THAT DAMIEN FELLOW, AND NO ONE ELSE.
THERE WAS NEVER ANY ASSURANCE.
YES, OF COURSE! IN ORDER TO CONFIRM THIS DIVINE ANSWER ...
... I'LL JUST ORDER ANOTHER CHAWANMUSHI ...
SHUDDER
WHAT IS THIS ...?
A PRESENCE, BEARING DOWN ON ME...
SLOW...
TURN
JOLT
...!!

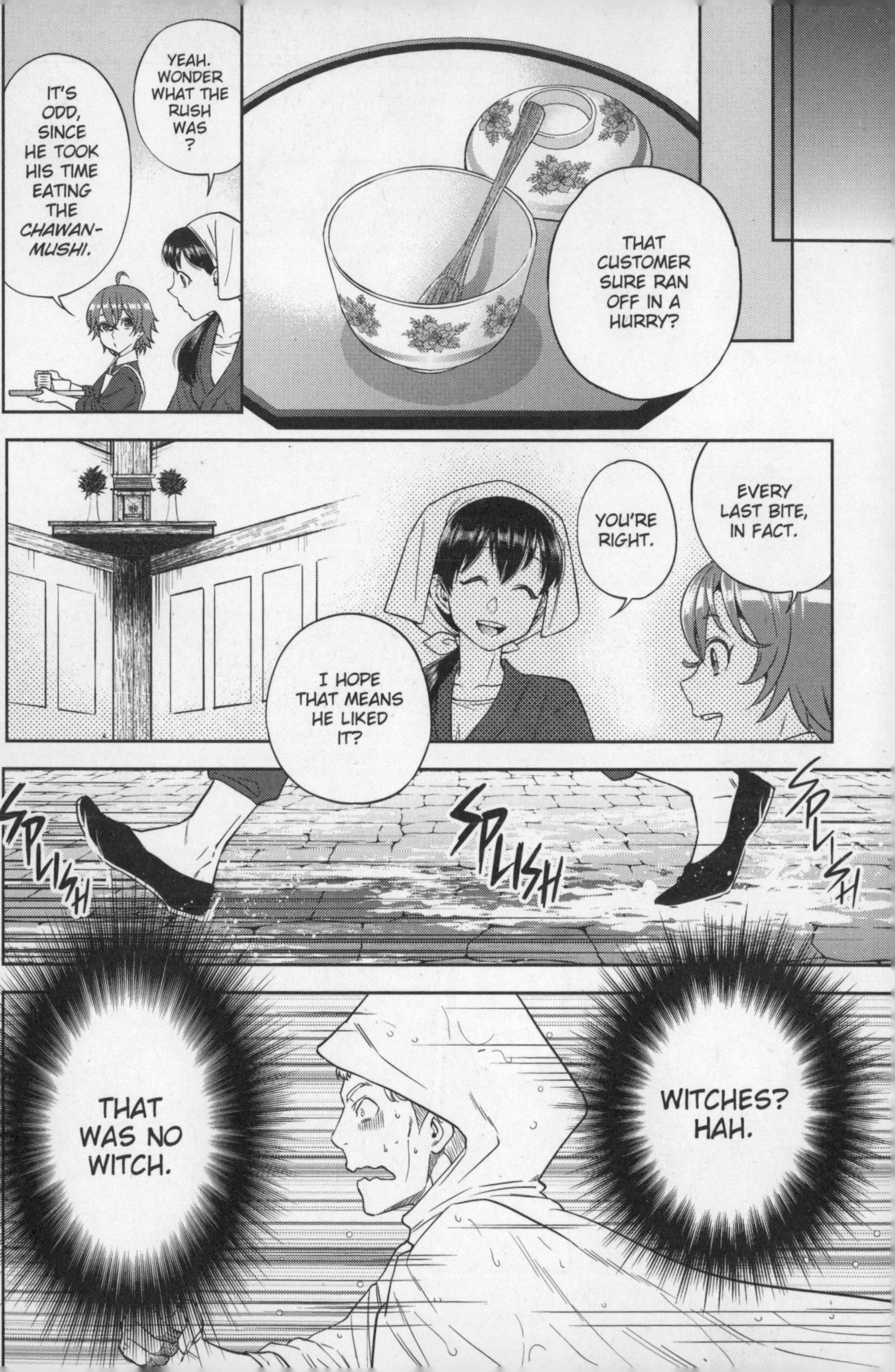
THAT CUSTOMER SURE RAN OFF IN A HURRY?
YEAH. WONDER WHAT THE RUSH WAS?
IT'S ODD, SINCE HE TOOK HIS TIME EATING THE CHAWAN-MUSHI.
EVERY LAST BITE, IN FACT.
YOU'RE RIGHT.
I HOPE THAT MEANS HE LIKED IT?
SPLISH
SPLISH
SPLISH
WITCHES? HAH.
THAT WAS NO WITCH.

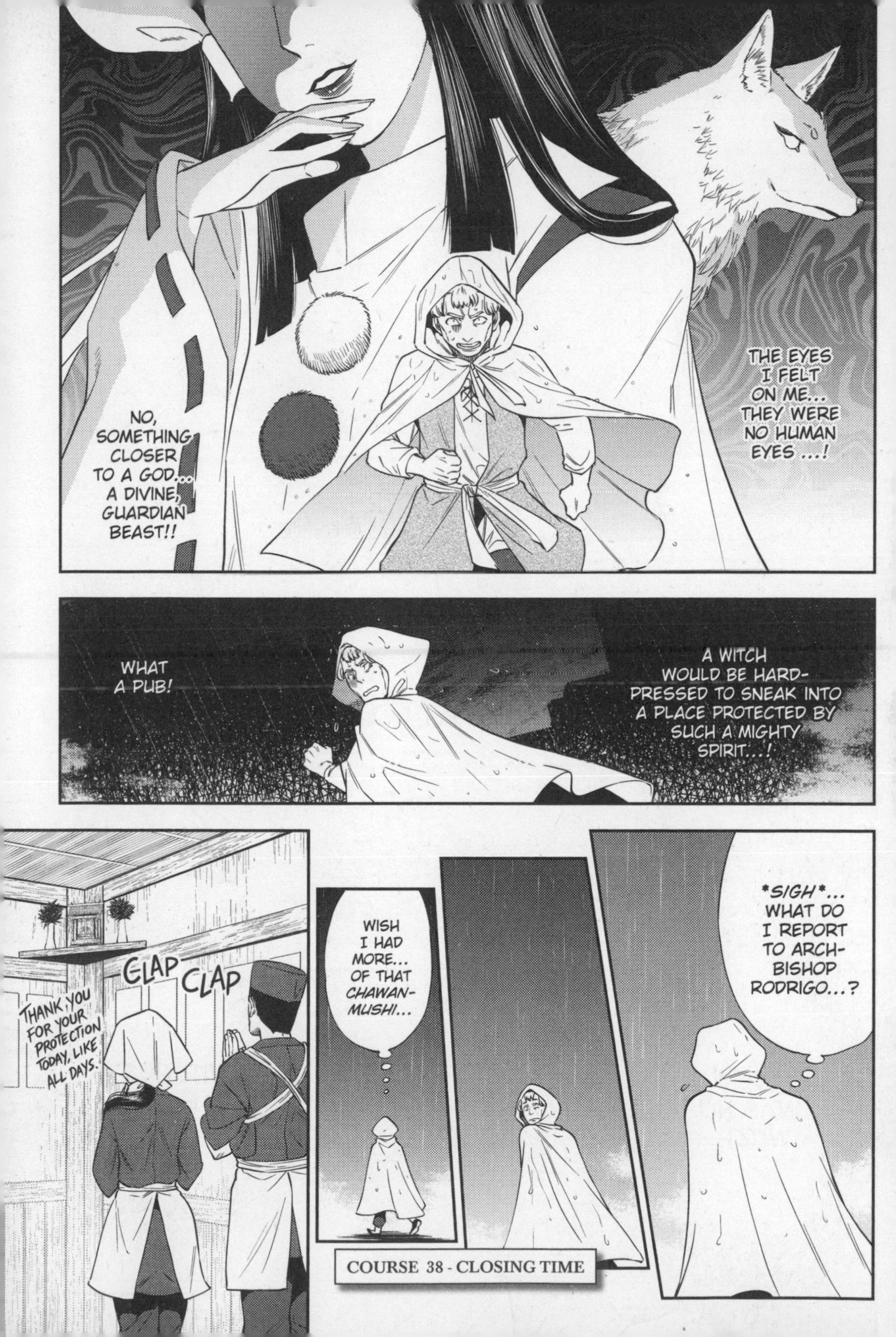
THE EYES I FELT ON ME... THEY WERE NO HUMAN EYES ...!
NO, SOMETHING CLOSER TO A GOD... A DIVINE, GUARDIAN BEAST!!
A WITCH WOULD BE HARD-PRESSED TO SNEAK INTO A PLACE PROTECTED BY SUCH A MIGHTY SPIRIT...!
WHAT A PUB!
SIGH... WHAT DO I REPORT TO ARCH-BISHOP RODRIGO...?
WISH I HAD MORE... OF THAT CHAWAN-MUSHI...
COURSE 38 - CLOSING TIME
CLAP CLAP
THANK YOU FOR YOUR PROTECTION TODAY, LIKE ALL DAYS.

Chawanmushi

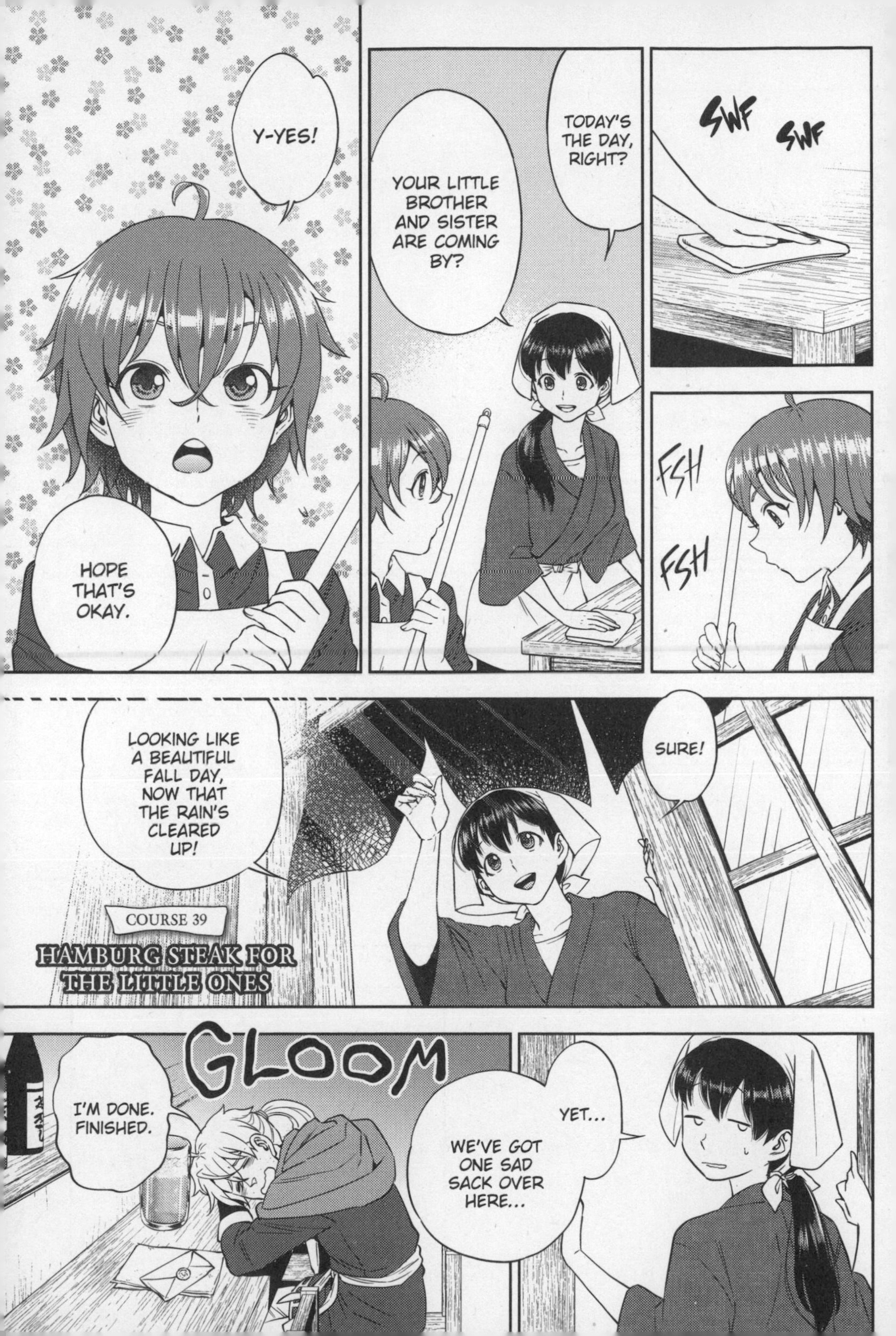
SWF
SWF
FSH
FSH
TODAY'S THE DAY, RIGHT?
YOUR LITTLE BROTHER AND SISTER ARE COMING BY?
Y-YES!
HOPE THAT'S OKAY.
LOOKING LIKE A BEAUTIFUL FALL DAY, NOW THAT THE RAIN'S CLEARED UP!
SURE!
COURSE 39
HAMBURG STEAK FOR THE LITTLE ONES
YET...
WE'VE GOT ONE SAD SACK OVER HERE...
GLOOM
I'M DONE. FINISHED.

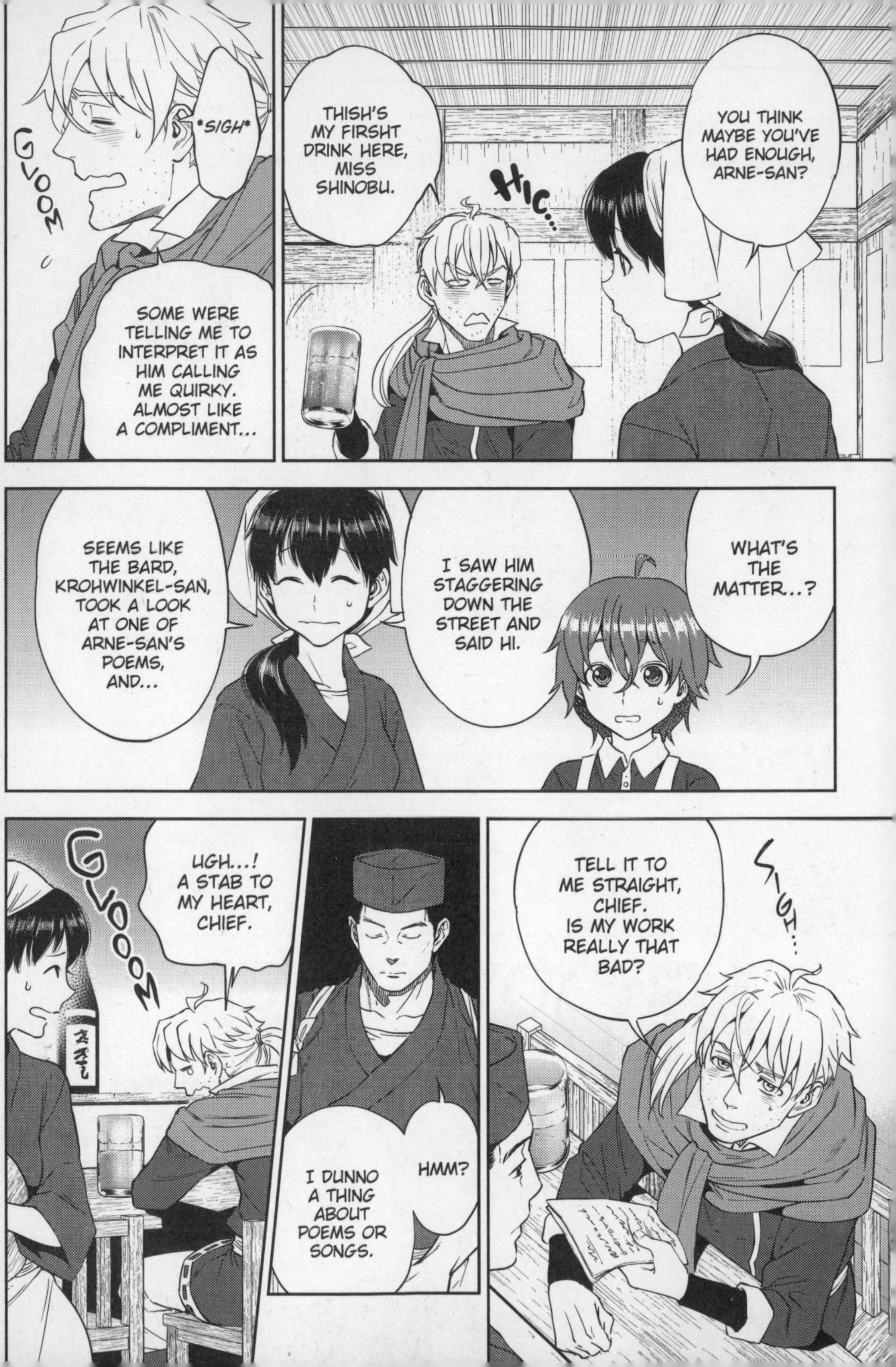
YOU THINK MAYBE YOU'VE HAD ENOUGH, ARNE-SAN?
HIC...
THISH'S MY FIRSHT DRINK HERE, MISS SHINOBU.
SIGH
GLOOM
SOME WERE TELLING ME TO INTERPRET IT AS HIM CALLING ME QUIRKY. ALMOST LIKE A COMPLIMENT...
WHAT'S THE MATTER...?
I SAW HIM STAGGERING DOWN THE STREET AND SAID HI.
SEEMS LIKE THE BARD, KROHWINKEL-SAN, TOOK A LOOK AT ONE OF ARNE-SAN'S POEMS, AND...
SIGH...
TELL IT TO ME STRAIGHT, CHIEF. IS MY WORK REALLY THAT BAD?
HMM?
I DUNNO A THING ABOUT POEMS OR SONGS.
UGH...! A STAB TO MY HEART, CHIEF.
GLOOOOM

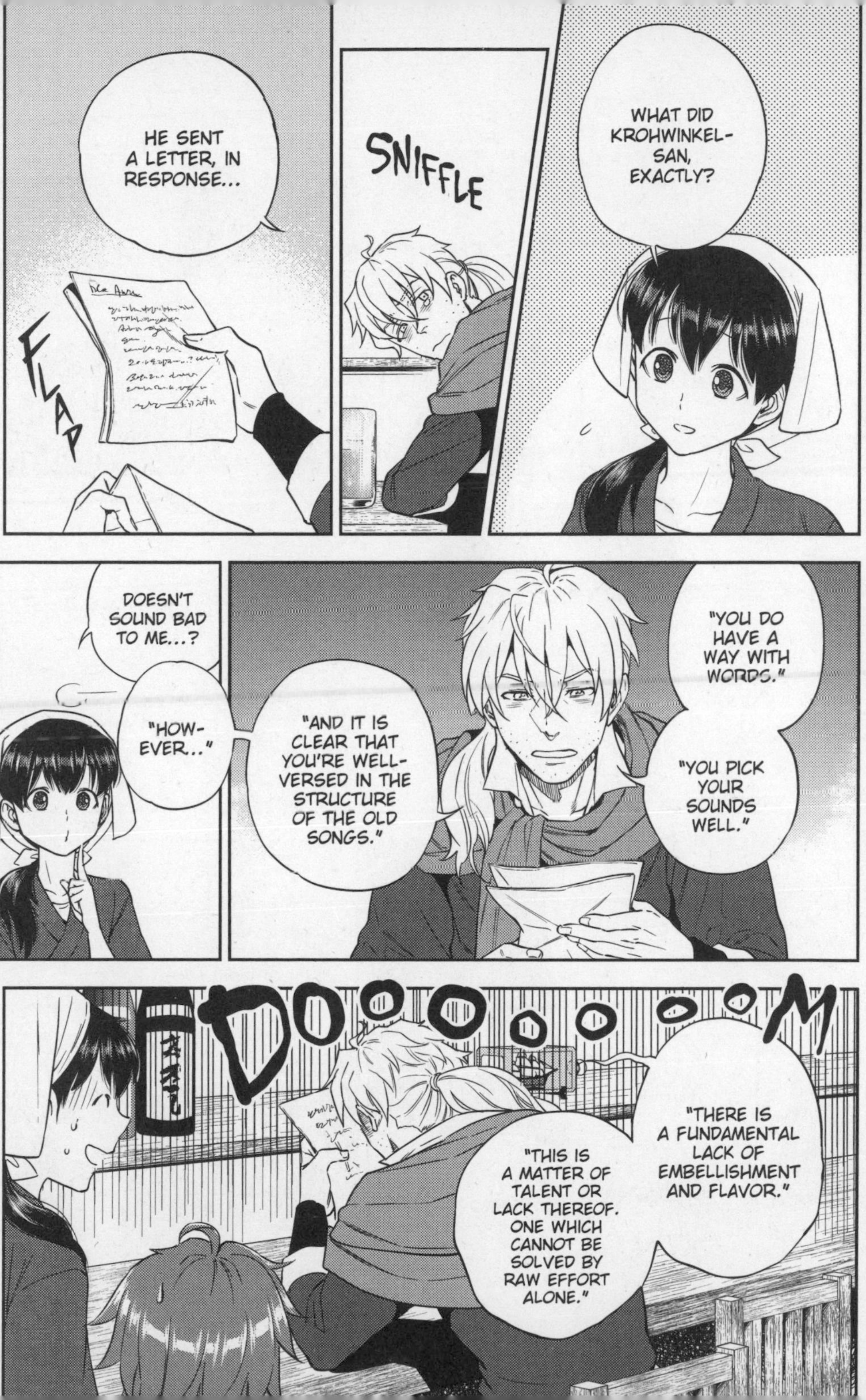
WHAT DID KROHWINKEL-SAN, EXACTLY?
SNIFFLE
HE SENT A LETTER, IN RESPONSE...
FLAP
"YOU DO HAVE A WAY WITH WORDS."
"YOU PICK YOUR SOUNDS WELL."
"AND IT IS CLEAR THAT YOU'RE WELL-VERSED IN THE STRUCTURE OF THE OLD SONGS."
DOESN'T SOUND BAD TO ME...?
"HOW-EVER..."
DOOOOOOM
"THERE IS A FUNDAMENTAL LACK OF EMBELLISHMENT AND FLAVOR."
"THIS IS A MATTER OF TALENT OR LACK THEREOF. ONE WHICH CANNOT BE SOLVED BY RAW EFFORT ALONE."

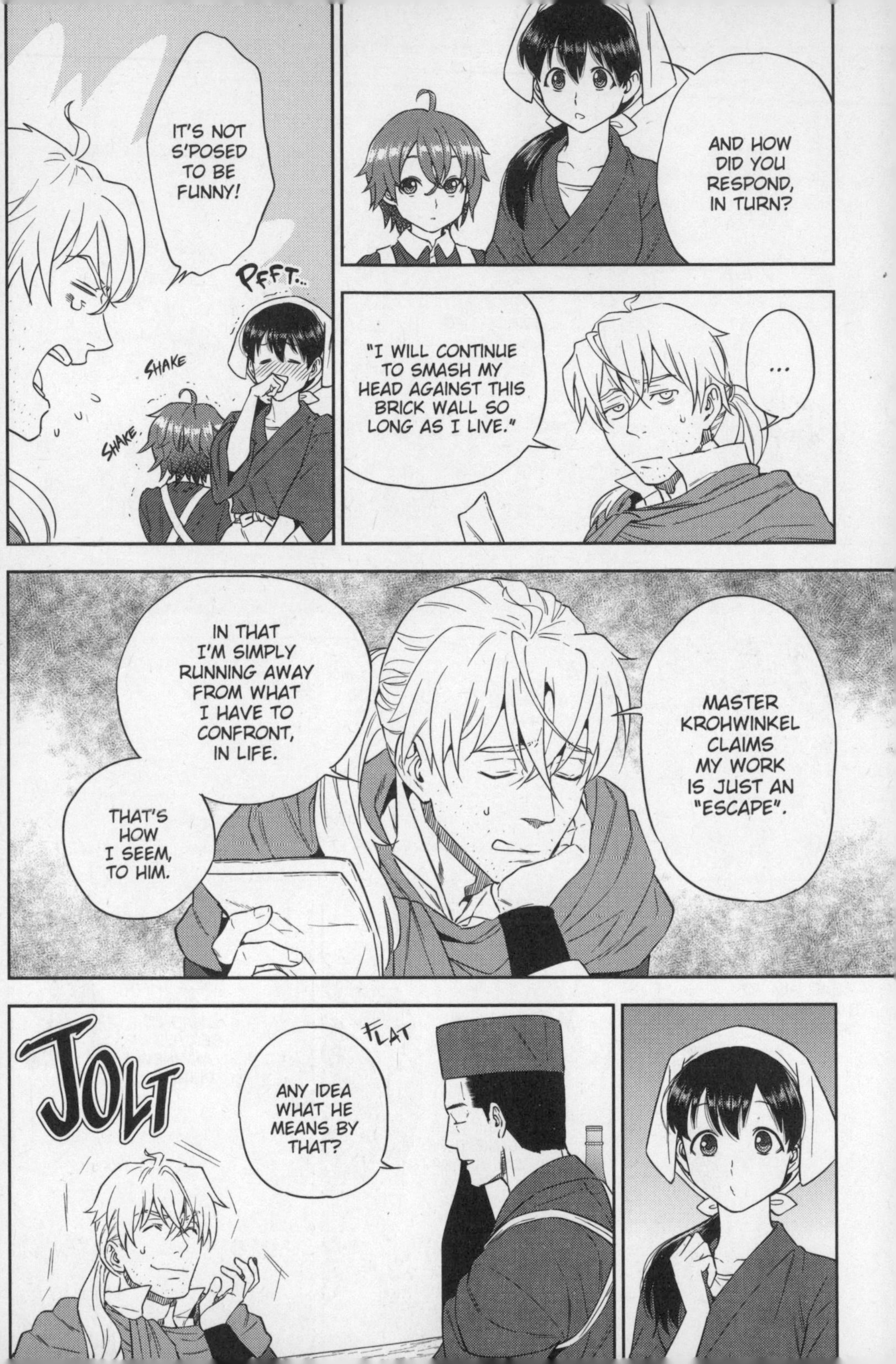
AND HOW DID YOU RESPOND, IN TURN?
...
"I WILL CONTINUE TO SMASH MY HEAD AGAINST THIS BRICK WALL SO LONG AS I LIVE."
IT'S NOT S'POSED TO BE FUNNY!
PFFT...
SHAKE
SHAKE
MASTER KROHWINKEL CLAIMS MY WORK IS JUST AN "ESCAPE".
IN THAT I'M SIMPLY RUNNING AWAY FROM WHAT I HAVE TO CONFRONT, IN LIFE.
THAT'S HOW I SEEM, TO HIM.
FLAT
ANY IDEA WHAT HE MEANS BY THAT?
JOLT

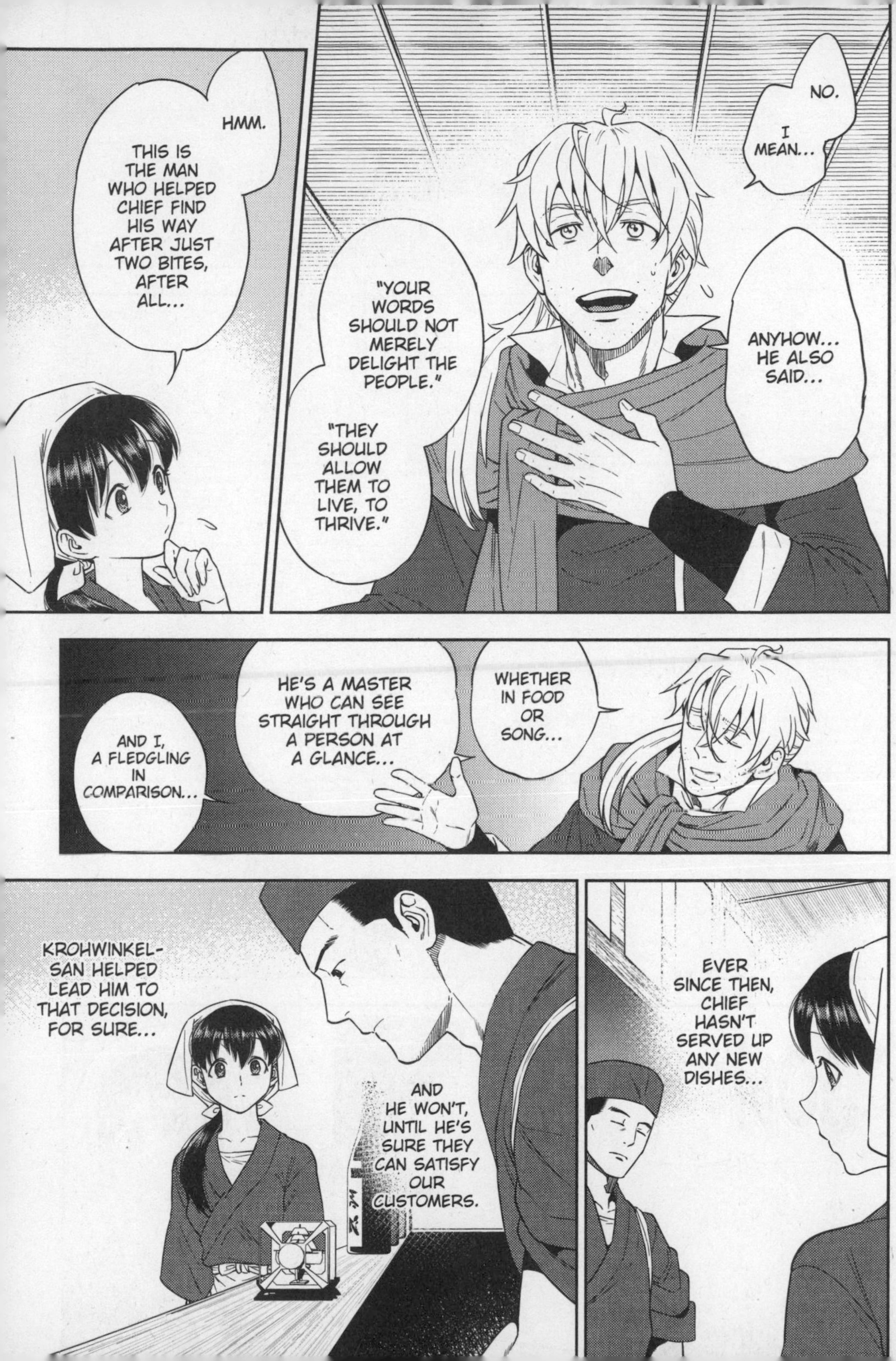
NO.
I MEAN...
ANYHOW... HE ALSO SAID...
"YOUR WORDS SHOULD NOT MERELY DELIGHT THE PEOPLE."
"THEY SHOULD ALLOW THEM TO LIVE, TO THRIVE."
HMM.
THIS IS THE MAN WHO HELPED CHIEF FIND HIS WAY AFTER JUST TWO BITES, AFTER ALL...
WHETHER IN FOOD OR SONG...
HE'S A MASTER WHO CAN SEE STRAIGHT THROUGH A PERSON AT A GLANCE...
AND I, A FLEDGLING IN COMPARISON...
EVER SINCE THEN, CHIEF HASN'T SERVED UP ANY NEW DISHES...
KROHWINKEL-SAN HELPED LEAD HIM TO THAT DECISION, FOR SURE...
AND HE WON'T, UNTIL HE'S SURE THEY CAN SATISFY OUR CUSTOMERS.

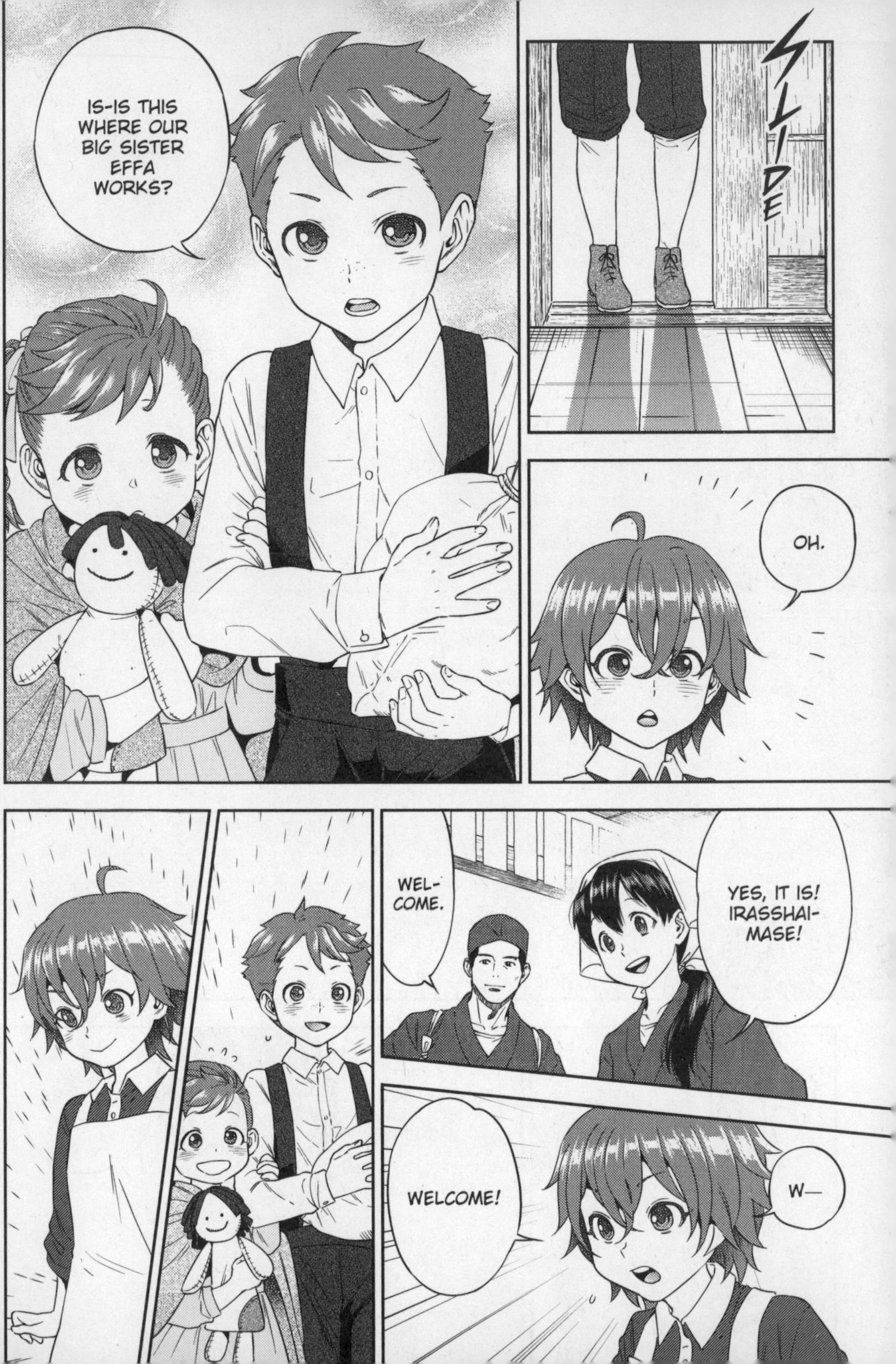
SLIDE
OH.
IS-IS THIS WHERE OUR BIG SISTER EFFA WORKS?
YES, IT IS! IRASSHAI-MASE!
WEL-COME.
W—
WELCOME!

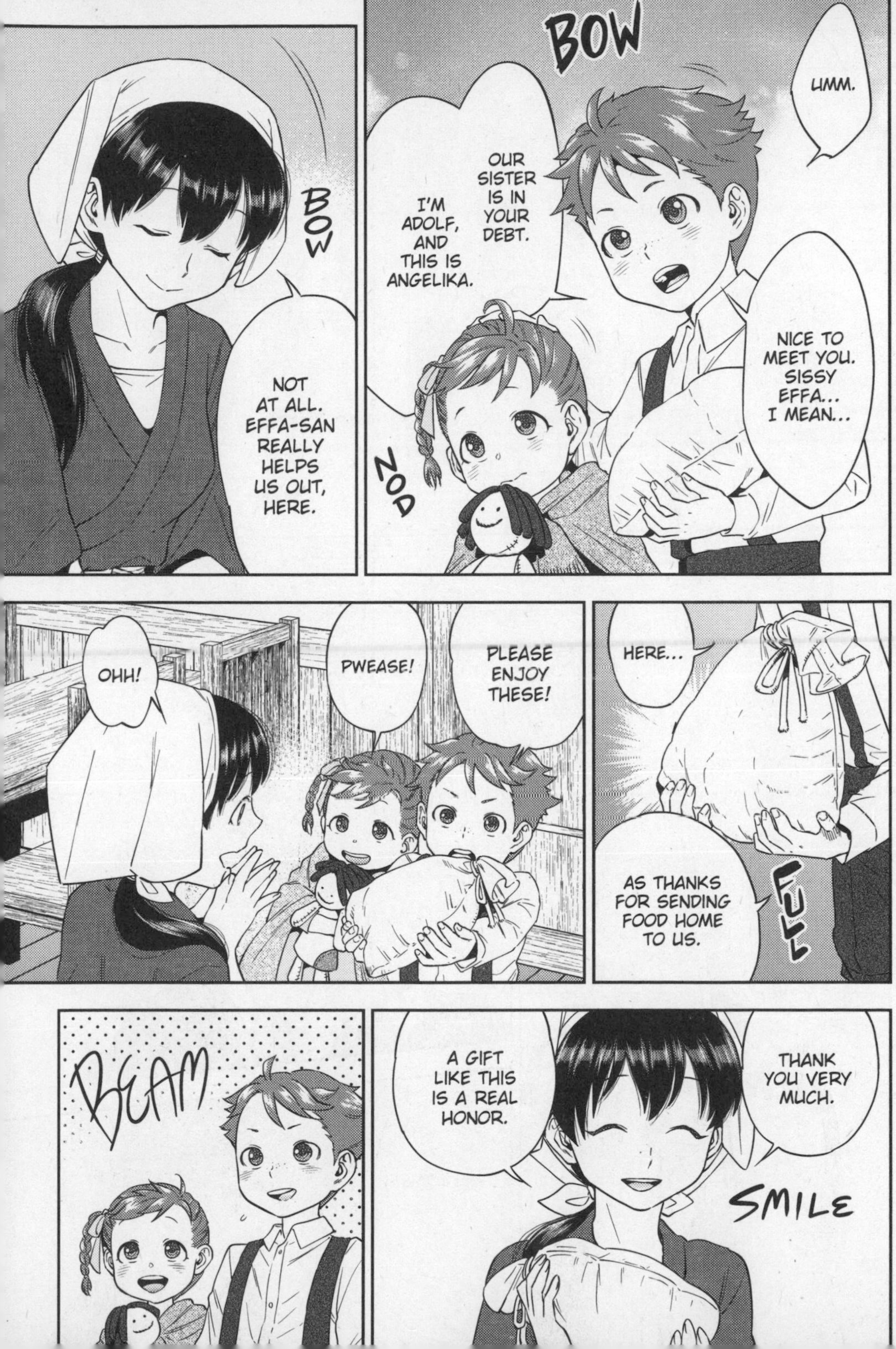
UMM.
BOW
OUR SISTER IS IN YOUR DEBT.
I'M ADOLF, AND THIS IS ANGELIKA.
NICE TO MEET YOU. SISSY EFFA... I MEAN...
NOD
BOW
NOT AT ALL. EFFA-SAN REALLY HELPS US OUT, HERE.
HERE...
AS THANKS FOR SENDING FOOD HOME TO US.
FULL
PLEASE ENJOY THESE!
PWEASE!
OHH!
THANK YOU VERY MUCH.
A GIFT LIKE THIS IS A REAL HONOR.
SMILE
BEAM

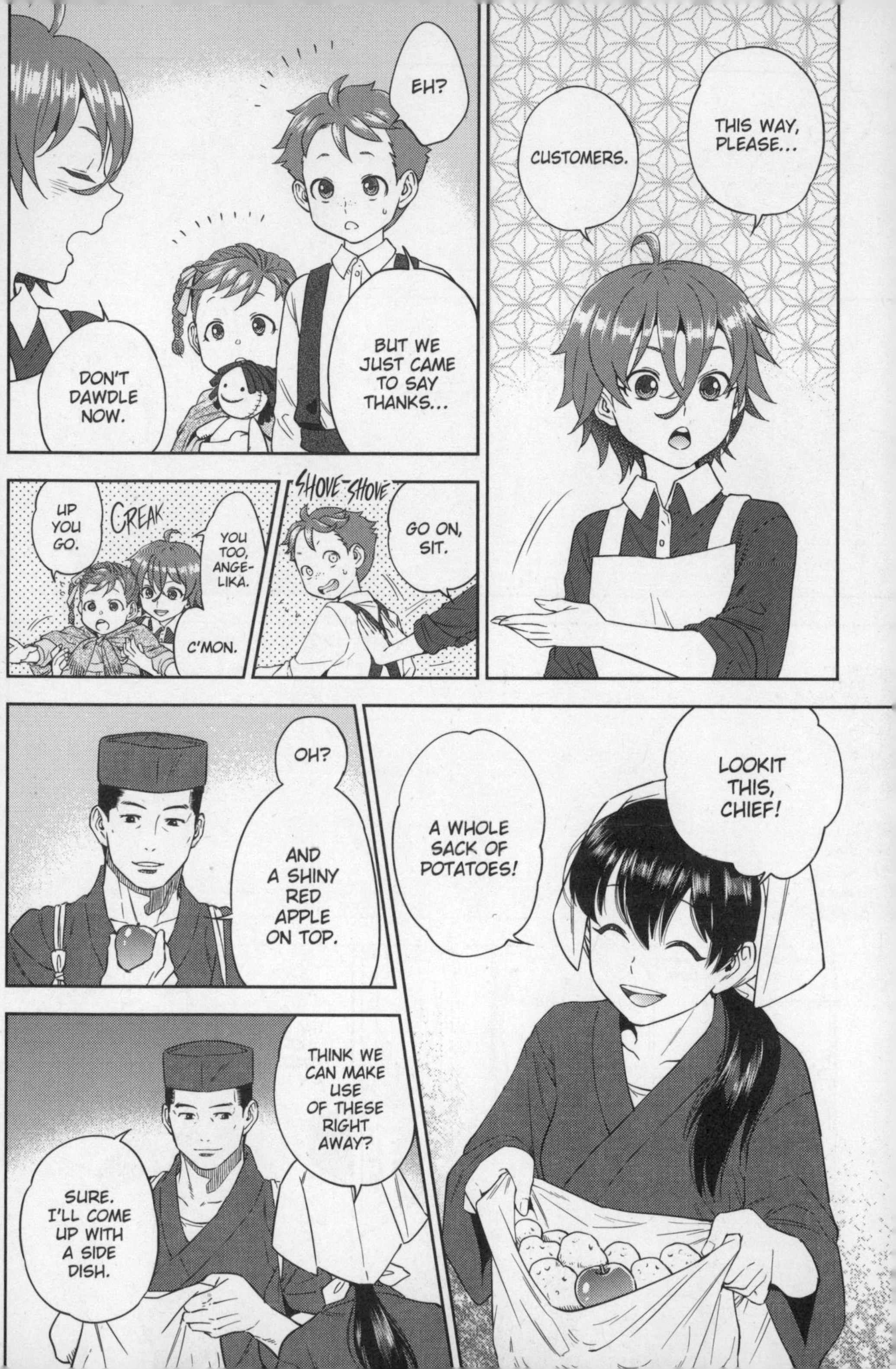
THIS WAY, PLEASE...
CUSTOMERS.
EH?
BUT WE JUST CAME TO SAY THANKS...
DON'T DAWDLE NOW.
SHOVE-SHOVE
GO ON, SIT.
YOU TOO, ANGE-LIKA.
CREAK
UP YOU GO.
C'MON.
LOOKIT THIS, CHIEF!
A WHOLE SACK OF POTATOES!
OH?
AND A SHINY RED APPLE ON TOP.
THINK WE CAN MAKE USE OF THESE RIGHT AWAY?
SURE. I'LL COME UP WITH A SIDE DISH.

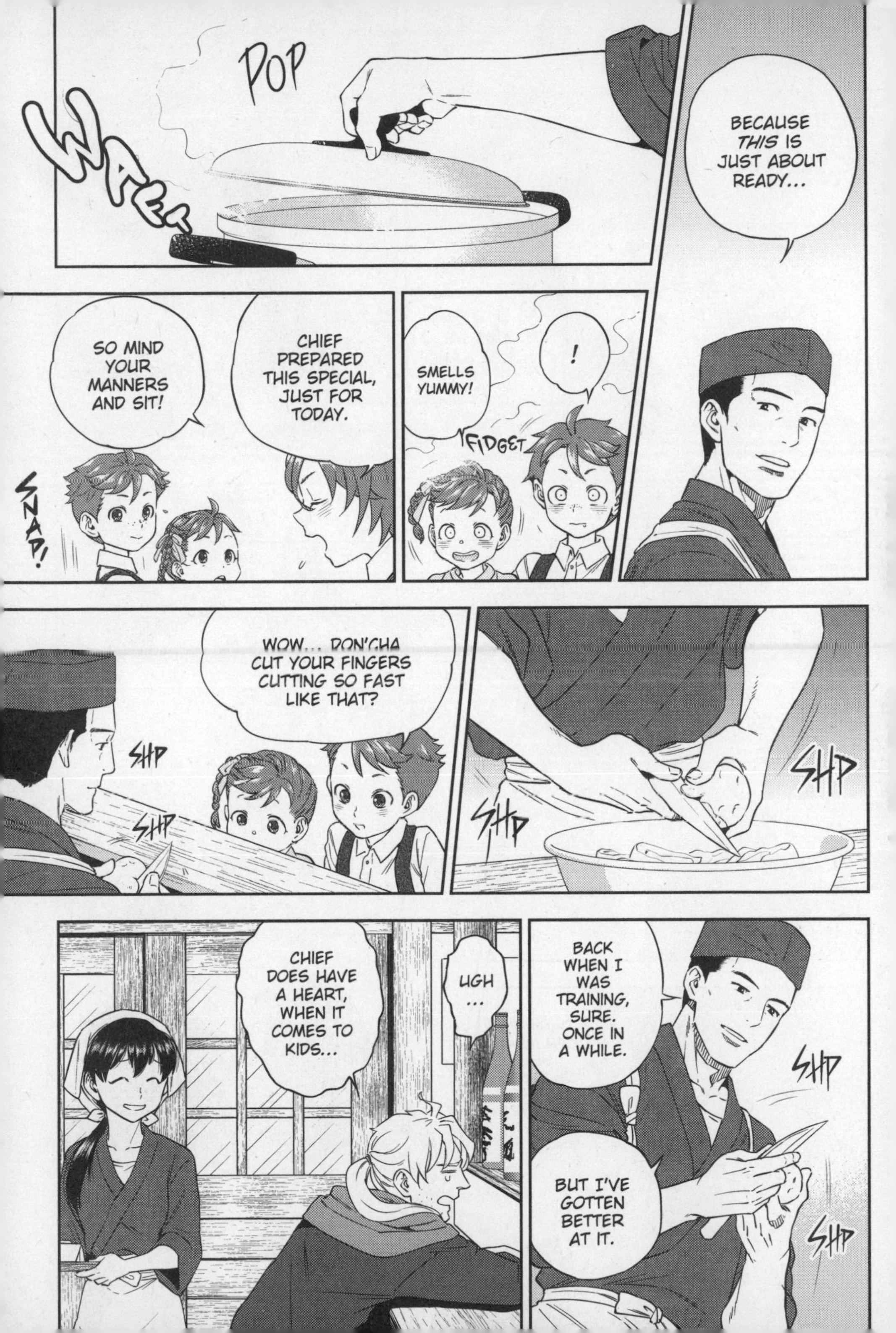
BECAUSE *THIS* IS JUST ABOUT READY...
POP
WAFT
!
SMELLS YUMMY!
FIDGET
CHIEF PREPARED THIS SPECIAL, JUST FOR TODAY.
SO MIND YOUR MANNERS AND SIT!
SNAP!
SHP
SHP
WOW... DON'CHA CUT YOUR FINGERS CUTTING SO FAST LIKE THAT?
SHP
SHP
BACK WHEN I WAS TRAINING, SURE. ONCE IN A WHILE.
SHP
BUT I'VE GOTTEN BETTER AT IT.
SHP
UGH ...
CHIEF DOES HAVE A HEART, WHEN IT COMES TO KIDS...

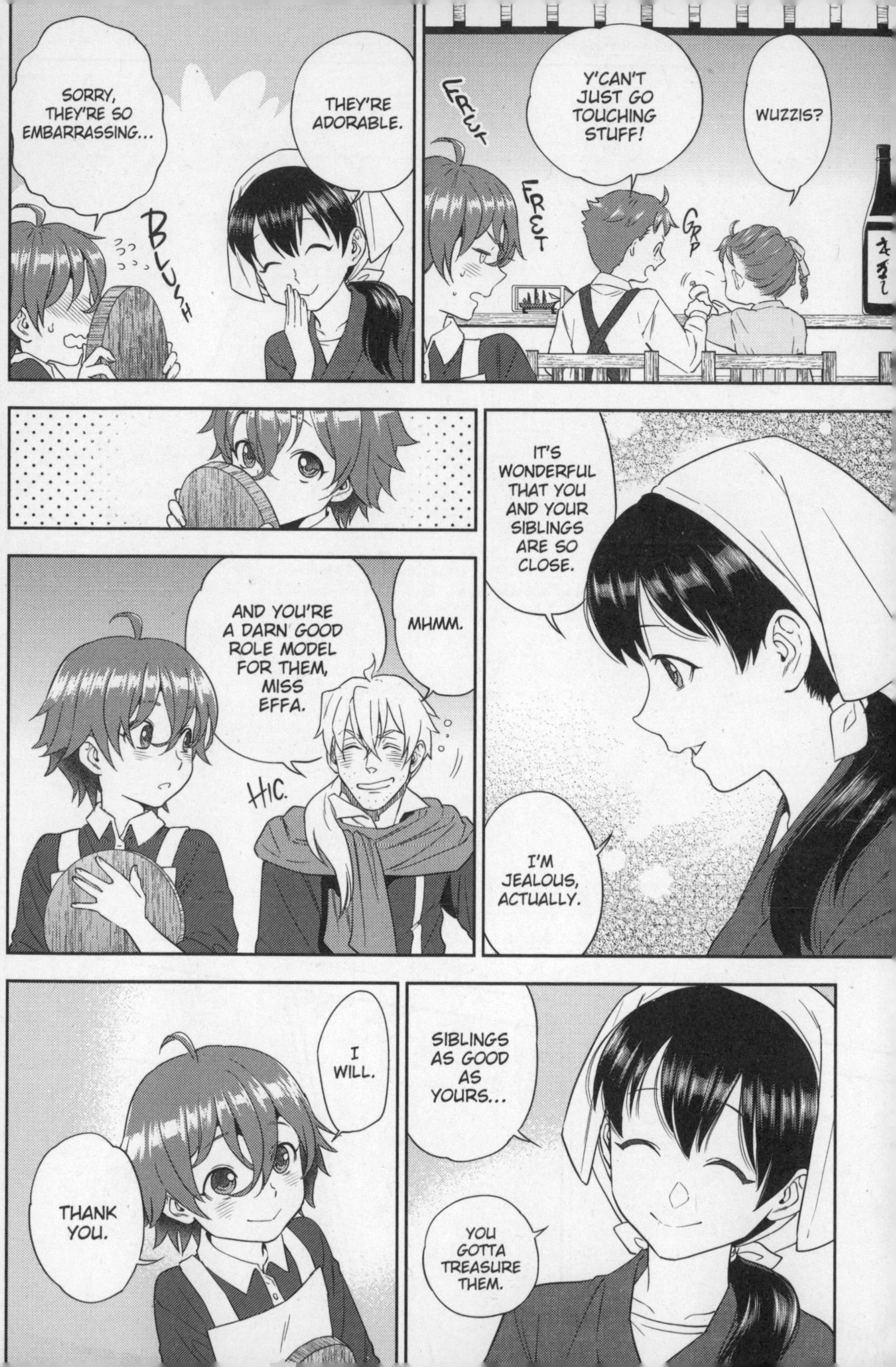

WUZZIS?
Y'CAN'T JUST GO TOUCHING STUFF!
GRP
FRET
FRET
THEY'RE ADORABLE.
SORRY, THEY'RE SO EMBARRASSING...
BLUSH
IT'S WONDERFUL THAT YOU AND YOUR SIBLINGS ARE SO CLOSE.
I'M JEALOUS, ACTUALLY.
MHMM.
AND YOU'RE A DARN GOOD ROLE MODEL FOR THEM, MISS EFFA.
HIC.
SIBLINGS AS GOOD AS YOURS...
YOU GOTTA TREASURE THEM.
I WILL.
THANK YOU.

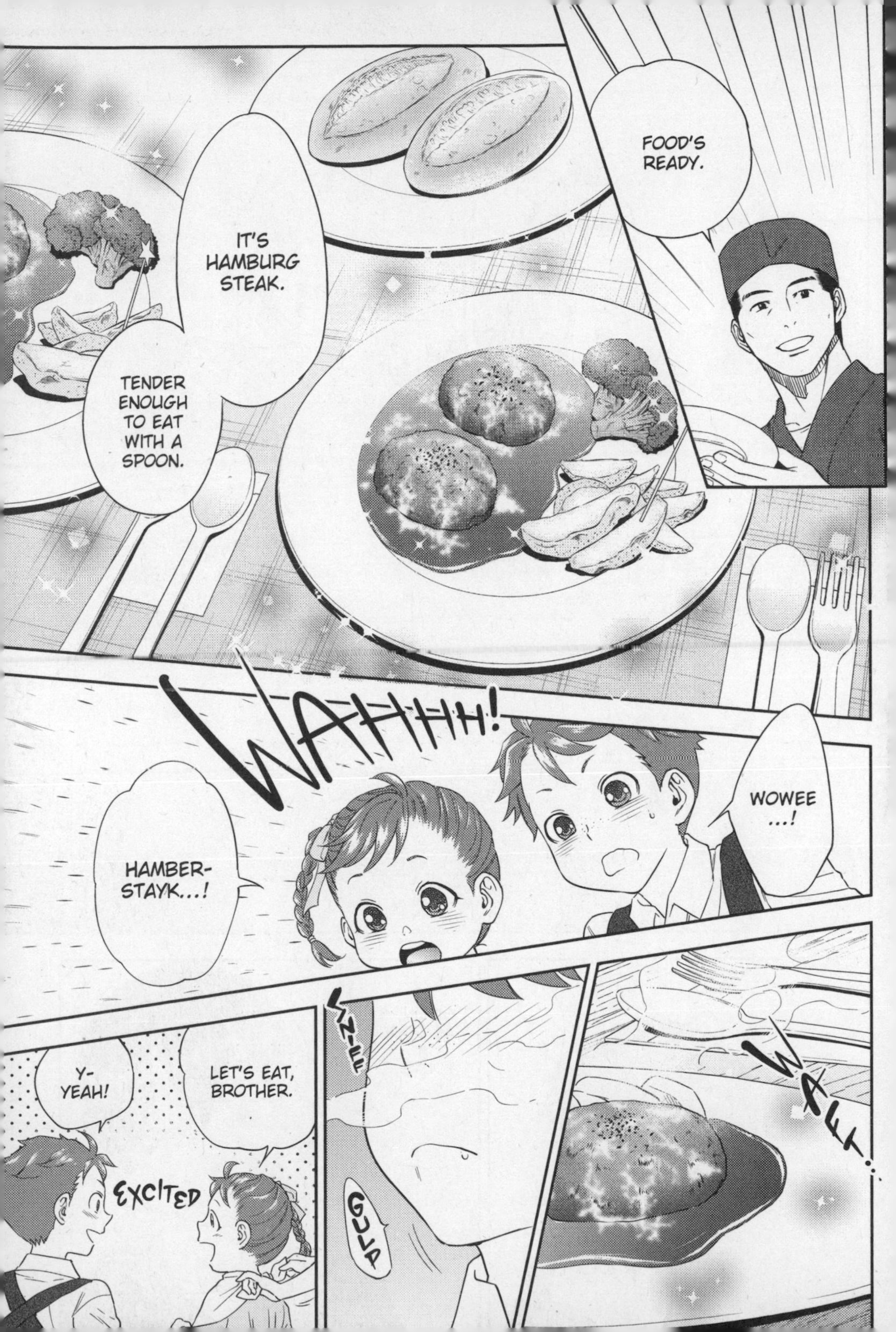
FOOD'S READY.
IT'S HAMBURG STEAK.
TENDER ENOUGH TO EAT WITH A SPOON.
WAHHHH!
WOWEE ...!
HAMBER-STAYK...!
WAFT...
SNIFF
GULP
LET'S EAT, BROTHER.
Y-YEAH!
EXCITED

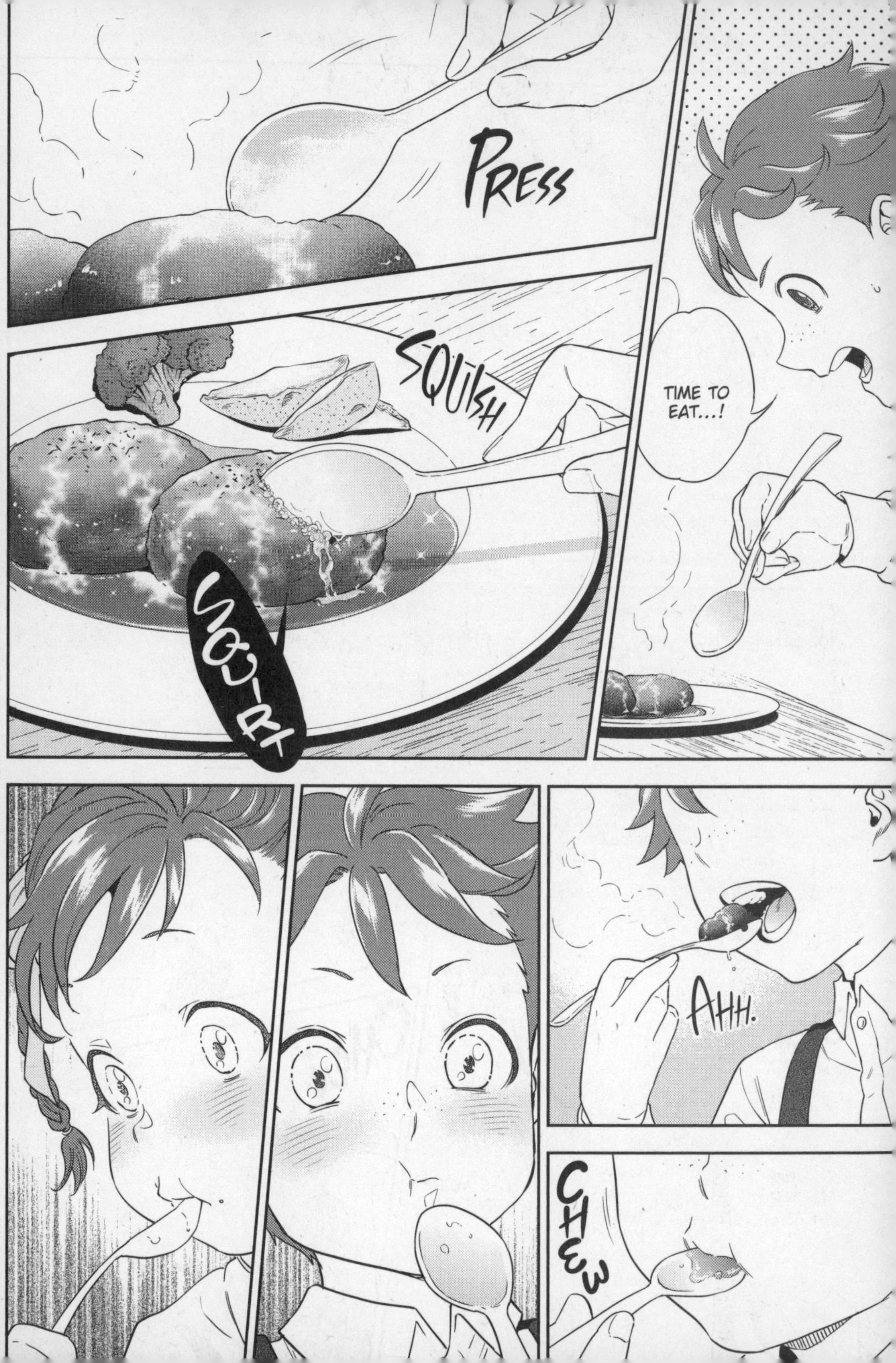
TIME TO EAT...!
PRESS
SQUISH
SQUIRT
AHH.
CHEW

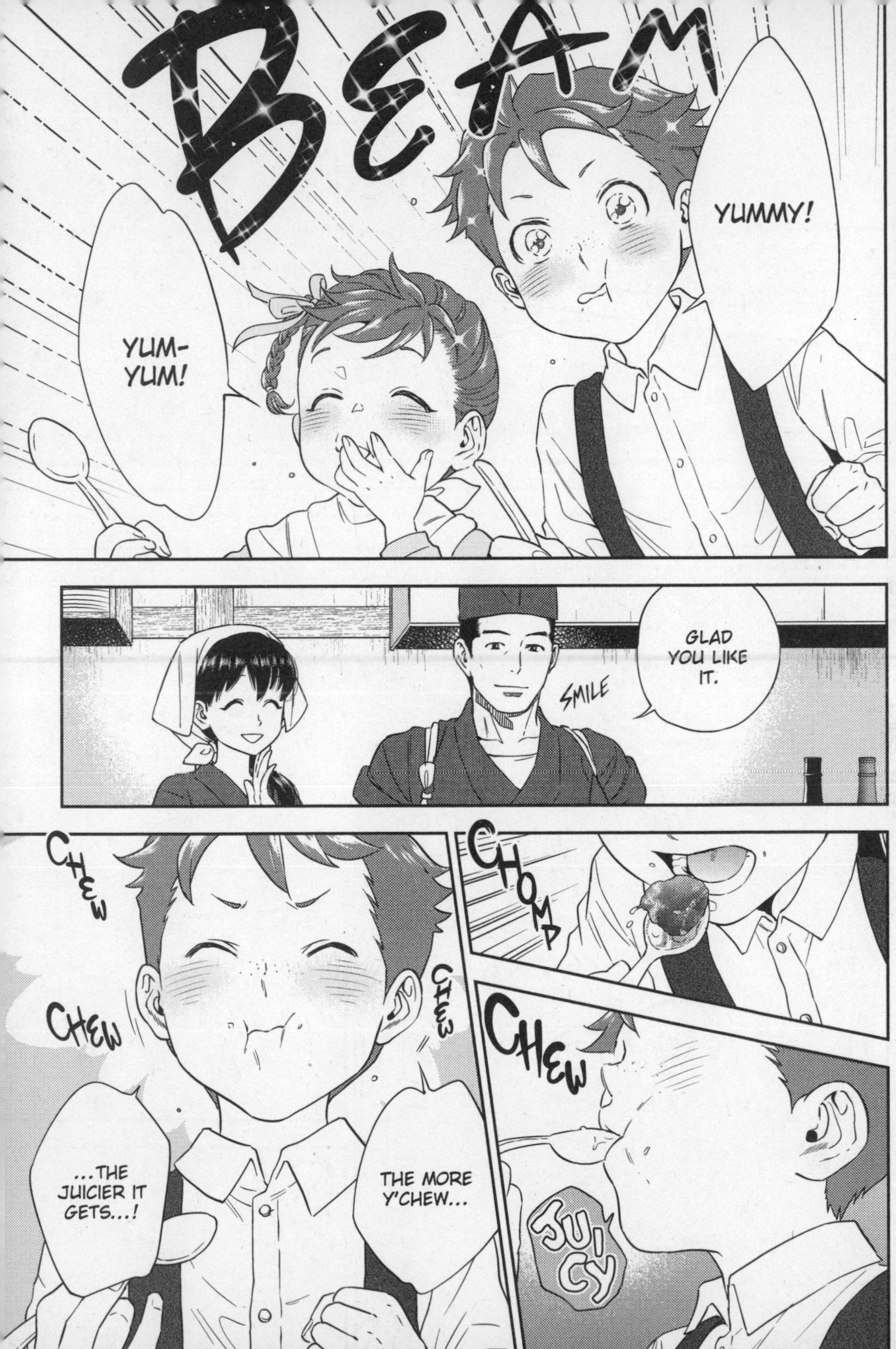
BEAM
YUMMY!
YUM-YUM!
GLAD YOU LIKE IT.
SMILE
CHOMP
CHEW
JUICY
CHEW
CHEW
CHEW
THE MORE Y'CHEW...
...THE JUICIER IT GETS...!

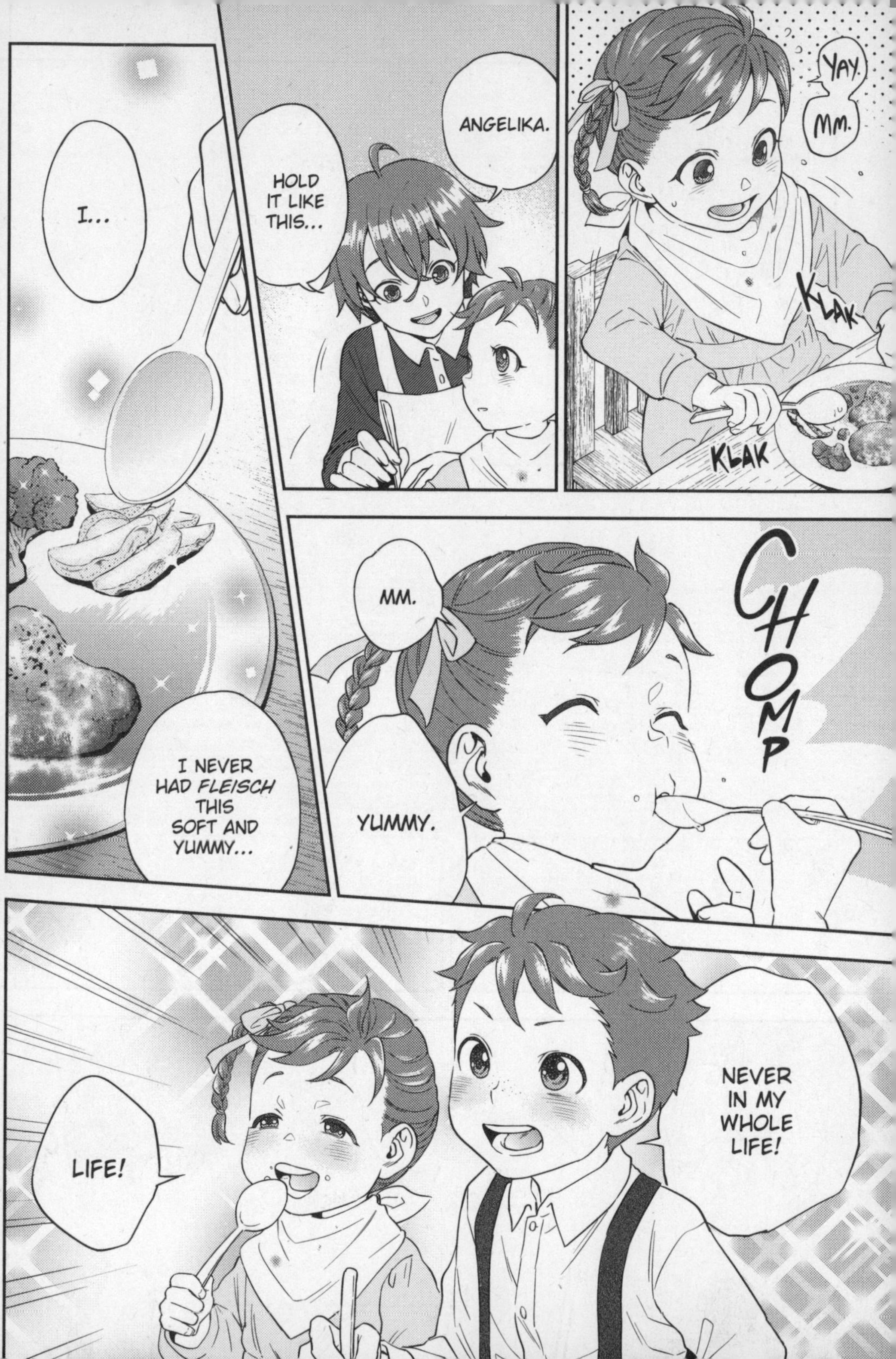
YAY.
MM.
KLAK-
KLAK
ANGELIKA.
HOLD IT LIKE THIS...
CHOMP
MM.
YUMMY.
I...
I NEVER HAD *FLEISCH* THIS SOFT AND YUMMY...
NEVER IN MY WHOLE LIFE!
LIFE!

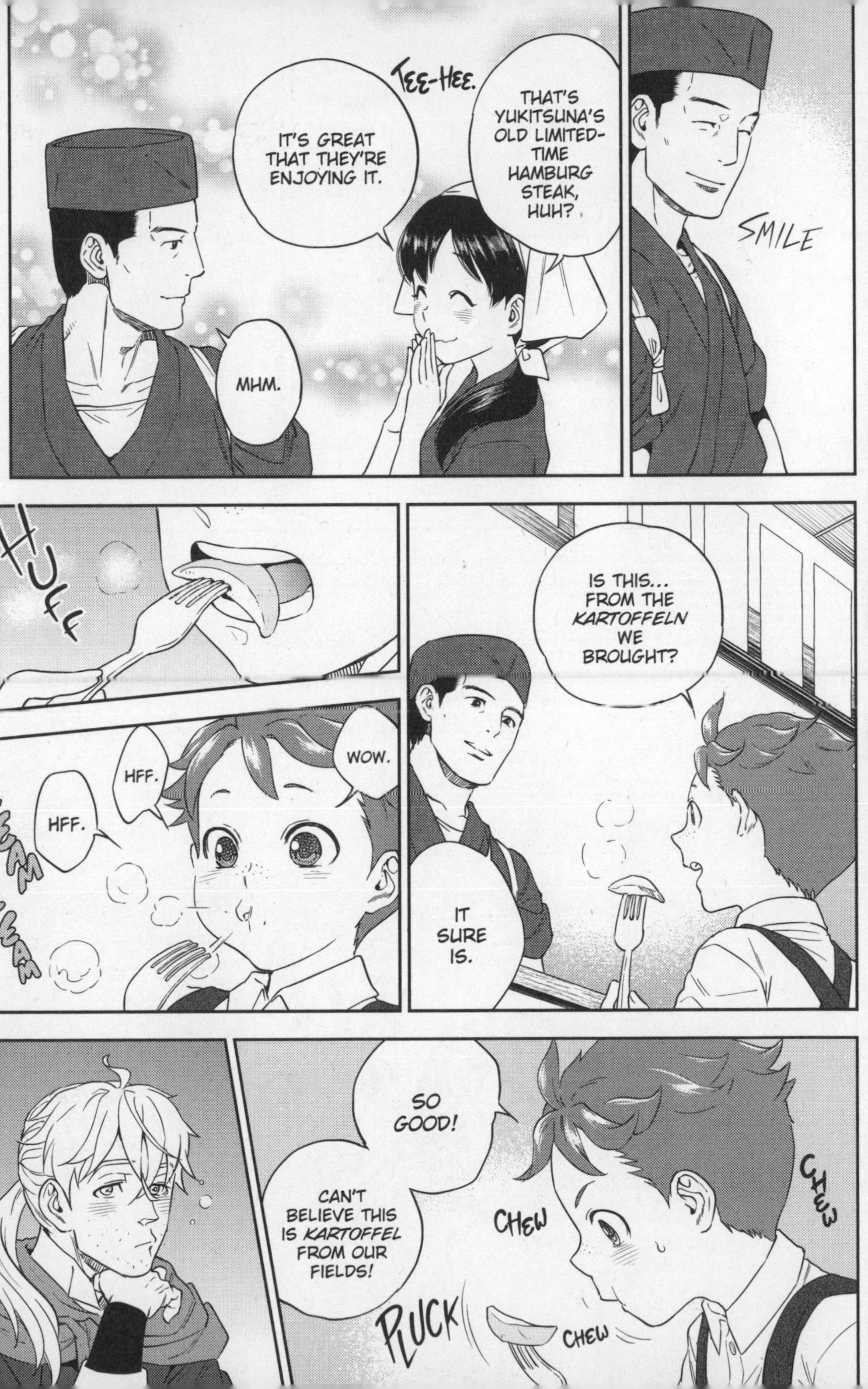
SMILE
TEE-HEE.
THAT'S YUKITSUNA'S OLD LIMITED-TIME HAMBURG STEAK, HUH?
IT'S GREAT THAT THEY'RE ENJOYING IT.
MHM.
IS THIS... FROM THE *KARTOFFELN* WE BROUGHT?
IT SURE IS.
HUFF
WOW.
HFF.
HFF.
STEAM
STEAM
SO GOOD!
CHEW
CHEW
CAN'T BELIEVE THIS IS *KARTOFFEL* FROM OUR FIELDS!
PLUCK
CHEW

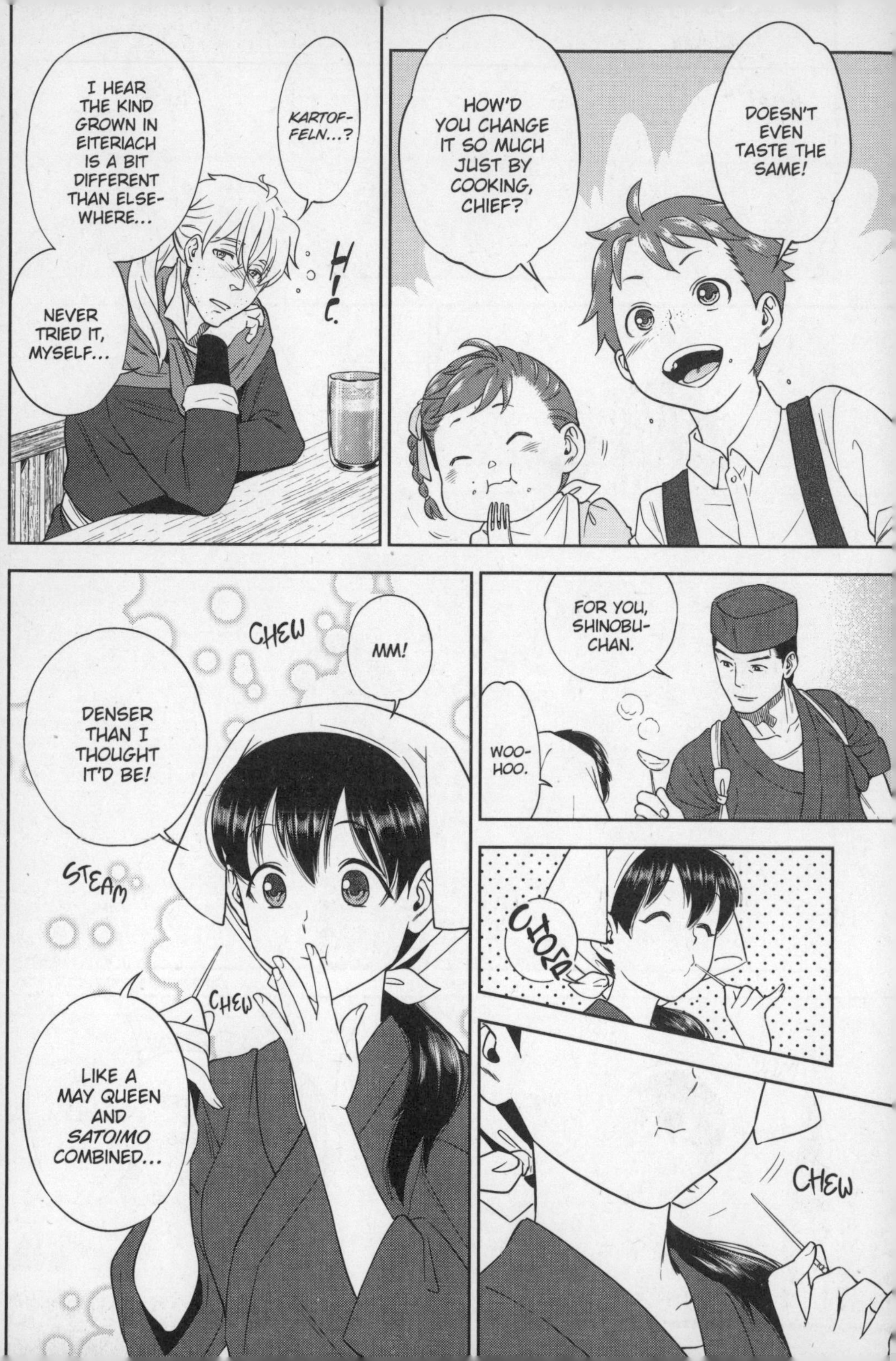
DOESN'T EVEN TASTE THE SAME!
HOW'D YOU CHANGE IT SO MUCH JUST BY COOKING, CHIEF?
KARTOF-FELN...?
I HEAR THE KIND GROWN IN EITERIACH IS A BIT DIFFERENT THAN ELSE-WHERE...
HIC
NEVER TRIED IT, MYSELF...
FOR YOU, SHINOBU-CHAN.
WOO-HOO.
CHOMP
CHEW
MM!
CHEW
DENSER THAN I THOUGHT IT'D BE!
STEAM
CHEW
LIKE A MAY QUEEN AND *SATOIMO* COMBINED...

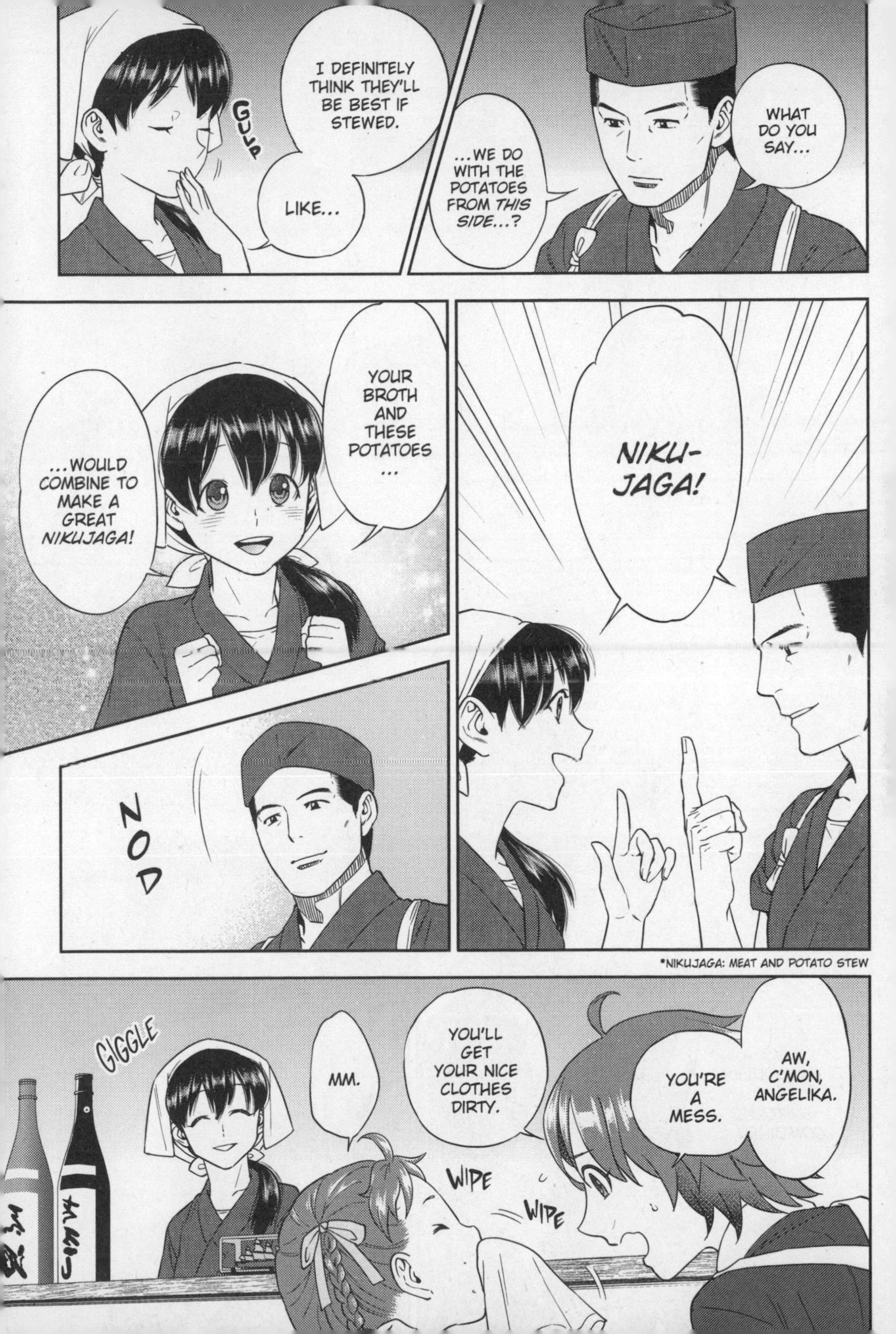
WHAT DO YOU SAY...
...WE DO WITH THE POTATOES FROM THIS SIDE...?
I DEFINITELY THINK THEY'LL BE BEST IF STEWED.
GULP
LIKE...
NIKU-JAGA!
YOUR BROTH AND THESE POTATOES...
...WOULD COMBINE TO MAKE A GREAT NIKUJAGA!
NOD
AW, C'MON, ANGELIKA.
YOU'RE A MESS.
YOU'LL GET YOUR NICE CLOTHES DIRTY.
MM.
WIPE
WIPE
GIGGLE

*NIKUJAGA: MEAT AND POTATO STEW

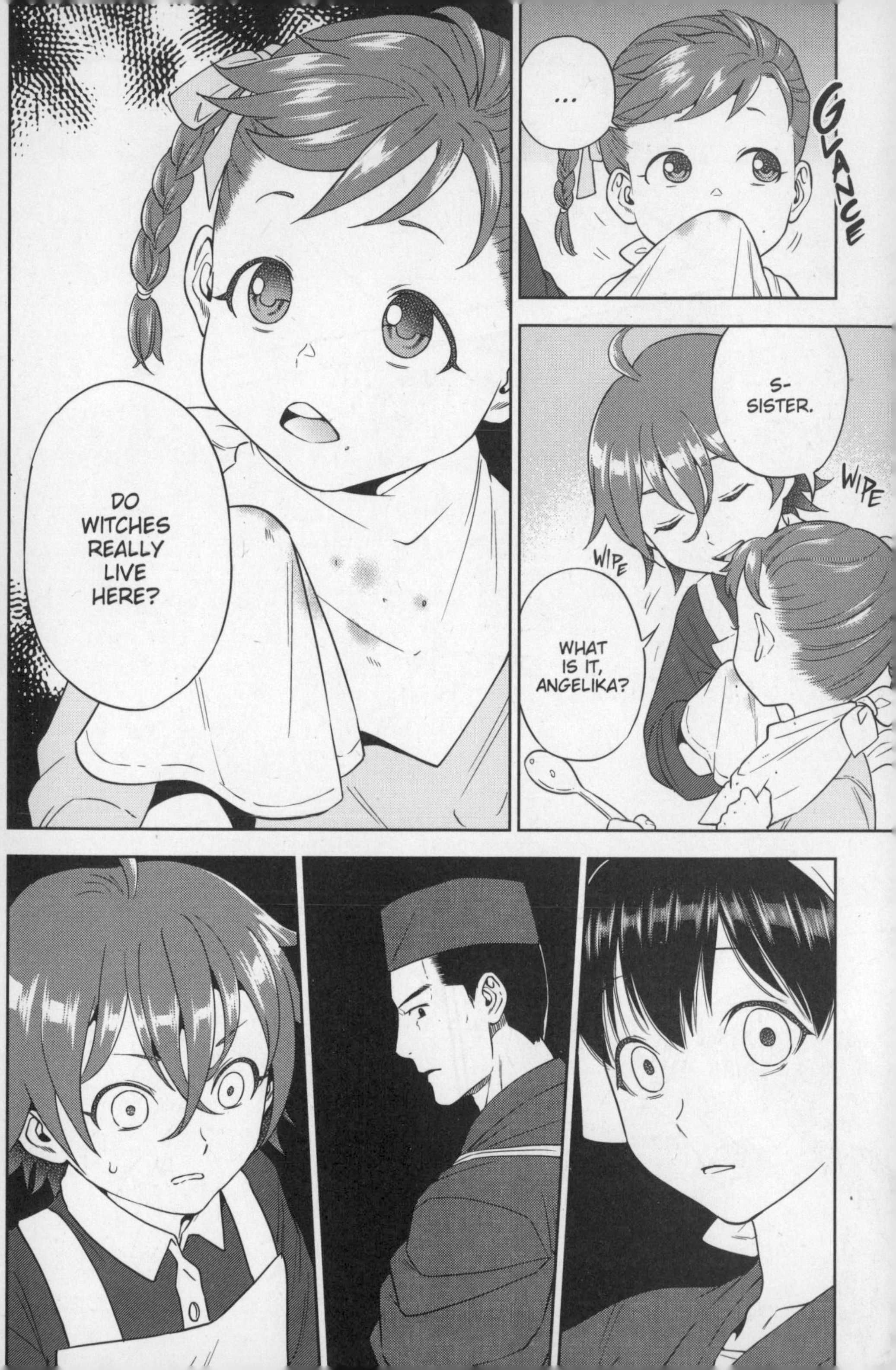
...
GLANCE
S-SISTER.
WIPE
WIPE
WHAT IS IT, ANGELIKA?
DO WITCHES REALLY LIVE HERE?

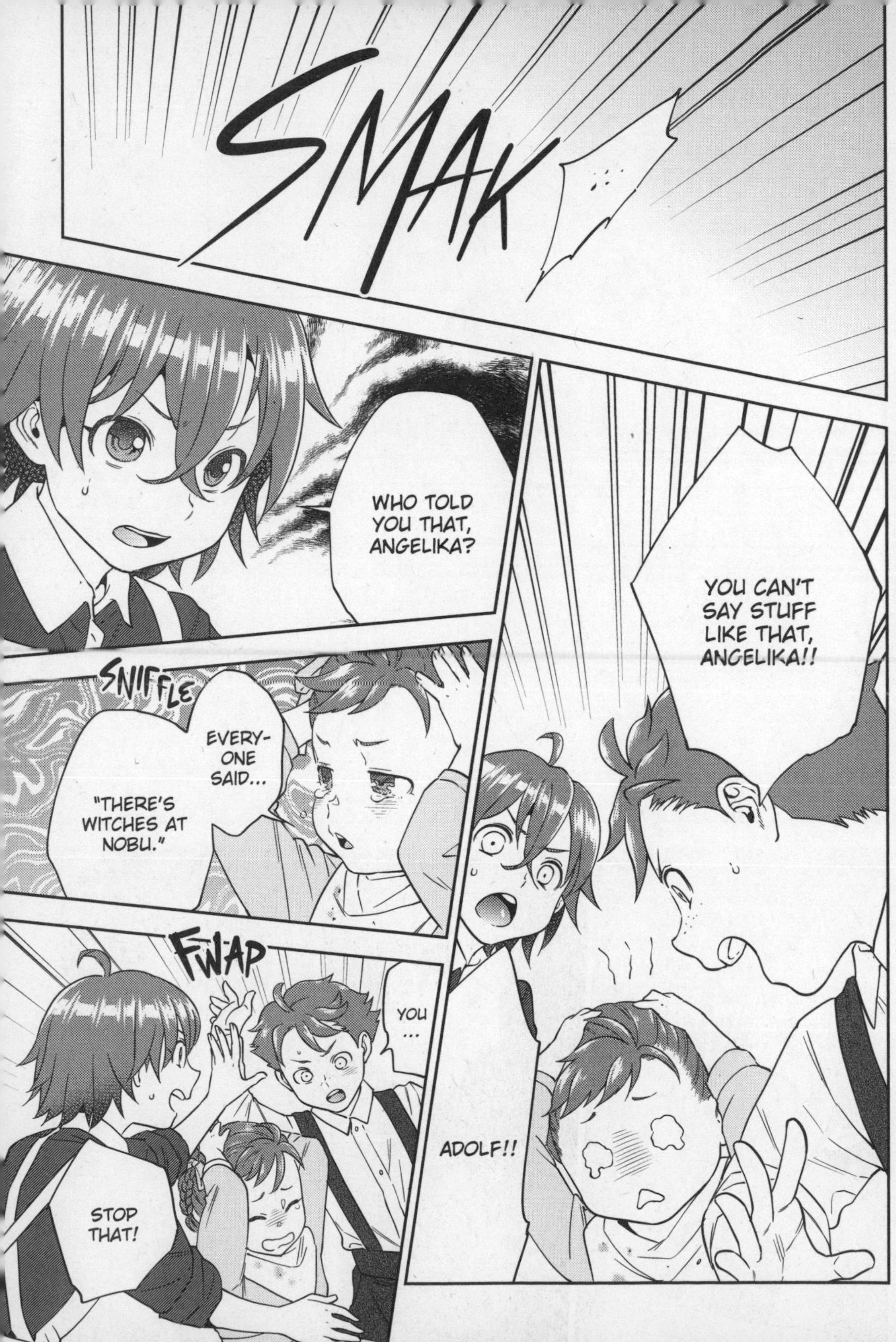
SMAK
YOU CAN'T SAY STUFF LIKE THAT, ANGELIKA!!
ADOLF!!
WHO TOLD YOU THAT, ANGELIKA?
SNIFFLE
EVERY-ONE SAID...
"THERE'S WITCHES AT NOBU."
FWAP
YOU ...
STOP THAT!

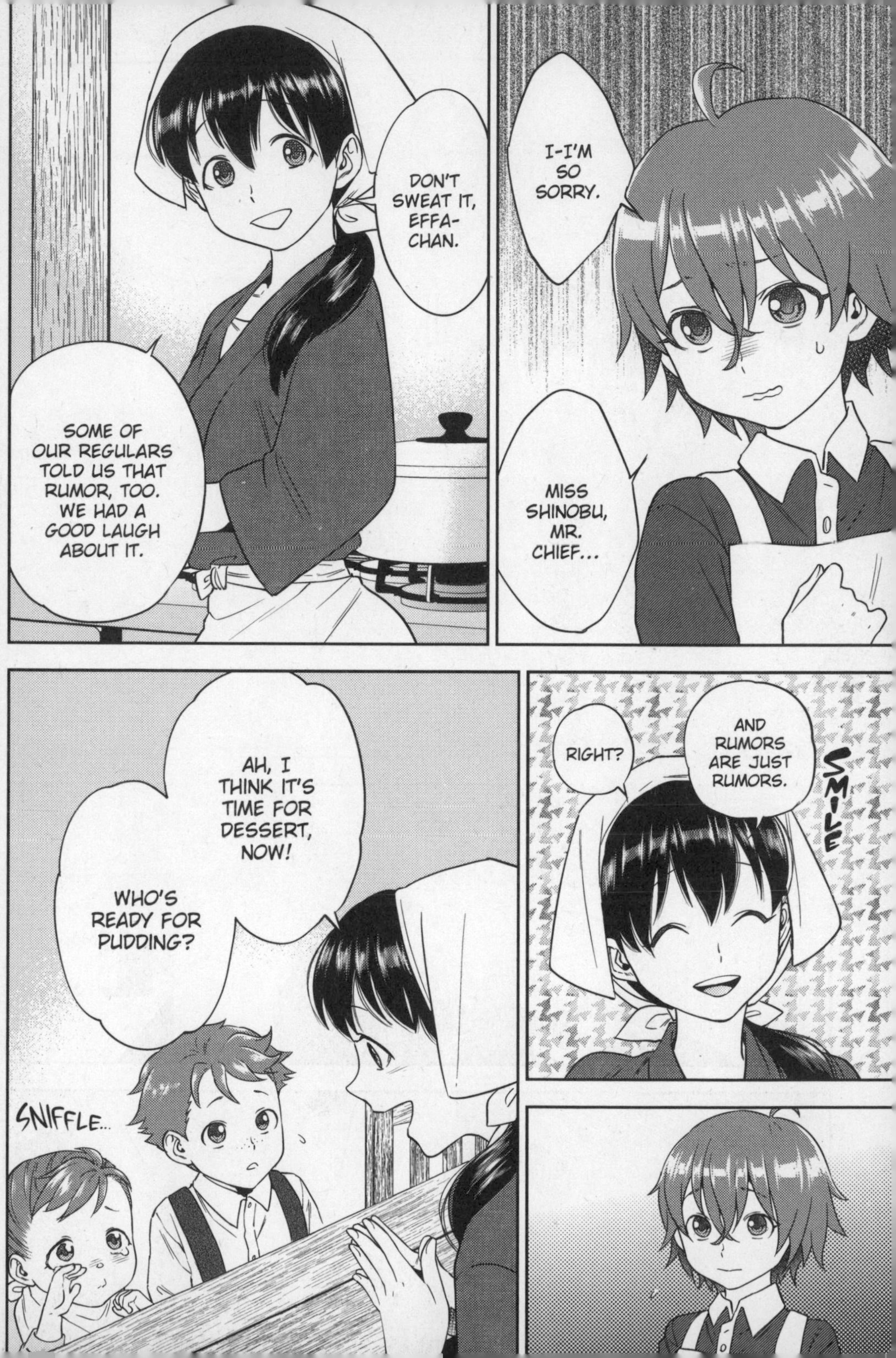
I-I'M SO SORRY.
MISS SHINOBU, MR. CHIEF...
DON'T SWEAT IT, EFFA-CHAN.
SOME OF OUR REGULARS TOLD US THAT RUMOR, TOO. WE HAD A GOOD LAUGH ABOUT IT.
AND RUMORS ARE JUST RUMORS.
RIGHT?
SMILE
AH, I THINK IT'S TIME FOR DESSERT, NOW!
WHO'S READY FOR PUDDING?
SNIFFLE...

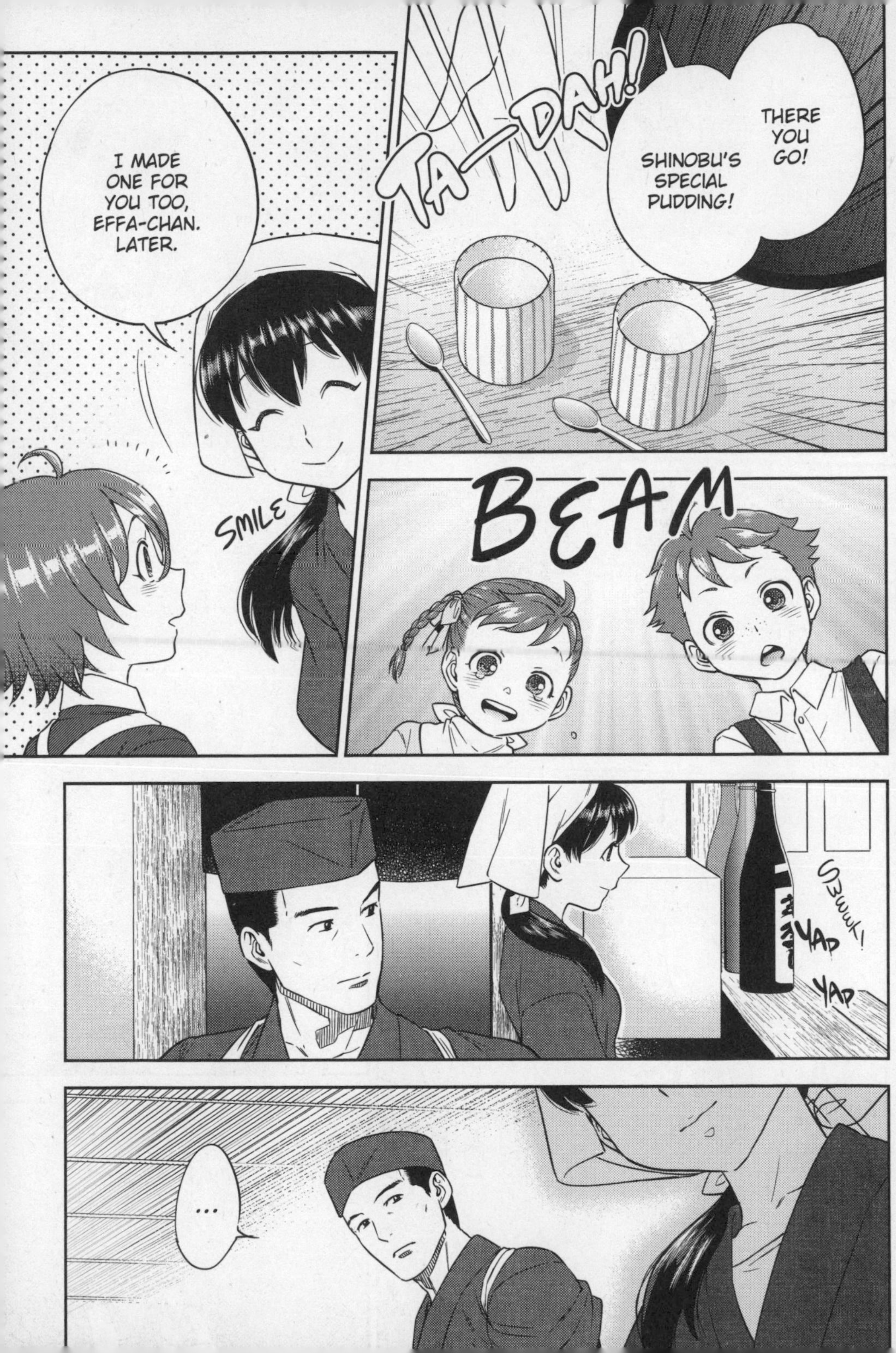
THERE YOU GO!
SHINOBU'S SPECIAL PUDDING!
TA-DAH!
BEAM
I MADE ONE FOR YOU TOO, EFFA-CHAN. LATER.
SMILE
SWWWK!
YAP
YAP
...

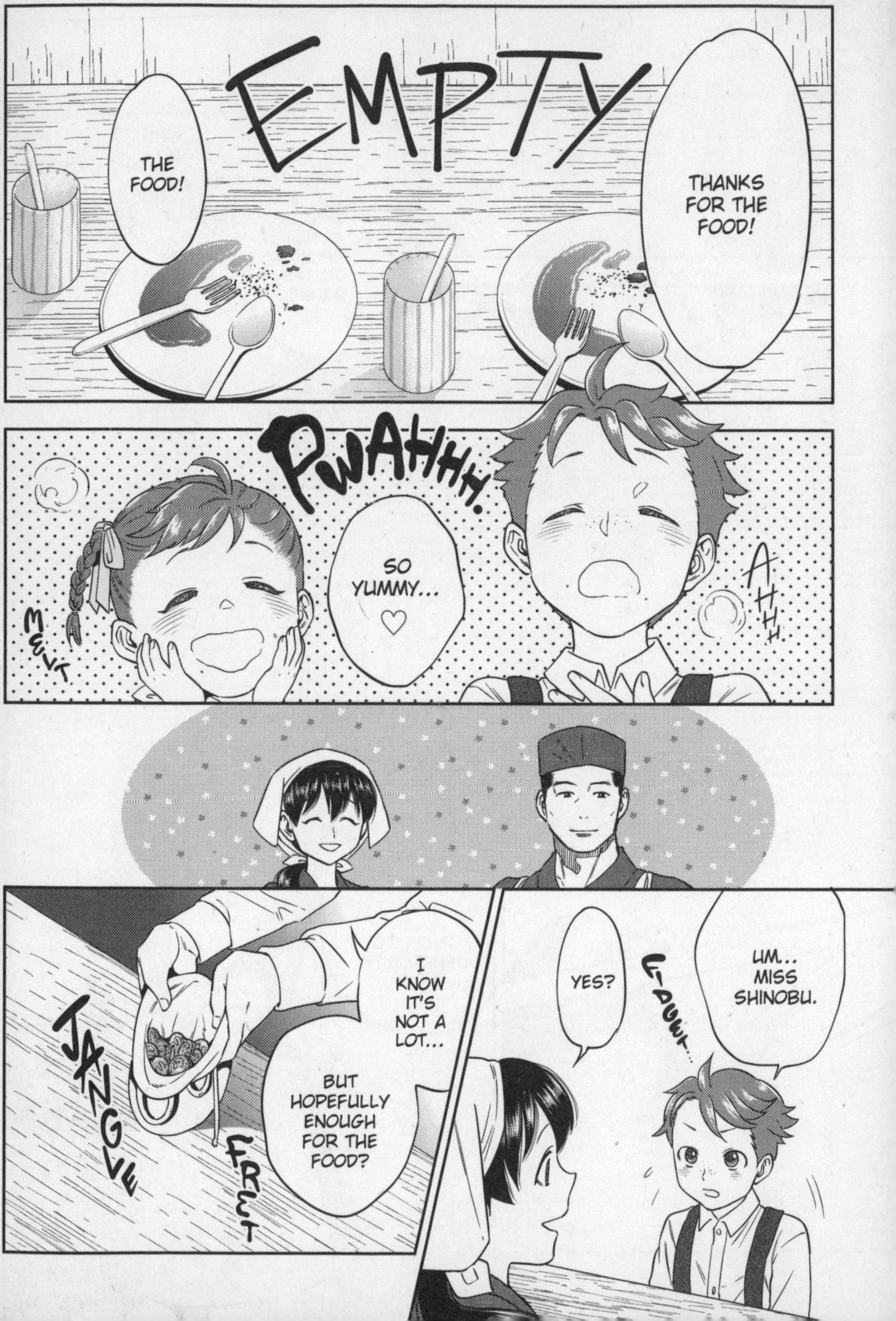
THANKS FOR THE FOOD!
EMPTY
THE FOOD!
PWAHHH.
AHHH.
SO YUMMY... ♡
MELT
UM... MISS SHINOBU.
FIDGET...
YES?
I KNOW IT'S NOT A LOT...
BUT HOPEFULLY ENOUGH FOR THE FOOD?
FRET
JANGLE

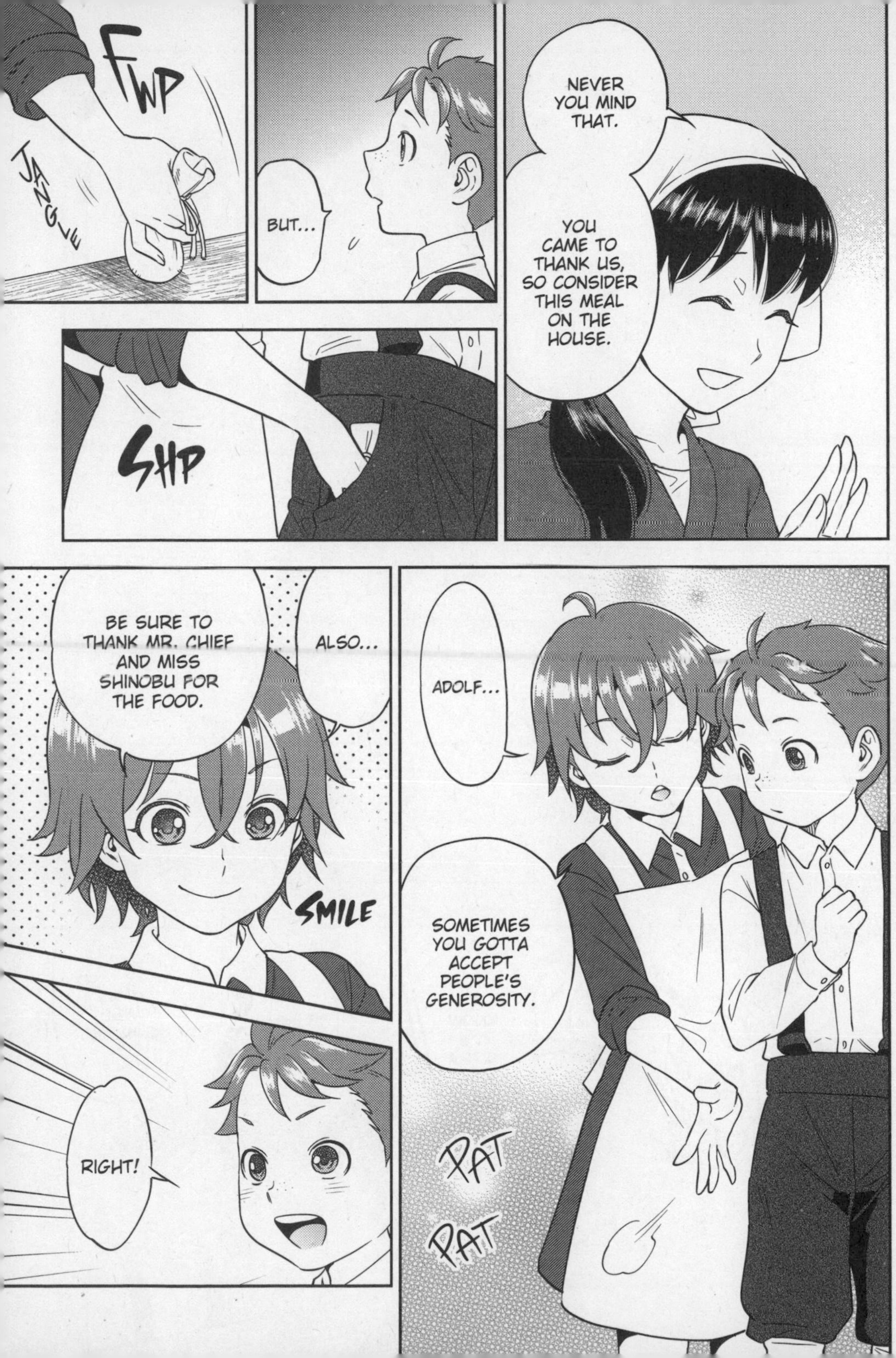
NEVER YOU MIND THAT.
YOU CAME TO THANK US, SO CONSIDER THIS MEAL ON THE HOUSE.
BUT...
FWP
JANGLE
SHP
ADOLF...
SOMETIMES YOU GOTTA ACCEPT PEOPLE'S GENEROSITY.
PAT
PAT
ALSO...
BE SURE TO THANK MR. CHIEF AND MISS SHINOBU FOR THE FOOD.
SMILE
RIGHT!

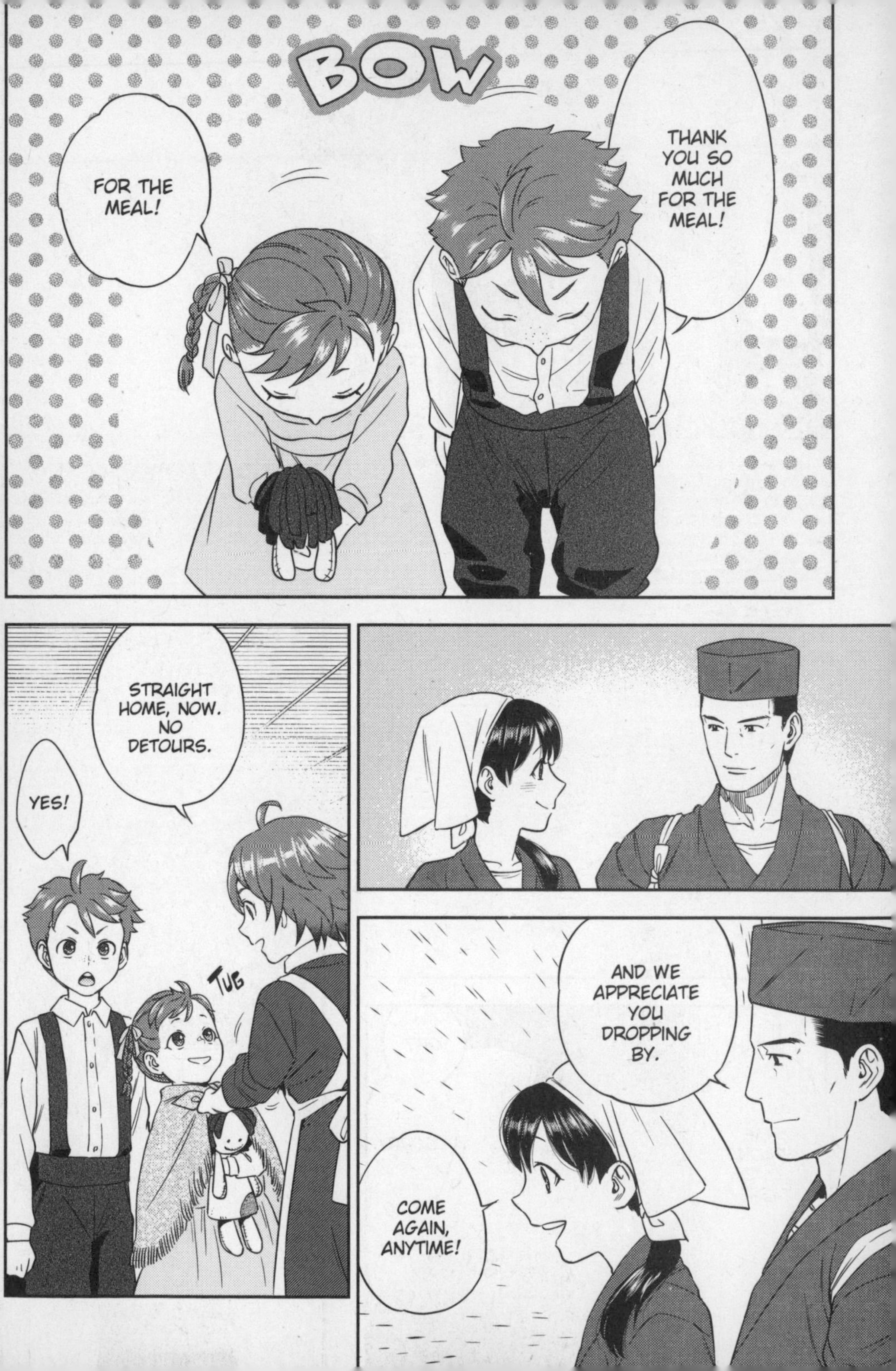
THANK YOU SO MUCH FOR THE MEAL!
BOW
FOR THE MEAL!
AND WE APPRECIATE YOU DROPPING BY.
COME AGAIN, ANYTIME!
STRAIGHT HOME, NOW. NO DETOURS.
YES!
TUG

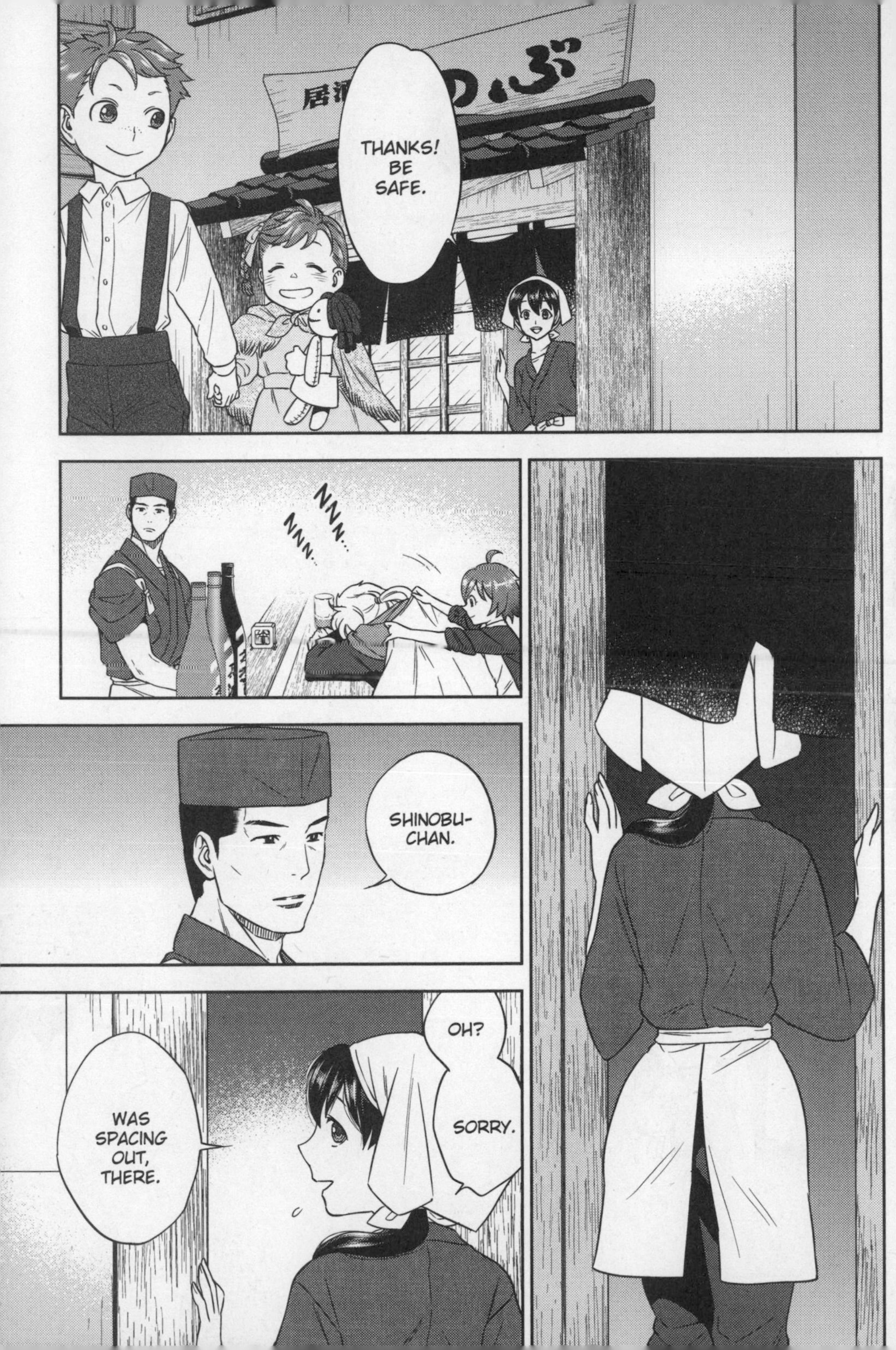
THANKS! BE SAFE.
NNN... NNN...
SHINOBU-CHAN.
OH?
SORRY.
WAS SPACING OUT, THERE.

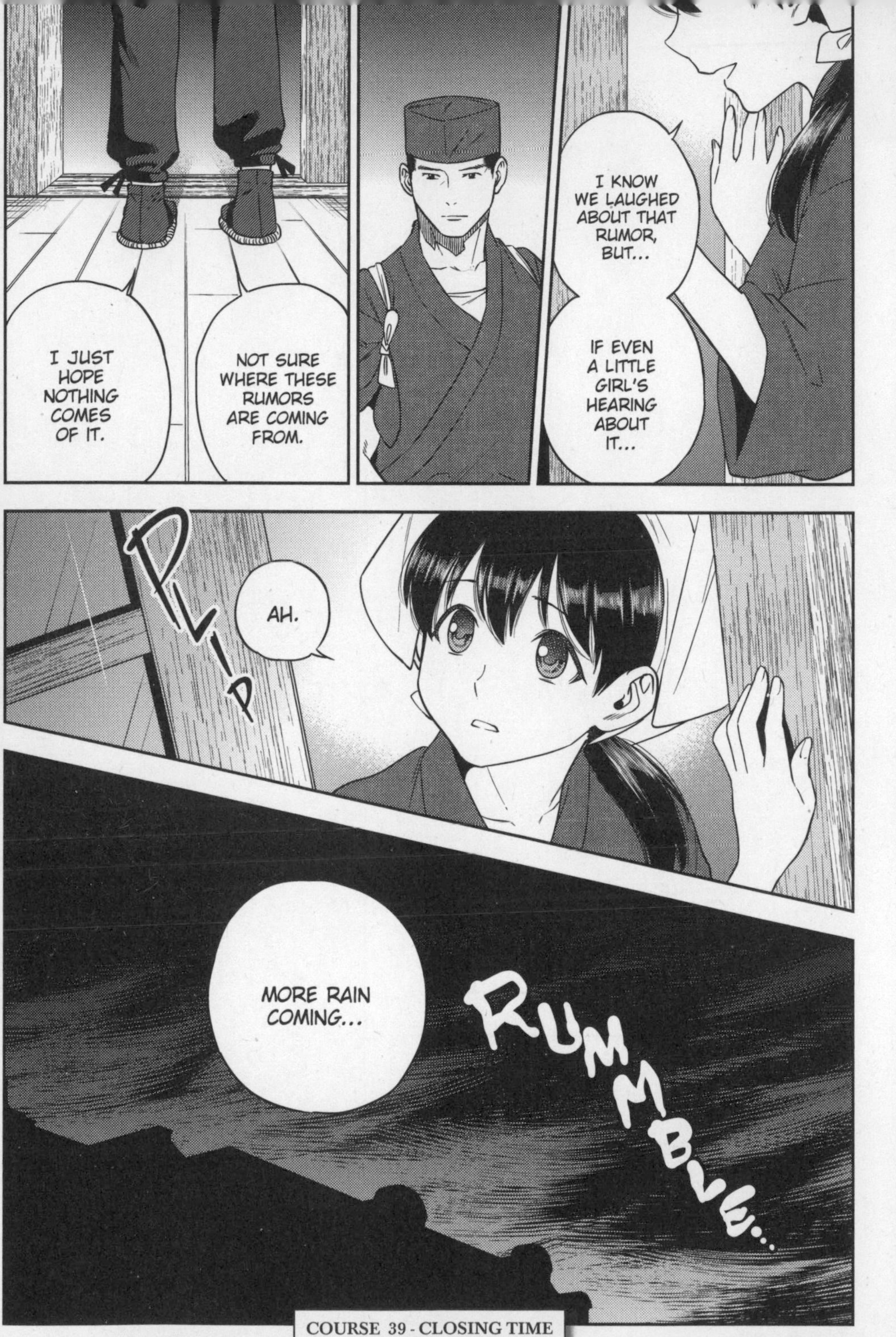
I KNOW WE LAUGHED ABOUT THAT RUMOR, BUT...
IF EVEN A LITTLE GIRL'S HEARING ABOUT IT...
NOT SURE WHERE THESE RUMORS ARE COMING FROM.
I JUST HOPE NOTHING COMES OF IT.
PLIP
AH.
MORE RAIN COMING...
RUMMBLE...

COURSE 39 - CLOSING TIME

Hamburg Steak

M E N U

FOOD VOCABULARY ENCOUNTERED IN THIS BOOK:

The fantasy world of "Nobu" brings together speakers of Japanese and German for a delicious cross-cultural exchange. Hans, Nikolaus, Chief, Shinobu, and the gang use a variety of foreign food vocabulary throughout, so here's a quick review of what came up in this volume!

GERMAN

Brot: bread
Ei(er): egg(s)
Eintopf: stew
Fisch: fish
Fleisch: meat
Garnele(n): shrimp(s)
Kartoffel(n): potato(es)
Käse: cheese
Knoblauch: garlic
Mehl: flour
Öl: oil
Olivenöl: olive oil
Pilz(e): mushroom(s)
Reis: rice
Reisbrei: porridge
Schnitzel: meat that's been pounded thin and fried
Suppe: soup
Wein: wine
Zwiebel: onion

SPANISH

Ajillo: a type of tapas stir-fry with oil, garlic, and hot peppers

ITALIAN

Olio e peperoncino: a pasta that literally means "oil and pepperoncino" (a type of hot pepper). If Chief hadn't used up the garlic, it would be "aglio e olio"

JAPANESE

Ankake yudofu: boiled tofu topped with viscous ankake sauce
Atsukan: hot sake
Chawanmushi: hot egg pudding filled with any number of cooked ingredients
Dashimaki tamago: rolled omelette flavored with dashi broth
Doteyaki: beef tendon stewed in miso, sake, and sugar
Hamburg steak: a patty of ground beef, served without a bun, adapted from the German dish
Kakiage: a type of tempura that combines chopped vegetables and seafood
Kamaboko: processed white fish, formed into a firm loaf and chopped into slices
Konnyaku: stiff, hearty jelly made from processed potatoes and cut into cubes
Maitake: hen-of-the-woods mushroom
Mitsuba: Japanese parsley
Nikujaga: meat and potato stew
Oshibori: the hot, rolled towels provided to restaurant customers before the meal
Satoimo: taro root
Tempura: Japanese deep-frying technique that uses flour and egg batter
Yagen nankotsu kara-age: fried chicken cartilage; yagen means "medicine mortar" and refers to the curved shape
Yakionigiri: the traditional riceball (onigiri), slathered with soy sauce and grilled

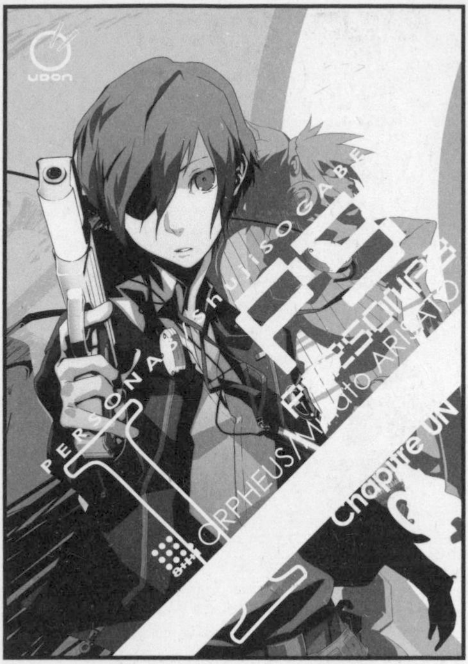
UDON
Chapitre UN

PERSONA 3 VOL.1
ISBN-13: 978-1927925850

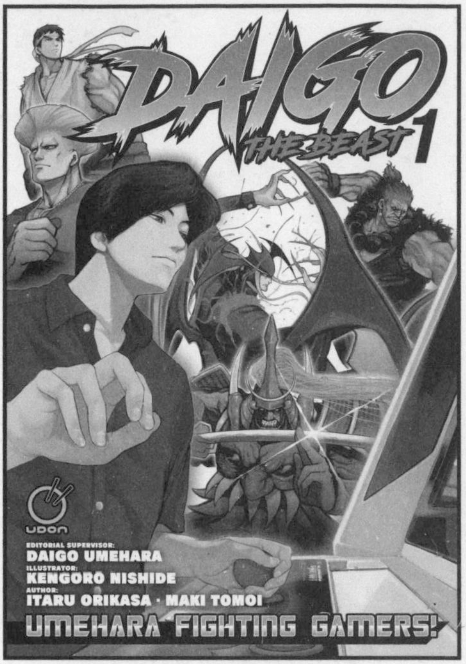
DAIGO
THE BEAST 1
UDON
EDITORIAL SUPERVISOR:
DAIGO UMEHARA
ILLUSTRATOR:
KENGORO NISHIDE
AUTHOR:
ITARU ORIKASA · MAKI TOMOI
UMEHARA FIGHTING GAMERS!

DAIGO THE BEAST VOL.1
ISBN-13: 978-1772940572

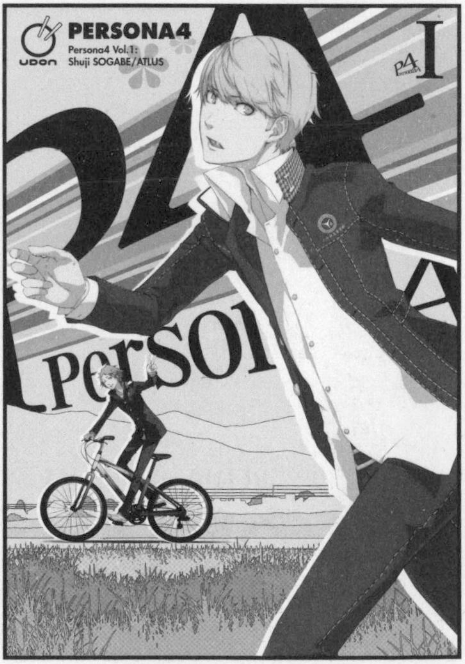
UDON
PERSONA4
Persona4 Vol.1:
Shuji SOGABE/ATLUS
P4 I

PERSONA 4 VOL.1
ISBN-13: 978-1927925577

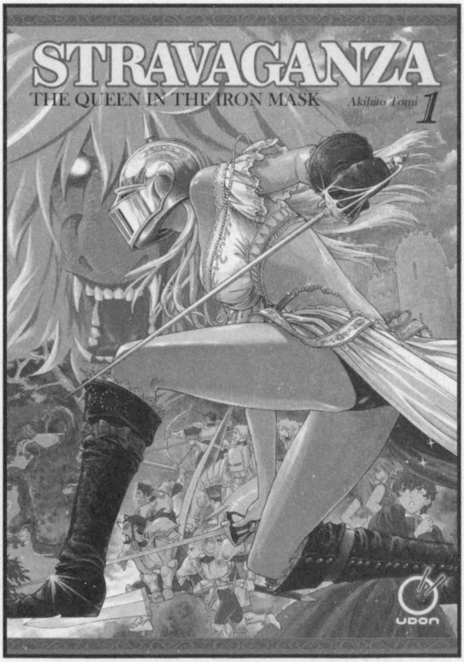
STRAVAGANZA
THE QUEEN IN THE IRON MASK
Akihito Tomi 1
UDON

STRAVAGANZA VOL.1
ISBN-13: 978-1772941036

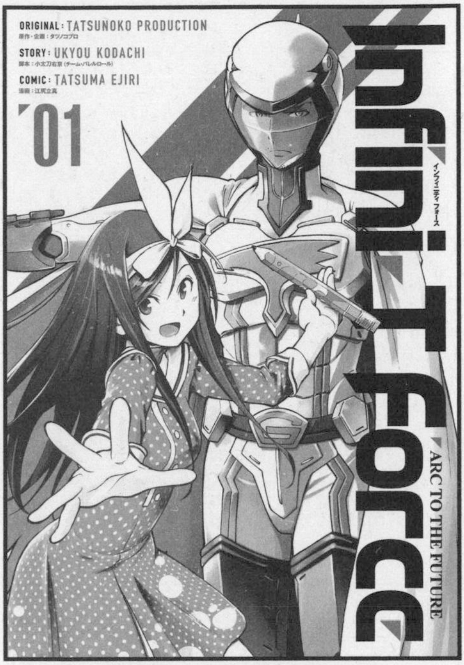
ORIGINAL: TATSUNOKO PRODUCTION
STORY: UKYOU KODACHI
COMIC: TATSUMA EJIRI
01
Infini-T Force
ARC TO THE FUTURE

INFINI-T FORCE VOL.1

ISBN-13: 978-1772940503

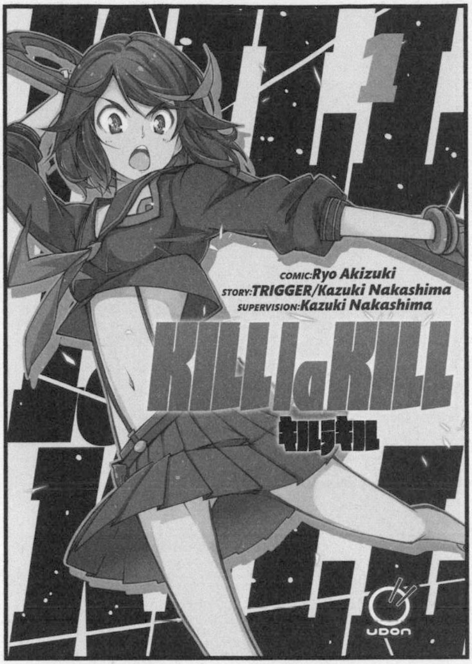
1
COMIC: Ryo Akizuki
STORY: TRIGGER/Kazuki Nakashima
SUPERVISION: Kazuki Nakashima
KILL la KILL
キルラキル
UDON

KILL LA KILL VOL.1

ISBN 13: 978 1927925492

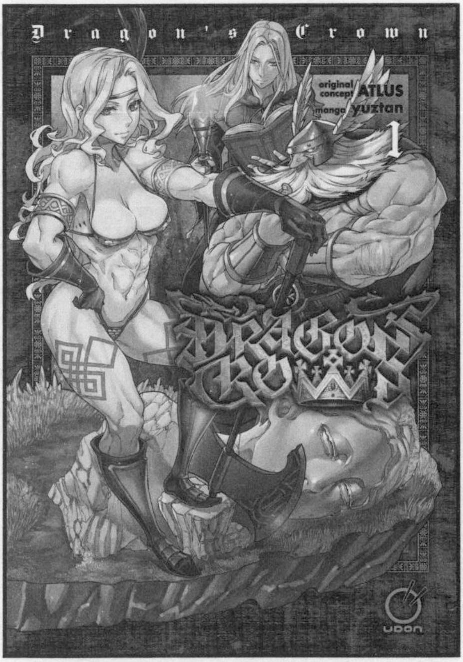
Dragon's Crown
original concept ATLUS
manga yuztan
1
DRAGON'S CROWN
UDON

DRAGON'S CROWN VOL.1

ISBN-13: 978-1772940480

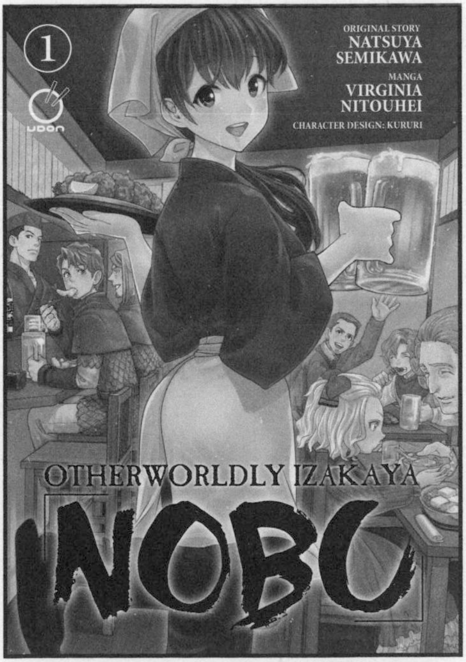
1
UDON
ORIGINAL STORY
NATSUYA SEMIKAWA
MANGA
VIRGINIA NITOUHEI
CHARACTER DESIGN: KURURI
OTHERWORLDLY IZAKAYA
NOBU

OTHERWORLDLY IZAKAYA NOBU VOL.1

ISBN-13: 978-1772940671

OTHERWORLDLY IZAKAYA
NOBU ⑥

ENGLISH EDITION
Translation: CALEB D. COOK
Typesetting: MIYOKO HOSOYAMA
Sound Effects: EK WEAVER
Associate Editor: M. CHANDLER

UDON STAFF
Chief of Operations: ERIK KO
Director of Publishing: MATT MOYLAN
VP of Business Development: CORY CASONI
Director of Marketing: MEGAN MAIDEN
Japanese Liaisons: STEVEN CUMMINGS
ANNA KAWASHIMA

Original Story
NATSUYA SEMIKAWA

Manga
VIRGINIA NITOUHEI

Character Design
KURURI

ISEKAI IZAKAYA "NOBU" Volume 6

First published in Japan in 2018 by KADOKAWA CORPORATION, Tokyo.
English translation rights arranged with KADOKAWA CORPORATION, Tokyo
through TUTTLE–MORI AGENCY, INC., Tokyo.

English language version published by UDON Entertainment Inc.
118 Tower Hill Road, C1, PO Box 20008
Richmond Hill, Ontario, L4K 0K0 CANADA

www.UDONentertainment.com

First Printing: February 2020
ISBN-13: 978-1-77294-109-8
ISBN-10: 1-77294-109-3

Printed in Canada